The Civil R

Uncovering the Past: Documentary Readers in American History
Series Editors: Steven F. Lawson and Nancy A. Hewitt

The books in this series introduce students in American history courses to two important dimensions of historical analysis. They enable students to engage actively in historical interpretation, and they further students' understanding of the interplay between social and political forces in historical developments.

Consisting of primary sources and an introductory essay, these readers are aimed at the major courses in the American history curriculum, as outlined further below. Each book in the series will be approximately 225–50 pages, including a 25–30 page introduction addressing key issues and questions about the subject under consideration, a discussion of sources and methodology, and a bibliography of suggested secondary readings.

Published

Paul G. E. Clemens
The Colonial Era: A Documentary Reader

Sean Patrick Adams
The Early American Republic: A Documentary Reader

Stanley Harrold
The Civil War and Reconstruction: A Documentary Reader

Steven Mintz
African American Voices: A Documentary Reader, 1619–1877

Robert P. Ingalls and David K. Johnson
The United States Since 1945: A Documentary Reader

Camilla Townsend
American Indian History: A Documentary Reader

Steven Mintz
Mexican American Voices: A Documentary Reader

Brian Ward
The 1960s: A Documentary Reader

Nancy Rosenbloom
Women in American History Since 1880: A Documentary Reader

Jeremi Suri
American Foreign Relations Since 1898: A Documentary Reader

Carol Faulkner
Women in American History to 1880: A Documentary Reader

David Welky
America Between the Wars, 1919–1941: A Documentary Reader

William A. Link and Susannah J. Link
The Gilded Age and Progressive Era: A Documentary Reader

G. Kurt Piehler
The United States in World War II: A Documentary Reader

Leslie Brown
African American Voices: A Documentary Reader, 1863–Present

David Freund
The Modern American Metropolis: A Documentary Reader

Edward Miller
The Vietnam War: A Documentary Reader

James Giesen and Bryant Simon
Food and Eating in America: A Documentary Reader

John A. Kirk
The Civil Rights Movement: A Documentary Reader

The Civil Rights Movement

A Documentary Reader

Edited by John A. Kirk

WILEY Blackwell

Registered Office
John Wiley & Sons, Inc., 111 River Street, Hoboken, NJ 07030, USA

Editorial Office
111 River Street, Hoboken, NJ 07030, USA

For details of our global editorial offices, customer services, and more information about Wiley products visit us at www.wiley.com.

Library of Congress Cataloging-in-Publication Data
Names: Kirk, John A., 1970– editor.
Title: The civil rights movement: a documentary reader / edited by
    John A. Kirk.
Description: Hoboken: Wiley, 2020. | Series: Uncovering the past:
    documentary readers in American history | Includes bibliographical
    references and index.
Identifiers: LCCN 2019052197 (print) | LCCN 2019052198 (ebook) | ISBN
    9781118737163 (paperback) | ISBN 9781119583646 (adobe pdf) | ISBN
    9781119583622 (epub)
Subjects: LCSH: African Americans–Civil rights–History–20th
    century–Sources. | Civil rights movements–United States–History–20th
    century–Sources. | African Americans–Civil rights–History–20th
    century–Sources–Textbooks. | Civil rights movements–United
    States–History–20th century–Sources–Textbooks.
Classification: LCC E185.61 .C6146 2020 (print) | LCC E185.61 (ebook) |
    DDC 323.1196/073–dc23
LC record available at https://lccn.loc.gov/2019052197
LC ebook record available at https://lccn.loc.gov/2019052198

Cover Design: Wiley
Cover Image: © Yevhenii Dubinko/Getty Images

Set in 10/12.5pt Sabon by SPi Global, Pondicherry, India

Printed in the United States of America

V10018108_031720

Contents

Series Editors' Preface

Primary sources have become an essential component in the teaching of history to undergraduates. They engage students in the process of historical interpretation and analysis and help them understand that facts do not speak for themselves. Rather, students see how historians construct narratives that recreate the past. Most students assume that the pursuit of knowledge is a solitary endeavor; yet historians constantly interact with their peers, building upon previous research and arguing among themselves over the interpretation of sources and their larger meaning. The documentary readers in this series highlight the value of this collaborative creative process and encourage students to participate in it.

Each book in the series introduces students in American history courses to two important dimensions of historical analysis. They enable students to engage actively in historical interpretation, and they further students' understanding of the interplay among social, cultural, economic, and political forces in historical developments. In pursuit of these goals, the sources in each text embrace a broad range, including such items as illustrations of material artifacts, letters and diaries, sermons, maps, photographs, song lyrics, selections from fiction and memoirs, legal statutes, court decisions, presidential orders, speeches, and political cartoons.

Each volume in the series is edited by a specialist in the field who is concerned with undergraduate teaching. The goal is not to offer a comprehensive selection of material but to provide items that reflect major themes and debates; that illustrate significant social, cultural, political, and economic dimensions of an era or subject; and that inform, intrigue and inspire undergraduate students. The editor of each volume has written an introduction that discusses the central questions that have occupied historians in this field and the ways historians have used primary sources to answer them. In addition, each introductory essay contains an explanation of the kinds of materials available to investigate a particular subject, the methods by which scholars analyze them, and the considerations that go into interpreting them. Each source selection is introduced by a short head note that gives students the necessary information and a context for understanding the document. Also, each section of the volume includes questions to guide student reading and stimulate classroom discussion.

John A. Kirk's *The Civil Rights Movement: A Documentary Reader* offers an interactive synthesis of the most important social and political movement of the twentieth century. Within the framework of a "long civil rights movement" he concentrates on the two most pivotal decades – the 1950s and 1960s – that distinguish the modern civil rights movement from its predecessors. Rather than a "long" approach, he embraces a "wide" view of the civil rights movement. Alongside the "top-down" narrative focusing on Dr. Martin Luther King and national leaders, which only tells part of the story, Kirk examines the black freedom rights struggle from the wider, "bottom-up" frame of reference of local movement participants.

Balancing multiple perspectives, this wide-ranging primary-source reader includes presidential executive orders and speeches; federal, district and local court decisions; congressional legislation; government commission reports; campaign materials and party platforms; newspaper and magazine editorials, articles and reports; and books, memoirs, essays, and pamphlets. Illuminating "bottom-up" perceptions of marginalized people, Kirk provides a rich array of oral histories and interviews; songs and music; sermons and speeches; field reports of grassroots organizers; and visual sources such as movement photographs.

Steven F. Lawson and Nancy A. Hewitt
Series Editors

Acknowledgments

The challenge of compiling, editing and writing about the primary sources in this book has provided me with yet another new way of thinking about and approaching the study of the civil rights movement. I am grateful to series editors Nancy Hewitt and Steven Lawson for inviting me to contribute this volume, and for their always gentle and instructive comments, guidance, and wisdom. Given that Steven Lawson is one of the leading scholars in civil rights studies, his expertise has been a particularly welcome benefit, and it has kept me even more attentive to the subject matter.

I thank Peter Coveney at Wiley for signing up this project, even though it has outlasted his retirement from the publisher by several years. A number of people at the press have had a hand in seeing the project through from the beginning to the end, and I am thankful for the professionalism and patience of acquisitions editor Jennifer Manias, editorial assistant Elizabeth Saucier, and project editors Denisha Sahadevan, Janani Govindankutty, and Niranjana Vallavan. The anonymous reviewers' reports on the proposal and draft manuscript were extremely useful in determining the scope and content of the book, and in pointing toward primary sources that may otherwise have escaped my attention. Of course, I take full responsibility for the final material and commentaries in the book that were ultimately shaped by my editorial choices and decisions.

The book was written and compiled at the University of Arkansas at Little Rock. I appreciate the university supporting my research leave that allowed the project to achieve its final completion. Part of the time spent working on the book overlapped with my five years as chair of the History Department. Most of it was concurrent with the past three years serving as director of the university's Anderson Institute on Race and Ethnicity. UA Little Rock Chancellor Joel E. Anderson's interest in issues of race and ethnicity, and his recognition of their crucial role in shaping the city and state, played a significant part in my recruitment to the university. Now that he is Chancellor Emeritus, I am delighted to serve as director of the Institute that is his legacy project. The role has provided me with welcome opportunities for engagement and insight beyond traditional scholarship and classroom teaching. I thank the Institute's long-serving program coordinator Tamisha Cheatham for her support, and particularly for sustaining the Institute while I was away on research leave. Two graduate assistants, Sarah Riva and Paola Cavallari, helped tremendously in tracking down the copyright holders of the primary sources.

Completing a book always makes one reflect on one's formative influences. Professionally, mentorship from some of the very best in the field of civil rights studies, including Richard King, Tony Badger, Adam Fairclough, and Brian Ward, has been invaluable. Personally, my mother and father, Anne and William; my brother and his wife, Alan and Louise; and my niece and nephew, Annabelle and Marcus, form the core of my family back in England. My wife Charlene and her extended family, and my daughter Sadie, form my expatriate family in the United States.

This book is dedicated to my family, with thanks and love.

John A. Kirk
Little Rock, Arkansas
October 2018

Introduction

What is the civil rights movement? To those historians who first asked that question, the answer was relatively straightforward: Martin Luther King, Jr was the civil rights movement and the civil rights movement was Martin Luther King, Jr. Early histories of the civil rights movement were therefore biographies of its talismanic figurehead that focused on his activism during the 1950s and 1960s. Starting in the year of his death in 1968, for two decades King cast a long shadow over the civil rights movement's history. This King-centered period of attention crested in the mid-1980s. In 1983, President Ronald Reagan signed into law a Martin Luther King, Jr national holiday, celebrated on the third Monday in January each year. The first observance of the holiday was in 1986. King was the first black American to be honored in this way and the recognition, which followed a concerted grassroots campaign to exert political pressure to achieve it, cemented his position in American historical folklore. Around the same time, the publication of three landmark books provided an exhaustive chronicling of King's life and the organization he led, the Southern Christian Leadership Conference (SCLC): David J. Garrow, *Bearing the Cross: Martin Luther King, Jr and the Southern Christian Leadership Conference* (William Morrow, 1986), Adam Fairclough, *To Redeem the Soul of America: The Southern Christian Leadership Conference and Martin Luther King, Jr* (University of Georgia Press, 1987), and Taylor Branch, *Parting the Waters: Martin Luther King and the Civil Rights Movement, 1954–63* (Simon and Schuster, 1988). Branch subsequently wrote another two hefty volumes: *Pillar of Fire: America in the King Years, 1963–65* (Simon and Schuster, 1998) and *At Canaan's Edge: America in the King Years, 1965–1968* (Simon and Schuster, 2006). The books written by Garrow, Fairclough, and Branch remain among the defining works written about King and his movement leadership. Garrow's book and Branch's first book both won Pulitzer Prizes. The television series *Eyes on the Prize: America's Civil Rights Years 1954–1965*, created and executive produced by Henry Hampton at the film company Blackside, Inc., first aired in 1987. The series is still considered one of the best multipart documentaries about the civil rights movement. Although not quite as intently focused on King's leadership, and incorporating a wider array of movement voices, nevertheless the chronology of the series identified the years in which King was prominent as being the movement's halcyon days.

The initial King-centered focus in telling the story of the civil rights movement established narrative conventions that still profoundly shape popular conceptions of civil rights history today. The concentration on one individual leader has created the impression of a "top-down" movement in which a few, namely King and other national civil rights leaders, influenced and led the many rank and file participants. King's interaction with presidents and other prominent national political leaders reinforced the notion that the civil rights movement's focus was exclusively about winning national legislation and changing laws. In this rendition, King's life and death frame the chronology of the movement. King rose to prominence through his local leadership in the Montgomery, Alabama bus boycott from 1955 to 1956 and died from an assassin's bullet in Memphis, Tennessee in 1968. Indeed, many early accounts created an even shorter "Montgomery to Selma" movement narrative, beginning with King's bus boycott leadership and ending with the passage of the Civil Rights Act of 1964 and the Voting Rights Act of 1965, the latter in part a result of King's and the SCLC's campaign for the vote in Selma, Alabama. It was this timeframe that the first series of *Eyes on the Prize* adopted. The books by Garrow, Fairclough, and Branch did extend the "Montgomery to Selma" narrative to a "Montgomery to Memphis" narrative covering the entire length of King's life. In doing so, they began to draw attention to the more complex challenges in addressing structural and institutional racism that King and the movement faced after 1965, which did not fit quite as comfortably with the more triumphalist "Montgomery to Selma" narrative that ended with the successful passage of civil rights legislation.

Beginning in earnest in the 1980s, a second wave of civil rights studies emerged that challenged many of the basic assumptions found in King-centered studies. These new studies were rooted in community-based approaches to the civil rights movement from a "bottom-up" perspective that viewed events mainly through the lens of local and state level activists. Initially, many of these studies focused on communities that were national flashpoints in the "Montgomery to Memphis" narrative and relocated those nationally known events within the context of local and state struggles. As the number of community studies proliferated, they gradually moved beyond the familiar locales of civil rights activism and explored an extensive and expansive story of black struggles for freedom and equality nationwide. Collectively, these community studies have reshaped our understanding of the civil rights movement, and the locus of civil rights studies has increasingly moved away from national legislation, and national figures and organizations, to local concerns, local leadership, and community organizations and institutions. Community studies revealed that although sometimes there were overlapping agendas between national and local activists, at other times they were quite different from one another, and sometimes even directly at odds with each other. The move to examine communities beyond those that King and the SCLC engaged with in the 1950s and 1960s signaled the vibrancy and extent of local civil rights organizing that stretched well beyond King, the SCLC, and their immediate orbit of influence. They chimed with the claim of movement activist Ella Baker that "The movement made Martin rather than Martin making the movement." Community studies also suggested that civil rights activism had a much longer history than an exclusive focus on the national picture in the 1950s and 1960s revealed. Viewed from the "bottom-up," civil rights struggles appeared to both predate and outlast the established King-centered movement chronology by decades.

The questions about when the civil rights movement began and when it ended have been a major source of debate. In the mid-1980s, at the height of King-centered studies, historian Clayborne Carson insisted that the civil rights movement should be reimagined as part of a longer and continuing "black freedom struggle" driven by activists at a local level. Almost 20 years later, Jacquelyn Dowd Hall argued that the black freedom struggle was part of a "long" civil rights movement, with its roots in the "liberal and radical milieu of the late 1930s." At the same time, Hall rejected the well-worn "declension narrative" about the movement's demise in the late 1960s and early 1970s, instead claiming that the movement's legacies continue down to the present day, as do those of the successive white "backlash" resistance movements that opposed it. In a provocative rejoinder, on the face of it Peniel Joseph essentially agreed with many of the points that Hall made: he too called for a longer movement chronology, an engagement with the uses and abuses of black freedom struggle history, and a more involved and nuanced discussion about movement legacies. However, Joseph, at the forefront of the emergent field of "Black Power Studies," more fundamentally maintained that these issues should be explored not within the framework of a "long" civil rights movement, but rather within the framework of a "long" black power movement, giving primacy to the black power movement rather than to the civil rights movement as the most authentic expression of a longer black freedom struggle. Very much in line with these developments, in 1990 Henry Hampton and Blackside, Inc. produced *Eyes on the Prize II: America at the Racial Crossroads 1965–1985* that extended the narrative arc of the first series.

Meanwhile, despite the ascendency of the *longue durée* approach in civil rights studies, there have been plenty of observers sounding notes of caution about dispensing quite so quickly with what movement activist Bayard Rustin called the "classical" phase of the civil rights movement in the 1950s and 1960s (for this usage, see Rustin's essay "From Protest to Politics" in Chapter 10). Civil rights activist Hugh Murray has been among the bluntest of these voices complaining, "The people who were involved in the movement in the 1950s and 1960s called it the civil rights movement. Historians in pipe-smoked rooms ought not to try to rename it." A number of historians have articulated their own particular reservations. Richard H. King, whose work has explored the distinct meanings of freedom that emerged during the classical civil rights movement, warns that, "the freshness, even inexplicability, of the movement should not be underplayed for the sake of historical pedigree." Adam Fairclough, whose work embodies the shifts that have taken place in civil rights studies, with his first major study one of King and the SCLC, and his second a state study of Louisiana, asserts that, "Too much stress on continuity smooths out history's peaks and valleys, producing a bland, featureless landscape," which can lead to an ungainly "homogenized mush." Sundiata Keita Cha-Jua and Clarence Lang have argued forcefully and at length about the need to understand the specificity and uniqueness of the classical civil rights movement as a product of its own historical moment.

How, then, do we navigate this increasingly fractious and fragmented terrain when studying the civil rights movement? Some historians have attempted to point the way, each in a similar vein looking to incorporate the insights of a long black freedom struggle while not losing the distinctiveness of the classical civil rights movement. As Steven Lawson puts it, the movement of the "1950s and 1960s [...] needs to be identified for the characteristics that made it distinct from earlier efforts without forgetting the links that connected them." Eric Arnesen echoes these sentiments deeming it, "possible – and necessary – to appreciate the distinctiveness of the modern phase of the movement while simultaneously recognizing its deeper roots." In a useful collection of essays edited by Emilye Crosby, *Civil Rights History From the Ground Up: Local Struggles, A National Movement* (University of Georgia Press, 2011), Crobsy's essay "The Politics of Writing and Teaching Movement History," calls for an "interactive synthesis" between the long/classical and local/national historical perspectives, "one that seriously engages the collective insights of local studies, while simultaneously considering the full-range of movement scholarship – from top-down studies of leaders, organizations, and federal (in)action to those works addressing previously neglected or distorted topics, including analyses of women/gender, religion, segregationists, the role and impact of class, northern bases of structural inequality, community based Black Power, civil rights unionists, and much more." It is precisely this approach that I pursue in this edited collection of primary sources.

Informed by my own past three decades of working within the rapidly shifting sands of civil rights historiography, this primary source reader draws on my experiences in writing and publishing movement histories that have included both King-centered studies focusing on the 1950s and 1960s, along with community-focused studies written within the framework of the long civil rights movement. Equally, the collection reflects my experiences in teaching civil rights history in three different universities in three different countries. Throughout, a course on "Martin Luther King, Jr and the Civil Rights Movement" (which at some point, revealingly, became shortened to just "The Civil Rights Movement") has been at the core of my intellectual journey as a teacher and scholar. Yet the course I teach today is almost entirely different from the one I first constructed in the early 1990s, an important lesson itself in understanding that the past is never a fixed point but that it is always changing as it is reconsidered in the light of new research, new approaches, and new understandings. What has not changed about my course is the chronological timeframe it employs, which is still unapologetically rooted in the 1950s and 1960s. I have always wanted to focus intently on those decades to convey a sense of what was distinctive about the black freedom struggle during that specific time period, and to understand why collectively many movement participants saw themselves as belonging to something that they self-consciously referred to as the civil rights movement (and later, the black power movement). Based on the same convictions, the main focus of this collection is on those two pivotal decades. This does not mean that I reject or that I am not mindful of the importance of the insights offered by a longer chronological perspective. Rather, I think that framing the longer story belongs to a different, if equally valid project. In teaching survey courses on African-American history and the history of race and ethnicity in the United States, I have gained the opportunity to explore and apply the insights from the longer reach of black (and other peoples') struggles for freedom and equality in those classes.

Having said that, the influences of long and local civil rights movement studies still profoundly shape my research, my teaching, and this book. Given the descriptors of long and local, it is tempting to define these developments as being purely chronological and geographical in their scope. Though these factors are important in their own right, the two approaches have changed the landscape of civil rights studies far beyond those immediately apparent terms. Importantly, they have concurrently created what we might term a "wide" civil rights movement. That is, as Crosby indicates above, they have opened up civil rights scholarship to a much broader array of themes, issues, and concerns than ever before. Even if we preserve the focus on the 1950s and 1960s, we can no longer credibly view them in the same way that King-centered studies once did. To be sure, King still has a role to play, as do many of the topics that emerged during that first wave of works on the movement. But we now understand that King and the "top-down" narrative tells us only part of the story of the civil rights movement, which also needs to be understood within the context of wider perspectives that include the multiple and intersecting stories of other movement participants from the "bottom-up." It is this reframing of the narrative to incorporate a more expansive body of views and perspectives that has most radically transformed my own approach to the subject and the one that I want to primarily showcase in this book.

In what follows, I demonstrate how an interactive synthesis of insights from civil rights studies can reshape our collective understanding of the civil rights movement. Collating a multi-perspective history necessarily means drawing on a large and diverse selection of primary sources. Some of the sources used in this book reflect "top-down" perspectives, including presidential executive orders and speeches; federal, district, and local court decisions; legal opinions and briefs; congressional legislation; government commission reports; campaign materials; and party platforms. Some sources traverse "top-down" and "bottom-up" perspectives, including newspaper and magazine editorials, articles, and reports; books, essays, and pamphlets; press releases; field reports; media interviews; speeches and addresses; letters; memoirs and autobiographies; political tracts and manifestos; and constitutions and by-laws. In capturing "bottom-up" perspectives, oral histories and interviews have often proved essential in gaining access to hitherto marginalized voices not represented in the existing written record. Songs and music, represented here as transcribed lyrics, also because of the limitations of the written word, give at least a reminder of the aural cadences that were a vital aspect of movement culture, as do sermons and speeches delivered from pulpit and podium – although in all of these instances they can never fully capture the range of meanings conveyed by their live performance. Fortunately, through the Internet, more people have more access to more of these sources beyond the written word than ever before, and I encourage readers to pursue them in both their aural and visual forms to gain a stronger sense of their full performative power. Visual sources are essential in gaining a sense of the high drama and street theater contained in direct action protests. The movement worked hard to thoughtfully and consciously frame the issues involved, and in the case of photographs and television coverage, quite literally so. Again, the limitations of the paper and print format of this volume prohibit the incorporation of moving images, which, again, can be remedied by recourse to the Internet and various other visual mediums. Though televised coverage was important, movement photography should not be overlooked as an art form and as a potent propaganda tool in its own right. The civil rights movement produced some of the most iconic photographs of the twentieth century. The use of maps, tables, and graphs in this collection provide further visual sources, and quantitative as well as qualitative movement measures.

In the rest of this introduction, I provide an overview of and orientation to each of the book's chapters. The purpose is to give a sense of the material that is covered in each chapter, to show how each chapter relates to the others in forming an overarching narrative, and to highlight the themes that thread throughout the entire book. At the end of each individual book chapter there are several "Discussion Questions" that relate to the material covered. Many of these questions tackle issues that stretch beyond individual chapters. While in this introduction and throughout the collection I draw attention to the main themes and ideas contained within the primary sources, the myriad potential connections between them are something that readers are encouraged to think about and pursue further. How can the dots between the primary sources within and between chapters be connected? Which sources speak to and echo the others? What other themes can possibly be identified for future study and discussion? Considering these questions can lead to a more dynamic and inter-active interrogation of the material. The primary sources and the context I provide are the beginning, not the end point for their investigation. A "Further Reading" section at the end of each chapter serves as a useful guide in this respect. Of course, any selection of sources chosen to represent the ever-expanding universe of civil rights studies is open to scrutiny and criticism. From "How could document/chapter x possibly be omitted?" to "Why on earth was document/chapter y included?" there is plenty of scope for debate. Readers may like to engage with those questions alongside movement scholars, since they are also helpful in sharpening the senses, and yet another way to critically approach this collection. All the while, it is worth remembering that there are no right and wrong answers in these circumstances, just different perspectives and approaches, limitations of time and space, and therefore ulti-mately the need for editorial decisions to determine priorities, for which I take full responsibility. Thoughtful critiques are the main way that intellectual growth happens and that new insights occur. I dare say I may even agree with some of them.

Chapter 1 contains a nod to the origins of the civil rights movement and highlights just some of the developments that laid the groundwork for what came later. A number of the sources show how tactics that became synonymous with the movement were already being adopted and trialed in earlier decades, from bus boycotts in Harlem in 1941 and Baton Rouge in 1953, to a 1942 sit-in in Chicago, to a 1947 Journey of Reconciliation that was a prototype of the Freedom Rides, to Brotherhood of Sleeping Car Porters Union (BSCPU) president A. Philip Randolph's 1941 call for a March on Washington. US Supreme Court decisions such as *Smith v. Allwright* (1944) were beginning to remove some of the obstacles to the vote for blacks in the South, such as all-white party primaries, while as Henry Lee Moon's 1948 book *Balance of Power* points out, burgeoning urban black communities in the North were beginning to exert their collective voting strength to draw attention to racial issues at both local and national levels. This newfound voting strength, in turn, elicited a response from national politicians like President Harry S. Truman, who depended on black votes for his successful election to office in 1948. Truman's Committee on Civil Rights drafted a platform for change in *To Secure These Rights* before the election, and the president tried to implement some of its recommendations with executive orders to desegregate the federal workforce and the armed forces afterwards. Standing in the way of further reforms were powerful southern politicians blocking legislation in Congress. A cohort of these politicians rebelled against Truman and the national Democratic Party in 1948 by creating their own States' Rights Democratic Party, better known as the Dixiecrats. By contrast to *To Secure These Rights*, the Dixiecrat Party platform outlines an anti-civil rights agenda. At a local level, black women activists such as Annie L. McPheeters in Atlanta were preparing and equipping people in communities to take full advantage of the changes that were taking place at the time and for those that lay ahead, while black women leaders such as Dorothy Height were influential in organizing national women's networks for change. Finally, the inclusion of the Fifth Pan-African Congress' Declaration to the Colonial Workers, Farmers and Intellectuals and congressman Jacob K. Javits's press release on segregation and discrimination in the armed forces in this chapter, serve as a reminder that there were ever-present global dimensions to national civil rights struggles in the United States. These included an increasing number of decolonization and independence movements worldwide and a rapidly shifting international relations context with the end of World War II and the beginning of the Cold War.

Chapter 2 examines one of the defining events in the birth of a new era of civil rights activism in the 1950s, the US Supreme Court ruling in the case of *Brown v. Board of Education* (1954) and responses to it. The *Brown* decision was a culmination of attacks on the legal basis of segregation led by the National Association for the Advancement of Colored People (NAACP). Formed in 1909, the NAACP is one of the oldest and longest-serving civil rights organizations still in operation in the United States today. In the 1930s, NAACP lawyer Charles Hamilton Houston drew up the blueprints for a legal attack on segregation. Hamilton's protégé Thurgood Marshall, later appointed as the first black US Supreme Court justice in 1967, led the way in the 1940s as director-counsel of the NAACP Legal Defense and Educational Fund (NAACP LDF). Marshall began the legal assault on segregation with numerous victories in teachers' salary equalization suits in public schools before switching focus to black graduate education. In 1950, two US Supreme Court rulings in *McLaurin v. Oklahoma* and *Sweatt v. Painter* rolled back segregation in higher education as far as it could go without actually abolishing it. These rulings encouraged Marshall to "go for the jugular" and try to get the courts to overrule altogether the legal doctrine of "separate but equal" established in *Plessy v. Ferguson* (1896) that provided the legal justification for all segregated facilities. In 1954, the US Supreme Court did just that in the *Brown* decision by specifically outlawing segregation in public schools. The decision and its impact have been much debated. On the one hand, some have noted that *Brown* further galvanized black communities by providing them with legal impetus and a mandate for change. On the other hand, some have pointed toward the galvanizing effect *Brown* had on white communities, particularly in the South, in mobilizing resistance to change. There were those in the federal government who viewed the *Brown* decision as an important propaganda coup in the Cold War's battle for hearts and minds worldwide. The murder of 14-year-old Chicagoan Emmett Till in 1955 while visiting family in Mississippi dramatically demonstrated to the nation the extent to which southern whites were willing to go to preserve white supremacy. From the local and state level organizing of White Citizens' Councils to prevent school desegregation, to a national level "Southern Manifesto" that was signed by the vast majority of southern congressmen condemning the *Brown* decision as unconstitutional, the white South girded for a campaign of massive resistance to the Court's decision.

It was against this backdrop that the Montgomery bus boycott took place. Chapter 3 charts the boycott and its aftermath. Early "top-down" accounts revolved around the story of the tired seamstress Rosa Parks who refused to give up her seat on a city bus. A "bottom-up" analysis reveals a different and more complex story. Rosa Parks was not an unwitting agent of history; rather, she was a seasoned activist who had been involved in women's issues for decades, who had served as local branch secretary for the NAACP, and who had attended out-of-state training sessions in social change. Although Parks's refusal to give up her seat was not a premeditated act of defiance, she was fully conscious of what her actions meant and their potential consequences. Parks's arrest mobilized key community actors and institutions. Civil rights attorney Fred D. Gray, one of the few black attorneys in the state, and one of the fewer still willing to take the risk of provoking white wrath by defending a civil rights case, agreed to represent her in court. Edgar Daniel (E.D.) Nixon, president of the local BSCPU, suggested the idea of a bus boycott. Nixon connected with Jo Ann Robinson, a teacher at Montgomery's Alabama State College and head of the local organization the Women's Political Council that had raised concerns about the treatment of black bus passengers in the past. Robinson took charge of publicizing the bus boycott. Only then, with the boycott already gaining momentum, did Martin Luther King, Jr enter the picture. When community leaders decided to form the Montgomery Improvement Association to coordinate the bus boycott, they chose King as its head because they thought the young and pliable newcomer would be an acceptable, non-threatening compromise candidate. Importantly, King was also one of the few black ministers in the city willing to accept the position. As the bus boycott grew beyond its initially planned protest of a few days, and into weeks and months, capturing national news headlines in the process, King became the prime focus of media attention. That notwithstanding, it is often forgotten that it was the NAACP's successful legal battle in the courts alongside the bus boycott that ultimately led to the desegregation of Montgomery buses in the case of *Browder v. Gayle* (1956). King and other movement leaders sought to capitalize on King's growing national standing by creating the SCLC and instating him as its president. However, the SCLC's attempts to extend bus boycotts to other communities proved largely unsuccessful.

As King and others pondered how to translate the mass activism of the Montgomery bus boycott into a regionwide movement, the battle over school desegregation reached its climax in Little Rock, Arkansas, which is the focus of Chapter 4. Little Rock was an unlikely place for such a confrontation. The capital of Arkansas was regarded as a relatively moderate city in a relatively moderate upper South state, as opposed to the lower or deep South states of Louisiana, Mississippi, Alabama, Georgia, and South Carolina that were recognized hotbeds of resistance. Little Rock Superintendent of Schools Virgil T. Blossom was among the first in the South to draw up a desegregation plan. Yet when Blossom subsequently built and opened two new segregated schools, the NAACP challenged his plan in the courts. Daisy Bates, president of the Arkansas NAACP State Conference of branches, and who along with her husband L.C. Bates was the co-owner of the Little Rock-based *Arkansas State Press* newspaper, fronted local efforts to desegregate schools. The federal courts upheld the Blossom Plan and continued to maintain oversight of its implementation. The day before Central High School was due to admit its first black students, Gov. Orval E. Faubus called out the Arkansas National Guard to prevent their entry. When one of the black students, Elizabeth Eckford, turned up to school the following day, she was turned away at bayonet point by state troops and hounded by a white mob. The photograph of white student Hazel Bryan screaming vitriol at Elizabeth became the enduring image of events across the world. Faubus was eventually ordered by the courts to remove the National Guard, but mob rule continued. Finally, President Dwight D. Eisenhower federalized the National Guard and sent in federal troops to accompany the Little Rock Nine students into Central High with 2,000 white students. The following year, Faubus closed all of the public high schools to prevent their desegregation. In the landmark ruling of *Cooper v. Aaron* (1958), the US Supreme Court gave its strongest backing to *Brown* since it had handed down its original decision four years earlier. The Court said that violence and disruption could not be used as excuses for delaying school desegregation plans. Little Rock's public high schools reopened in 1959 on a token desegregated basis. District by district, black students and their families across the South bore the burden of school desegregation in the face of white hostility, which was even targeted at elementary students, as six year-old Ruby Bridges discovered in 1960 when she became the first black student to desegregate an elementary school in New Orleans. Meanwhile, the struggle to desegregate higher education continued. When James Meredith attempted to enroll at the University of Mississippi in 1962 he met with armed mob resistance. The federal government sent in reinforcements to ensure that he was finally admitted.

Chapters 5 and 6 analyse two developments, the sit-ins and the Freedom Rides, which crystalized and dramatically expanded the use of nonviolent direct action in the civil rights movement. The sit-in movement began in Greensboro, North Carolina, on 1 February 1960, when four students from North Carolina Agricultural and Technical College requested service at the Woolworth's department store lunch counter. When they were refused service, they sat at the lunch counter until the store closed for business at the end of the day. The students cited Indian independence leader Mohandas K. Gandhi and the Little Rock Nine as much as they did Martin Luther King, Jr as their source of inspiration for the nonviolent protest. The next day, the students came back again, with other students accompanying them. The demonstrations spread to other lunch counters in the city, and then to other cities in North Carolina, and eventually right across the South. Black colleges and universities provided a valuable information hub and support network to sustain the protests. As the sit-in movement expanded, other networks in the black community mobilized to support the students' actions. Nationwide, the NAACP assisted in coordinating economic boycotts against stores that had branches in the South. The sit-ins met with mixed results. In the upper South, many businesses decided to desegregate their lunch counters rather than endure continuing disruption. Others decided to do away with their lunch counters altogether rather than desegregate them. As was true in other efforts to end segregation, the lower South states formed the bedrock of resistance to change. One of the most important developments that grew out of the sit-ins was the formation of a new civil rights organization, the Student Nonviolent Coordinating Committee (SNCC – pronounced "snick"). SNCC was a vital incubator of student activism in the 1960s that ensured the youthful idealism that drove the sit-ins would continue to be nurtured. Ella Baker, one of the key people who had helped in the formation and early running of the SCLC, encouraged students to retain an independent voice rather than be subsumed into an adult-led organization. Baker was also influential in cultivating a different way of operating within SNCC than in other civil rights organizations. SNCC typically followed a participatory democracy model of organizing by working intently at the grassroots level to equip and empower local people to articulate and act on their community needs and concerns.

The 1961 Freedom Rides followed the sit-ins after a US Supreme Court ruling ordered an end to segregation in bus terminal facilities. The *Boynton v. Virginia* (1960) ruling was a result of Howard University student Bruce

Boynton's impromptu sit-in at a lunch counter terminal in Richmond, Virginia. The Congress of Racial Equality (CORE) decided to follow its earlier Journey of Reconciliation, which had tested the desegregation of interstate buses following the *Morgan v. Virginia* (1946) decision, with Freedom Rides. An interracial group of 13 freedom riders, which split between two buses, set off on a journey through the South in May 1961. After initial success in testing bus terminal facilities, the riders were attacked in Alabama. In the face of extreme white hostility, and with the bus companies refusing to transport them any further, the freedom riders decided to abandon their journey. A group of students based in Nashville, Tennessee, who had bonded together during the sit-in movement there, and who became an influential collective voice in SNCC, were determined to continue the Freedom Rides. They reasoned that if they did not, it would only serve to convince segregationists that the civil rights movement could be ground to a halt through the use of violence and intimidation. The pressure the students exerted finally moved the federal government, in the shape of Attorney General Robert Kennedy, to broker a deal to move them along their way to Montgomery. When they reached Montgomery, Alabama governor John Patterson reneged on a deal to keep the freedom riders safe and they were once again attacked by a white mob. Robert Kennedy sent in US federal marshals to protect them. The attorney general then brokered another deal with Mississippi governor James O. Eastland to get the freedom riders to their final destination of Jackson, Mississippi. This time, the riders arrived safely at their destination, but as part of the deal they were arrested and sent to unwelcoming Mississippi jails. Once the Kennedy administration had the freedom riders out of sight, they were also out of mind. To keep up the pressure, national civil rights organizations banded together to orchestrate and fund more Freedom Rides over the summer of 1961. The Kennedy administration finally agreed to petition the Interstate Commerce Commission (ICC) to ban segregation in interstate travel and in interstate travel terminal facilities. The ICC ban went into effect on 1 November 1961.

Martin Luther King, Jr played a cameo role in both the sit-ins and the Freedom Rides, but for the most part he watched from the wings as developments unfolded. Chapter 7 looks at the events that shaped King's understanding of where he and the SCLC best fit into the unfolding civil rights movement. Two campaigns between 1961 and 1963 were a steep learning curve. SNCC had already begun organizing in Albany, Georgia, in 1961, forming an alliance with other local civil rights groups in the city under the umbrella name of the Albany Movement. King was a latecomer to events when he agreed to visit the city at the request of local leaders. What he found there was a fractious black leadership and, in Laurie Pritchett, a chief of police who had given considerable thought to handling nonviolent direct action demonstrations. Pritchett believed that the best way to limit the movement's effectiveness was by diffusing protests as swiftly and calmly as possible. In the absence of any visible signs of extensive conflict to attract news headlines, the Kennedy administration looked the other way. King beat a retreat without gaining any concessions, even as the local movement continued on. King's defeat in Albany, as the story was styled, led to a good deal of reflection and much greater consideration of the location of the SCLC's next campaign. In Birmingham, Rev. Fred Shuttlesworth was the outspoken leader of the SCLC-affiliated Alabama Christian Movement for Human Rights (ACMHR). Shuttlesworth convinced King and the SCLC to stage protests in the city. Though things did not go strictly to plan, the SCLC improvised to adapt to local circumstances. Most controversially, SCLC field secretary James Bevel decided to recruit schoolchildren to participate in demonstrations. When director of public safety T. Eugene "Bull" Connor ordered snarling police dogs and spray from high-powered fire hoses turned on the children, President John F. Kennedy and the rest of the nation finally sat up and took notice. The scenes prompted President Kennedy to initiate civil rights legislation to end segregation. The civil rights movement appropriated the March on Washington for Jobs and Freedom that was being organized in 1963 by A. Philip Randolph and Bayard Rustin to place pressure on Congress to pass Kennedy's proposed legislation. The title of the event was shortened to the March on Washington and the rhetoric was toned down to make it less hostile to the Kennedy administration. In the end, it was the spectacle of the march rather than its substance that was remembered. King's celebrated "I Have a Dream" speech fully reflected that, with its stirring imagery and emotion very much to the fore, glossing over the fact that it made few concrete demands. Attention on the triumphal mass rally in Washington, DC turned to a tragedy in Birmingham soon after when a white terrorist bombing of a black church killed four young girls – Addie Mae Collins, Denise McNair, Carole Robertson, and Cynthia Wesley – who were attending Sunday school.

Another death – that of President Kennedy, who was assassinated in Dallas, Texas, in November 1963 – brought his vice president Lyndon B. Johnson into office. As a Texan, Johnson was considered a southerner, but he was even more committed to civil rights than Kennedy. A long-serving politician, Johnson was one of the few southerners in Congress who refused to sign the "Southern Manifesto" opposing the *Brown* decision. Against the odds, Johnson used all of his political know-how and guile to get the Civil Rights Act of 1964 passed and signed into law in July that year. Chapter 8 analyses the Civil Rights Act and the events of the 1964 Freedom Summer. Among its many provisions, the most immediate impact of the Civil Rights Act was to target an end to segregation in public accommodations and facilities. Attention then turned to the issue of voting rights. SNCC had been working on voter registration in Mississippi since 1961. The Kennedy administration had encouraged the civil rights movement to channel its efforts into voter registration since it believed it would prove less confrontational and less controversial than nonviolent direct action protests. The Kennedy administration was wrong. Efforts to secure the vote in Mississippi were resisted every bit as fiercely as other forms of civil rights activism, as SNCC workers soon discovered. After holding a Freedom Vote in 1963 to continue the process of voter education and mobilization in Mississippi, the following year SNCC recruited a cadre of volunteers, many of them white students from northern colleges, to expand those efforts in a 1964 Freedom Summer. In June, the disappearance and subsequent discovery of the bodies of three students, black Mississippian James Chaney and two white New Yorkers, Andrew Goodman and Michael Schwerner, drew national attention to Mississippi. In November 1964, Mississippi Freedom Democratic Party (MFDP) candidates elected during Freedom Summer tried to gain formal recognition at the Democratic National Convention. They resisted accepting a compromise for partial representation put forward by party officials, but their efforts did open up future conventions to greater diversity and wider participation. While Freedom Summer centered on the vote, it contained numerous other initiatives and experiments in community organizing and mobilization. Freedom Schools were set up and health clinics were founded to address the shortcomings of Mississippi's education and healthcare provisions for its black population. Both followed the SNCC ethos of encouraging local people to shape and to ultimately take control over running their own community institutions. The intense and close-quarters nature of Freedom Summer brought individual relationships under scrutiny, not just between blacks and whites, but also between men and women. As SNCC extolled its egalitarian philosophy, women began to question why that philosophy only applied to race relations and not to sex and gender relations too.

King and the SCLC launched their own voting rights campaign in Selma in early 1965. By contrast to SNCC's "bottom-up" community empowerment model of 1964's Freedom Summer, King and the SCLC targeted their short burst of community activism campaigns at a national audience to win support for "top-down" presidential and congressional action to pass voting rights legislation. The Selma campaign, covered in Chapter 9, was to voting rights legislation in 1965 what King and the SCLC's Birmingham campaign had been to civil rights legislation in 1963. A letter and tape recording from FBI assistant director William C. Sullivan sent anonymously to King prefaced the campaign. A straightforward blackmail attempt, the letter appeared to advise King to either kill himself or to withdraw from public life to avoid salacious revelations about his private life allegedly contained in the tape recording. The ineptitude of the SCLC's postal system meant that King did not receive the letter or the tape recording until after the campaign was already underway. In concert with SNCC and other local civil rights groups, the SCLC ran a nonviolent direct action campaign that culminated in a dramatic showdown on Selma's Edmund Pettus Bridge. When state troopers charged at protestors on horseback, wielding batons and firing tear gas, the national headlines it produced brought thousands of supporters from across the country to Selma in support of the movement. President Johnson made a powerful speech to Congress urging the passage of voting rights legislation. The Voting Rights Act of 1965 became law in August that year and contained a number of measures to provide greater access to the ballot for black voters. The Act remains a cornerstone in safeguarding voting rights today. But the campaign came at a cost. Three people, local black youth Jimmie Lee Jackson, northern white minister Rev. James B. Reeb, and a northern white volunteer Viola Gregg Liuzzo, were killed during its course. The campaign ended for King and the SCLC with a march from Selma to Montgomery, with King delivering a speech on the steps of the Alabama courthouse. SNCC workers, including Stokely Carmichael, stayed on in places such as Alabama's Lowndes County to continue their community-organizing efforts.

The usual convention at this point is to note that the passage of the Civil Rights Act of 1964 and the Voting Rights Act of 1965 marked the culmination of one phase of the southern civil rights movement in securing two of its major goals, the desegregation of public facilities and accommodations and voting rights. The movement then moved on to other issues and to other places. Outside the South, a different sort of *de facto* ("in fact") segregation rather than *de jure* ("in law") segregation held sway. This posed different sorts of problems for the movement to tackle. There is some kernel of truth in all this, but it is also a gross oversimplification, as more research is currently demonstrating. The southern movement's goals were never solely about desegregation and voting rights. Conditions that blacks encountered outside of the South, such as housing discrimination, limited access to education and employment opportunities, and white-dominated community policing, were just as pervasive inside the South. Equally, a focus on the southern civil rights movement in most narratives obscures much of the civil rights movement elsewhere. Only one historian, Thomas Sugrue, *Sweet Land of Liberty: The Forgotten Struggle for Civil Rights in the North* (Random House, 2008), has made a determined attempt to construct a coherent narrative of a northern civil rights movement, although a number of other scholars have turned their attention to various northern-based grassroots civil rights struggles – a good introduction to and overview of this work is Jeanne Theoharis and Komozi Woodard, eds. *Freedom North: Black Freedom Struggles outside the South, 1940–1980* (Palgrave Macmillan, 2003). Quintard Taylor, *In Search of the Racial Frontier: African Americans in the American West, 1528–1990* (W.W. Norton, 1998), has drawn attention to black freedom struggles in the West. Much still remains to be done. Will new regional histories of the civil rights movement emerge in the North,

Mid-West, Southwest, West, and elsewhere? Or will scholars artfully craft a national civil rights narrative that incorporates them all into one story? Mostly, the jury is still out on those questions.

Chapter 10, then, should be viewed as a window into a much larger and emerging field of scholarship, and not just an addendum or an aside to the main story. There seems little doubt that those in the movement understood that 1965 was a turning point of sorts. The passage of the Voting Rights Act of 1965 contrasted starkly with the violence that erupted in the Watts neighborhood of Los Angeles just five days later. Beginning as a local conflict between black residents and a white highway patrolman, events quickly escalated and extended into six days of unrest, resulting in 35 deaths. Watts was not the first urban uprising to occur in the 1960s, nor was it the last in what became termed the "long, hot summers" of the mid to late 1960s. When a government commission investigated the causes of unrest at the request of President Johnson, the resulting report, released in 1968, was damning in its observations about the role played by persistent racism in American society. Against this backdrop, movement thinkers and tacticians deliberated over the next step for action. Bayard Rustin advocated moving away from nonviolent direct action protests and entering into and influencing mainstream politics, building lasting coalitions with other groups, and strengthening institutions and power bases in black communities. Whitney Young, Jr, executive director of the National Urban League, called for a massive economic investment in impoverished black urban communities, a "National Marshall Plan" akin to the money the United States had dedicated to rebuilding devastated European nations after World War II. At first, Martin Luther King, Jr and the SCLC seemed convinced that they could transplant their southern campaign tactics to the North. However, in seeking to do so from 1965 to 1966 in Chicago, they discovered a very different sort of environment. The scale and size of the city and the issues it faced were quite different from those that King and the SCLC had primarily sought to tackle in the South. The task of simplifying the multifaceted issues of urban poverty and racism that afflicted Chicago, and finding ways to address them, proved far more difficult. King and the SCLC came away from Chicago with few concessions. The Chicago campaign forced King and the SCLC to rethink how they were going to navigate the post-1965 landscape. One of the things that King discovered in Chicago was that the depth of white grassroots resistance to civil rights was every bit as entrenched in the North as it was in the South. Sometimes this was expressed differently and sometimes it was all too familiar. In the early to mid-1970s, when Boston adopted a plan for the two-way busing of black and white students between segregated neighborhoods to achieve school desegregation – a method initially devised and mandated by the courts for use in southern school districts – massive resistance proved every bit as fierce as it had been in the South 20 years earlier.

Chapter 11 explores the black power movement. As with the previous chapter, the chapter on black power could well be extended into its own book-length collection of primary sources, and likewise it should be taken as another window into current research rather than any attempt at a comprehensive overview. Black power studies has expanded rapidly as a field in the past decade or so, and a number of its proponents have persuasively argued that it represents its own discrete era in the black freedom struggle, demanding attention in its own right rather than merely being an appendage to the civil rights movement. Much as the civil rights movement did, the black power movement drew upon longer traditions in the black freedom struggle while creating something fresh, innovative, and distinctive. The black power movement's much-publicized advocacy of armed self-defense had deep roots in black communities, particularly in the rural South where shotgun ownership was often the only deterrent to white violence. North Carolina's Robert F. Williams drew attention to this tradition in the early 1960s with the formation of a Black Armed Guard and the publication of his 1962 book *Negroes with Guns*. Nation of Islam (NOI) minister Malcolm X, who was assassinated in 1965 before the "black power" slogan became widely popularized, was nevertheless a strong influence on the movement. Malcolm transmitted longstanding black nationalist and black separatist traditions into the 1960s. SNCC worker, and from 1966 new SNCC chair, Stokely Carmichael, popularized the "black power" slogan on a 1966 March Against Fear instigated by James Meredith, the man who in 1962 desegregated the University of Mississippi. Carmichael's understanding of black power was developed in the rural South through his involvement in organizing the Black Panther Party in Lowndes County after the 1965 Selma-to-Montgomery march. Though the Black Panther Party originated in the rural South, it is today best known in popular culture as the derivative Black Panther Party for Self-Defense that was founded by Huey P. Newton and Bobby Seale in Oakland, California. The black power movement had a wide-ranging impact that introduced new styles and sensibilities to express black identity and culture. A good example of this is the Black Arts Movement that flourished in the late 1960s and early 1970s. Though the black power movement is sometimes characterized as being an expression of black hyper-masculinity, black women, as in the civil rights movement, played important roles at all levels. Discussions about the intersecting roles of race, gender, and class identity in the black power movement proved just as robust. One of the most iconic women associated with the black power movement was Angela Davis, whose activism on behalf of the imprisoned Soledad Brothers reflected the black power movement's concern with the relationship between the criminal justice system and racial discrimination.

Alongside the emergence of the black power movement, two issues loomed large in Martin Luther King Jr's final years of life: the Vietnam War and economic justice. Chapter 12 maps developments in those two areas. In the latter half of the 1960s, American involvement in Vietnam became a dominant concern that risked eclipsing the civil rights and black power movements in the headlines. The black population was disproportionately affected by the war. Blacks were more likely than whites to be drafted and they therefore bore an unequal share of the casualties. Movement activists claimed that they were drafted as a way to get rid of "troublemakers" at home. Some organizations, such as SNCC, questioned whether they should be fighting people of color overseas at all while they continued to face racial discrimination in the United States. King's initial concerns about the war in his public pronouncements were centered on the way it diverted attention and funds away from the civil rights movement and President Johnson's War on Poverty programs. King's wariness about cutting ties with the Johnson administration over the Vietnam War precluded a more strident approach, but on 4 April 1967, a year to the day before his assassination, at New York's Riverside Church King delivered a stinging rebuke to America's involvement in Vietnam, echoing SNCC's earlier Statement on Vietnam about the moral bankruptcy of American foreign and domestic policy. King and the SCLC also began to formulate plans for a Poor People's Campaign (PPC) as part of wider antipoverty efforts taking place in the latter half of the 1960s that included many nongovernmental initiatives such as the formation of the National Welfare Rights Organization (NWRO). As preparations got underway, King became involved in a labor dispute in Memphis, where black sanitation workers who belonged to the American Federation of State, County and Municipal Employees (AFSCME) union were striking for better pay and conditions. King felt that the issues at stake vividly illustrated the intersection between race and economic injustice. Attempts to carry out a nonviolent march in support of the sanitation workers in March 1968 went awry as violence broke out. Some blamed the local Memphis black power group the Invaders for the trouble, although they protested their innocence and offered to help organize another march. While legal wrangles over another march continued, on 4 April King was assassinated on his Lorraine Motel room balcony. King's friend and fellow minister Ralph Abernathy took over as SCLC president and inherited the responsibility of running the PPC. The PPC climaxed in Washington, DC in May and June 1968 with mixed results. Demonstrations were finally abandoned prematurely. The PPC was the last major SCLC campaign of the 1960s.

Chapter 13 continues the attention on economic justice in looking at the development of the idea of affirmative action and responses to it from the 1960s through the 1980s. President Kennedy's 1961 Executive Order 10925 first coined the term "affirmative action" but only attached a very vague definition to it. Kennedy's 1963 Executive Order 11114 described affirmative action in terms of "the elimination of discrimination" in employment. This language was adopted in the Civil Rights Act of 1964, which extended nondiscriminatory mandates to cover all firms (not just, as previously, government-related and government-funded employment) with over 25 employees. In a 1965 speech at Howard University, President Johnson went further still, stating that the aim was to move beyond opening up "opportunity" to the actual "achievement" of a more diverse workplace. Building on the policies of Democratic presidents Kennedy and Johnson, in 1969 Republican president Richard M. Nixon's administration set "specific goals of minority manpower utilization" for federal construction contracts in Philadelphia. Affirmative action policies worked in achieving better employment opportunities for blacks in the 1970s, albeit circumscribed by other factors such as a faltering economy, a gender stratified workplace, and the geographical coordinates of new employment opportunities that were more abundant in the predominantly white suburbs than in the disproportionately black cities. By the late 1970s, and more concertedly under Republican President Ronald Reagan and an increasingly conservative leaning US Supreme Court since the 1980s, affirmative action came under legal attack. In *Regents of the University of California v. Bakke* (1978) the Court struck down the use of racial "quotas" in higher education (that is, setting aside a certain number of places for "disadvantaged" – meaning minority – students), while keeping the door open to the consideration of a student's racial and ethnic background, among other factors, in making admissions decisions. In *Firefighters Local Union No. 1784 v. Stotts* (1984) the Court struck down an affirmative action program in Memphis in favor of a "last hired, first fired" seniority policy that advantaged white workers.

Fully encapsulating the legacies of the civil rights and black power movements in a limited number of sources is an impossible task, but Chapter 14 begins to trace just some of the main threads to which many others may comfortably be attached. The civil rights and black power movements became the blueprint and inspiration for a movement culture that grew out of and continued beyond the 1960s. The first three sources in this chapter touch upon and introduce three of these movements. The Young Lords was a Puerto Rican-oriented organization that found ethnic solidarity in a program and platform that held distinct similarities to that of the Black Panther Party for Self-Defense. The gay (more commonly referred to today as the LGBTQ+) rights movement embraced a growing collective voice and mustered concerted action related to issues of sexual orientation and gender identity. The Combahee River Collective coined the term "identity politics" in exploring the intersections of race, class, gender, and sexuality. King's role as leader of the civil rights movement was seared into the national consciousness with the establishment of a national holiday in his honor. The debates that revolved around establishing the holiday, and the meanings attached to King and the civil rights movement in those deliberations, revealed the still contested nature of King's and the movement's legacies. Nelson Mandela's dramatic rise from long-term political prisoner to president of South Africa in the space of four years during the early 1990s highlighted once more the international scope of black freedom struggles. In a visit to Atlanta shortly after his release from prison, Mandela made clear his debt to King and the civil rights movement as a source of inspiration. While the movement's influence was evident overseas, it continued to fight both new and old battles at home. Environmental racism and the role of what commentators refer to as the school-to-prison pipeline that entwines schools with the criminal justice system were among the newly articulated concerns, although, as we see throughout this book, "new" concerns can almost always be identified as having much earlier origins. At the same time, some of the "old" battles were very familiar, for example in fighting to uphold school desegregation, voting rights, and affirmative action, all of which have come under renewed threat. Economic justice remains elusive as the massive wealth gap that exists between blacks and whites testifies. And yet, there are signs that the movement's legacies are still vital and flourishing, from the "top-down" election of America's first black president Barack Obama in 2008, and his re-election in 2012, to the "bottom-up" emergence of the social media-inspired Black Lives Matter movement. The omnipresent white "backlash" to both of these developments, among others, suggests that the struggle for freedom and equality remains as intensely alive and contested today as it ever was.

Further Reading

Branch, Taylor. *Parting the Waters: Martin Luther King and the Civil Rights Movement, 1954–63* (Simon and Schuster, 1988).

Branch, Taylor. *Pillar of Fire: America in the King Years, 1963–65* (Simon and Schuster, 1998).

Branch, Taylor. *At Canaan's Edge: America in the King Years, 1965–1968* (Simon and Schuster, 2006).

Fairclough, Adam. *To Redeem the Soul of America: The Southern Christian Leadership Conference and Martin Luther King, Jr* (University of Georgia Press, 1987).

Fairclough, Adam. *Better Day Coming: Blacks and Equality, 1890–2000* (New York: Penguin, 2001).

Garrow, David J. *Bearing the Cross: Martin Luther King, Jr and the Southern Christian Leadership Conference* (William Morrow, 1986).

Hampton, Henry, and Steve Fayer, eds. *Voices of Freedom: An Oral History of the Civil Rights Movement from the 1950s through the 1980s* (Vintage, 1994).

Kirk, John A. *Martin Luther King, Jr* (Pearson Longman, 2005).

Kirk, John A. *Martin Luther King, Jr and the Civil Rights Movement: Controversies and Debates* (Palgrave Macmillan, 2007).

Lawson, Steven F. *Running for Freedom: Civil Rights and Black Politics Since 1941* (Wiley Blackwell, 2014, fourth edition).

Marable, Manning. *Race, Reform and Rebellion: The Second Reconstruction in Black America, 1945–1982* (University of Mississippi, 2007, third edition).

O'Reilly, Kenneth. *Nixon's Piano: Presidents and Racial Politics from Washington to Clinton* (Free Press, 1995).

Raines, Howell, ed. *My Soul is Rested: Movement Days in the Deep South Remembered* (Penguin, 1983).

Theoharis, Jeanne. *A More Beautiful and Terrible History: The Uses and Misuses of Civil Rights History* (Beacon Press, 2018).

Chapter 1   Origins of the Civil Rights Movement

1.1 *New York Amsterdam Star-News*, "Bus Boycott Ends in Victory," 1941

The Montgomery bus boycott of 1955–1956 has become a landmark event in civil rights history. But, like so many developments in the civil rights movement in the 1950s and 1960s, it echoed and built upon the past. Almost 15 years before events in Montgomery made headlines, residents in the predominantly black neighborhood of Harlem, New York City, successfully ran a bus boycott to win demands for better and more employment opportunities. There were distinct similarities between the two events. Notably, the leadership of Adam Clayton Powell, Jr, a dynamic leader of Harlem's biggest church, Abyssian Baptist, who advocated peaceful and nonviolent protest, provides a parallel to Martin Luther King Jr's ministerial leadership of the bus boycott in Montgomery. Both Harlem and Montgomery bus boycotts depended upon urbanized black communities that could be energized, organized, and mobilized to achieve their goals. Yet there were differences too. The Harlem bus boycott was about jobs, whereas the later Montgomery bus boycott protested segregation. This speaks to the differences in conditions that blacks faced in the North and South of the United States at mid-century. Many blacks had migrated north to escape segregation, disenfranchisement, economic exploitation, and racial violence in the South. What they discovered in the North was persistent racial discrimination, sometimes manifested in the same ways as in the South, sometimes different. These different experiences and environments helped in turn to shape different black responses to them. Powell worked with the Harlem Labor Union and other black groups in New York to form a United Bus Strike Committee to first

The Civil Rights Movement: A Documentary Reader, First Edition. Edited by John A. Kirk.
© 2020 John Wiley & Sons, Inc. Published 2020 by John Wiley & Sons, Inc.

support and then to follow up on a strike by the city's Transport Workers Union against the Fifth Avenue Coach Company and the New York Omnibus Corporation. For a month, the boycott kept 60,000 people a day off the buses at an estimated daily loss of $3,000 in fares. The boycott led to an agreement to hire 100 black drivers and 70 mechanics, as well as an undertaking to increase the number of black employees on buses to 17% of the workforce in line with the percentage of blacks who lived in Manhattan at the time.

Bus Boycott Ends in Victory

———

Local Groups Planning Big Celebration

———

Contract Provides for Hiring 100 Drivers and 70 Mechanics

———

Harlem dropped its hard pressed picket campaign against the bus companies last Saturday and moved to celebrate a victory which assured the employment of Negroes as drivers on New York City buses and workers as mechanics in maintenance shops. The contract ended a four-week bus strike, in which it was said, Omnibus and Fifth Avenue Coach Company lost more than $3,000 a day.

The agreement, which was signed on April 19, provides among other things that "A minimum of one hundred Negro drivers will be employed as operators of buses before other drivers are employed" and "A minimum of seventy Negro workers will be employed as maintenance men in all categories before other workers are employed in this division" and an additional number of Negro employees on the ratio "of one Negro to one white man until the total number of Negro workers employed" by the bus companies "shall be equal to seventeen per cent of all workers employed by them exclusively in New York City."

The contract, which bound the bus company to hire Negroes, "subject, however, to the working agreements, policies and conditions" of the companies and the agreement, failed to specify any time limit for the hiring of Negroes. But the bus companies did agree "to commence training immediately a group of Negroes in the practice and details of operation of buses on the highways of New York City," but retained to themselves the right to determine "the membership and size of such a group."

Before any Negroes will be employed as drivers by the Fifth Avenue Coach Company ninety-one laid-off employees, who are to be entitled to seniority rights must be rehired.

In the meantime, the United Negro Bus Association is laying plans for its monster victory parade and open air mass meeting on Saturday, May 3, from 1 to 4 p.m., at Colonial Park, 15th St and Broadhurst Ave., when Michael Quill, international president, and other officials of the Transport Workers Union, officials of the bus companies and leaders of the bus strike are expected to address the people of Harlem.

Source: *New York Amsterdam Star-News*, 26 April 1941, p. 1.

1.2 A. Philip Randolph, "Call to Negro America to March on Washington for Jobs and Equal Participation in National Defense," 1941

The United States' preparations for and eventual entry into World War II provided an important context for the victory in the Harlem bus boycott and in other black gains during the 1940s. Labor shortages on the home front and the potential opening up of new jobs from which blacks had previously been excluded convinced many that the time had come to take decisive action to seize the opportunities on offer. Moreover, blacks were fighting to defend the United States overseas against avowedly undemocratic and racist enemies in a strictly segregated military while still fighting for democracy and against racism at home. These very apparent contradictions led the black newspaper the Pittsburgh Courier *to launch a campaign for a "double V" for victory, which encouraged blacks to fight for greater democracy and recognition of their role in the war effort on the home front as well as fighting the enemy overseas. One area of possibility for new black jobs was in wartime defense industries. Just as in the segregated military, however, blacks faced discrimination in wartime employment.*

Labor leader A. Philip Randolph, president of the Brotherhood of Sleeping Car Porters Union (BSCPU), the largest black union in the United States at the time, led the call for President Franklin D. Roosevelt to introduce legislation to end discrimination in wartime industries, in government hiring, and in the armed forces. Randolph declared that he would lead 10,000 (later upped to 100,000) marchers on Washington, DC to back up his demands. In response, Roosevelt signed Executive Order 8802 in June 1941, which banned "discrimination in the employment of workers in defense industries or government because of race, creed, color, or national origin." Randolph called off the march, although he later reprised the idea in the 1963 March on Washington for Jobs and Freedom. The Fair Employment Practices Committee (FEPC) that was created to implement and oversee Roosevelt's executive order struggled to combat racial discrimination. Roosevelt made further moves to strengthen the FEPC in 1943 by increasing its budget and by increasing the scope of its mission and the number of its staff. At the beginning of the war, blacks had held 3% of wartime industry jobs. By the end of the war, that number had grown to 8%. The number of government jobs for blacks grew threefold. After the war ended, Congress cut the FEPC's budget and it formally dissolved in 1946.

The eventual desegregation of the armed forces came in 1948. Though its gains were relatively limited and short-lived, the FEPC offered a glimmer of hope that federal action could combat racial discrimination – something that the civil rights movement looked to build upon further in the postwar era.

We call upon you to fight for jobs in National Defense. We call upon you to struggle for the integration of Negroes in the armed forces [...]

We call upon you to demonstrate for the abolition of Jim-Crowism in all Government departments and defense employment.

This is an hour of crisis. It is a crisis of democracy. It is a crisis of minority groups. It is a crisis of Negro Americans. What is this crisis?

To American Negroes, it is the denial of jobs in Government defense projects. It is racial discrimination in Government departments. It is widespread Jim-Crowism in the armed forces of the Nation.

While billions of the taxpayers' money are being spent for war weapons, Negro workers are finally being turned away from the gates of factories, mines and mills – being flatly told, "NOTHING DOING." Some employers refuse to give Negroes jobs when they are without "union cards," and some unions refuse Negro workers union cards when they are "without jobs."

What shall we do?

What a dilemma!

What a runaround!

What a disgrace!

What a blow below the belt!

Though dark, doubtful and discouraging, all is not lost, all is not hopeless. Though battered and bruised, we are not beaten, broken, or bewildered.

Verily, the Negroes' deepest disappointments and direst defeats, their tragic trials and outrageous oppressions in these dreadful days of destruction and disaster to democracy and freedom, and the rights of minority peoples, and the dignity and independence of the human spirit, is the Negroes' greatest opportunity to rise to the highest heights of struggle for freedom and justice in Government, in industry, in labor unions, education, social service, religion, and culture.

With faith and confidence of the Negro people in their own power for self-liberation, Negroes can break down those barriers of discrimination against employment in National Defense. Negroes can kill the deadly serpent of race hatred in the Army, Navy, Air and Marine Corps, and smash through and blast the Government, business and labor-union red tape to win the right to equal opportunity in vocational training and re-training in defense employment.

Most important and vital of all, Negroes, by the mobilization and coordination of their mass power, can cause PRESIDENT ROOSEVELT TO

ISSUE AN EXECUTIVE ORDER ABOLISHING DISCRIMINATIONS IN ALL GOVERNMENT DEPARTMENT, ARMY, NAVY, AIR CORPS AND NATIONAL DEFENSE JOBS.

Of course, the task is not easy. In very truth, it is big, tremendous and difficult.

It will cost money.

It will require sacrifice.

It will tax the Negroes' courage, determination and will to struggle. But we can, must and will triumph.

The Negroes' stake in national defense is big. It consists of jobs, thousands of jobs. It may represent millions, yes hundreds of millions of dollars in wages. It consists of new industrial opportunities and hope. This is worth fighting for.

But to win our stakes, it will require an "all-out," bold and total effort and demonstration of colossal proportions.

Negroes can build a mammoth machine of mass action with a terrific and tremendous driving and striking power that can shatter and crush the evil fortress of race prejudice and hate, if they will only resolve to do so and never stop, until victory comes.

Dear fellow Negro Americans, be not dismayed by these terrible times. You possess power, great power. Our problem is to harness and hitch it up for action on the broadest, daring and most gigantic scale.

In this period of power politics, nothing counts but pressure, more pressure, and still more pressure, through the tactic and strategy of broad, organized, aggressive mass action behind the vital and important issues of the Negro. To this end, we propose that ten thousand Negroes MARCH ON WASHINGTON FOR JOBS IN NATIONAL DEFENSE AND EQUAL INTEGRATION IN THE FIGHTING FORCES OF THE UNITED STATES.

An "all-out" thundering march on Washington, ending in a monster and huge demonstration at Lincoln's Monument will shake up white America.

It will shake up official Washington.

It will give encouragement to our white friends to fight all the harder by our side, with us, for our righteous cause.

It will gain respect for the Negro people.

It will create a new sense of self-respect among Negroes.

But what of national unity?

We believe in national unity which recognizes equal opportunity of black and white citizens to jobs in national defense and the armed forces, and in all other institutions and endeavors in America. We condemn all dictatorships, Fascist, Nazi and Communist. We are loyal, patriotic Americans all.

But if American democracy will not defend its defenders; if American democracy will not protect its protectors; if American democracy will not give jobs to its toilers because of race or color; if American democracy will not insure equality of opportunity, freedom and justice to its citizens, black and white, it is a hollow mockery and belies the principles for which it is supposed to stand [...]

Today we call on President Roosevelt, a great humanitarian and idealist, to [...] free American Negro citizens of the stigma, humiliation and insult of discrimination and Jim-Crowism in Government departments and national defense.

The Federal Government cannot with clear conscience call upon private industry and labor unions to abolish discrimination based on race and color as long as it practices discrimination itself against Negro Americans.

Source: *Black Worker* 14 (May 1941), n.p. http://www.wwnorton.com/college/history/archive/resources/documents/ch30_02.htm

1.3   James Farmer Recalls the Congress of Racial Equality's Chicago Sit-In in 1942

The misconception that the Montgomery bus boycott was the first bus boycott to protest racial discrimination is paralleled in the way we also often mistakenly assume that the 1960 Greensboro, North Carolina, sit-ins were the first protests of their kind. In fact, the idea of a sit-in was adapted from the sit-down labor strikes originating in the 1930s when workers occupied their workplaces to halt production until management listened to their concerns. And it was the Committee (changed a year later to Congress) of Racial Equality (CORE) that first adopted the tactic of a sit-in demonstration for civil rights in Chicago in 1942. CORE was formed in 1942 as an outgrowth of the pacifist organization the Fellowship of Reconciliation (FOR). Inspired by Indian independence leader Mohandas K. Gandhi's use of civil disobedience and nonviolence, the interracial group borrowed from Gandhi's tactics and redeployed them in the struggle against racial discrimination in the United States. CORE's first target was segregation in Chicago's Jack Spratt restaurant chain. Below, James Farmer, a co-founder and later the national director of CORE, narrates what happened.

On that day in May 1942, we began what I believe to be the first organized civil rights sit-in in American history. A group of twenty-eight persons entered Jack Spratt in parties of two, three and four. In each party, there was one black man or woman. With the discipline of peacefulness strictly observed, we occupied all available seating spaces at the counter and in booths.

The small restaurant staff was thrown into confusion. The man who we believed to be the manager was not there. The woman with whom our negotiation team had talked was in charge. Waitresses looked at each other and shrugged. Then they looked at the white woman in charge for a cue, but none was forthcoming. All the while, we sat smoking and quietly chatting.

Two whites, who were not obviously members of our group and were sitting some distance from each other at the counter, were served. One, a well-dressed middle-aged woman, thanked the waitress when her food arrived, but sitting with hands in her lap, did not touch it. The other, a man, also older, promptly passed his food to the black beside him, who proceeded to eat it.

The woman in charge went to the lady who had been served and asked, "Is your dinner all right ma'am?"

"Oh, I'm sure it's just fine."

"But you aren't eating it."

"I know. You see, it wouldn't be very polite for me to begin eating before my friends also had been served."

An elderly couple dining in one booth inquired what was going on.

When informed by one of our people in the next booth, they discussed it between themselves and then passed the word to us that they agreed with us and would eat no more of their food until all of us were served. And they would not leave until we left.

This evoked a silent applause from the neighboring booths. Other customers, not in our groups, had stopped eating, too, or were eating very slowly; they did not want to miss any of this drama. They had, in effect, joined the sit-in out of curiosity if nothing else.

After making a phone call, the woman in charge swept past me and spoke to Jimmy Robinson [the white CORE treasurer]. "If the colored people in your group will go to the basement, I'll have them served there."

I responded: "No, ma'am. We will not eat in the basement."

"Well," she said, still speaking to Jimmy, not to me, "if you'll clear out the two rear booths, then all the colored people can sit there, and I will have them served."

"No, thank you," I said. "We're quite comfortable where we are."

"I'll call the police," she said, and now she was looking directly at me with a triumphant expression on her face.

I told her I thought that might be the appropriate thing for her to do. (I had phoned the police precinct just before the demonstration, telling them precisely what we were going to do and exactly how. I had explained the discipline of nonviolence and had refreshed their memory about the little-used state civil rights law in Illinois. This was in line with the Gandhian principle of being open and above board with the authorities.)

Within minutes, two of Chicago's finest walked in. After casting their eyes around the restaurant, they walked to her and one of them asked, "What did you call us for, lady? I don't see anybody disturbing the peace. What do you want us to do?"

"I want you to throw these people out, of course," she replied.

"Lady, we can't do that. What're they doing wrong? You're open for business aren't you? They're not trespassing."

"Well, now, won't you throw them out," she asked, "on the grounds that we reserve the right to seat our patrons and would serve some of them in the basement?"

The policeman slapped his thigh in exasperation. He went into the phone booth and made a call. When he came out he said, "No, lady, there's nothing in the law that allows us to do that. You must either serve them or solve the problem yourself the best way you can."

The cops left, one winking at me as he passed by.

The woman in charge ordered the waitresses to serve everyone.

After dining and leaving good tips for the waitresses, to compensate them for the time we had occupied the seats, we paid our bills and left. The money was not thrown out this time.

Jimmy wrote Jack Spratt a letter thanking them for the service and congratulating them on their change in policy. Subsequent tests over the next fortnight by small mixed and all-black groups confirmed that the policy had, in fact, changed.

Source: James Farmer, *Lay Bare the Heart: An Autobiography of the Civil Rights Movement* (New York: Arbor House, 1985), pp. 106–8.

1.4 US Supreme Court, *Smith v. Allwright*, 1944

A large obstacle to black freedom and equality in the South was disenfranchisement, which denied the vast majority of blacks the ability to participate in local and state politics. The right to vote had been established by the Fifteenth Amendment, ratified in 1870, which prevented discrimination on the grounds of "race, color, or previous condition of servitude." However, from the 1890s onward, southern states employed a number of different devices to disenfranchise black people. Some implemented poll taxes to price blacks out of voting, while others instituted literacy tests administered by white election officials. Another instrument of exclusion from the political process in some states was the all-white party primary. In a solidly Democratic Party-dominated South, the Democratic Party's primary elections were the most important part of the electoral process. Whoever won the party nomination was virtually guaranteed to win the general election; in many instances, this occurred without any opposition from other party candidates. White Democrats excluded blacks from party primaries, contending that they were private elections run by party officials and therefore not subject to the provisions of the Fourteenth and Fifteenth Amendments, which only covered actions taken by government officials. The National Association for the Advancement of Colored People's Legal Defense and Educational Fund (NAACP LDF) challenged this contention in a number of lawsuits, insisting that party primaries were in fact an integral part of the electoral process and covered by constitutional amendments. In the Texas case of Smith v. Allwright *(1944), the US Supreme Court upheld the NAACP LDF's legal argument and abolished all-white party primaries. While many other obstacles to the vote still remained, the* Smith *decision gave further encouragement to blacks that the federal government was willing to act to protect civil rights. The case also provided the NAACP LDF with a signal court victory that helped pave the way for others to follow.*

The right of a Negro to vote in the Texas primary has been considered heretofore by this Court. The first case was *Nixon v. Herndon*, 273 US 536. At that time, 1924, the Texas statute, Art. 3093a, afterwards numbered Art. 3107 (Rev. Stat. 1925) declared "in no event shall a Negro be eligible to participate in a Democratic Party primary election in the State of Texas." [Dr. L.A.] Nixon was refused the right to vote in a Democratic primary and brought a suit for damages against the election officers under R. S. §§ 1979 and 2004, the present §§ 43 and 31 of Title 8, USC, respectively. It was urged to this Court that the denial of the franchise to Nixon violated his Constitutional rights under the Fourteenth and Fifteenth Amendments. Without consideration of the Fifteenth, this Court held that the action of Texas in denying the ballot to Negroes by statute was in violation of the equal protection clause of the Fourteenth Amendment and reversed the dismissal of the suit.

The legislature of Texas reenacted the article but gave the State Executive Committee of a party the power to prescribe the qualifications of its members for voting or other participation. This article remains in the statutes. The State Executive Committee of the Democratic party adopted a resolution that white Democrats and none other might participate in the primaries of that party. Nixon was refused again the privilege of voting in a primary and again brought suit for damages by virtue of § 31, Title 8, USC. This Court again reversed the dismissal of the suit for the reason that the Committee action was deemed to be state action and invalid as discriminatory under the Fourteenth Amendment. The test was said to be whether the Committee operated as representative of the State in the discharge of the State's authority. *Nixon v. Condon*, 286 US 73. The question of the inherent power of a political party in Texas "without restraint by any law to determine its own membership" was left open.

In *Grovey v. Townsend*, 295 US 45, this Court had before it another suit for damages for the refusal in a primary of a county clerk, a Texas officer with only public functions to perform, to furnish petitioner, a Negro, an absentee ballot. The refusal was solely on the ground of race. This case differed from *Nixon v. Condon, supra*, in that a state convention of the Democratic party had passed the resolution of May 24, 1932, hereinbefore quoted. It was decided that the determination by the state convention of the membership of the Democratic party made a significant change from a determination by the Executive

Committee. The former was party action, voluntary in character. The latter, as had been held in the *Condon* case, was action by authority of the State. The managers of the primary election were therefore declared not to be state officials in such sense that their action was state action. A state convention of a party was said not to be an organ of the State. This Court went on to announce that to deny a vote in a primary was a mere refusal of party membership with which "the State need have no concern," *loc. cit.* at 55, while for a State to deny a vote in a general election on the ground of race or color violated the Constitution. Consequently, there was found no ground for holding that the county clerk's refusal of a ballot because of racial ineligibility for party membership denied the petitioner any right under the Fourteenth or Fifteenth Amendment.

Since *Grovey* v. *Townsend* and prior to the present suit, no case from Texas involving primary elections has been before this Court. We did decide, however, *United States* v. *Classic*, 313 US 299. We there held that § 4 of Article I of the Constitution authorized Congress to regulate primary as well as general elections, 313 US at 316, 317, "where the primary is by law made an integral part of the election machinery." 313 US at 318. Consequently, in the *Classic* case, we upheld the applicability to frauds in a Louisiana primary of §§ 19 and 20 of the Criminal Code. Thereby corrupt acts of election officers were subjected to Congressional sanctions because that body had power to protect rights of federal suffrage secured by the Constitution in primary as in general elections. 313 US at 323. This decision depended, too, on the determination that under the Louisiana statutes the primary was a part of the procedure for choice of federal officials. By this decision the doubt as to whether or not such primaries were a part of "elections" subject to federal control, which had remained unanswered since *Newberry* v. *United States*, 256 US 232, was erased. The *Nixon Cases* were decided under the equal protection clause of the Fourteenth Amendment without a determination of the status of the primary as a part of the electoral process. The exclusion of Negroes from the primaries by action of the State was held invalid under that Amendment. The fusing by the *Classic* case of the primary and general elections into a single instrumentality for choice of officers has a definite bearing on the permissibility under the Constitution of excluding Negroes from primaries. This is not to say that the *Classic* case cuts directly into the rationale of *Grovey* v. *Townsend*. This latter case was not mentioned in the opinion. *Classic* bears upon *Grovey* v. *Townsend* not because exclusion of Negroes from primaries is any more or less state action by reason of the unitary character of the electoral process but because the recognition of the place of the primary in the electoral scheme makes clear that state delegation to a party of the power to fix the qualifications of primary elections is delegation of a state function that may make the party's action the action of the State. When *Grovey* v. *Townsend* was written, the Court looked upon the denial of a vote in a primary as a mere refusal by a party of party membership. 295 US at 55. As the Louisiana statutes for holding primaries are similar to those of Texas, our ruling in *Classic* as to the unitary character of the electoral process calls for a reexamination as to whether or not the exclusion of Negroes from a Texas party primary was state action.

The statutes of Texas relating to primaries and the resolution of the Democratic party of Texas extending the privileges of membership to white citizens only are the same in substance and effect today as they were when *Grovey* v. *Townsend* was decided by a unanimous Court. The question as to whether the exclusionary action of the party was the action of the State persists as the determinative factor. In again entering upon consideration of the inference to be drawn as to state action from a substantially similar factual situation, it should be noted that *Grovey* v. *Townsend* upheld exclusion of Negroes from primaries through the denial of party membership by a party convention. A few years before, this Court refused approval of exclusion by the State Executive Committee of the party. A different result was reached on the theory that the Committee action was state authorized and the Convention action was unfettered by statutory control. Such a variation in the result from so slight a change in form influences us to consider anew the legal validity of the distinction which has resulted in barring Negroes from participating in the nominations of candidates of the Democratic party in Texas. Other precedents of this Court forbid the abridgement of the right to vote. *United States v. Reese*, 92 US 214, 217; *Neal v. Delaware*, 103 US 370, 388; *Guinn v. United States*, 238 US 347, 361; *Myers v. Anderson*, 238 US 368, 379; *Lane v. Wilson*, 307 US 268.

It may now be taken as a postulate that the right to vote in such a primary for the nomination of candidates without discrimination by the State, like the right to vote in a general election, is a right secured by the Constitution. *United States v. Classic*, 313 US at 314; *Myers v. Anderson*, 238 US 368; *Ex parte Yarbrough*, 110 US 651, 663 *et seq.* By the terms of the Fifteenth Amendment that right may not be abridged by any State on account of race. Under our Constitution the great privilege of the ballot may not be denied a man by the State because of his color.

Source: US Supreme Court, *Smith v. Allwright*, 321 US 649 (1944), https://supreme.justia.com/cases/federal/us/321/649/case.html

1.5 Annie L. McPheeters Interview on Grassroots Voter Registration in Atlanta in the 1930s and 1940s

While the NAACP LDF and its attorneys battled through the courts, it took an army of workers on the ground to pave the way at local and state levels for the

national gains that would follow. Securing changes in the law was one side of the struggle; implementing them and making them a tangible day-to-day reality in the lives of black people was another. Black women such as Atlanta's Annie McPheeters played vital roles in preparing black communities for change. A number of black women held positions that gave them access to valuable community resources that could be harnessed in civil rights struggles. In McPheeters's case, she acted in her capacity as a professional librarian to support black literacy initiatives that were essential in overcoming literacy tests at the polls and in securing better jobs. The library also formed a hub for connecting the local community to regionwide and nationwide networks, bringing in outside speakers and exposing patrons to new ideas and information. Equally, the library acted as a community information exchange and as a point of contact for political education and voter mobilization. Since blacks had been denied the vote for decades, reviving an interest in voting rights and educating patrons about how to claim the vote and how to use it effectively once they had secured it was essential if the black community was going to make its political voice heard. The Negro Women's Voters League and the League of Women Voters that McPheeters worked with helped to educate black voters through raising consciousness about the importance of the vote as well as attending to more directly practical matters, such as how to use a voting machine. In many ways, reviving and instilling a political culture among a long disenfranchised community of people was as much of a struggle as securing the vote itself.

[A]fter completing my work as a professional librarian, I began working in the public library. The public library service was my main interest in library service. And, as has been recorded, the public library is one with the public school, in that it teaches people how to know how to read, provides them with books and materials; and, last of all, the public library works with people in their various efforts in learning how to become good citizens. And, this, of course, was one of the main purposes of our public library. And, in addition to that type of service, the whole community as a result, would be better educated if they became members of the public library. This was one of the things that we, in our attempts in the public library, did to bring citizens into close contact with the public library – so that down through the years we did various – our staff was organized so that we could bring the citizen and his library into close contact. I was the librarian, head of the library, and head of the Negro Department. I organized the staff in this manner: I, as the head librarian, would be in charge of the adult education programs and do the outreach programs. And the children's librarian would work with the children and the young people; and then we had another, non-professional who did the clerical work and who did the publicity for our branch. Then, we had a library page who came in and served – slipped and shelved the books and placed those books on the shelves [...]

Th[e Adult Education] program was an excellent program for those persons who participated in it. As I said, various persons from the community were brought in to speak to the groups. We had the college presidents who came in, our president from Atlanta University and several others. And, at that time, also, one of the outstanding discussion groups centered around Gandhi and his movement. And we had several programs directly connected with the Gandhi movement. Then, there were other aspects that were discussed, too, during this adult education program. So, it lasted from 1931 to 1934. It was in 1934 that I came to the library, and just before that adult education project closed. And I was able to learn a good bit about how an adult education project would function. And when that project closed, then I was able to work out an adult education program for our library – although we could not – we did not have the staff to carry out the project as much as it had been done under the Adult Education Program – but we did follow through as much as we could in that respect [...]

One of the first groups that I knew about and had worked with was the Negro Women's Voters League. This League, as I understand it, was formed by Mrs Ruby Blackburn. Mrs Blackburn was an outstanding person, a very active person in the community – and she was most interested in voters – in voting – and she knew the lack of interest on the part of black voters to turn out and vote. One of her main objectives was to go into the various meetings and anywhere in the community that she had a chance – she was always interested in talking with those groups and encouraging them to vote and to participate in the various voters leagues. And, as a result, as I said, she formed what was known as the Negro Women's Voters League. That name was "Negro Women's Voters League" [more often referred to as: League of Negro Women Voters] – yes, she called it. It was organized, I think around 1947 or 1949. And although she was an uneducated woman – she had her work, basically, for her livelihood, she was a beautician; but she was so interested in politics and civic activities that she went all over the city and even out of the city. She went to Washington and other places like that, carrying the message and interesting people in their right to vote and in their right to participate in voting activities.

And the other group that our library staff worked closely with was the League of Women Voters. This group of women was very instrumental each year when that time came, they would collect a lot of material on the various persons running for office. And they would distribute this material to the various libraries. Well, it was a long time before we knew, in the library, much about the League of Women Voters because at that time segregation was still the outstanding aspect in our community and we did learn later about the League of Women Voters and their activity. And I contacted them, and they would come to the library and give us materials for use to pass out to the various citizens.

One of the things that they were instrumental in doing, as well as the Negro Women Voters League, was to assist citizens in learning how to use the voting machines. During those early years, after we stopped casting our ballot – just marking a ballot and dropping it in a box, then, the voting machines became popular. But the citizens – many of them – stayed away and were afraid to use them. And, as a result, they did not know how to use these voting machines. And so the League of Women Voters and the Negro Women Voters League would come to the library and teach citizens how to use these machines because we had asked that the voting machines be placed in all of the branches and also placed at the main library. And so we were able to teach many citizens how to use those voting machines.

Source: Annie L. McPheeters interviewed by Kathryn Nasstrom, 8 June 1992. Georgia Government Documentation Project, Georgia State University, and Southern Oral History Program, University of North Carolina, Louis Round Wilson Special Collections Library, University of North Carolina, Chapel Hill, http://dc.lib.unc.edu/cdm/compoundobject/collection/sohp/id/11526/rec/1

1.6 Fifth Pan-African Congress, Declaration to the Colonial Workers, Farmers and Intellectuals, 1945

Black struggles for freedom and equality in the United States did not take place in isolation; rather, they unfolded within a larger global context. An illustration of this is the Pan-African Congress movement, which involved a series of meetings held by black leaders in various locations around the world between World War I and World War II that tackled a number of issues related to African diaspora peoples. That diaspora included black Americans, and black American leader W.E.B. Du Bois, one of the founding members of the NAACP and the editor of its newspaper The Crisis, *played a prominent role in organizing the congresses. In 1944, a Pan-African Federation was founded in Manchester, England, that was dedicated to promoting the wellbeing and unity, the self-determination and independence, and the civil rights and eradication of racial discrimination through the cooperation of all African peoples. In October 1945, the Fifth Pan-African Congress held in Manchester brought together a number of influential leaders in subsequent African diaspora independence movements including Du Bois, Trinidadian journalist and author George Padmore, Ghanaian independence leader Kwame Nkrumah, and Kenyan independence leader Jomo Kenyatta. The below Declaration to the Colonial Workers, Farmers and Intellectuals that emerged from the Fifth Pan-African Congress reflects the anti-capitalist and anti-imperialist influences on that movement. In its urging of "Colonial and Subject Peoples of the World" to "Unite!" it identified all freedom struggles by people of color as stemming from and organizing against common systems of oppression. It was no coincidence that black independence struggles around the world emerged parallel with the civil rights movement in the United States, and that its respective leaders saw mutual solidarity in, and drew mutual inspiration from, those developments.*

DECLARATION TO THE COLONIAL WORKERS, FARMERS AND INTELLECTUALS.

The delegates of the Fifth Pan-African Congress believe in the right of all peoples to govern themselves. We affirm the right of all Colonial peoples to control their own destiny. All Colonies must be free from foreign imperialist control, whether political or economic. The peoples of the Colonies must have the right to elect their own governments, without restrictions from foreign powers. We say to the peoples of the Colonies that they must fight for these ends by all the means at their disposal.

The object of imperialist powers is to exploit. By granting the right to Colonial peoples to govern themselves that object is defeated. Therefore, the struggle for political power by Colonial and subject peoples is the first step towards, and the necessary prerequisite to, complete social, economic and political emancipation.

The Fifth Pan-African Congress therefore calls on the workers and farmers of the Colonies to organise effectively. Colonial workers must be in the front of the battle against Imperialism. Your weapons – the Strike and the Boycott – are invincible.

We also call upon the intellectuals and professional classes of the Colonies to awaken to their responsibilities. By fighting for trade union rights, the right to form cooperatives, freedom of the press, assembly, demonstration and strike, freedom to print and read the literature which is necessary for the education of the masses, you will be using the only means by which your liberties will be won and maintained. Today there is only one road to effective action – the organisation of the masses. And in that organisation the educated Colonials must join.

Colonial and Subject Peoples of the World – Unite!

Source: Fifth Pan-African Congress, Declaration to the Colonial Workers, Farmers and Intellectuals, 1945.

1.7 Journey of Reconciliation, 1947

In 1944, Irene Morgan was arrested and jailed in Virginia for refusing to sit in the segregated section of a Greyhound bus on her interstate journey to Baltimore, Maryland. NAACP LDF attorney William H. Hastie, along with Thurgood Marshall as co-counsel, argued Morgan's case before the US Supreme Court. The NAACP LDF attorneys contended that since Morgan was on an interstate journey, state segregation laws should not have been enforced. The Court agreed that under the Commerce Clause of the Constitution, which gave the federal government the right to regulate commerce between the states, federal nondiscriminatory laws took precedence over state segregation laws in interstate travel.

The only way to make sure that transportation carriers were in fact complying with the new law was to actually test their services. That is precisely what 16 men from CORE, eight black and eight white, set out to do in April 1947. The group planned an integrated ride from Virginia through North Carolina, Tennessee, and Kentucky, all states with segregation laws. The ride met with different receptions in the places they visited. The most serious trouble came in North Carolina. A number of arrests were made in Durham and Ashville, while in Chapel Hill five riders were dragged off the bus and beaten before being handed over to the local police. Some of the riders served time on a prison chain gang. The Journey of Reconciliation underscored the fact that changes in the law did not necessarily represent actual changes in the treatment of black riders on buses. Without the willingness of the federal government to protect the rights of those who sought to enforce the law, the riders were left at the mercy of local and state authorities. Despite this, the Journey of Reconciliation did further the use of nonviolent direct action in the civil rights struggle and the tactic was reprised to greater effect in the 1961 Freedom Rides.

Source: Journey of Reconciliation, Documents Collection Center, Yale Law School Lillian Goldman Law Library, https://documents.law.yale.edu/journey-reconciliation

1.8 President's Committee on Civil Rights, *To Secure These Rights*, 1947

Established by Democratic President Harry S. Truman's Executive Order 9808 in 1946, the President's Committee on Civil Rights was charged with investigating the status of civil rights in the United States and proposing measures to strengthen and protect them. The report the committee produced was wide-ranging in its recommendations, which are summarized in the extract below. Section I suggested ways to institutionalize the defense of civil rights at federal, state, and local levels. Section II addressed ways to combat racial violence and to uphold civil liberties, including a proposal for an anti-lynching act. Section III dealt with safeguarding voting rights and citizenship rights, as well as proposing an end to segregation in the military. Section IV looked to uphold freedom of speech and conscience. Section V was largest in scope, including recommendations to end racial discrimination in employment, education, housing, health services, public services, and the federally controlled areas of Washington, DC and the Panama Canal Zone. The same section revealed disagreements within the committee over how to best achieve its goals: the majority favored strong federal action, while a minority concluded that educating people at a state level to improve race relations was the way forward – an indication of the delicate balance that existed between civil rights, states' rights, and the role of the federal government as an arbiter between them.

Truman urged Congress to act on the recommendations of the report to little effect. Southern congressmen, many of whom held office because of widespread disenfranchisement and political corruption in the South, were opposed to any civil rights measures. Their collective power in Congress was strong enough to prevent any action from being taken. This set up a political conundrum: the Supreme Court and the president, representing the judicial and executive branches of federal government, indicated that they were both increasingly predisposed to act to uphold civil rights. A significant section of Congress, the legislative branch of federal government, was adamantly opposed. This federal political standoff played a crucial role in shaping the context of civil rights struggles over the following years.

The Committee's Recommendations

I. *To strengthen the machinery for the protection of civil rights, the President's Committee recommends*:

1. The reorganization of the Civil Rights Section of the Department of Justice [...]
2. The establishment within the FBI of a special unit of investigators trained in civil rights work [...]
3. The establishment by the state governments of law enforcement agencies comparable to the federal Civil Rights Section [...]
4. The establishment of a permanent Commission on Civil Rights in the Executive Office of the President, preferably by Act of Congress;

And the simultaneous creation of a joint Standing Committee on Civil Rights in Congress [...]

5. The establishment by the states of permanent commissions on civil rights to parallel the work of the federal Commission at the state level [...]

6. The increased professionalization of state and local police forces [...]

II. *To strengthen the right to safety and security of the person, the President's Committee recommends:*

1. The enactment by Congress of new legislation to supplement Section 51 of Title 18 of the United States Code which would impose the same liability on one person as is now imposed by that statute on two or more conspirators [...]

2. The amendment of Section 51 to remove the penalty provision which disqualifies persons convicted under the Act from holding public office [...]

3. The amendment of Section 52 to increase the maximum penalties that may be imposed under it from a $1,000 fine and a one-year prison term to a $5,000 fine and a ten-year prison term, thus bringing its penalty provisions into line with those in Section 51 [...]

4. The enactment by Congress of a new statute, to supplement Section 52, specifically directed against police brutality and related crimes [...]

5. The enactment by Congress of an anti-lynching act [...]

6. The enactment by Congress of a new criminal statute on involuntary servitude, supplementing Sections 443 and 444 of Title 18 of the United States Code [...]

7. A review of our wartime evacuation and detention experience looking toward the development of a policy which will prevent the abridgment of civil rights of any person or groups because of race or ancestry [...]

8. Enactment by Congress of legislation establishing a procedure by which claims of evacuees for specific property and business losses resulting from the wartime evacuation can be promptly considered and settled [...]

III. *To strengthen the right to citizenship and its privileges, the President's Committee recommends:*

1. Action by the states or Congress to end poll taxes as a voting prerequisite [...]

2. The enactment by Congress of a statute protecting the right of qualified persons to participate in federal primaries and elections against interference by public officers and private persons [...]

3. The enactment by Congress of a statute protecting the right to qualify for, or participate in, federal or state primaries or elections against discriminatory action by state officers based on race or color, or depending on any other unreasonable classification of persons for voting purposes [...]

4. The enactment by Congress of legislation establishing local self government for the District of Columbia; and the amendment of the Constitution to extend suffrage in presidential elections, and representation in Congress to District residents [...]

5. The granting of suffrage by the States of New Mexico and Arizona to their Indian citizens [...]

6. The modification of the federal naturalization laws to permit the granting of citizenship without regard to the race, color, or national origin of applicants [...]

7. The repeal by the states of laws discriminating against aliens who are ineligible for citizenship because of race, color, or national origin [...]

8. The enactment by Congress of legislation granting citizenship to the people of Guam and American Samoa [...]

9. The enactment by Congress of legislation, followed by appropriate administrative action, to end immediately all discrimination and segregation based on race, color, creed, or national origin, in the organization and activities of all branches of the Armed Services [...]

10. The enactment by Congress of legislation providing that no member of the armed forces shall be subject to discrimination of any kind by any public authority or place of public accommodation, recreation, transportation, or other service or business [...]

IV. *To strengthen the right to freedom of conscience and expression the President's Committee recommends*:

1. The enactment by Congress and the state legislatures of legislation requiring all groups, which attempt to influence public opinion, to disclose the pertinent facts about themselves through systematic registration procedures [...]

2. Action by Congress and the executive branch clarifying the loyalty obligations of federal employees, and establishing standards and procedures by which the civil rights of public workers may be scrupulously maintained [...]

V. *To strengthen the right to equality of opportunity, the President's Committee recommends*:

1. In general:
   The elimination of segregation, based on race, color, creed, or national origin, from American life.

   The separate but equal doctrine has failed in three important respects. First, it is inconsistent with the fundamental equalitarianism of the American way of life in that it marks groups with the brand of inferior status. Secondly, where it has been followed, the results have been separate and unequal facilities for minority peoples. Finally, it has kept people apart despite incontrovertible evidence that an environment favorable to civil rights is fostered whenever groups are permitted to live and work together. There is no adequate defense of segregation [...]

The conditioning by Congress of all federal grants-in-aid and other forms of federal assistance to public or private agencies for any purpose on the absence of discrimination and segregation based on race, color, creed, or national origin.

We believe that federal funds, supplied by taxpayers all over the nation, must not be used to support or perpetuate the pattern of segregation in education, public housing, public health services, or other public services and facilities generally. We recognize that these services are indispensable to individuals in modern society and to further social progress. It would be regrettable if federal aid, conditioned on non-segregated services, should be rejected by sections most in need of such aid. The Committee believes that a reasonable interval of time may be allowed for adjustment to such a policy. But in the end it believes that segregation is wrong morally and practically and must not receive financial support by the whole people.

A minority of the Committee favors the elimination of segregation as an ultimate goal but opposes the imposition of a federal sanction. It believes that federal aid to the states for education, health, research and other public benefits should be granted provided that the states do not discriminate in the distribution of the funds. It dissents, however, from the majority's recommendation that the abolition of segregation be made a requirement, until the people of the states involved have themselves abolished the provisions in their state constitutions and laws which now require segregation. Some members are against the non-segregation requirement in educational grants on the ground that it represents federal control over education. They feel, moreover, that the best way ultimately to end segregation is to raise the educational level of the people in the states affected; and to inculcate both the teachings of religion regarding human brotherhood and the ideals of our democracy regarding freedom and equality as a more solid basis for genuine and lasting acceptance by the peoples of the states.

2. For employment:

The enactment of a federal Fair Employment Practice Act prohibiting all forms of discrimination in private employment, based on race, color, creed, or national origin [...]

The enactment by the states of similar laws [...]

The issuance by the President of a mandate against discrimination in government employment and the creation of adequate machinery to enforce this mandate [...]

3. For education:

Enactment by the state legislatures of fair educational practice laws for public and private educational institutions, prohibiting discrimination in the admission and treatment of students based on race, color, creed, or national origin [...]

4. For housing:

The enactment by the states of laws outlawing restrictive covenants;

Renewed court attack, with intervention by the Department of Justice, upon restrictive covenants.

5. For health services:

The enactment by the states of fair health practice statutes forbidding discrimination and segregation based on race, creed, color, or national origin, in the operation of public or private health facilities [...]

6. For public services:

The enactment by Congress of a law stating that discrimination and segregation, based on race, color, creed, or national origin, in the rendering of all public services by the national government is contrary to public policy;

The enactment by the states of similar laws [...]

The establishment by act of Congress or executive order of a unit in the federal Bureau of the Budget to review the execution of all government programs, and the expenditures of all government funds, for compliance with the policy of nondiscrimination [...]

The enactment by Congress of a law prohibiting discrimination or segregation, based on race, color, creed, or national origin, in interstate transportation and all the facilities thereof, to apply against both public officers and the employees of private transportation companies [...]

The enactment by the states of laws guaranteeing equal access to places of public accommodation, broadly defined, for persons of all races, colors, creeds, and national origins [...]

7. For the District of Columbia:

The enactment by Congress of legislation to accomplish the following purposes in the District;

Prohibition of discrimination and segregation, based on race, color, creed, or national origin, in all public or publicly-supported hospitals, parks, recreational facilities, housing projects, welfare agencies, penal institutions, and concessions on public property;

The prohibition of segregation in the public school system of the District of Columbia;

The establishment of a fair educational practice program directed against discrimination, based on race, color, creed, or national origin, in the admission of students to private educational institutions;

The establishment of a fair health practice program forbidding discrimination and segregation by public or private agencies, based on race, color, creed, or national origin, with respect to the training of doctors and nurses, the admission of patients to hospitals, clinics, and similar institutions, and the right of doctors and nurses to practice in hospitals;

The outlawing of restrictive covenants;

Guaranteeing equal access to places of public accommodation, broadly defined, to persons of all races, colors, creeds, and national origins.

8.   The enactment by Congress of legislation ending the system of segregation in the Panama Canal Zone [...]

A long term campaign of public education to inform the people of the civil rights to which they are entitled and which they owe to one another.

Source: President's Committee on Civil Rights, *To Secure These Rights: The Report of the President's Committee on Civil Rights* (Washington, DC: Governmental Printing Office, 1947), pp. 152–75, https://www.trumanlibrary.org/civilrights/srights4.htm#chap4

1.9 President Harry S. Truman, Executive Order 9981, 1948

Although President Truman was unsuccessful in convincing Congress to act on the proposals in To Secure These Rights, *he did issue two executive orders to implement two of its recommendations. The first was Executive Order 9980, which ordered the desegregation of the federal workforce. The second was Executive Order 9981, which ordered an end to racial discrimination in the armed forces. The second order established a committee to investigate and to make recommendations to the civilian leadership in the military to implement the policy. Even so, the move encountered resistance and took some time to take effect. Secretary of the Army Kenneth Claiborne Royall was forced into retirement in 1949 for refusing to take any action. The first war the United States fought after the executive order was the Korean War between 1950 and 1953. Yet segregated black units continued to exist. In the end, it was as much military necessity as political pressure that drove desegregation: white units in Korea that were understrength because of casualties had little choice but to take black soldiers as reinforcements. By the end of the war, more than 90% of black troops served in formerly all-white units. However, not until Republican President Dwight D. Eisenhower's term in office was the last of the all-black units disbanded in September 1954, and military schools, hospitals, and bases desegregated.*

WHEREAS it is essential that there be maintained in the armed services of the United States the highest standards of democracy, with equality of treatment and opportunity for all those who serve in our country's defense:

NOW, THEREFORE, by virtue of the authority vested in me as President of the United States, by the Constitution and the statutes of the United States, and as Commander in Chief of the armed services, it is hereby ordered as follows:

1. It is hereby declared to be the policy of the President that there shall be equality of treatment and opportunity for all persons in the armed services without regard to race, color, religion or national origin. This policy shall be put into effect as rapidly as possible, having due regard to the time required to effectuate any necessary changes without impairing efficiency or morale.

2. There shall be created in the National Military Establishment an advisory committee to be known as the President's Committee on Equality of Treatment and Opportunity in the Armed Services, which shall be composed of seven members to be designated by the President.

3. The Committee is authorized on behalf of the President to examine into the rules, procedures and practices of the armed services in order to determine in what respect such rules, procedure and practices may be altered or improved with a view to carrying out the policy of this order. The Committee shall confer and advise with the Secretary of Defense, the Secretary of the Army, the Secretary of the Navy, and the Secretary of the Air Force, and shall make such recommendations to the President and to said Secretaries as in the judgment of the Committee will effectuate the policy thereof.

4. All executive departments and agencies of the Federal Government are authorized and directed to cooperate with the Committee in its work, and to furnish the Committee such information or the services of such persons as the Committee may require in the performance of its duties.

5. When requested by the Committee to do so, persons in the armed services or in any of the executive departments and agencies of the Federal Government shall testify before the Committee and shall make available for the use of the Committee such documents and other information as the Committee may require.

6. The Committee shall continue to exist until such time as the President shall terminate its existence by Executive Order.

[Signature of Harry Truman]
The White House
July 26, 1948

Source: President Harry S. Truman, Executive Order 9981, https://www.trumanlibrary.org/9981.htm

1.10 Henry Lee Moon, *Balance of Power: The Negro Vote*, 1948

President Truman's motives in taking a more forthright stand for civil rights were not purely altruistic but also a matter of political pragmatism. When the Fifteenth Amendment was ratified in 1870, blacks voted overwhelmingly for the Republican Party as the party of President Abraham Lincoln and the party of Emancipation. The Democratic Party was the party of the defeated southern confederacy. When Reconstruction came to an end in 1877, white southerners coalesced around the Democratic Party to reestablish white supremacy in the region. During the 1930s, at the national level the Democratic Party emerged under President Franklin D. Roosevelt as the most liberal leaning party. Roosevelt's New Deal coalition built a national voting block of various different groupings including labor unions and blue-collar workers as well as racial, ethnic, and religious minorities. Blacks were encouraged by Roosevelt's use of federal government resources to assist them during the Great Depression, even if those efforts often fell well short of what blacks wanted and needed. As a consequence, those blacks that had access to the vote decisively shifted allegiances from the Republican Party to the Democratic Party.

The shift in votes gave the national Democratic Party a greater investment in supporting measures that would appeal to black voters and increase the black vote. The influx of black workers from the South into northern, midwestern, and western cities for wartime industry jobs created a large block of newly enfranchised black voters. For Truman, in his close-run 1948 presidential election, this new voting block proved vital. For the first time in US electoral history, the black vote made the difference in the outcome of a presidential election, handing Truman a narrow victory over Republican candidate Thomas E. Dewey. This consolidated the ties between the national Democratic Party and the black vote. As more blacks voted Democrat, Democrats outside of the South became more supportive of civil rights measures.

Below, black journalist and NAACP public relations director Henry Lee Moon provides a commentary on the political developments taking place by examining how new black votes could influence American politics at local as well as at national levels.

[T]he Negro citizen, possessed of the greatest ballot potential in his history, faces the presidential year of 1948. His full voting strength in the states beyond the borders of the old Confederacy amounted in 1940 to 2,540,000. This basic strength has been augmented by the migration of more than 700,000 Negro workers, mostly adults, seeking employment in war industries in the North and West. Of this number, 121,000 settled in five congested production areas in the West, the Census Bureau estimates. Another 83,000 crowded into the Detroit-Willow Run area of Michigan. The Chicago-Gary area absorbed 60,000; Baltimore, 40,000; Philadelphia, 36,000; Cleveland and St. Louis, 15,000 each, and Cincinnati and Indianapolis, 8000 each. Additional thousands sought jobs and refuge in New England cities, in the Buffalo-Niagara falls area, and in the smaller industrial cities of the Midwest. An undetermined number continued to stream into New York City. While there was much migration of white workers to these centers, many of them also from the South, the percentage increases owing to migration were much greater for the Negro populations. In the Portland-Vancouver and San Francisco areas the percentage increases of Negroes were 437 and 227, respectively. In the Detroit-Willow Run area the Negro increase was 60.2 compared to a 47-per-cent increase of the white population. While fewer in absolute numbers, the Negro migrants contributed a much greater percentage growth to the colored populations among whom they settled than did white migrants to the local white populations.

The Negro's political influence in national elections derives not so much from its numerical strength as from its strategic diffusion in the balance-of-power and marginal states whose electoral votes are generally considered vital to the winning candidate. In the 1944 elections there were twenty-eight states in which a shift of 5 per cent or less of the popular vote would have reversed the electoral votes cast by these states. In twelve of these, with a total of 228 electoral college votes, the potential Negro vote exceeds the number required to shift the state from one column to the other. Two of these marginal states – Ohio with 25 votes and Indiana with 13 – went Republican. The ten remaining states – New York, New Jersey, Pennsylvania, Illinois, Michigan, Missouri, Delaware, Maryland, West Virginia and Kentucky – gave to Mr Roosevelt 190 electoral college votes essential to his victory. The closeness of the popular vote in the marginal states accented the decisive potential of the Negro's ballot. While in the year of the great Roosevelt landslide, 1936, balance of power could be imputed to no particular segment of the America electorate, it may well be that we shall not soon see again another such overwhelming victory.

An alert, well-organized Negro electorate can be an effective factor in at least seventy-five congressional districts in eighteen northern and border states. Increasing political activity in the Democratic primaries in the South should result in the removal or silencing of some of the most rabidly anti-Negro politicians who have owed their seats in Congress to the suppression of the Negro vote and the elimination of a competitive political system. With the wartime migration, the expanded black ghettos in northern and western industrial towns have inevitably spilled over, consolidating Negro voting strength in additional congressional districts.

Source: *Balance of Power: The Negro Vote* by Henry Lee Moon, pp. 197–9, copyright 1948 Henry Lee Moon. Used by permission of Doubleday, an imprint of the Knopf Doubleday Publishing Group, a division of Penguin Random House LLC. All rights reserved.

1.11 States' Rights Democratic Party, Platform of the States' Rights Democratic Party, 1948

The support for cultivating black voters and civil rights measures in the national Democratic Party brought a backlash from the Democratic Party's southern wing. Democratic support in the South depended upon the party's historical ties to white supremacy. Southern Democrats were often more conservative than either national Democrats or Republicans. Trying to keep white southern Democrats and their votes in a party that increasingly also became the party of civil rights nationally was a tricky balancing act to say the least. In 1948, southern Democrats broke away from the national Democratic Party and formed their own States' Rights Democratic Party, more popularly known as the Dixiecrats. With South Carolina's governor James Strom Thurmond as its presidential nominee, the Dixiecrats claimed victories in the lower South states of South Carolina, Alabama, Mississippi, and Louisiana in the 1948 presidential election. The Dixiecrat revolt turned out to be, at least in the short term, just a shot across the bow of the national Democratic Party. Most Dixiecrats went back into the Democratic fold after the election. In the mid to longer term, the election marked the beginning of a complicated and acrimonious divorce between the Democratic Party and the South that would have profound political consequences. The Dixiecrat platform below indicates the touchstones of southern Democratic beliefs deeply rooted in the politics and culture of the region, namely support for states' rights over a strong federal government, and support for segregation and white supremacy over civil rights.

– 1 –

We believe that the Constitution of the United States is the greatest charter of human liberty ever conceived by the mind of man.

– 2 –

We oppose all efforts to invade or destroy the rights guaranteed by it to every citizen of this republic.

– 3 –

We stand for social and economic justice, which, we believe can be guaranteed to all citizens only by a strict adherence to our Constitution and the avoidance of any invasion or destruction of the constitutional rights of the states and individuals. We oppose the totalitarian, centralized bureaucratic government and the police nation called for by the platforms adopted by the Democratic and Republican Conventions.

– 4 –

We stand for the segregation of the races and the racial integrity of each race; the constitutional right to choose one's associates; to accept private employment without governmental interference, and to earn one's living in any lawful way. We oppose the elimination of segregation, the repeal of miscegenation statutes, the control of private employment by Federal bureaucrats called for by the misnamed civil rights program. We favor home-rule, local self-government and a minimum interference with individual rights.

– 5 –

We oppose and condemn the action of the Democratic Convention in sponsoring a civil rights program calling for the elimination of segregation, social equality by Federal fiat, regulations of private employment practices, voting, and local law enforcement.

– 6 –

We affirm that the effective enforcement of such a program would be utterly destructive of the social, economic and political life of the Southern people, and of other localities in which there may be differences in race, creed or national origin in appreciable numbers.

– 7 –

We stand for the check and balances provided by the three departments of our government. We oppose the usurpation of legislative functions by the executive and judicial departments. We unreservedly condemn the effort to establish in the United States a police nation that would destroy the last vestige of liberty enjoyed by a citizen.

– 8 –

We demand that there be returned to the people to whom of right they belong, those powers needed for the preservation of human rights and the discharge of our responsibility as democrats for human welfare. We oppose a denial of those by political parties, a barter or sale of those rights by a political convention, as well as any invasion or violation of those rights by the Federal

Government. We call upon all Democrats and upon all other loyal Americans who are opposed to totalitarianism at home and abroad to unite with us in ignominiously defeating Harry S. Truman, Thomas E. Dewey and every other candidate for public office who would establish a Police Nation in the United States of America.

– 9 –

We, therefore, urge that this Convention endorse the candidacies of J. Strom Thurmond and Fielding H. Wright for the President and Vice-president [...]

Source: States' Rights Democratic Party, Platform of the States' Rights Democratic Party, 14 August 1948, http://www.presidency.ucsb.edu/ws/index.php?pid=25851

1.12 Congressman Jacob K. Javits, Press Release on Segregation and Discrimination in the Armed Forces, 1950

Increasingly during the post-World War II era, it was not just regional and national politics that entered into the debate over civil rights, but also international relations and foreign policy. After the end of World War II the United States and the Soviet Union became embroiled in an ideological Cold War of capitalism versus communism that lasted the next four decades. The emergence of Communist China under Mao Zedong in 1949, together with the Soviet Union becoming the second nuclear superpower that same year, fueled fears that the United States was falling behind in the Cold War. In a geopolitical struggle for hearts and minds, much of it waged in nonwhite countries, the treatment of black people in the United States came under intense scrutiny. This added to the perceived urgency in tackling civil rights issues.

Below, Jacob Javits, a white New York congressman, and a liberal Republican, calls for greater efforts in implementing President Truman's executive order to desegregate the armed forces. Javits, like many other Americans, had experienced first-hand the questions that people overseas were asking about the United States' treatment of black people and its apparent contradiction with the nation's aspirations to be a bastion of liberal democracy and the leader of the free world.

Representative Jacob K. Javits (R-L, NY) today introduced a resolution calling for a Select Committee to investigate segregation and discrimination on grounds of race, creed, color or national origin in the armed services. The resolution calls for a special committee of nineteen to be appointed by the Speaker from the legislative committee on Armed Services, Education and Labor, Foreign Affairs and Expenditures in the Executive Departments. A report by the special committee is required not later than June 1, 1950.

In introducing the resolution, Mr Javits said: "The Navy, the Air Force and the Army have each developed separate policies respecting the question of segregation and discrimination in response to the President's Executive Order of July 26, 1948 and to the directive of the Secretary of Defense of April 6, 1949. Persistent charges have been made that practices of segregation and discrimination continue in the Army. Nothing could be more useful as propaganda material to the Communist propagandists in the 'cold war.' During my recent visit to Europe with the European Study Mission of the Foreign Affairs Committee, both in Germany (which is a main front of the cold war) and other western democracies, I was impressed by the questioning of people in all walks of life about our race relations policies about segregation and discrimination in employment, housing, and education, and in the armed services. The Communist propagandists in West Germany and Western Europe seek to build up the alleged evils and to magnify them, but there is enough to them to damage us seriously in the cold war. I so advised the Secretary of Defense on December 22 in announcing that I would introduce this resolution. The situation among the peoples of Asia and Africa is even worse. With Communist China as a propaganda base, segregation and discrimination on grounds of race, creed or color in the United States can be used to win tens of millions to the Communist cause."

"The least which is required," Congressman Javits continued, "is a complete hearing of the facts. Certainly our constitutional democracy cannot tolerate discrimination of segregation among men who wear the uniform of the United States and are sworn to uphold its national security at the cost of their very lives. Good faith with respect to a civil rights program requires nothing less than an investigation such as this. Civil rights must be the subject of bi-partisan policy if effective action is to be had and this would be the first step toward that goal. It is difficult to see how at least such an investigation can be refused by the Congressional leadership consistent with the President's civil rights stand. The question has become one relative to the foreign policy of the United States as well as to the economy and efficiency of administration of the Department of Defense and general policies of equality of opportunity in the United States. Hence I have proposed that the standing committees charged with these responsibilities respectively contribute to the special committee. The investigation needs to include all these questions."

Source: Press Release, 12 January 1950. Record Group 220: Records of the President's Committee on Equality of Treatment and Opportunity in the Armed Services, Miscellaneous. Rep. Jacob Javits (Resolution). Harry S. Truman Presidential Library & Museum, https://www.trumanlibrary.org/whistlestop/study_collections/desegregation/large/documents/index.php?documentid=11-10&pagenumber=1

1.13 *The Crusader,* "Boycott of City Bus Company in Baton Rouge Forces End of Absolute Jimcrow," 1953

The Harlem bus boycott of 1941 demonstrated that such a tactic could be effectively used in the North as leverage for black demands. The tactic had an even longer tradition in the South where black boycotts of streetcars to protest the introduction of segregated seating arrangements in the late nineteenth and early twentieth century occurred in a number of cities. At that time, however, there was little national support for the enforcement of civil rights. Encouraged by postwar developments and increasingly positive responses to defending civil rights at the federal level, more black communities were emboldened to take action.

In June 1953, blacks in Baton Rouge, Louisiana, boycotted buses for one week, in part to protest the city revoking the licenses of black-owned bus companies in 1950 that gave black bus passengers no alternative but to ride white-owned segregated buses. In January 1953, Rev. Theodore Judson (T.J.) Jemison, pastor of Baton Rouge's largest black church Mt Zion First Baptist, negotiated a modified segregated system on buses with the city council. White bus drivers went on strike against the new system and it was overturned on the grounds that it violated existing segregation ordinances. Jemison, along with other black community leaders, formed the United Defense League and organized a bus boycott and an alternative "fair lift" transportation system. Since blacks composed 80% of the city's bus riders, the boycott hit the white bus company hard. Another compromise over segregated seating arrangements was reached and the boycott was called off.

Jemison insisted the compromise was the best solution. Others in the black community felt that they were in a position to press for even more far-reaching changes. The Baton Rouge bus boycott was the largest boycott of a segregated southern bus system at the time and it inspired the more extensive and more successful Montgomery bus boycott that occurred a couple of years later. In the article below, Jemison denies that the action was a boycott since many southern states such as Louisiana had anti-boycott laws that would have rendered such a protest illegal.

Boycott Of City Bus Company In Baton Rouge Forces End Of Absolute Jimcrow: Organize Auto "Fair Lift" To Carry Workers

Baton Rouge, La – (ANP) – Negroes, banding together as one pulled a ninety percent effective boycott here last week and forced the end of absolute jimcrow on the local buses of Baton Rouge, the state capital of Louisiana.

As a result of their unified fight, colored riders gained the right to sit anywhere on the buses except from the two side seats at the front. Whites may sit anywhere on local transit lines except the rear seat across the back of the bus.

The city council of Baton Rouge in an emergency action approved the above plan which it considers an acceptable arrangement in an effort to end a week-long boycott of the Baton Rouge Bus company by Negroes.

Company Drivers Strike

The trouble all started two weeks ago when the city council passed an ordinance ending segregation indirectly on the city buses in keeping with a campaign promise made by the city's mayor. Under the new law Negroes could keep their seats in front of the bus if they boarded before whites did and would not have to move to the rear as seats were emptied. They also could sit up front if no rear seats were available.

Because of this law, the company's white bus drivers refused to take their posts. They went on a four-day strike. This resulted in an opinion by Fred S. Leblanc, state attorney general, that the city ordinance violated the state segregation laws. When this ruling was announced the white bus drivers returned to work.

This in turn drove the city's Negroes, who make up two thirds of the bus line's passengers, into action. They refused to ride the bus lines, making these demands:

1. The company abide by the new city ordinance.
2. The company hire Negro bus drivers or the city issue a separate franchise to allow Negroes to operate their own bus lines.

Organize "Fair Lift"

To demonstrate their intentions, the Negroes then organized what they called a "fair lift" free automobile service to replace the bus service. Under the program about 150 automobiles were utilized to transport people.

Thru the United Defense League which operated the fair lift, more than $1,000 was raised to support the venture. Three service stations sold gasoline at wholesale prices for the private car transportation system, and a system of pickup points was established for passengers.

The Rev. T.J. Jemison, president of the UDL, said the action was not a boycott. He declared, "That's illegal. We're just not riding."

Source: *The Crusader* (Rockford, Illinois), 3 July 1953, p. 1.

1.14 Dorothy Height Recalls Her Work with the National Council of Negro Women from the 1930s to the 1950s

Women and women's organizations played important roles in the civil rights movement although they were often overshadowed by the attention given to men and male-dominated organizations. Educator and political leader Mary McLeod Bethune founded the National Council of Negro Women (NCNW) in 1935 as a focal point for coordinating the activities of black women's organizations when she was advisor of minority affairs in President Franklin D. Roosevelt's "Black Cabinet," an informal group of black advisors. The NCNW worked in a range of fields including employment, housing, voting rights, anti-lynching legislation, and the desegregation of the armed forces and education. Bethune died in 1955, and soon after Dorothy Height became the NCNW's fourth national president and led the Council for the next 40 years through the civil rights movement and beyond.

Born in Richmond, Virginia, Height attended New York University, Columbia University, and the New York School of Social Work. Height was a caseworker for the New York City Welfare Department when she became involved with the NCNW, and she also served on the national staff of the Young Women's Christian Association (YWCA) and as national president of the Delta Sigma Theta sorority. During the 1960s, she organized "Wednesdays in Mississippi" (later "Workshops in Mississippi") that supplemented voting rights activism with attempts to establish interracial, interregional, and interfaith dialog between black and white women from the North and South. Height had the ear of influential white leaders including First Lady Eleanor Roosevelt, President Dwight D. Eisenhower, who she encouraged to desegregate schools, and President Lyndon B. Johnson, who she assisted in appointing black women to government positions. She was also a founding member of the Council for United Civil Rights Leadership (CUCRL), which was formed in 1963 to coordinate the March on Washington for Jobs and Freedom. Height remained active in civil rights and women's issues, earning the Presidential Medal of Freedom in 1994 and the Congressional Gold Medal in 2004. She died in 2010 at the age of 98.

From the moment I met Mary McLeod Bethune at the Harlem branch of the YWCA in 1937, I was pleased to do whatever I could to help her cause. She had founded the NCNW in 1935, and until 1944 its business was conducted where Mrs Bethune lived, in a small rented apartment in Washington, DC. During the first seven years there was no paid staff. Mrs Bethune simultaneously administered the National Council of Negro Women, the Bethune-Cookman College in Florida, and the Division of Negro Affairs of the National Youth Administration, and she was the acknowledged leader of Franklin Roosevelt's "Black Cabinet." In spite of these demanding responsibilities, during the fourteen years that Mrs Bethune served as president she established NCNW as a major player working for child labor laws, public housing, the minimum wage, and quality desegregated education.

From 1939 to 1944, when I was employed by the Phyllis Wheatley YWCA, I would work at my regular job during the day and for the NCNW most evenings and many weekends. Perhaps my greatest contribution was to help Mrs Bethune see that she needed a full-time NCNW staff. With her blessing and board support, we recruited our first executive director,

Jeanetta Welch Brown, who had been national affairs director for Alpha Kappa Alpha Sorority. Mrs Bethune made me chair of the personnel committee to develop policies and help with board-staff relations, and I continued to serve her successors, Dorothy Boulding Ferebee and Vivian Carter Mason, as president.

I wish I could have been president of the NCNW while Mrs Bethune was still alive, even for just one year. If that had been possible, I believe some of the things that have been so difficult to accomplish could have been done much more easily. Mrs Bethune was a dreamer, but she was a realist too. Though a great deal of her vision had been expressed, she knew when she died in 1955 that very little of it had been realized.

When I was elected president of the NCNW in 1958, three years after her death, we had two full-time staff members and one part-timer, and we faced a major financial challenge. Mrs Bethune had depended heavily on members of means and a few wealthy white donors to tide the organization over during times of financial crisis. On my first day in office I received a certified letter calling for immediate payment of a $7,500 loan from the industrial bank of Washington. I quickly realized that we had a problem and called my cousin, Campbell C. Johnson, who was on the bank's board. He interceded, and the bank kindly allowed us to pay off the loan in installments.

There was good reason to get our financial house in order: our work was more urgent than ever. In the early sixties the momentum of the war on poverty and the civil rights movement thrust the NCNW into a position of leadership.

Source: Dorothy Height, *Open Wide the Freedom Gates: A Memoir* (New York: PublicAffairs, 2003), pp. 155–7.

Discussion Questions

1. What tactics did the early civil rights movement adopt, and why?
2. Compare and contrast the roles of the president, the Supreme Court, and Congress in early civil rights struggles.
3. Examine the relationship between national developments and grassroots community mobilization in the early civil rights movement.
4. In what ways did the early civil rights movement encounter white opposition?
5. Assess the international relations and foreign policy dimensions of early civil rights struggles.
6. How did gender roles shape participation in the early civil rights movement?

Further Reading

Brown-Nagin, Tomiko. *Courage to Dissent: Atlanta and the Long History of the Civil Rights Movement* (Oxford University Press, 2011).

Bynum, Cornelius L. *A. Philip Randolph and the Struggle for Civil Rights* (University of Illinois Press, 2010).

Catsam, Derek Charles. *Freedom's Main Line: The Journey of Reconciliation and the Freedom Rides* (University Press of Kentucky, 2009).

Farmer, James. *Lay Bare the Heart: An Autobiography of the Civil Rights Movement* (Arbor House, 1985).

Frederickson, Kari. *The Dixiecrat Revolt and the End of the Solid South, 1932–1968* (University of North Carolina Press, 2001).

Geselbracht, Raymond H. *The Civil Rights Legacy of Harry S. Truman* (Truman State University Press, 2007).

Height, Dorothy. *Open Wide the Freedom Gates: A Memoir* (PublicAffairs, 2003).

Hine, Darlene Clark. *Black Victory: The Rise and Fall of the White Primary in Texas* (KTO Press, 1979).

Lucander, David. *Winning the War for Democracy: The March on Washington Movement, 1941–1946* (University of Illinois Press, 2014).

Mershon, Sherie, and Steven Schlossman. *Foxholes and Color Lines: Desegregating the U.S. Armed Forces* (Johns Hopkins University Press, 1998).

Morris, Aldon D. *Origins of the Civil Rights Movement: Black Communities Organizing for Change* (Free Press, 1984).

Powell, Adam Clayton, Jr. *Adam by Adam: The Autobiography of Adam Clayton Powell, Jr* (Dial Press, 1971).

Reed, Merle E. *Seedtime for the Modern Civil Rights Movement: The President's Committee on Fair Employment Practice, 1941–1946* (Louisiana State University Press, 1991).

Von Eschen, Penny. *Race against Empire: Black Americans and Anti-Colonialism, 1937–1957* (Cornell University Press, 1997).

Chapter 2

Brown v. Board of Education and Massive Resistance, 1954–6

2.1 US Supreme Court, *McLaurin v. Oklahoma State Regents*, 1950

The National Association for the Advancement of Colored People Legal Defense and Educational Fund (NAACP LDF) fought segregation and racial discrimination in the courts on a number of fronts. Education was an enticing option for lawsuits since racial inequalities were transparent and they directly affected many of the NAACP's constituents. Thurgood Marshall began by attacking unequal teacher salaries, questioning why black teachers were paid less than white teachers to do the same jobs in the same public schools systems. Successful in a number of teacher salary equalization suits, the focus then began to shift to graduate education. In Missouri ex rel. Gaines v. Canada (1938), the US Supreme Court ruled that states could not provide black graduate students with out-of-state scholarships to avoid their own responsibility to provide black graduate education. In Sipuel v. Oklahoma State Regents (1948), the Court upheld the idea of "separate but equal" graduate education when the University of Oklahoma furnished separate law school facilities for Ada Louis Sipuel, the one black student in the state who applied for admission. When more black graduate students applied to attend various other graduate programs at the university, it became clear that the university could not support "separate but equal" facilities on the scale required. Instead, the university admitted black graduate students to formerly all-white graduate schools while implementing demeaning segregated arrangements such as forcing black students to sit partitioned from whites by a screen in classrooms, providing segregated library facilities, and limiting the use of the refectory to inconvenient hours.

The Civil Rights Movement: A Documentary Reader, First Edition. Edited by John A. Kirk.
© 2020 John Wiley & Sons, Inc. Published 2020 by John Wiley & Sons, Inc.

When the NAACP LDF challenged this in McLaurin v. Oklahoma State Regents *(1950), the Court upheld the contention that it did not provide a truly "equal" education. The day after, in* Sweatt v. Painter *(1950), the Court declared that the entirely separate law school provided for black graduates in Texas was not equal to that of whites because it did not provide exactly the same learning experiences and opportunities. By implication the Court indicated that unless graduate facilities were absolutely identical for whites and blacks they were unconstitutional. Although the Court did not explicitly declare an end to segregation, it rendered segregated graduate education practically indefensible. The ruling opened up the possibility of an attack on the very legal foundations of segregation in the doctrine of "separate but equal" facilities originally established in* Plessy v. Ferguson *(1896). The NAACP LDF eagerly accepted that challenge and in doing so shifted its focus to the more far-reaching and expansive segregation that existed in public schools.*

MR CHIEF JUSTICE VINSON delivered the opinion of the Court.

In this case, we are faced with the question whether a state may, after admitting a student to graduate instruction in its state university, afford him different treatment from other students solely because of his race. We decide only this issue; see *Sweatt* v. *Painter, ante*, p. 629.

Appellant is a Negro citizen of Oklahoma. Possessing a Master's Degree, he applied for admission to the University of Oklahoma in order to pursue studies and courses leading to a Doctorate in Education. At that time, his application was denied, solely because of his race. The school authorities were required to exclude him by the Oklahoma statutes, 70 Okla. Stat. (1941) ßß 455, 456, 457, which made it a misdemeanor to maintain or operate, teach or attend a school at which both whites and Negroes are enrolled or taught. Appellant filed a complaint requesting injunctive relief, alleging that the action of the school authorities and the statutes upon which their action was based were unconstitutional and deprived of the equal protection of the laws. Citing our decisions in *Missouri ex rel. Gaines* v. *Canada*, 305 U.S. 337 (1938), and *Sipuel* v. *Board of Regents*, 332 U.S. 631 (1948), a statutory three-judge District Court held that the State had a Constitutional duty to provide him with the education he sought as soon as it provided that education for applicants of any other group. It further held that to the extent the Oklahoma statutes denied him admission they were unconstitutional and void. On the assumption, however, that the State would follow the constitutional mandate, the court refused to grant the injunction, retaining jurisdiction of the cause with full power to issue any necessary and proper orders to secure McLaurin the equal protection of the laws.

Following this decision, the Oklahoma legislature amended these statutes to permit the admission of Negroes to institutions of higher learning attended by white students, in cases where such institutions offered courses not available in the Negro schools. The amendment provided, however, that in such cases the program of instruction "shall be given at such colleges or institutions of higher education upon a segregated basis." Appellant was thereupon admitted to the University of Oklahoma Graduate School. In apparent conformity with the amendment, his admission was made subject to "such rules and regulations as to segregation as the President of the University shall consider to afford to Mr G.W. McLaurin substantially equal educational opportunities as are afforded to other persons seeking the same education in the Graduate College," a condition which does not appear to have been withdrawn. Thus he was required to sit apart at a designated desk in an anteroom adjoining the class-room; to sit at a designated desk on the mezzanine floor of the library, but not to use the desks in the regular reading room; and to sit at a designated table and to eat at a different time from the other students in the school cafeteria.

To remove these conditions, appellant filed a motion to modify the order and judgment of the District Court. That court held that such treatment did not violate the provisions of the Fourteenth Amendment and denied the motion. This appeal followed.

In the interval between the decision of the court below and the hearing in this Court, the treatment afforded appellant was altered. For some time, the section of the classroom in which appellant sat was surrounded by a rail on which there was a sign stating, "Reserved For Colored," but these have been removed. He is now assigned to a seat in the classroom in a row specified for colored students; he is assigned to a table in the library on the main floor; and he is permitted to eat at the same time in the cafeteria as other students, although here again he is assigned to a special table.

It is said that the separations imposed by the State in this case are in form merely nominal. McLaurin uses the same classroom, library and cafeteria as students of other races; there is no indication that the seats to which he is assigned in these rooms have any disadvantage of location. He may wait in line in the cafeteria and there stand and talk with his fellow students, but while he eats he must remain apart.

These restrictions were obviously imposed in order to comply, as nearly as could be, with the statutory requirements of Oklahoma. But they signify that the State, in administering the facilities it affords for professional and graduate study, sets McLaurin apart from the other students. The result is that appellant is handicapped in his pursuit of effective graduate instruction. Such restrictions impair and inhibit his ability to study, to engage in discussions and exchange views with other students, and, in general, to learn his profession.

Our society grows increasingly complex, and our need for trained leaders increases correspondingly. Appellant's case represents, perhaps, the epitome of that need, for he is attempting to obtain an advanced degree in education, to become, by definition, a leader and trainer of others. Those who will come under his guidance and influence must be directly affected by the education he receives. Their own education and development will necessarily suffer to the extent that his training is unequal to that of his classmates. State-imposed restrictions which produce such inequalities cannot be sustained [...]

We conclude that the conditions under which this appellant is required to receive his education deprive him of his personal and present right to the equal protection of the laws. See *Sweatt* v. *Painter, ante,* p. 629. We hold that under these circumstances the Fourteenth Amendment precludes differences in treatment by the state based upon race. Appellant, having been admitted to a state-supported graduate school, must receive the same treatment at the hands of the state as students of other races.

Source: US Supreme Court, *McLaurin v. Oklahoma State Regents* 339 U.S. 637 (1950), https://supreme.justia.com/cases/federal/us/339/637/case.html

2.2   United States, Brief as *Amicus Curiae, Brown v. Board of Education,* 1952

Civil rights as a Cold War imperative entered into legal battles after World War II when the US Justice Department under President Truman began to file amicus curiae *("friend of the court") briefs in civil rights cases. This indicated just how serious a threat to the United States' world standing the denial of civil rights was deemed to be. The first case the Justice Department entered as* amicus curiae *was* Shelley v. Kraemer *(1948) that struck down the enforcement of restrictive covenants placed in house contracts to prevent resale to blacks or other people of color. The Justice Department filed further* amicus *briefs in* Henderson v. United States *(1950) that dealt with segregation in railroad dining cars, and in the* McLaurin v. Oklahoma State Regents *(1950) and* Sweatt v. Painter *(1950) higher education cases. In each of these cases, the Justice Department highlighted the threat to American foreign policy that racial discrimination constituted.*

The Justice Department became involved in school desegregation cases through Bolling v. Sharpe *(1954), a corollary case to those school desegregation cases collectively decided in* Brown v. Board of Education *(1954).* Bolling *originated as a complaint about segregated schools in Washington, DC, a particular embarrassment since it occurred in the heart of the nation's capital. The Justice Department's* amicus curiae *brief in* Brown *included a powerful letter from US Secretary of State Dean Acheson to US Attorney General James P. McGranery testifying about the negative impact segregated schools had on perceptions of the United States around the world. Although a Republican president Dwight D. Eisenhower assumed office just a month after the* Brown *amicus curiae brief was filed, he understood just as well the integral connections between race relations and international relations.*

It is in the context of the present world struggle between freedom and tyranny that the problem of racial discrimination must be viewed. The United States is trying to prove to the people of the world, of every nationality, race, and color, that a free democracy is the most civilized and most secure form of government yet devised by man. We must set an example for others by showing firm determination to remove existing flaws in our democracy.

The existence of discrimination against minority groups in the United States has an adverse effect upon our relations with other countries. Racial discrimination furnishes grist for the Communist propaganda mills, and it raises doubts even among friendly nations as to the intensity of our devotion to democratic faith. In response to the request of the Attorney General for an authoritative statement on the effects of racial discrimination in the United States upon the conduct of foreign relations, the Secretary of State has written as follows:

* * * I wrote the Chairman of the Fair Employment Practices Committee on May 8, 1946, that the existence of discrimination against minority groups was having an adverse effect upon our relations with other countries. At that time I pointed out that discrimination against such groups in the United States created suspicion and resentment in other countries, and that we would have better international relations were these reasons for suspicion and resentment to be removed.

During the past six years, the damage to our foreign relations attributable to this source has become progressively greater. The United States is under constant attack in the foreign press, over the foreign radio, and in such international bodies as the United Nations because of various practices of discrimination against minority groups in this country. As might be expected, Soviet spokesmen regularly exploit this situation in propaganda against the United States, both within the United Nations and through radio broadcasts and the press, which reaches all corners of the world. Some of these attacks against us are based on falsehood or distortion; but the undeniable existence of racial discrimination gives unfriendly governments the most effective kind of ammunition for their propaganda warfare. The hostile reaction among normally friendly peoples, many of whom are particularly sensitive in regard to the status of non-European races, is growing in alarming proportions. In such countries the view is expressed more and more vocally that the United States is hypocritical in claiming to be the champion of democracy while permitting practices of racial discrimination here in this country.

The segregation of school children on a racial basis is one of the practices in the United States that has been singled out for hostile foreign comment in the United Nations and elsewhere. Other peoples cannot understand how such a practice can exist in a country which professes to be a staunch supporter of freedom, justice, and democracy. The sincerity of the United States in this respect will be judged by its deeds as well as its words.

Although progress is being made, the continuance of racial discrimination in the United States remains a source of constant embarrassment to this Government in the day-to-day conduct of its foreign relations; and it jeopardizes the effective maintenance of our moral leadership of the free and democratic nations of the world.

Source: Brief for the United States as *Amicus Curiae*, p. 6, *Brown v. Board of Education*, 347 US 483 (1954) (filed December 1952), http://archive.oah.org/special-issues/teaching/2008_12/sources/ex1src2.pdf

2.3 US Supreme Court, *Brown v. Board of Education*, 1954

The NAACP LDF achieved its signal victory against segregation in 1954 when the US Supreme Court called time on the legal doctrine of "separate but equal" and ordered the desegregation of public schools in the landmark case of Brown v. Board of Education. *In making its decision, the Court cited the new role that public education played in the mid-twentieth century in determining life chances and success in modern American society. Sweepingly, and controversially, the Court ruled that the very fact of racial separation in schools conferred a "feeling of inferiority" on black students that made "Separate educational facilities [...] inherently unequal."*

Materially, there was a clear and demonstrable difference in segregated schools that could easily be determined, for example by examining the amount of money spent in each southern state per black and white student. There was a remedy to that in equalizing spending and making conditions more equal. However, by declaring that segregated education did psychological damage to black students, the ruling narrowed the remedy solely to desegregation. The Court drew on the experiments of black psychologist Kenneth B. Clark who had performed his "doll tests" in southern schools by presenting black and white students with black and white dolls and asking them which was the most intelligent doll, the most beautiful doll, and so on. White students invariably chose the white doll. Strikingly, black students chose the white doll too. Clark concluded that segregated education worked to internalize the idea of racial inferiority at a very early age.

Knowing that the Brown *decision would be controversial, the nine justices on the Court sought a united front in reaching a unanimous decision. To achieve this, they agreed that in the first instance they would rule purely upon the point of law that schools should desegregate. As a compromise, they temporarily left aside the thorny issue of how to actually implement school desegregation. It took just over a year until the* Brown *implementation order was handed down in 1955. In the meantime, the Court solicited advice at federal and state government levels to try to build a consensus for the best way to achieve desegregated public schools.*

In approaching this problem, we cannot turn the clock back to 1868 when the [Fourteenth] Amendment was adopted, or even to 1896 when *Plessy* v. *Ferguson* was written. We must consider public education in the light of its full development and its present place in American life throughout the Nation. Only in this way can it be determined if segregation in public schools deprives these plaintiffs of the equal protection of the laws.

Today, education is perhaps the most important function of state and local governments. Compulsory school attendance laws and the great expenditures for education both demonstrate our recognition of the importance of education to our democratic society. It is required in the performance of our most basic public responsibilities, even service in the armed forces. It is the very foundation of good citizenship. Today it is a principal instrument in awakening the child to cultural values, in preparing him for later professional training, and in helping him to adjust normally to his environment. In these days, it is doubtful that any child may reasonably be expected to succeed in life if he is denied the opportunity of an education. Such an opportunity, where the state has undertaken to provide it, is a right which must be made available to all on equal terms.

We come then to the question presented: Does segregation of children in public schools solely on the basis of race, even though the physical facilities and other "tangible" factors may be equal, deprive the children of the minority group of equal educational opportunities? We believe that it does.

In *Sweatt v. Painter, supra*, in finding that a segregated law school for Negroes could not provide them equal educational opportunities, this Court relied in large part on "those qualities which are incapable of objective measurement but which make for greatness in a law school." In *McLaurin v. Oklahoma State Regents, supra*, the Court, in requiring that a Negro admitted to a white graduate school be treated like all other students, again resorted to intangible considerations: "his ability to study, to engage in discussions and exchange views with other students, and, in general, to learn his profession."

Such considerations apply with added force to children in grade and high schools. To separate them from others of similar age and qualifications solely because of their race generates a feeling of inferiority as to their status in the community that may affect their hearts and minds in a way unlikely ever to be undone. The effect of this separation on their educational opportunities was well stated by a finding in the Kansas case by a court which nevertheless felt compelled to rule against the Negro plaintiffs:

"Segregation of white and colored children in public schools has a detrimental effect upon the colored children. The impact is greater when it has the sanction of the law; for the policy of separating the races is usually interpreted as denoting the inferiority of the negro group. A sense of inferiority affects the motivation of a child to learn. Segregation with the sanction of law, therefore, has a tendency to [retard] the educational and mental development of negro children and to deprive them of some of the benefits they would receive in a racial[ly] integrated school system."

Whatever may have been the extent of psychological knowledge at the time of *Plessy* v. *Ferguson*, this finding is amply supported by modern authority. Any language in *Plessy* v. *Ferguson* contrary to this finding is rejected.

We conclude that in the field of public education the doctrine of "separate but equal" has no place. Separate educational facilities are inherently unequal. Therefore, we hold that the plaintiffs and others similarly situated for whom the actions have been brought are, by reason of the segregation complained of, deprived of the equal protection of the laws guaranteed by the Fourteenth Amendment. This disposition makes unnecessary any discussion whether such segregation also violates the Due Process Clause of the Fourteenth Amendment.

Because these are class actions, because of the wide applicability of this decision, and because of the great variety of local conditions, the formulation of decrees in these cases presents problems of considerable complexity. On reargument, the consideration of appropriate relief was necessarily subordinated to the primary question – the constitutionality of segregation in public education. We have now announced that such segregation is a denial of the equal protection of the laws. In order that we may have the full assistance of the parties in formulating decrees, the cases will be restored to the docket, and the parties are requested to present further argument on Questions 4 and 5 previously pro-pounded by the Court for the reargument this Term. The Attorney General of the United States is again invited to participate. The Attorneys General of the states requiring or permitting segregation in public education will also be permitted to appear as *amici curiae* upon request to do so by September 15, 1954, and submission of briefs by October 1, 1954.

It is so ordered.

Source: US Supreme Court, *Brown v. Board of Education,* 347 U.S. 483 (1954), https://supreme.justia.com/cases/federal/us/347/483/case.html

2.4 *Arkansas State Press*, "After the Court's Decision – Now What?" 1954

The Brown *decision was the cause of much celebration in black America, but it was also greeted with a good deal of caution too. Finally, the nation had confessed to the damage done to black students by segregated education and it had admitted that such racial discrimination was unlawful. The legal argument had been won. At the same time, many black Americans wondered what would happen next. As always with court rulings, to win the legal argument was one thing but to actually claim those rights in practice was another. The Court's lack of a tangible plan for the implementation of its school desegregation decision was cause for concern.*

White southerners had forcefully resisted attempts to challenge white supremacy in the past, even to the point of civil war. To many, it seemed, the battle for school desegregation had only really just begun. The editorial below by Lucius Christopher (L.C.) Bates calls for a calm but uncompromising implementation of the Brown *decision. Bates was the co-owner of the Little Rock black newspaper the* Arkansas State Press *along with his wife Daisy Bates, who was president of the Arkansas NAACP State Conference of branches. L.C. Bates's editorial articulates both the hopes and fears of black America in the wake of the* Brown *decision. As we shall see in the next chapter, the Bateses soon found themselves at the very heart of the struggle to desegregate public schools.*

After the Court's Decision – Now What?

Now that the Supreme Court has passed down the long anticipated opinion, outlawing segregation in dixie schools, just where do we go from here?

Yes, we like most of the people, are pleased because we have seen the ruling on something that we have felt illegal all along. But when we said it we were branded a radical, a trouble-maker, and in many instances, a Communist. So it is natural that the Court's opinion is pleasing to us, because it gives us the opportunity to say something that every one every now and then gets a kick out of: "I told you so." But following this opinion, things are going to be too serious for any "getting back" at any person. This is no time to invent pretext for inflammatory arguments. It is a time that calls for calmness, and an unhysterical appraisal of our new venture into hitherto undiscovered democracy.

We are sorry that we cannot take the Court's opinion as optimistically as many. By no stretch of the imagination can we see the southerner relinquishing his claim on the phony luxury that he has cherished throughout the years without further fighting. However, there is one thing that makes the court opinion a little encouraging, and that is the younger generation of the white southerner is more receptive to reasoning than the older generation. But irrespective of that the pattern is set and the die is cast. The south is going to have integration in public schools.

We feel that the proper approach would be for the leaders among Negro race-leaders, not clabber mouths, Uncle Toms, or grinning appeasers – to get together and counsel with the school heads and try to get relief from school ills. This might work in some instances. If it does, it will save time, money, and a lot of emotionalism. Let the school officials understand that we are going to get a square deal in education. We want it peacefully if possible.

Source: *Arkansas State Press*, 21 May 1954, p. 4. Reproduced with the permission of the *Arkansas State Press*.

2.5 US Supreme Court, *Brown v. Board of Education*, 1955

When the US Supreme Court announced its implementation order for the Brown *decision, which became known as* Brown II, *it proved a disappointment to those looking for decisive action. After* Brown, *the Court found itself politically isolated. Southern congressmen were furious at the decision. President Dwight D. Eisenhower was lukewarm in support at best. The South girded for a grassroots campaign of massive resistance to school desegregation. The consensus for change that the Court hoped it could build had failed to materialize. There were some bright spots, notably in the border South states and some parts of the upper South that moved to desegregate their schools immediately after* Brown. *Typically, these were in places with lower black school populations where providing a dual segregated school system was an unwanted financial burden. Across the rest of the South, most school districts were steadfast in doing nothing at all until the Court explicitly told them exactly how they should proceed.*

In part because of the seeming lack of consensus and support for its original decision, the Court handed down what many regarded as a weak implementation order, amounting to a "go slow under the circumstances" approach. The Court did not define what exactly constituted school desegregation or precisely when or how it was supposed to be achieved. It handed the responsibility for overseeing implementation to local school districts and local courts, many of which were opposed to, or at the very least subject to election by people who were opposed to, school desegregation. Brown II *even appeared to conveniently list the types of things that might be used as viable excuses for delay. The implementation order is peppered with ambiguous language such as "a prompt and reasonable start" (what does prompt and reasonable mean?), "good faith compliance" (determined how?), and "with all deliberate speed" (how fast is that?). It would take decades to untangle those complicated and unresolved questions.*

MR CHIEF JUSTICE WARREN delivered the opinion of the Court.

These cases were decided on May 17, 1954. The opinions of that date, declaring the fundamental principle that racial discrimination in public education is unconstitutional, are incorporated herein by reference. All provisions of federal, state, or local law requiring or permitting such discrimination must yield to this principle. There remains for consideration the manner in which relief is to be accorded.

Because these cases arose under different local conditions and their disposition will involve a variety of local problems, we requested further argument on the question of relief. In view of the nationwide importance of the decision, we invited the Attorney General of the United States and the Attorneys General of all states requiring or permitting racial discrimination in public education to present their views on that question. The parties, the United States, and the States of Florida, North Carolina, Arkansas, Oklahoma, Maryland, and Texas filed briefs and participated in the oral argument.

These presentations were informative and helpful to the Court in its consideration of the complexities arising from the transition to a system of public education freed of racial discrimination. The presentations also demonstrated that substantial steps to eliminate racial discrimination in public schools have already been taken, not only in some of the communities in which these cases arose, but in some of the states appearing as *amici curiae*, and in other states as well. Substantial progress has been made in the District of Columbia and in the communities in Kansas and Delaware involved in this litigation. The defendants in the cases coming to us from South Carolina and Virginia are awaiting the decision of this Court concerning relief.

Full implementation of these constitutional principles may require solution of varied local school problems. School authorities have the primary responsibility for elucidating, assessing, and solving these problems; courts will have to consider whether the action of school authorities constitutes good faith implementation of the governing constitutional principles. Because of their proximity to local conditions and the possible need for further hearings, the courts which originally heard these cases can best perform this judicial appraisal. Accordingly, we believe it appropriate to remand the cases to those courts.

In fashioning and effectuating the decrees, the courts will be guided by equitable principles. Traditionally, equity has been characterized by a practical flexibility in shaping its remedies and by a facility for adjusting and reconciling public and private needs. These cases call for the exercise of these traditional attributes of equity power. At stake is the personal interest of the plaintiffs in admission to public schools as soon as practicable on a nondiscriminatory basis. To effectuate this interest may call for elimination of a variety of obstacles in making the transition to school systems operated in accordance with the constitutional principles set forth in our May 17, 1954, decision. Courts of equity may properly take into account the public interest in the elimination of such obstacles in a systematic and effective manner. But it should go without saying that the vitality of these constitutional principles cannot be allowed to yield simply because of disagreement with them.

While giving weight to these public and private considerations, the courts will require that the defendants make a prompt and reasonable start toward full compliance with our May 17, 1954, ruling. Once such a start has been made, the courts may find that additional time is necessary to carry out the ruling in an effective manner. The burden rests upon the defendants to establish that such time is necessary in the public interest and is consistent with good faith compliance at the earliest practicable date. To that end, the courts may consider problems related to administration, arising from the physical condition of the school plant, the school transportation system, personnel, revision of school districts and attendance areas into compact units to achieve a system of determining admission to the public schools on a nonracial basis, and revision of local laws and regulations which may be necessary in solving the foregoing problems. They will also consider the adequacy of any plans the defendants may propose to meet these problems and to effectuate a transition to a racially nondiscriminatory school system. During this period of transition, the courts will retain jurisdiction of these cases.

The judgments below, except that in the Delaware case, are accordingly reversed and the cases are remanded to the District Courts to take such proceedings and enter such orders and decrees consistent with this opinion as are necessary and proper to admit to public schools on a racially nondiscriminatory basis with all deliberate speed the parties to these cases. The judgment in the Delaware case – ordering the immediate admission of the plaintiffs to schools previously attended only by white children – is affirmed on the basis of the principles stated in our May 17, 1954, opinion, but the case is remanded to the Supreme Court of Delaware for such further proceedings as that Court may deem necessary in light of this opinion.

It is so ordered.

Source: US Supreme Court, *Brown v. Board of Education*, 349 US 294 (1955), https:// supreme.justia.com/cases/federal/us/349/294/case.html

2.6 *Chicago Defender*, "Blood on Their Hands ... An Editorial," [Emmett Till] 1955

The Brown *decision's impact reached far beyond schools. Encouraged by the legal backing of the US Supreme Court, blacks became ever more emboldened in their efforts to end racial discrimination. White southerners, dismayed at what they perceived as an attack on their regional mores, doubled down on their insistence in defending white supremacy.*

The murder of Emmett Till occurred in this context of racial polarization. Till, a 14-year-old boy from Chicago, was visiting relatives in Mississippi in the summer of 1955. One day, Till allegedly tried to impress his friends by flirting with a white women, Carolyn Bryant, at a local store. Several nights later, so the most repeated story goes, her husband Roy and his half-brother J.W. Milam abducted Till from his great-uncle's where he was staying. The two white men beat, shot, and mutilated Till before dumping his body in the Tallahatchie River tied to a cotton gin fan. Three days later, Till's body was retrieved and sent back to Chicago. Till's mother, Mamie Till Bradley, in a powerful act of protest, insisted on an open casket funeral so that everyone could witness her son's disfigured body. Bryant and Milam were tried for murder in Mississippi and acquitted by an all-white jury in a segregated courtroom. Protected against double jeopardy (the law does not allow prosecution of the same crime twice based on the same or similar charges and on

the same facts) they later admitted their guilt and sold their story to Look
magazine.

*The black press and much of the white press outside the South was outraged
by the events and expressed disgust. Although there was some criticism from
within the South initially, ultimately white southerners closed ranks in defending
Bryant and Milam and the values of white supremacy that they were seeking to
uphold. The murder of Emmett Till convinced many blacks of a need to take a
stand, while further solidifying sentiment in the white South that their way of life
must be preserved at all costs.*

The lynching of 14-year-old Emmett Louis "Bo" Till of Chicago in Mississippi
last week is an outrage to all decent American citizens, white, and colored, and
dramatically points out to the world the ugliest aspects of life in our Democracy.

The Chicago youth vacationing in Mississippi was kidnapped from the home
of relatives and brutally lynched after he was accused of whistling at the wife
of a storekeeper in Money, Miss.

The blood of "Bo" Till is on the hands of the five candidates for governor of
Mississippi who campaigned on an anti-Negro platform in the recent elections.
They charged the atmosphere of the state for acts of violence.

We accuse these racist rabble-rousers with contributing directly to the murder
of "Bo" Till and the lynching of American reputation for decency and respect
for law and order in the eyes of the entire world.

No country that tolerates the barbarous hate-filling of a child within its
midst deserves nor can it expect the respect of the civilized world. There can
be no compromise this time. Your child can be the next victim of white
supremacists.

It is up to the administration in Washington to begin action once and for all
to end the crime of lynching that has degraded our nation. Full justice must be
meted out to the two men now being held for this dastardly crime. A federal
anti-lynching law must be passed and in addition, it should be made a federal
offense to interfere with or attack any religious or racial group in elections.
Republicans and Democrats alike have been too quick to appease and forgive
bigotry and its consequent acts of violence.

Unless the Administration acts at once to stop this wanton and ruthless
taking of lives, the blood of "Bo" Till, Rev. George Lee, Lamar Smith and the
long line of martyrs in the fight for first class citizenship for the Negro in
America will be on its hands and "all the perfumes of Arabia will not wash
it away."

Source: "Blood on Their Hands ... An Editorial," 10 September 1955, *Chicago Defender*
(National edition), p. 1.

2.7 R.B. Patterson, "Organization of a Local Citizens' Council," 1955

Grassroots opposition to school desegregation, and opposition to civil rights and voting rights more broadly, came through the organization of White Citizens' Councils in the South. The Citizens' Councils formed the vanguard of massive resistance to the Brown *decision at local, county, and state levels. The first Citizens' Council was founded in Mississippi in July 1954 and chapters soon spread across the region. Robert B. Patterson, from Indianola, Mississippi, a plantation manager and a former football team captain at Mississippi State University, became the recognized leader of the movement. Unlike the mostly clandestine activities of the Ku Klux Klan at the time, the Citizens' Councils met and worked out in the open, attracted sizable memberships, and included people from different walks of life, including middle-class professionals and elected politicians. This lent the Councils a greater air of respectability. In most instances, rather than employing outright violence, the Citizens' Councils used threats and intimidation, although the seditious climate they created often led others to commit acts of violence, as the Emmett Till case testifies.*

The incentive to organize a Citizens' Council must come from within the Community itself. Certain leading citizens must decide that they need a local organization in order that their community can do its part to protect itself and to unite with their State and their section of the country in destroying the monster of integration that threatens our Nation.

One of the local leaders must take it upon himself to call a meeting from ten to twenty Community leaders. Advantages of local organization are discussed and a vote is taken as to whether or not this group should organize. A Temporary Chairman is elected, a meeting date is set for the next week and each man present is told to bring several of his friends who are sympathetic towards the movement to the next meeting. A nominating committee should be appointed from this group to have a satisfactory slate of officers to present for election at the second meeting.

At the second meeting, a speaker can address the gathering, telling them of the erroneous doctrines behind the "Black Monday" decision of the Supreme Court and further stress the need for local, state and regional organization.

The group can next elect permanent officers to include Chairman, Vice-Chairman, Secretary and Treasurer, and a Board of Directors. The Chairman and Directors can appoint the four committees as follows:

1. Information and Education
2. Legal Advisory
3. Membership and Finance
4. Political and Elections

In rural counties it might be better to have a countywide organization with directors from each small district who could call a meeting in their precincts or areas. In large cities it might be better to organize by precinct. In counties with two or three large cities it might be better to form two or three or more separate councils. This, of course, will vary according to the population and geographical layout of the county.

In Mississippi prominent, level headed and courageous leadership has been found in each instance, and the members that belong to our Councils come from every walk of life. Every man who is a patriotic law-abiding American who loves his state and nation should be proud to take part in this movement.

Source: R.B. Patterson, "Organization of a Local Citizens' Council," *The Citizens' Council* (Jackson, Miss.) Vol. 1, No. 2, November 1955, p. 1.

2.8 Southern US Congressmen, "Declaration of Constitutional Principles," 1956

Opposition to school desegregation came not only from the grassroots mobilization of Citizens' Councils, but it also received collective backing from the South's most senior politicians in Congress. In March 1956, 101 southern congressmen (99 Democrats and 2 Republicans) signed and released a "Declaration of Constitutional Principles," which became more popularly known as the "Southern Manifesto." South Carolina's Sen. James Strom Thurmond, who had been the presidential candidate for the Dixiecrats in 1948, came up with the initial draft, and Georgia's Sen. Richard Russell wrote the final version.

The statement lambasted the Brown *decision as a "clear abuse of judicial power" and argued that the US Supreme Court did not have the constitutional right to end segregation in schools. Harking back to the same arguments fought over in the American Civil War almost a century before, the congressmen upheld the notion that states' rights took precedence over "federal encroachment." In calling for "lawful means" of resistance and asking southerners to "refrain from disorder and lawless acts," it stressed opposition within the law, while using incendiary language that only further stoked the flames of resistance already burning brightly in the South.*

Not every southern congressman signed. Notably absent was future president and at the time Texas's Sen. Lyndon B. Johnson, and Tennessee's Sen. Albert Gore, Sr, whose son Al Gore, Jr later became vice president in William Jefferson "Bill" Clinton's presidential administration from 1993 to 2001. Such voices of dissent were a rarity in the South at the time. Increasingly, political races in the region were dominated by the school desegregation question, and those taking the hardest line against it stood the best chance of winning.

THE DECISION OF THE SUPREME COURT IN THE SCHOOL CASES – DECLARATION OF CONSTITUTIONAL PRINCIPLES

Mr [Walter F.] GEORGE. Mr President, the increasing gravity of the situation following the decision of the Supreme Court in the so-called segregation cases, and the peculiar stress in sections of the country where this decision has created many difficulties, unknown and unappreciated, perhaps, by many people residing in other parts of the country, have led some Senators and some Members of the House of Representatives to prepare a statement of the position which they have felt and now feel to be imperative.

I now wish to present to the Senate a statement on behalf of 19 Senators, representing 11 States, and 77 House Members, representing a considerable number of States likewise [...]

DECLARATION OF CONSTITUTIONAL PRINCIPLES

The unwarranted decision of the Supreme Court in the public school cases is now bearing the fruit always produced when men substitute naked power for established law.

The Founding Fathers gave us a Constitution of checks and balances because they realized the inescapable lesson of history that no man or group of men can be safely entrusted with unlimited power. They framed this Constitution with its provisions for change by amendment in order to secure the fundamentals of government against the dangers of temporary popular passion or the personal predilections of public officeholders.

We regard the decisions of the Supreme Court in the school cases as a clear abuse of judicial power. It climaxes a trend in the Federal Judiciary undertaking to legislate, in derogation of the authority of Congress, and to encroach upon the reserved rights of the States and the people.

The original Constitution does not mention education. Neither does the 14th Amendment nor any other amendment. The debates preceding the submission of the 14th Amendment clearly show that there was no intent that it should affect the system of education maintained by the States.

The very Congress which proposed the amendment subsequently provided for segregated schools in the District of Columbia.

When the amendment was adopted in 1868, there were 37 States of the Union [...]

Every one of the 26 States that had any substantial racial differences among its people, either approved the operation of segregated schools already in existence or subsequently established such schools by action of the same law-making body which considered the 14th Amendment.

As admitted by the Supreme Court in the public school case (*Brown* v. *Board of Education*), the doctrine of separate but equal schools "apparently originated in *Roberts* v. *City of Boston* (1849), upholding school segregation against attack as being violative of a State constitutional guarantee of equality." This constitutional doctrine began in the North, not in the South, and it was followed not only in Massachusetts, but in Connecticut, New York, Illinois, Indiana, Michigan, Minnesota, New Jersey, Ohio, Pennsylvania and other northern states until they, exercising their rights as states through the constitutional processes of local self-government, changed their school systems.

In the case of *Plessy* v. *Ferguson* in 1896 the Supreme Court expressly declared that under the 14th Amendment no person was denied any of his rights if the States provided separate but equal facilities. This decision has been followed in many other cases. It is notable that the Supreme Court, speaking through Chief Justice Taft, a former President of the United States, unanimously declared in 1927 in *Lum* v. *Rice* that the "separate but equal" principle is "within the discretion of the State in regulating its public schools and does not conflict with the 14th Amendment."

This interpretation, restated time and again, became a part of the life of the people of many of the States and confirmed their habits, traditions, and way of life. It is founded on elemental humanity and commonsense, for parents should not be deprived by Government of the right to direct the lives and education of their own children.

Though there has been no constitutional amendment or act of Congress changing this established legal principle almost a century old, the Supreme Court of the United States, with no legal basis for such action, undertook to exercise their naked judicial power and substituted their personal political and social ideas for the established law of the land.

This unwarranted exercise of power by the Court, contrary to the Constitution, is creating chaos and confusion in the States principally affected. It is destroying the amicable relations between the white and Negro races that have been created through 90 years of patient effort by the good people of both races. It has planted hatred and suspicion where there has been heretofore friendship and understanding.

Without regard to the consent of the governed, outside mediators are threatening immediate and revolutionary changes in our public schools systems. If done, this is certain to destroy the system of public education in some of the States.

With the gravest concern for the explosive and dangerous condition created by this decision and inflamed by outside meddlers:

We reaffirm our reliance on the Constitution as the fundamental law of the land.

We decry the Supreme Court's encroachment on the rights reserved to the States and to the people, contrary to established law, and to the Constitution.

We commend the motives of those States which have declared the intention to resist forced integration by any lawful means.

We appeal to the States and people who are not directly affected by these decisions to consider the constitutional principles involved against the time when they too, on issues vital to them may be the victims of judicial encroachment.

Even though we constitute a minority in the present Congress, we have full faith that a majority of the American people believe in the dual system of government which has enabled us to achieve our greatness and will in time demand that the reserved rights of the States and of the people be made secure against judicial usurpation.

We pledge ourselves to use all lawful means to bring about a reversal of this decision which is contrary to the Constitution and to prevent the use of force in its implementation.

In this trying period, as we all seek to right this wrong, we appeal to our people not to be provoked by the agitators and troublemakers invading our States and to scrupulously refrain from disorder and lawless acts.

Signed by:

MEMBERS OF THE UNITED STATES SENATE

Walter F. George, Richard B. Russell, John Stennis, Sam J. Ervin, Jr, Strom Thurmond, Harry F. Byrd, A. Willis Robertson, John L. McClellan, Allen J. Ellender, Russell B. Long, Lister Hill, James O. Eastland, W. Kerr Scott, John Sparkman, Olin D. Johnston, Price Daniel, J.W. Fulbright, George A. Smathers, Spessard L. Holland.

MEMBERS OF THE UNITED STATES HOUSE
OF REPRESENTATIVES

Alabama: Frank W. Boykin, George M. Grant, George W. Andrews, Kenneth A. Roberts, Albert Rains, Armistead I. Selden, Jr, Carl Elliott, Robert E. Jones, George Huddleston, Jr.

Arkansas: E.C. Gathings, Wilbur D. Mills, James W. Trimble, Oren Harris, Brooks Hays, W.F. Norrell.

Florida: Charles E. Bennett, Robert L.F. Sikes, A.S. Herlong, Jr, Paul G. Rogers, James A. Haley, D.R. Matthews.

Georgia: Prince H. Preston, John L. Pilcher, E.L. Forrester, John James Flynt, Jr, James C. Davis, Carl Vinson, Henderson Lanham, Iris F. Blitch, Phil M. Landrum, Paul Brown.

Louisiana: F. Edward Hebert, Hale Boggs, Edwin E. Willis, Overton Brooks, Otto E. Passman, James H. Morrison, T. Ashton Thompson, George S. Long.

Mississippi: Thomas G. Abernathy, Jamie L. Whitten, Frank E. Smith, John Bell Williams, Arthur Winstead, William M. Colmer.

North Carolina: Herbert C. Bonner, L.H. Fountain, Graham A. Barden, Carl T. Durham, F. Ertel Carlyle, Hugh Q. Alexander, Woodrow W. Jones, George A. Shuford.

South Carolina: L. Mendel Rivers, John J. Riley, W.J. Bryan Dorn, Robert T. Ashmore, James P. Richards, John L. McMillan.

Tennessee: James B. Frazier, Jr, Tom Murray, Jere Cooper, Clifford Davis.

Source: *Congressional Record*, 84th Congress Second Session. Vol. 102, part 4 (12 March 1956) (Washington, DC: Governmental Printing Office, 1956), pp. 4459–60.

Discussion Questions

1. Outline and assess the reasoning of the US Supreme Court that led to the 1954 *Brown* decision.
2. In what ways, if any, could the US Supreme Court have drawn up a more effective implementation order for the *Brown* decision?
3. Account for the virulent white southern opposition to the *Brown* decision.

Further Reading

Day, John Kyle. *The Southern Manifesto: Massive Resistance and the Fight to Preserve Segregation* (University Press of Mississippi, 2014).

Klarman, Michael. *From Jim Crow to Civil Rights: The Supreme Court and the Struggle for Racial Equality* (Oxford University Press, 2004).

Kluger, Richard. *Simple Justice: The History of Brown v. Board of Education and Black America's Struggle for Equality* (Alfred A. Knopf, 1976).

Lewis, George. *Massive Resistance: The White Response to the Civil Rights Movement* (Hodder and Arnold, 2006).

McMillen, Neil R. *The Citizens' Council: Organized Resistance to the Second Reconstruction, 1955–1964* (University of Illinois Press, 1971).

Patterson, James T. *Brown v. Board of Education: A Civil Rights Milestone and Its Troubled Legacy* (Oxford University Press, 2001).

Peltason, J. W. *Fifty-Eight Lonely Men: Southern Federal Judges and School Desegregation* (University of Illinois Press, 1971).

Tyson, Timothy B. *The Blood of Emmett Till* (Simon and Schuster, 2017).

Webb, Clive, ed. *Massive Resistance: Southern Opposition to the Second Reconstruction* (Oxford University Press, 2005).

Wilkinson, J. Harvie, III. *From Brown to Bakke: The Supreme Court and School Integration: 1954–1978* (Oxford University Press, 1979).

Chapter 3

The Montgomery Bus Boycott and the Southern Christian Leadership Conference, 1955–7

3.1 Rosa Parks Recalls Her Role in the Montgomery Bus Boycott in 1955

Rosa Parks's arrest aboard a Montgomery bus on 1 December 1955 has become an iconic moment in the civil rights movement. Interpretations of what that event means have changed significantly over time. Early representations of Parks's actions, notably in Martin Luther King, Jr's account of the bus boycott, Stride Toward Freedom *(Harper & Row, 1958), portrayed Parks as a tired seamstress who spontaneously decided to defy segregation laws because her feet hurt. This was part of a conscious attempt at the time to depoliticize Parks's actions and to instead emphasize the human element of the bus boycott, not least to avoid the common charge of communist-inspired agitation against activists that was prevalent in the wake of Sen. Joseph McCarthy's anticommunist crusades that had gripped the nation.*

More recently historians have become aware of Parks's longstanding commitment to racial and social justice struggles. Before making her protest, Parks had been the secretary in the local Montgomery National Association for the Advancement of Colored People (NAACP) branch, she had attended classes in social justice at Highlander Folk School in Tennessee, and she had been involved in women's issues, including investigations into the rape of black women by white men. Parks was well connected to activist networks in the local black and white communities. While her actions on 1 December do not appear to have been part of any formally preconceived plan to trigger a bus boycott, Parks made a politically conscious and informed choice in the context of decades of personal activism to defy segregation law on a Montgomery bus.

The Civil Rights Movement: A Documentary Reader, First Edition. Edited by John A. Kirk.
© 2020 John Wiley & Sons, Inc. Published 2020 by John Wiley & Sons, Inc.

When I got off from work that evening of December 1, I went to Court Square as usual to catch the Cleveland Avenue bus home. I didn't look to see who was driving when I got on, and by the time I recognized him, I had already paid my fare. It was the same driver who had put me off the bus back in 1943, twelve years earlier. He was still tall and heavy, with red, rough-looking skin. And he was still mean-looking. I didn't know if he had been on that route before – they switched the drivers around sometimes. I do know that most of the time if I saw him on a bus, I wouldn't get on it.

I saw a vacant seat in the middle section of the bus and took it. I didn't even question why there was a vacant seat even though there were quite a few people standing in the back. If I had thought about it at all, I would probably have figured maybe someone saw me get on and did not take the seat but left it vacant for me. There was a man sitting next to the window and two women across the aisle.

The next stop was the Empire Theater, and some whites got on. They filled up the white seats, and one man was left standing. The driver looked back and noticed the man standing. Then he looked back at us. He said, "Let me have those front seats," because they were the front seats of the black section. Didn't anybody move. We just sat right where we were, the four of us. Then he spoke a second time: "Y'all better make it light on yourselves and let me have those seats."

The man in the window seat next to me stood up, and I moved to let him pass by me, and then I looked across the aisle and saw that the two women were also standing. I moved over to the window seat. I could not see how standing up was going to "make it light" for me. The more we gave in and complied, the worse they treated us.

I thought back to the time when I used to sit up all night and didn't sleep, and my grandfather would have his gun right by the fireplace, or if he had his one-horse wagon going anywhere, he always had his gun in the back of the wagon. People always say I didn't give up my seat because I was tired, but that isn't true. I was not tired physically, or no more tired than I usually was at the end of a working day. I was not old, although some people have an image of me as being old then. I was forty-two. No, the only tired I was, was tired of giving in.

The driver of the bus saw me still sitting there, and he asked was I going to stand up. I said, "No." He said, "Well, I'm going to have you arrested." Then I said, "You may do that." These were the only words we said to each other. I didn't even know his name, which was James Blake, until we were in court together. He got out of the bus and stayed outside for a few minutes, waiting for the police.

As I sat there, I tried not to think about what might happen. I knew that anything was possible. I could have been manhandled or beaten. I could be arrested. People have asked me if it occurred to me then that I could be the test case the NAACP had been looking for. I did not think about that at all. In fact if I had let myself think too deeply about what might happen to me, I might have gotten off the bus. But I chose to remain.

3.2 Fred D. Gray Recalls His Role in the Montgomery Bus Boycott in 1955

News of Rosa Parks's arrest began to mobilize key community figures and existing black networks in Montgomery. An important voice in the black community in the age of segregation belonged to the small but influential black middle-class. A segregated community required segregated services and the black middle-class provided those services. This included attorneys like Fred D. Gray. Black attorneys were far fewer in number than white attorneys, and of the few black attorneys that did exist, many were reticent about taking on civil rights cases for fear of retribution by whites. Fearless and pioneering local black attorneys like Fred D. Gray, who agreed to take on Rosa Parks's case, helped push back against racial discrimination at a local level.

Gray contacted other community leaders like E.D. Nixon and Jo Ann Robinson to formulate a plan of action. Initially, Parks and Nixon contacted white attorney Clifford Durr, who along with his wife Virginia Durr were among a small number of whites in Montgomery who were also opposed to segregation. Parks had previously worked for the Durrs as a seamstress. Gray had already defended a black woman, Claudette Colvin, who was arrested in March 1955 for breaking segregation laws on Montgomery buses. Colvin's case was similar to Parks's, but when it was discovered that the 15-year-old Colvin was pregnant, the NAACP Legal Defense and Educational Fund (NAACP LDF) felt that she would attract criticism as a lead plaintiff in the case. By contrast, Parks was viewed as a paragon of respectability and beyond reproach. Momentum for a broad-based community protest in response to Parks's arrest, a possibility that had been discussed before, began to take shape as the legal proceedings continued.

Upon my return [from out of town] on the early evening I had many calls from Mrs Parks, Mr Nixon, Jo Ann Robinson, and just everybody, telling me that Rosa Parks had been arrested. Of course, by the time of my return, Mr Nixon, with the assistance of attorney Durr, had posted her bond and she had been released. In fact, she was never actually jailed. The normal procedure of the police department in such a case at that time would be to arrest her on the bus, place her in a police car, take her to city jail (then located on North Ripley

Street), fingerprint her, "book" her, and then give her an opportunity to make a phone call so that bond could be arranged. All of this had already occurred by the time I arrived back into town that evening [...]

Rosa and Raymond Parks lived in the Cleveland Court Apartments, not far from downtown on Montgomery's west side. At Mrs Parks's invitation, I immediately went over to her house. She told me what had happened and asked me to represent her, and I took it from there. I left her apartment and went the short distance to Mr Nixon's house on Clinton Avenue, where he and I discussed the matter at length. I told him that I would be working on her case over the weekend. We also discussed the fact that now was the time for us to do whatever we should to solve the problems on the buses. Of course he was one hundred percent in support of any effort in that direction and had already been busily making calls to arrange a meeting of Montgomery black leaders.

I left Mr Nixon's house and went to Jo Ann Robinson's house and we discussed the incident. During the course of our discussion, we concluded:

1. If we were ever going to have a bus protest in Montgomery, Alabama, we must have it now.
2. For the bus protest to be successful, the African American community must support it. It must have the wholehearted support of the African American preachers and of both E.D. Nixon and Coach Rufus Lewis.
3. A leader must be selected who would be able to organize, motivate, and keep the people together. Jo Ann believed that her pastor, a young newcomer to Montgomery, the Rev. Martin Luther King Jr, could be that person.

Source: Fred D. Gray, *Bus Ride to Justice: The Life and Works of Fred D. Gray* (Montgomery: New South Books, revised edition 2013, originally published 1995), pp. 50–1.

3.3 E.D. Nixon Recalls His Role in the Montgomery Bus Boycott in 1955

Edgar Daniel (E.D.) Nixon was head of the Brotherhood of Sleeping Car Porters Union (BSCPU) in Montgomery and held influence with local union members. Also through the BSCPU, Nixon had links with a national organization that could potentially lend outside help and expertise. Nixon had considered protests against bus segregation before. Arrests that had been made on the buses in Montgomery for violating segregation laws over the previous ten months had begun to cement that idea. Since the Brown *decision had abolished segregation in the schools, it in turn implicitly cast legal doubt on the veracity of other segregation laws too. Nixon's job as a Pullman car porter had taken him around the United States and he had witnessed life outside of the segregated South. What he saw and experienced there made southern segregation seem even more of an anathema. Nixon dreamed of doing something to bring about change in his own community. Yet taking a stand came with significant risks attached. With Rosa Parks's case offering a tangible legal test and a direct opportunity for community mobilization, Nixon decided that the time had finally come to act.*

On the night of December 1st, 1955, I sat for a long while on the edge of my bed. After a time I turned to my wife and said, "You know, I think every Negro in town should stay off the buses for one day in protest at Mrs Parks' arrest." My wife looked at me as if I was crazy. Then I asked her, "What do you think?" "I think you ought to stop day dreaming, and turn out the light and get some sleep."

As I began to think about the three women who had been arrested in the last ten months for violating the Jim Crow law on the buses, my mind turned back thirty years. I began to think about the days when I first traveled out of Montgomery as a pullman porter. I remembered seeing Negroes in the North sitting anywhere they wanted on streetcars and trains. I remembered how I had seen black men holding public office – how they had freedoms which are still being denied us in Alabama. I began to wonder how long we were going to put up with being pushed around.

I remembered, how years ago, I had first asked myself, "What can I do to help bring freedom to the Negro in Alabama?" Naturally, one person alone could not bring about many changes in a deeply rooted tradition. But I believed that one person could kindle a spark that might cause others to see light and work.

I recalled that it had taken a long time before I had the courage to begin. Most of the people I talked to called me crazy. Others told me to take it easy if I wanted to live. They told me that Southern white people were different from those up North. Nevertheless I kept believing that Negroes could be free [...]

Then all of a sudden, as I sat there on the edge of my bed, some ideas came to me: Why not ask the people of Montgomery to stand up and be counted? Why not start a protest for Mrs Parks? Why not stay out of the buses? Why not start a Montgomery Improvement Association? I decided that it was time for mass action in spite of my wife's reaction. I felt that the Negroes in Montgomery were at last anxious to move, prepared to sacrifice and ready to endure whatever came.

Source: E.D. Nixon, "How It All Started," *Liberation* (December 1956), p. 10, cited in Peter B. Levy ed., *Let Freedom Ring: A Documentary History of the Modern Civil Rights Movement* (New York and Westport, CT: Praeger, 1992), pp. 54–5.

3.4 Jo Ann Robinson Recalls Her Role in the Montgomery Bus Boycott in 1955

E.D. Nixon was not the only community member in Montgomery poised to act. Jo Ann Robinson and the Women's Political Council (WPC) had also been making plans to take a stand. Robinson, like many others in the WPC, was a teacher. Teachers made up the largest single group in the black middle-class. Black schools and colleges were important centers of community life and resources, and an obvious home base for protests. There were also drawbacks: whites still controlled state institutions under the existing segregated system, and most crucially their finances. Teachers who took a stand for civil rights could quickly find themselves feeling economic pressure by being fired or having their contracts non-renewed. Black educators walked a tightrope between exerting their considerable influence and retaining their jobs.

Jo Ann Robinson indicates below the sorts of resources that teachers had access to that could be useful in community protests: materials for making signs and flyers, a copier for multiplying them, and teachers and students able to distribute them widely. Inadvertently, the white media assisted in getting the message out by discovering the existence of the flyers and reporting on their contents. A one-day bus boycott was called for 5 December, the day of Rosa Parks's trial. The decision by the city police department to have a motorcycle patrolman follow each bus on that day, intended to prevent any interference with black riders who wanted to ride the buses, backfired by intimidating more blacks into not riding. When Robinson looked out of her window on the morning of 5 December, she could see from the paucity of black riders on the buses that the WPC's efforts at reaching the black community had been successful.

Fred Gray told me Rosa Parks was arrested. Her case would be on Monday. He said to me, "Jo Ann, if you have ever planned to do anything with the council, now is your time." I called all the officers of the three chapters, I called as many of the men who had supported us as I could reach, and I told them that Rosa Parks had been arrested and would be tried. They said, "You have the plans, put them into operation." We had worked for at least three years getting that thing organized.

The Women's Political Council had begun in 1946, after just dozens of black people had been arrested on the buses for segregation purposes. By 1955, we had members in every elementary, junior high, and senior high school, and in federal, state, and local jobs. Wherever there were more than ten blacks employed, we had members there. We were prepared to the point that we knew in a matter of hours we could corral the whole city.

I didn't go to bed that night. I cut stencils and took them to the college. The fellow who let me in during the night, John Cannon, is dead now, but he was in the business department. We ran off thirty-five thousand copies. After I had talked with every WPC member in the elementary, junior high, and senior high schools to have somebody on campus during the day so I could deliver them,

I took them to school with me in my car. I taught classes from eight o'clock to ten o'clock. When my ten o'clock class was over, I took two senior students with me and I had the flyers in my car, bundled and ready to be given out. I would drive to the place of dissemination, and a kid would be there to grab them. I was on the campus and off before anybody knew that I was there.

Most of the people got the message, but there were outlying areas that didn't. And one lone black woman, who was so faithful to her white lady, as she called it went back to work and took one of the circulars to this woman so she would know what the blacks had planned. When the woman got it, she immediately called the media. After that, the television, the radio, the evening newspapers told those persons whom we had not reached that there would be the boycott. So the die was cast.

Monday morning, December the fifth, 1955, I shall never forget because many of us had not gone to bed that night. It was the day of the boycott. We had been up waiting for the first buses to pass to see if any riders were on them. It was a cold morning, cloudy, there was a threat of rain, and we were afraid that if it rained the people would get on the bus. But as the buses began to roll, and there were one or two on some of them, none on some of them, then we began to realize that the people were cooperating and that they were going to stay off the bus that first day. What helped us keep them off, too, was that the police department had decided that they would put a police on a motorcycle with a white cap who would accompany the buses and any of the blacks who wanted to get on. They would help them to get on without what they called "the goon squads" keeping them from riding. And that helped out the cause because those few blacks who were going to ride were afraid that the police who were following the buses would hurt them. So they didn't ride. As a result, a very negligible number of riders rode that first day.

Source: Jo Ann Robinson interview from *Voices of Freedom: An Oral History of the Civil Rights Movement from the 1950s through the 1980s* by Henry Hampton and Steve Fayer, pp. 22–3, copyright © 1990 by Blackside, Inc. Used by permission of Bantam Books, an imprint of Random House, a division of Penguin Random House LLC. All rights reserved.

3.5 Martin Luther King, Jr, "Holt Street Baptist Church Speech," 1955

How did Martin Luther King, Jr emerge as the leader of the Montgomery bus boycott? As we have already seen, a number of people played central roles in getting the bus boycott started. King was a relative newcomer to events. Born in Atlanta, Georgia, in 1929, King grew up in a church family; his father Martin Sr, known as "Daddy" King, inherited his church pulpit from King's maternal grandfather. King attended Morehouse College in Atlanta before completing a divinity degree at Crozer Theological Seminary in Pennsylvania and embarking upon a PhD in systematic theology at Boston University, where he met and married Coretta Scott King. Before completing his PhD thesis, in 1954 King was offered the position as pastor at Montgomery's Dexter Avenue Baptist Church. The congregation, made up largely of middle-class blacks, had fired its previous pastor Vernon Johns for being too active in civil rights issues.

When E.D. Nixon called King to ask if a meeting could be held at his church to discuss the bus boycott, King at first hesitated, knowing full well the many risks involved both to him and his family. King later reluctantly agreed. Black churches were at the heart of black community networks and were one of the few entirely black-owned spaces that black people could use as meeting place. Black ministers were paid by their congregations, and therefore unlike black teachers enjoyed a degree of economic independence from whites. King's church contained relatively well-to-do black community members who owned vehicles that would prove useful in a car pool to provide an alterative transport system to buses during the boycott.

When community leaders agreed to form a new organization, the Montgomery Improvement Association (MIA), to run the bus boycott, the question was raised about who should lead it. Existing community leaders were all wary about their rivals holding the position. King, a new, young, and raw recruit to the community seemed like a capable and non-threatening compromise figure – and he was one of the few preachers in the city who was actually willing to do the job. Other ministers feared repercussions from the white community if they put themselves forward to lead what was bound to be a controversial and possibly dangerous bus boycott. After agreeing to take on the role, King stepped out to deliver a speech at Holt Street Baptist Church at the end of the first day of the bus boycott. There were one thousand people inside the church and four thousand more outside listening over loudspeakers. The italicized text in brackets below represents the audience responses to King's speech in the traditional call-and-response pattern of black church sermons.

My friends, we are certainly very happy to see each of you out this evening. We are here this evening for serious business. (*Yes*) We are here in a general sense because first and foremost we are American citizens (*That's right*) and we are determined to apply our citizenship to the fullness of its meaning. (*Yeah, That's right*) We are here also because of our love for democracy, (*Yes*) because of our deep-seated belief that democracy transformed from thin paper to thick action (*Yes*) is the greatest form of government on earth. (*That's right*)

But we are here in a specific sense, because of the bus situation in Montgomery. (*Yes*) We are here because we are to get the situation corrected. This situation is not at all new. The problem has existed over endless years. (*That's right*) For many years now Negroes in Montgomery and so many other areas have been inflicted with the paralysis of crippling fears (*Yes*) on buses in our community. (*That's right*) On so many occasions, Negroes have been intimidated and humiliated and impressed – oppressed – because of the sheer fact that they were Negroes. (*That's right*) I don't have time this evening to go into the history of these numerous cases. Many of them now are lost in the thick fog of oblivion, (*Yes*) but at least one stands before us now with glaring dimensions. (*Yes*)

Just the other day, just last Thursday to be exact, one of the finest citizens in Montgomery (*Amen*) – not one of the finest Negro citizens (*That's right*) but one of the finest citizens in Montgomery – was taken from a bus (*Yes*) and carried to jail and arrested (*Yes*) because she refused to get up to give her seat to a white person. (*Yes, That's right*) Now the press would have us believe that she refused to leave a reserved section for Negroes, (*Yes*) but I want you to know this evening that there is no reserved section. (*All right*) The law has never been clarified at that point. (*Hell no*) Now I think I speak with, with legal authority – not that I have any legal authority, but I think I speak with legal authority behind me (*All right*) – that the law, the ordinance, the city ordinance has never been totally clarified. (*That's right*)

Mrs Rosa Parks is a fine person. (*Well, well said*) And since it had to happen I'm happy that it happened to a person like Mrs Parks, for nobody can doubt the boundless outreach of her integrity. (*Sure enough*) Nobody can doubt the height of her character, (*Yes*) nobody can doubt the depth of her Christian commitment and devotion to the teachings of Jesus. (*All right*) And I'm happy since it had to happen, it happened to a person that nobody can call a disturbing factor in the community. (*All right*) Mrs Parks is a fine Christian person, unassuming, and yet there is integrity and character there. And just because she refused to get up, she was arrested.

And you know, my friends, there comes a time when people get tired of being trampled over by the iron feet of oppression. [*Thundering applause*] There comes a time, my friends, when people get tired of being plunged across the abyss of humiliation where they experience the bleakness of nagging despair. (*Keep talking*) There comes a time when people get tired of being pushed out of the glittering sunlight of life's July, and left standing amid the piercing chill of an alpine November. (*That's right*) [*Applause*] There comes a time. (*Yes sir, Teach*) [*Applause continues*]

We are here, we are here this evening because we're tired now. (*Yes*) [*Applause*] And I want to say, that we are not here advocating violence. (*No*) We have never done that. (*Repeat that, Repeat that*) [*Applause*] I want it to be known throughout Montgomery and throughout this nation (*Well*) that we are Christian people. (*Yes*) [*Applause*] We believe in the Christian religion. We believe in the teachings of Jesus. (*Well*) The only weapon that we have in our hands this evening is the weapon of protest. (*Yes*) [*Applause*] That's all.

Source: "MIA Mass Meeting at Holt Street Baptist Church," 5 December 1955, Martin Luther King, Jr Papers website, http://mlk-kpp01.stanford.edu/kingweb/ publications/papers/vol3/551205.004-MIA_Mass_Meeting_at_Holt_Street_ Baptist_Church.htm

3.6 US Supreme Court, *Browder v. Gayle*, 1956

*As the bus boycott continued, NAACP LDF attorneys were enlisted to fight the
legal case against segregation on buses in the courts. Initially, the MIA only
requested a modified system of segregation on buses that would treat black patrons
more humanely. When the city and bus line refused point-blank to consider this,
the MIA prepared a court challenge to Alabama state laws and Montgomery city
ordinances requiring bus segregation.*

*Following its established policy, the NAACP LDF would only agree to help if
segregation laws were challenged directly. Attorney Fred D. Gray, with the
assistance of NAACP LDF attorneys, filed the case in the federal District Court on
1 February 1956. Rosa Parks was not among the plaintiffs. Instead, four other
women were chosen, including Claudette Colvin, who had been discriminated
against by white bus drivers in Montgomery in the past. The plaintiffs were
selected on the basis of which represented the best legal cases for challenging state
and city laws.*

*On 5 June 1956, the District Court ruled that segregation on buses in
Montgomery was unconstitutional. The city appealed the case to the US Supreme
Court. The boycott of buses in Montgomery continued. Finally, on 13 November
1956, the Court upheld the District Court's ruling. It took another month until, on
20 December, Montgomery's Mayor William Gayle was served notice by federal
marshals to desegregate the city's buses. The next morning, King was up bright and
early and among the first to take a desegregated bus ride.*

The purpose of this action is to test the constitutionality of both the statutes of
the State of Alabama and the ordinances of the City of Montgomery which
require the segregation of the white and colored races on the motor buses of
the Montgomery City Lines, Inc., a common carrier of passengers in said City
and its police jurisdiction.

The plaintiffs are four Negro citizens who bring this action for themselves
and on behalf of all other Negroes similarly situated. The defendants are the
members of the Board of Commissioners and the Chief of Police of the City of
Montgomery, the members of the Alabama Public Service Commission, The
Montgomery City Lines, Inc., and two of its employee drivers.

Each of the four named plaintiffs has either been required by a bus driver or
by the police to comply with said segregation laws or has been arrested and
fined for her refusal so to do. The plaintiffs, along with most other Negro citizens of the City of Montgomery, have since December 5, 1955, and up to the
present time, refrained from making use of the transportation facilities provided by Montgomery City Lines, Inc. Plaintiffs and other Negroes desire and
intend to resume the use of said buses if and when they can do so on a non-segregated basis without fear of arrest.

The members of the Board of Commissioners and the Chief of Police of the
City of Montgomery in their answers to the complaint admit "that they seek to

enforce the statutes of the State of Alabama and the ordinances of the City of Montgomery, Alabama," and further aver that "segregation of privately owned buses within cities within the State of Alabama is in accordance with the laws of the State of Alabama and the City of Montgomery."

[...]

[T]he separate but equal doctrine can no longer be safely followed as a correct statement of the law. In fact, we think that Plessy v. Ferguson has been impliedly, though not explicitly, overruled, and that, under the later decisions, there is now no rational basis upon which the separate but equal doctrine can be validly applied to public carrier transportation within the City of Montgomery and its police jurisdiction. The application of that doctrine cannot be justified as a proper execution of the state police power.

We hold that the statutes and ordinances requiring segregation of the white and colored races on the motor buses of a common carrier of passengers in the City of Montgomery and its police jurisdiction violate the due process and equal protection of the law clauses of the Fourteenth Amendment to the Constitution of the United States. This holding does not, however, become effective until the entry of formal judgment. The parties are requested to submit to the Court in writing within two weeks from the date of this opinion their views as to the form of judgment to be entered, and as to whether such judgment should be stayed in the event of an appeal.

Source: US Supreme Court, *Browder v. Gayle* 142 F. Supp 707 (1956), https://law.justia.com/cases/federal/district-courts/FSupp/142/707/2263463/

3.7 *Chicago Defender,* "Bus Boycotts in 3 Cities," 1956

As the below report from the Chicago Defender *illustrates, even before it ended, the Montgomery bus boycott was inspiring other black communities to take similar action. Students in Tallahassee, Florida, began a bus boycott. The local NAACP branches in Miami, Florida, and Memphis, Tennessee, challenged bus segregation laws there. Others followed in the next few years.*

But none of the bus boycotts proved as successful as the one in Montgomery, either in the extent of community organization or in longevity. Some cities, in the wake of the successful bus boycott in Montgomery, desegregated their bus systems to avoid a lawsuit and to forestall any demonstrations of black community unity. Some cities scrapped their bus systems altogether rather than desegregate. Some cities did not have a large enough black population to make the same economic impact as the bus boycott in Montgomery. It appeared that what had happened in Montgomery was, in many ways, a unique set of circumstances.

One outcome of the boycott's success in Montgomery was renewed efforts by whites to put the NAACP out of business. The success of the NAACP LDF in winning court decisions to desegregate schools and buses convinced many whites that if they got rid of the NAACP, then black protest movements would ground to a halt. State, county, and local authorities began to harass the NAACP and its members. Alabama even banned the NAACP's operations in the state altogether. In addition to school desegregation and the bus boycott, the NAACP LDF had successfully assisted in desegregating the University of Alabama in February 1956 when black graduate student Autherine Lucy enrolled for a degree in library science. Lucy was expelled within a matter of weeks under controversial circumstances.

The attack on the NAACP led to other organizations sprouting up to continue the movement, such as the Alabama Christian Movement for Human Rights (ACMHR) in Birmingham under the leadership of Rev. Fred Shuttlesworth. As the ACMHR name suggests, many of these new organizations were church-led, drawing their inspiration from Martin Luther King, Jr's leadership in the Montgomery bus boycott.

Bus Boycotts in 3 Cities

US Court Rules Out Seating Bias

Segregated bus seating in three neighboring Southern states has turned US civil rights "topsy turvy" for the time being.

In one state a boycott has protested and a federal court decision has banned it. In the other two states two boycotts and a civil suit are threatening to wipe it out of existence.

This is the score:

In Montgomery, Ala., a federal court decision last week banned segregated seating, but the bus boycott that started six months ago is continuing. And boycott leaders have given indication that the boycott will continue until their full demands have been guaranteed.

In Tallahassee, Fla., where A and M college students started boycotting city buses two weeks ago over segregation, enough steam was generated to start rolling similar action in Miami.

The president of the Miami chapter of the NAACP, the Rev. Theo R. Gibson, declared last week that Negroes may call a boycott of city buses if segregation in the vehicles is not abolished.

Then in Memphis, Tenn., last week, the NAACP filed suit attacking the constitutionality of state laws requiring bus segregation and urging "a speedy hearing" before a three-judge federal court panel.

The Montgomery federal court struck down Alabama's segregation laws involving intrastate travel in a 2–1 decision holding that state laws requiring bus segregated seating were unconstitutional.

Judge Richard T. Rives and Frank M. Johnson held that enforced segregation violates the due process and equal protection clauses of the Federal Constitution. The third judge, Seaborn A. Lynn, submitted a dissenting opinion.

The court gave city and bus officials two weeks to appeal the decision before making the ruling effective.

Southeast of Alabama, in the neighboring state of Florida, the city of Tallahassee has become more unsettled than it was two weeks ago when some several thousand students at A and M college touched off a boycott against city buses over segregated seating.

The Tallahassee boycott, as late as Friday, seemed to be gaining momentum despite improved conditions offered by City and Transit company officials. Negro leaders of the boycott refused a compromise agreement and the city commission responded by not only discontinuing the route near the college but also a route in another section of the city which is predominantly Negro.

The impact of the Tallahassee bus boycott winged its way to Miami where NAACP and civic leaders organized a special committee to "fight segregation in Miami's buses."

Members of the Miami NAACP said that a possible boycott of the Miami Transit company is being considered. They added that petitions asking that segregation be ended will be circulated among both white and Negro residents of the Florida city.

Just north of Alabama, in Memphis, Tenn., a civil suit aimed at cracking open Tennessee's laws calling for segregated bus seating was filed in District Court by members of the Memphis NAACP.

The suit was filed at the request of O.Z. Evers, 31, one of two men who left a cross town bus April 26 after the driver called police when he and another passenger, G.L. Myers, 46, took front seats and refused to move.

Police gave the men a choice of leaving the bus or being arrested.

Flanked on both sides by anti-segregation forces, Alabama, already reeling from within after being struck with a six-month old boycott, attempted to strike back last week by enjoining the NAACP from further activity within the state on the grounds that it was a "foreign corporation."

In the same city where the boycott was born, Circuit Judge Walter Jones approved a temporary injunction against the organization which was chartered in New York.

The petition charged that the NAACP failed to file certain documents with the state and pay a "non-residents" fee. The petition also specifically inferred that the organization was behind the Autherine Lucy school riots and the boycott.

In a counter move against the NAACP ban, more than 500 cheering Negroes last week organized a new organization dedicated to wiping out racial segregation. They named it "The Alabama Christian Movement for Human Rights."

The Rev. Fred Shuttlesworth, elected head of the group, said the organization was not connected with the NAACP.

Thus, in three neighboring southern states, Tennessee, Alabama and Florida a federal court decision, a civil suit, a new human rights organization and two powerful bus boycotts are threatening to not only force bus segregation out of existence, but push forward the whole civil rights fight in the United States.

Source: "Bus Boycotts in 3 Cities," *The Chicago Defender* (National edition), 16 June 1956, p. 1.

3.8 Southern Christian Leadership Conference, Constitution and By-Laws, 1957

The Montgomery bus boycott propelled Martin Luther King, Jr onto the national stage. As the boycott moved into 1956, the national press began to focus more on King's leadership. Only 26 years old when the boycott started, King felt the weight of expectation that rested on his young shoulders. After the boycott ended, three experienced civil rights activists worked with King to help form a new organization, the Southern Christian Leadership Conference (SCLC). Bayard Rustin had worked with A. Philip Randolph's BSCPU and with the Congress of Racial Equality (CORE). During the Montgomery bus boycott he had been sent to the city to help tutor King in nonviolence. Ella Baker had worked with New Deal agencies in the 1930s and later with the NAACP as a national field secretary and then director of branches. Stanley Levison was a white attorney who had worked with the American Jewish Congress and the NAACP. All three had previously met as part of a group called In Friendship organized by A. Philip Randolph.

After several planning meetings, the SCLC was launched in August 1957 with the motto "To Redeem the Soul of America." The organization provided a national platform for King's leadership for just over a decade in his role as SCLC president. As the name suggests, black southern ministers dominated the SCLC leadership. To avoid possible competition and thereby conflict with the NAACP, the SCLC did not solicit individual memberships but rather worked through affiliates, composed mainly of church-led organizations, voter registration organizations, and civic groups.

Aims and Purposes
I.   The Southern Christian Leadership Conference has the basic aim of achieving full citizenship rights, equality, and the integration of the Negro in all aspects of American life.

II. Social and economic forces are bringing about great changes in the South.
     Urbanization, industrialization, scientific agriculture and mass education are making it possible to remove the barriers to a prosperous, free and creative life for all Southerners. However, these barriers will not disappear automatically.

Accordingly, the responsibility of the Southern Negro in the struggle for a better society is two-fold:

A. The Negro must join with other Southerners in solving Southern problems; and

B. Since the South is part of the nation, the Negro (and other Southerners) must cherish and defend our fundamental, democratic heritage. Thus, simultaneously, he will be fulfilling his obligations to his country and to himself as a first-class citizen.

To secure these ends, the Southern Christian Leadership Conference is established, dedicating itself to justice, refusing to cooperate with evil, appealing to the conscience of man, and working for social change but always in a spirit of good will and non-violence.

III.   The Southern Christian Leadership Conference is organized as a service agency to facilitate coordinated action of local protest groups and to assist in their sharing of resources and experiences. The magnitude of the problem calls for the maximum commitment of resources of all institutions in Negro life, North and South. The Southern Christian Leadership Conference seeks to cooperate with all existing agencies attempting to bring full democracy to our great nation.

Source: Constitution and By-Laws of the Southern Christian Leadership Conference, Atlanta, Georgia, 1957, http://www.crmvet.org/docs/sclc_const.pdf

3.9 Martin Luther King, Jr, "Give Us the Ballot," 1957

The first campaign led by the SCLC was an effort to multiply bus boycotts across the South. For various reasons, outlined above, attempts to replicate the Montgomery bus boycott failed. Next, the SCLC turned its focus to more traditional civil rights work in voter registration campaigns. Again, the SCLC's efforts were not as successful as it had anticipated. Bureaucratic and organizational problems beset the SCLC and changes were made to try to address them. Notably, in 1960, King left his job at Dexter Avenue Baptist Church in Montgomery to share his father's pulpit at Ebenezer Baptist Church in Atlanta. This placed King in a larger city and in a transportation hub for the South and the nation that provided a more accessible base for his activities.

Nevertheless, there was a nagging feeling among some that King had not lived up to the promise of his leadership in the years immediately following the bus boycott. King and the SCLC struggled to translate the mass activism and the tactic of nonviolent direct action into an innovative and dynamic movement that could make an impact across the South. Over the following years the inspiration and direction to do that came from elsewhere, propelling the movement forward and forcing King and the SCLC to play catch-up.

King's speech below, delivered at a Prayer Pilgrimage for Freedom at the Lincoln Memorial in Washington, DC to mark the third anniversary of the Brown *decision, highlights both King's national standing in the years after the Montgomery bus boycott and his struggle to find a distinctive place in a newly emerging movement. The emphasis is very much on voting rights and school desegregation, rather than on nonviolent direct action. King does, however, show a keen awareness of the various key constituencies that would prove vital to his success as a leader: firstly, the federal government; secondly, white northern liberals; and thirdly, white southern moderates. King went on to define the fourth necessary source for the movement's success as strong black leadership.*

Mr Chairman, distinguished platform associates, fellow Americans. Three years ago the Supreme Court of this nation rendered in simple, eloquent, and unequivocal language a decision which will long be stenciled on the mental sheets of succeeding generations. For all men of goodwill, this May seventeenth decision came as a joyous daybreak to end the long night of human captivity. It came as a great beacon light of hope to millions of disinherited people throughout the world who had dared only to dream of freedom.

Unfortunately, this noble and sublime decision has not gone without opposition. This opposition has often risen to ominous proportions. Many states have risen up in open defiance. The legislative halls of the South ring loud with such words as "interposition" and "nullification."

But even more, all types of conniving methods are still being used to prevent Negroes from becoming registered voters. The denial of this sacred right is a tragic betrayal of the highest mandates of our democratic tradition. And so our most urgent request to the president of the United States and every member of Congress is to give us the right to vote. (*Yes*)

Give us the ballot, and we will no longer have to worry the federal government about our basic rights.

Give us the ballot (*Yes*), and we will no longer plead to the federal government for passage of an anti-lynching law; we will by the power of our vote write the law on the statute books of the South (*All right*) and bring an end to the dastardly acts of the hooded perpetrators of violence.

Give us the ballot (*Give us the ballot*), and we will transform the salient misdeeds of bloodthirsty mobs (*Yeah*) into the calculated good deeds of orderly citizens.

Give us the ballot (*Give us the ballot*), and we will fill our legislative halls with men of goodwill (*All right now*) and send to the sacred halls of Congress men who will not sign a "Southern Manifesto" because of their devotion to the manifesto of justice. (*Tell 'em about it*)

Give us the ballot (*Yeah*), and we will place judges on the benches of the South who will do justly and love mercy (*Yeah*), and we will place at the head of the southern states governors who will, who have felt not only the tang of the human, but the glow of the Divine.

Give us the ballot (*Yes*), and we will quietly and nonviolently, without rancor or bitterness, implement the Supreme Court's decision of May seventeenth, 1954. (*That's right*)

In this juncture of our nation's history, there is an urgent need for dedicated and courageous leadership. If we are to solve the problems ahead and make racial justice a reality, this leadership must be fourfold.

First, there is need for strong, aggressive leadership from the federal government. So far, only the judicial branch of the government has evinced this quality of leadership. If the executive and legislative branches of the government were as concerned about the protection of our citizenship rights as the federal courts have been, then the transition from a segregated to an integrated society would be infinitely smoother. But we so often look to Washington in vain for this concern. In the midst of the tragic breakdown of law and order, the executive branch of the government is all too silent and apathetic. In the midst of the desperate need for civil rights legislation, the legislative branch of the government is all too stagnant and hypocritical.

This dearth of positive leadership from the federal government is not confined to one particular political party. Both political parties have betrayed the cause of justice. (*Oh yes*) The Democrats have betrayed it by capitulating to the prejudices and undemocratic practices of the southern Dixiecrats. The Republicans have betrayed it by capitulating to the blatant hypocrisy of right wing, reactionary northerners. These men so often have a high blood pressure of words and an anemia of deeds. [*laughter*]

In the midst of these prevailing conditions, we come to Washington today pleading with the president and members of Congress to provide a strong, moral, and courageous leadership for a situation that cannot permanently be evaded. We come humbly to say to the men in the forefront of our government that the civil rights issue is not an Ephemeral, evanescent domestic issue that can be kicked about by reactionary guardians of the status quo; it is rather an eternal moral issue which may well determine the destiny of our nation (*Yeah*) in the ideological struggle with communism. The hour is late. The clock of destiny is ticking out. We must act now, before it is too late.

A second area in which there is need for strong leadership is from the white northern liberals. There is a dire need today for a liberalism which is truly liberal. What we are witnessing today in so many northern communities is a sort of quasi-liberalism which is based on the principle of looking sympathetically at all sides. It is a liberalism so bent on seeing all sides, that it fails to become committed to either side. It is a liberalism that is so objectively analytical that it is not subjectively committed. It is a liberalism which is neither hot nor cold, but lukewarm. (*All right*) We call for a liberalism from the North which will be thoroughly committed to the ideal of racial justice and will not be deterred by the propaganda and subtle words of those who say: "Slow up for a while; you're pushing too fast."

A third source that we must look to for strong leadership is from the moderates of the white South. It is unfortunate that at this time the leadership of the white South stems from the close-minded reactionaries. These persons gain prominence and power by the dissemination of false ideas and by deliberately appealing to the deepest hate responses within the human mind. It is my firm belief that this close-minded, reactionary, recalcitrant group constitutes a numerical minority. There are in the white South more open-minded moderates than appears on the surface. These persons are silent today because of fear of social, political and economic reprisals. God grant that the white moderates of the South will rise up coura-geously, without fear, and take up the leadership in this tense period of transition.

Source: Martin Luther King, Jr, "Give Us the Ballot," Address Delivered at the Prayer Pilgrimage for Freedom, 17 May 1957, https://kinginstitute.stanford.edu/king-papers/documents/give-us-ballot-address-delivered-prayer-pilgrimage-freedom

Discussion Questions

1. Outline and assess the different roles played by the various people involved in the beginning of the Montgomery bus boycott.
2. Do you think the bus boycott or the courts were the most important factor in bringing about desegregation on Montgomery buses, and why?
3. Account for the emergence of black ministers as some of the most promi-nent figures in the civil rights movement in the mid to late 1950s.

Further Reading

Brooks, Pamela E. *Boycotts, Buses, and Passes: Black Women's Resistance in the U.S. South and South Africa* (University of Massachusetts Press, 2008).

Burns, Stewart, ed. *Daybreak of Freedom: The Montgomery Bus Boycott* (University of North Carolina Press, 1997).

Gray, Fred D. *Bus Ride to Justice: Changing the System by the System: The Life and Works of Fred D. Gray, Preacher, Attorney, Politician: Lawyer for Rosa Parks* (Black Belt Press, 1999).

King, Coretta Scott. *My Life with Martin Luther King, Jr* (Holt, Rinehart and Winston, 1969).

King, Martin Luther, Jr. *Stride Toward Freedom: The Montgomery Story* (Harper and Row, 1958).

McGuire, Danielle L. *At the Dark End of the Street: Black Women, Rape, and Resistance—A New History of the Civil Rights Movement from Rosa Parks to the Rise of Black Power* (Alfred A. Knopf, 2010).

Morris, Aldon D. *Origins of the Civil Rights Movement: Black Communities Organizing for Change* (Free Press, 1984).

Robinson, Jo Ann, with David Garrow. *The Montgomery Bus Boycott and the Women Who Started It* (University of Tennessee Press, 1989).

Theoharis, Jeanne. *The Rebellious Life of Mrs. Rosa Parks* (Beacon Press, 2013).

Thornton, J. Mills. *Dividing Lines: Municipal Politics and the Struggle for Civil Rights in Montgomery, Birmingham, and Selma* (University of Alabama Press, 2002).

Chapter 4   The Little Rock Crisis and Desegregation in Education, 1957–62

4.1 Gov. Orval E. Faubus, Televised Speech, 1957

The struggle over school desegregation came to a head in Little Rock, Arkansas, in September 1957. Little Rock was regarded as a relatively moderate city in a relatively moderate state, where some limited progress had been made in desegregation. Little Rock superintendent of schools Virgil T. Blossom announced soon after the Brown *decision that the city would implement a gradual plan of school desegregation. The city had two main high schools, the black Dunbar High and the white Central High. Ominously, Blossom's plan included building two new high schools, one in an area of black residence and one in an area of white residence in the city's increasingly segregated neighborhoods. When the school in the predominantly black neighborhood opened in 1956, it had an all-black teaching staff assigned to it, clearly labeling it as a segregated school.*

The local branch of the National Association for the Advancement of Colored People (NAACP) challenged the Blossom Plan in the courts in the case of Aaron v. Cooper. *The courts upheld the Blossom Plan under the go-slow provisions of* Brown II, *but ordered that it must proceed as planned with the desegregation of Central High in September 1957. As the date approached, segregationists put pressure on the school board to abandon its desegregation plans. Meanwhile, Blossom began his selection process for black students to attend Central. Out of around 200 applicants, he whittled the number down to 17. Only nine black students eventually entered the school with around 2,000 white students.*

Arkansas elected Orval E. Faubus as governor in 1954. At first, Faubus seemed to be a moderate in keeping with the state's image and took the view that local communities should be left to their own devices to work out school desegregation. However, when contested in the Democratic Party primaries in 1956 by James D.

The Civil Rights Movement: A Documentary Reader, First Edition. Edited by John A. Kirk.
© 2020 John Wiley & Sons, Inc. Published 2020 by John Wiley & Sons, Inc.

Johnson, head of the White Citizens' Council in the state, Faubus took a hardline stance for segregation to ward off the competition. After his reelection, Faubus appeared to return to his earlier stance of moderation.

Yet the evening before Central High was due to desegregate, Faubus made a fateful decision to send Arkansas National Guard troops to the school, citing a threat of violence and disorder if desegregation went ahead. Faubus framed his actions as simply preserving the public peace, and appeared to be even-handed in saying that the troops would not be "segregationists or integrationists." But he rounded off his televised address with a swipe at "forcible integration" and an insistence that Little Rock schools would remain segregated.

I have undeniable reports of a telephone campaign of massive proportions going on in the City of Little Rock at this time, calling upon the mothers of White children to assemble peaceably upon the school grounds at 6:00 a.m. tomorrow, the opening day of school.

I have reports of caravans that will converge upon Little Rock from many points of the State, to assemble peaceably upon the school grounds in the morning. Some of these groups have already reached the city, and are here now. Some of the information about these caravans has come to me from school authorities themselves.

Telephone calls have come to me at the mansion in a constant stream. The expressions of all are the fear of disorder and violence, and of the harm that may occur tomorrow in this attempt at forcible integration of Central High School.

Other evidence of the alarm and concern comes from a Negro newspaper.

Coming as a boy from the hills, from a family of modest circumstances, I learned and have treasured many of the time-honored adages.

"A stitch in time saves nine." "An ounce of prevention is worth a pound of cure."

Remembering the wisdom of these maxims, and being aware of the overwhelming evidence of impending disorder which could lead to violence and even bloodshed, I have therefore, in accordance with the solemn responsibilities and my Oath of Office, made the decision to act and to act now. It is only good judgment to act before the situation gets out of hand – before the resulting violence creates lasting enmity, animosity, and hate between citizens of this community, which would do irreparable harm to the good relations that have existed between the races. I have, therefore, undertaken the following action:

Units of the Arkansas National Guard have been, or are now being mobilized, with the mission to maintain or restore the peace and order of the community. Advance units are already on duty on the grounds of Central High School.

I have briefed the Commanders as to the situation, and they already have or are now briefing the members of their commands.

I have informed Chief Lindsey, Director of Arkansas State Police, of the developments. He is now mobilizing a force to act as an arm of the state militia in maintaining or restoring the peace and order of the community, and to act in every way possible to protect the lives and property of the citizens of Pulaski County.

This decision I have reached prayerfully. It has been made after conferences with dozens of people, and after checking and verifying as many of the reports as possible.

The mission of the State Militia is to maintain or restore order and to protect the lives and property of citizens. They will act not as segregationists or integrationists, but as soldiers called to active duty to carry out their assigned tasks.

I must state here, in all sincerity, it is my firm conviction that it will not be possible to restore or to maintain order and protect the lives and property of the citizens, if forcible integration is carried out tomorrow in the schools of this community. The inevitable conclusion, therefore, must be that the schools in Pulaski County, for the time being, must be operated on the same basis as they have been operated in the past.

I appeal now for reason, clear thinking, and good order. Let us all be good citizens, and continue as a people and as a State, upon the road to progress on which we have so enthusiastically embarked.

THE PUBLIC PEACE WILL BE PRESERVED!

Source: Gov. Orval E. Faubus, 2 September 1957, box 496, folder 1, Orval E. Faubus Papers, Special Collections, University of Arkansas Libraries, Fayetteville.

4.2 Ira Wilmer "Will" Counts, Jr, Elizabeth Eckford and Hazel Bryan, 1957

Daisy and L.C. Bates emerged at the forefront of black community leadership as schools desegregated. Daisy Bates, as president of the Arkansas NAACP State Conference of branches, had worked with the Little Rock NAACP branch to help coordinate the legal challenge to the Blossom Plan in Aaron v. Cooper. *After losing that challenge, the Bateses' home became the headquarters for the NAACP and the Little Rock Nine – as the black students became collectively known – throughout unfolding events.*

On the morning of 4 September, plans had been made for the black students to meet with the Bateses and local ministers close to the school and then to proceed to Central High with a police escort. One of the students, Elizabeth Eckford, did not have a telephone, and Daisy Bates was unable to reach her. Elizabeth turned up at Central alone to face a howling white mob intent on preventing school desegregation, and Arkansas National Guard soldiers blocking her entrance. Arkansas Democrat *photographer Will Counts's below photograph depicts the pandemonium that ensued. White student Hazel Bryan's heckling of the bespectacled Elizabeth became the enduring image of the day's events in newspapers around the world.*

Realizing that she was at the mercy of a mob and that the Arkansas National Guard troops were not there to assist her, Elizabeth walked to the nearest bus stop and left. Shortly after, the other eight students – Minnijean Brown, Ernest Green, Thelma Mothershed, Melba Pattillo, Gloria Ray, Terrance Roberts, Jefferson Thomas, and Carlotta Walls – along with their chaperones were turned away from the school. The events placed the United States in a constitutional crisis. Faubus had called out the state militia to prevent the enactment of a federal order, directly bringing into question the authority of the federal government over states' rights.

Source: Ira Wilmer "Will" Counts, Jr, Elizabeth Eckford and Hazel Bryan, 4 September 1957, Archives Photograph Collection, Indiana University, Bloomington, http://webapp1.dlib.indiana.edu/archivesphotos/results/item.do?itemId=P0026600

4.3   Daisy Bates Recalls Events at Central High School in 1957

Gov. Faubus's actions led to a series of telegram exchanges with President Dwight D. Eisenhower. The two men subsequently met at Eisenhower's Newport, Rhode

Island retreat in search of an understanding about how to move forward. Little of substance was achieved.

Attention then turned back to the courts. On the same day that the black students were turned away from Central High, the school board asked the federal District Court for a delay in its desegregation plan because of potential violence and disorder. Attorneys from the NAACP's Legal Defense and Educational Fund (NAACP LDF) contested this. The Court turned down the school board's request for delay and instead granted an injunction against Faubus and Arkansas National Guard officials from interfering with school desegregation.

The judge who issued the ruling was Ronald N. Davies from Fargo, North Dakota, a temporary replacement on the bench. Through a quirk of political and legal geography, Arkansas was the only southern state in the Eighth Circuit Court of Appeals, which covered mainly northern and mid-western states. Davies was therefore less influenced by southern racial mores and merely followed the letter of the law. Faubus removed the Arkansas National Guard from Central High and headed to the Southern Governors' Conference in Georgia. Having created a crisis, he conveniently exited the city.

On Monday morning, 23 September, a white mob gathered at Central. An ill-prepared city police force that had now inherited the job of keeping law and order helped to escort the nine black students into the school. The mob refused to disperse and the police were in danger of losing control. False reports about the students being attacked inside the school circulated. Mid-morning, the nine black students were withdrawn from Central for their own safety. The school was now effectively under mob rule. The scenes brought an angry response from Eisenhower, who commanded the mob to cease and desist in its obstruction of justice. The next day, ignoring Eisenhower's command, the mob gathered at the school again. This time, the president took more decisive action. Below, Daisy Bates recalls the events of 23 September and the efforts of the Little Rock Nine to attend Central High School.

At last the call came from the police. They told us it would be safer to take a roundabout route to the school. They would meet us near Central and escort the children through a side entrance.

The white newsmen left my home for Central High. The Negro reporters remained, seating themselves around the kitchen table drinking coffee. They were: L. Alex Wilson, general manager and editor of the *Tri-State Defender*, of Memphis, Tennessee; James Hicks, managing editor of the *New York Amsterdam News*; Moses J. Newsome of the *Afro-American*, of Baltimore, Maryland, and Earl Davy, *State Press* photographer.

I told them they must take a different route from the one the children would take, but that if they were at the Sixteenth Street and Park Avenue Entrance to Central, they would be able to see the nine enter the school.

We had two cars. I went in the first car with some of the children and C.C. Mercer. Frank Smith, field secretary of the NAACP, followed with the rest of the nine. To this day I cannot remember which of the nine were in our car. Nor can they.

As we approached the side entrance to the school, the main body of the mob was moving away from us. I got out of the car and told the children to go quickly. From the sidewalk I watched the police escort them through the door of the school. Someone in the mob saw them enter and yelled, "They're in! The niggers are in!"

The people on the fringes of the mob started moving toward us. A policeman rushed up to me. "Get back in the car, Mrs Bates. Drive back the way you came, and fast!"

I tumbled into the car. Mr Mercer was waiting at the wheel. The car radio was on and a hoarse-voiced announcer was saying: "The Negro children are being mobbed in front of the school." I knew the children were in the school and, for the moment, at least, safe. But who was being mobbed?

We sped back to the house to reassure Mrs Brown and Mr Eckford. Then I called the other parents at work to quiet their fears.

A series of false radio reports followed. Newscasters, broadcasting from the school grounds, reported that the children were being beaten and were running down the halls of the school, bloodstained; that the police were trying to get them out, but the nine children, hysterical with fright, had locked themselves in an empty classroom.

A young white lawyer, who was very close to Assistant Chief of Police Gene Smith, devised a plan by which he would keep me informed of the goings on inside the school. When I called him, he assured me that the reports were false. After each report I would check with him, then call the parents. Once Mr Eckford screamed at me in exasperation, "Well, if it's not true why would they say such things on air?"

"*The children have barricaded themselves inside the school, the mob is breaking through the barricades, and the police are powerless to rescue the children,*" we heard one breathless newscaster announce. Again I called and demanded to know what was going on. I was told that the children were safe, but the police didn't know how much longer their forces could control the mob, which had now grown to over a thousand.

Later that day we learned that a white teen-age girl had been slipping in and out of the school, issuing false reports to the radio broadcasters. They had put her statements on the air without checking them. Gene Smith, Assistant Chief of Police, had finally caught up with her and ordered her arrested.

4.4 President Dwight D. Eisenhower, Executive Order 10730, 1957

The refusal of the mob to disperse at Central High forced President Eisenhower's hand. Although the president had never given strong backing to school desegregation, as a five-star general and supreme commander of the allied expeditionary forces in Europe during World War II, Eisenhower was certainly not ready to tolerate the insubordination of a state governor or succumb to a civilian mob. On 24 September, the president issued Executive Order 10730. As commander-in-chief of the armed forces, he federalized the Arkansas National Guard and sent 1,000 soldiers of the 101st Airborne Division of the US Army to Little Rock to uphold law and order.

On the morning of 25 September, federal troops arrived at the Bateses' home to collect the nine black students and escort them to Central High. With the world's media looking on, the nine students entered the school. The military escort became a staple of the students' daily routine that year. But their ordeal did not end there. Once inside the school, a group of white students harassed the black students to try to get them to leave. One black student, Minnijean Brown, was expelled for retaliating. The other eight students survived through to the end of the school year and Ernest Green, the only senior, became the first black student to graduate from Central in May 1958. Martin Luther King, Jr attended the graduation ceremony as one of the very few black people in the audience.

WHEREAS on September 23, 1957, I issued Proclamation No. 3204 reading in part as follows:

"WHEREAS certain persons in the state of Arkansas, individually and in unlawful assemblages, combinations, and conspiracies, have willfully obstructed the enforcement of orders of the United States District Court for the Eastern District of Arkansas with respect to matters relating to enrollment and attendance at public schools, particularly at Central High School, located in Little Rock School District, Little Rock, Arkansas; and

"WHEREAS such willful obstruction of justice hinders the execution of the laws of that State and of the United States, and makes it impracticable to enforce such laws by the ordinary course of judicial proceedings; and

"WHEREAS such obstruction of justice constitutes a denial of the equal protection of the laws secured by the Constitution of the United States and impedes the course of justice under those laws:

"NOW, THEREFORE, I, DWIGHT D. EISENHOWER, President of the United States, under and by virtue of the authority vested in me by the Constitution and Statutes of the United States, including Chapter 15 of Title 10 of the United

States Code, particularly sections 332, 333 and 334 thereof, do command all persons engaged in such obstruction of justice to cease and desist therefrom, and to disperse forthwith;" and

WHEREAS the command contained in that Proclamation has not been obeyed and willful obstruction of enforcement of said court orders still exists and threatens to continue:

NOW, THEREFORE, by virtue of the authority vested in me by the Constitution and Statutes of the United States, including Chapter 15 of Title 10, particularly sections 332, 333 and 334 thereof, and section 301 of Title 3 of the United States Code, It is hereby ordered as follows:

SECTION 1. I hereby authorize and direct the Secretary of Defense to order into the active military service of the United States as he may deem appropriate to carry out the purposes of this Order, any or all of the units of the National Guard of the United States and of the Air National Guard of the United States within the State of Arkansas to serve in the active military service of the United States for an indefinite period and until relieved by appropriate orders.

SEC. 2. The Secretary of Defense is authorized and directed to take all appropriate steps to enforce any orders of the United States District Court for the Eastern District of Arkansas for the removal of obstruction of justice in the State of Arkansas with respect to matters relating to enrollment and attendance at public schools in the Little Rock School District, Little Rock, Arkansas. In carrying out the provisions of this section, the Secretary of Defense is authorized to use the units, and members thereof, ordered into the active military service of the United States pursuant to Section 1 of this Order.

SEC. 3. In furtherance of the enforcement of the aforementioned orders of the United States District Court for the Eastern District of Arkansas, the Secretary of Defense is authorized to use such of the armed forces of the United States as he may deem necessary.

SEC. 4. The Secretary of Defense is authorized to delegate to the Secretary of the Army or the Secretary of the Air Force, or both, any of the authority conferred upon him by this Order.

DWIGHT D. EISENHOWER

THE WHITE HOUSE,

September 24, 1957.

Source: President Dwight D. Eisenhower, "Executive Order 10730: Providing Assistance for the Removal of an Obstruction of Justice Within the State of Arkansas," https://www.ourdocuments.gov/doc.php?flash=true&doc=89&page=transcript

4.5 Larry Lubenow Recalls Interviewing Louis Armstrong about Events in Little Rock in 1957

Events in Little Rock reverberated around the world. The treatment of the nine black students further hurt the United States' global image. When the United States leveled charges against the Soviet Union's human rights abuses in Eastern Europe, the Soviet Union pointed to the United States' treatment of black students in Little Rock. How could people of color in other countries, the Soviet Union asked, trust a United States that treated people of color in its own country so badly?

Similarly, some black people in the United States questioned how they could support their country's fight for democracy in other countries if the United States could not support democratic principles in the fight for black freedom at home. An outspoken critic of events in Little Rock was jazz musician Louis Armstrong, who had volunteered to perform overseas as an ambassador for the United States. Armstrong canceled his visit to the Soviet Union after watching the treatment of the Little Rock Nine and told white journalist Larry Lubenow in very forthright terms why.

In October 1957, events in Little Rock were edged out of the news headlines by the Soviet launch of Sputnik, the first satellite in space. The news of racial unrest in Little Rock contrasted starkly with the Soviet Union leaping ahead in the space race and further underscored the international damage of events in Arkansas. The Soviets took delight in reporting on national radio each time Sputnik flew over Little Rock.

SCOTT SIMON, host:
In September 1957, Louis Armstrong canceled his tour of the Soviet Union because of events in Little Rock, Arkansas. Nine black students attempted to integrate Central High School there. But when Orval Faubus supported the Arkansas National Guard to bar the door, Louis Armstrong decided he didn't want to make a tour of the Soviet Union sponsored by the US State Department.

Larry Lubenow was a reporter at that time, and he broke this story. He joins us now from member station KUT in Austin.

Mr Lubenow, thanks very much for being with us.

MR LARRY LUBENOW:	(Former Student-Journalist; Larry Lubenow & Associates): It's a pleasure to be here and to be a part of this.
SIMON:	You were a journalism student then, weren't you?

MR LUBENOW:	Yes, I was a senior in college, moonlighting at the paper.
SIMON:	You were working part time for the Grand Forks Herald, right?
MR LUBENOW:	Yes, I was.
SIMON:	And how did you happen to talk to Louis Armstrong?
MR LUBENOW:	I got a call from the editors that they wanted a reporter to go down to talk to Louis about music. I asked one question about music. And then I asked Louis if he knew that he was staying in the hometown of Judge Ronald Davies who made the decision at the 5th Circuit Court of Appeals on Little Rock. And he said he didn't. Then he went off.
SIMON:	He had some strong words for people in the US government then, didn't he?
MR LUBENOW:	Well, even stronger than that which was printed. He used expletives when he talked about Ike and John Foster Dulles and also Orval Faubus.
SIMON:	What did he call Governor Faubus?
MR LUBENOW:	Well, I can't repeat it, not on NPR. It's …
SIMON:	I thought it was just an ignorant plowboy. You can repeat that.
MR LUBENOW:	Well, that's what we went with, and Louis said, fine, go with it.
SIMON:	So let me get this straight. He didn't actually say ignorant plowboy. He said something else and you said, let's see if we can agree on …
MR LUBENOW:	Yes.
SIMON:	… an epithet here.
MR LUBENOW:	He said he's a no-good mother.
SIMON:	And he probably didn't mean mother. I see what you mean.
MR LUBENOW:	No. (Soundbite of laughter)
SIMON:	And so what did you say? Mr Armstrong, give me something that I can put in the paper?
MR LUBENOW:	Yeah, I sure did.
SIMON:	What did Louis Armstrong say in the interview about not going to the Soviet Union, do you recall?
MR LUBENOW:	Well, he said that as far as he was concerned, Ike and the government could go to hell. And he sang his version of the "Star-spangled Banner" to me with very

	dirty lyrics – oh, say can you mothers – M-F-see, by the M-F early light? He was very mad.
SIMON:	Yeah. I don't think I've ever heard that version. (Soundbite of laughter)
MR LUBENOW:	Yeah.
SIMON:	What happened to your story? Did you know you had a scoop?
MR LUBENOW:	I broke the story and I got all of $3.50 for the story, I think. Missed the concert and … (Soundbite of laughter)
MR LUBENOW:	Because I was busy putting out the story.
SIMON:	Now, when President Eisenhower eventually did order the 101st Airborne into Little Rock …
MR LUBENOW:	Yes.
SIMON:	… to integrate the schools.
MR LUBENOW:	Yes, he did. And some people think that it was because of Louis' words.
SIMON:	Mr Lubenow, awfully nice talking to you.
MR LUBENOW:	My pleasure, Scott.
SIMON:	Speaking with us from Austin, Texas, Larry Lubenow. And this is NPR News.

Source: ©2007 National Public Radio, Inc. News report titled "Remembering Louis Armstrong's Little Rock Protest" was originally broadcast on NPR's Weekend Edition Saturday on 22 September 2007, and is used with the permission of NPR.

4.6 US Supreme Court, *Cooper v. Aaron*, 1958

The legal battles over the desegregation of Central High continued during the 1957–1958 school year. In February 1958, the school board asked for a delay in its school desegregation plan. The federal District Court granted the delay. The NAACP LDF appealed the decision in the Eighth Circuit Court of Appeals, which overruled the delay. The school board then appealed the Eighth Circuit Court decision to the US Supreme Court.

On 28 August, the US Supreme Court sat in special session to hear the case, and on 12 September it ruled against further delay. In the landmark decision of Cooper v. Aaron, *the Court said that violence and disorder could not be used as excuses for failing to proceed with school desegregation. If the Court had ruled in favor of delay, it would have sent the message to segregationists that all they needed to do to prevent the implementation of* Brown *was to rabble rouse. By insisting that school desegregation should continue, the Court took its strongest stand in defense of the* Brown *decision since 1954.*

Gov. Faubus had other plans: he closed all of Little Rock's public high schools to prevent desegregation. He then held a referendum to let the people decide whether to keep the schools closed or to desegregate them. The majority white electorate chose to keep the schools closed. For the 1958–1959 school year, teachers sat in empty classrooms while students took correspondence classes or moved to other districts for their education.

Closed public schools caused huge disruption and brought a halt to outside economic investment in the city. A number of middle-class white women had formed the Women's Emergency Committee to Open Our Schools (WEC) in an unsuccessful attempt to keep the schools open in the referendum. The women continued to push for the reopening of schools, and for the city's male business and civic leaders to take a stand. When a segregationist-dominated school board started to fire schoolteachers and school administrators that they felt were sympathetic to school desegregation, a recall campaign initiated a battle over the control of the school board. Moderate business interests won out, and a new school board voted to reopen the schools on a limited and token desegregated basis.

Shortly after, the federal District Court ruled that the school closing laws passed by a Faubus-backed Arkansas General Assembly were unconstitutional. When schools reopened in August 1959, it brought the immediate conflict over school desegregation in the city to a close. The struggle to achieve meaningful desegregation that went beyond tokenism continued.

On May 20, 1954, three days after the first *Brown* opinion, the Little Rock District School Board adopted, and on May 23, 1954, made public, a statement of policy entitled "Supreme Court Decision – Segregation in Public Schools." In this statement, the Board recognized that

"It is our responsibility to comply with Federal Constitutional Requirements, and we intend to do so when the Supreme Court of the United States outlines the method to be followed."

Thereafter, the Board undertook studies of the administrative problems confronting the transition to a desegregated public school system at Little Rock. It instructed the Superintendent of Schools to prepare a plan for desegregation, and approved such a plan on May 24, 1955, seven days before the second *Brown* opinion. The plan provided for desegregation at the senior high school level (grades 10 through 12) as the first stage. Desegregation at the junior high and elementary levels was to follow. It was contemplated that desegregation at the high school level would commence in the fall of 1957, and the expectation was that complete desegregation of the school system would be accomplished by 1963. Following the adoption of this plan, the Superintendent of Schools discussed it with a large number of citizen groups in the city. As a result of these discussions, the Board reached the conclusion that "a large majority of the residents" of Little Rock were of "the belief ... that the Plan, although objectionable in principle" from the point of view of those supporting segregated schools, "was still the best for the interests of all pupils in the District."

Upon challenge by a group of Negro plaintiffs desiring more rapid completion of the desegregation process, the District Court upheld the School Board's plan, *Aaron v. Cooper,* 143 F.Supp. 855. The Court of Appeals affirmed, 243 F.2d 361. Review of that judgment was not sought here.

While the School Board was thus going forward with its preparation for desegregating the Little Rock school system, other state authorities, in contrast, were actively pursuing a program designed to perpetuate in Arkansas the system of racial segregation which this Court had held violated the Fourteenth Amendment. First came, in November, 1956, an amendment to the State Constitution flatly commanding the Arkansas General Assembly to oppose "in every Constitutional manner the Unconstitutional desegregation decisions of May 17, 1954, and May 31, 1955, of the United States Supreme Court," and, through the initiative, a pupil assignment law. Pursuant to this state constitutional command, a law relieving school children from compulsory attendance at racially mixed schools, and a law establishing a State Sovereignty Commission, were enacted by the General Assembly in February, 1957.

The School Board and the Superintendent of Schools nevertheless continued with preparations to carry out the first stage of the desegregation program. Nine Negro children were scheduled for admission in September, 1957, to Central High School, which has more than two thousand students. Various administrative measures, designed to assure the smooth transition of this first stage of desegregation, were undertaken.

On September 2, 1957, the day before these Negro students were to enter Central High, the school authorities were met with drastic opposing action on the part of the Governor of Arkansas, who dispatched units of the Arkansas National Guard to the Central High School grounds and placed the school "off limits" to colored students. As found by the District Court in subsequent proceedings, the Governor's action had not been requested by the school authorities, and was entirely unheralded. The findings were these:

"Up to this time [September 2], no crowds had gathered about Central High School and no acts of violence or threats of violence in connection with the carrying out of the plan had occurred. Nevertheless, out of an abundance of caution, the school authorities had frequently conferred with the Mayor and Chief of Police of Little Rock about taking appropriate steps by the Little Rock police to prevent any possible disturbances or acts of violence in connection with the attendance of the 9 colored students at Central High School. The Mayor considered that the Little Rock police force could adequately cope with any incidents which might arise at the opening of school. The Mayor, the Chief of Police, and the school authorities made no request to the Governor or any representative of his for State assistance in maintaining peace and order at Central High School. Neither the Governor nor any other official of the State government consulted with the Little Rock authorities about whether the Little

Rock police were prepared to cope with any incidents which might arise at the school, about any need for State assistance in maintaining peace and order, or about stationing the Arkansas National Guard at Central High School."

The Board's petition for postponement in this proceeding states:

"The effect of that action [of the Governor] was to harden the core of opposition to the Plan and cause many persons who theretofore had reluctantly accepted the Plan to believe there was some power in the State of Arkansas which, when exerted, could nullify the Federal law and permit disobedience of the decree of this [District] Court, and, from that date, hostility to the Plan was increased, and criticism of the officials of the [School] District has become more bitter and unrestrained."

The Governor's action caused the School Board to request the Negro students on September 2 not to attend the high school "until the legal dilemma was solved." The next day, September 3, 1957, the Board petitioned the District Court for instructions, and the court, after a hearing, found that the Board's request of the Negro students to stay away from the high school had been made because of the stationing of the military guards by the state authorities. The court determined that this was not a reason for departing from the approved plan, and ordered the School Board and Superintendent to proceed with it.

On the morning of the next day, September 4, 1957, the Negro children attempted to enter the high school, but, as the District Court later found, units of the Arkansas National Guard, "acting pursuant to the Governor's order, stood shoulder to shoulder at the school grounds and thereby forcibly prevented the 9 Negro students ... from entering," as they continued to do every school day during the following three weeks.

That same day, September 4, 1957, the United States Attorney for the Eastern District of Arkansas was requested by the District Court to begin an immediate investigation in order to fix responsibility for the interference with the orderly implementation of the District Court's direction to carry out the desegregation program. Three days later, September 7, the District Court denied a petition of the School Board and the Superintendent of Schools for an order temporarily suspending continuance of the program.

Upon completion of the United States Attorney's investigation, he and the Attorney General of the United States at the District Court's request, entered the proceedings and filed a petition on behalf of the United States, as *amicus curiae*, to enjoin the Governor of Arkansas and officers of the Arkansas National Guard from further attempts to prevent obedience to the court's order. After hearings on the petition, the District Court found that the School Board's plan had been obstructed by the Governor through the use of Arkansas National Guard troops, and granted a preliminary injunction on September 20, 1957, enjoining the Governor and the officers of the Guard from preventing the attendance of Negro children at Central High School, and from otherwise obstructing or interfering with the orders of the court in connection with the plan. The Arkansas National Guard was then withdrawn from the school.

The next school day was Monday, September 23, 1957. The Negro children entered the high school that morning under the protection of the Little Rock Police Department and members of the Arkansas State Police. But the officers caused the children to be removed from the school during the morning because they had difficulty controlling a large and demonstrating crowd which had gathered at the high school. 163 F.Supp. at 16. On September 25, however, the President of the United States dispatched federal troops to Central High School, and admission of the Negro students to the school was thereby effected. Regular army troops continued at the high school until November 27, 1957. They were then replaced by federalized National Guardsmen who remained throughout the balance of the school year. Eight of the Negro students remained in attendance at the school throughout the school year.

We come now to the aspect of the proceedings presently before us. On February 20, 1958, the School Board and the Superintendent of Schools filed a petition in the District Court seeking a postponement of their program for desegregation. Their position, in essence, was that, because of extreme public hostility, which they stated had been engendered largely by the official attitudes and actions of the Governor and the Legislature, the maintenance of a sound educational program at Central High School, with the Negro students in attendance, would be impossible. The Board therefore proposed that the Negro students already admitted to the school be withdrawn and sent to segregated schools, and that all further steps to carry out the Board's desegregation program be postponed for a period later suggested by the Board to be two and one-half years.

After a hearing, the District Court granted the relief requested by the Board. Among other things, the court found that the past year at Central High School had been attended by conditions of "chaos, bedlam and turmoil"; that there were "repeated incidents of more or less serious violence directed against the Negro students and their property"; that there was "tension and unrest among the school administrators, the classroom teachers, the pupils, and the latters' parents, which inevitably had an adverse effect upon the educational program"; that a school official was threatened with violence; that a "serious financial burden" had been cast on the School District; that the education of the students had suffered "and under existing conditions will continue to suffer"; that the Board would continue to need "military assistance or its equivalent"; that the local police department would not be able "to detail enough men to afford the necessary protection"; and that the situation was "intolerable."

The District Court's judgment was dated June 20, 1958. The Negro respondents appealed to the Court of Appeals for the Eighth Circuit and also sought there a stay of the District Court's judgment. At the same time, they filed a petition for certiorari in this Court asking us to review the District Court's judgment without awaiting the disposition of their appeal to the Court of Appeals, or of their petition to that court for a stay. That we declined to do. The Court of Appeals did not act on the petition for a stay, but, on August 18, 1958, after convening in special session on August 4 and hearing the appeal, reversed the District Court, 257 F.2d 33. On August 21, 1958, the Court of Appeals stayed its mandate to permit the School Board to petition this Court for certiorari. Pending the filing of the School Board's petition for certiorari, the Negro respondents, on August 23, 1958, applied to MR JUSTICE WHITTAKER, as Circuit Justice for the Eighth Circuit, to stay the order of the Court of Appeals withholding its own mandate, and also to stay the District Court's judgment. In view of the nature of the motions, he referred them to the entire Court. Recognizing the vital importance of a decision of the issues in time to permit arrangements to be made for the 1958–1959 school year [...] we convened in Special Term on August 28, 1958, and heard oral argument on the respondents' motions, and also argument of the Solicitor General who, by invitation, appeared for the United States as *amicus curiae,* and asserted that the Court of Appeals' judgment was clearly correct on the merits, and urged that we vacate its stay forthwith. Finding that respondents' application necessarily involved consideration of the merits of the litigation, we entered an order which deferred decision upon the motions pending the disposition of the School Board's petition for certiorari, and fixed September 8, 1958, as the day on or before which such petition might be filed, and September 11, 1958, for oral argument upon the petition. The petition for certiorari, duly filed, was granted in open Court on September 11, 1958, and further arguments were had, the Solicitor General again urging the correctness of the judgment of the Court of Appeals. On September 12, 1958, as already mentioned, we unanimously affirmed the judgment of the Court of Appeals in the per curiam opinion set forth in the margin at the outset of this opinion.

In affirming the judgment of the Court of Appeals which reversed the District Court, we have accepted without reservation the position of the School Board, the Superintendent of Schools, and their counsel that they displayed entire good faith in the conduct of these proceedings and in dealing with the unfortunate and distressing sequence of events which has been outlined. We likewise have accepted the findings of the District Court as to the conditions at Central High School during the 1957–1958 school year, and also the findings that the educational progress of all the students, white and colored, of that school has suffered, and will continue to suffer if the conditions which prevailed last year are permitted to continue.

The significance of these findings, however, is to be considered in light of the fact, indisputably revealed by the record before us, that the conditions they depict are directly traceable to the actions of legislators and executive officials of the State of Arkansas, taken in their official capacities, which reflect their own determination to resist this Court's decision in the *Brown* case and which have brought about violent resistance to that decision in Arkansas. In its petition for certiorari filed in this Court, the School Board itself describes the situation in this language:

"The legislative, executive, and judicial departments of the state government opposed the desegregation of Little Rock schools by enacting laws, calling out troops, making statements vilifying federal law and federal courts, and failing to utilize state law enforcement agencies and judicial processes to maintain public peace."

One may well sympathize with the position of the Board in the face of the frustrating conditions which have confronted it, but, regardless of the Board's good faith, the actions of the other state agencies responsible for those conditions compel us to reject the Board's legal position. Had Central High School been under the direct management of the State itself, it could hardly be suggested that those immediately in charge of the school should be heard to assert their own good faith as a legal excuse for delay in implementing the constitutional rights of these respondents, when vindication of those rights was rendered difficult or impossible by the actions of other state officials. The situation here is in no different posture because the members of the School Board and the Superintendent of Schools are local officials; from the point of view of the Fourteenth Amendment, they stand in this litigation as the agents of the State.

The constitutional rights of respondents are not to be sacrificed or yielded to the violence and disorder which have followed upon the actions of the Governor and Legislature.

Source: US Supreme Court, *Cooper v. Aaron*, 358 US 1 (1958), https://supreme.justia. com/cases/federal/us/358/1/case.html

4.7 Ruby Bridges Recalls School Desegregation in New Orleans in 1960

The Little Rock Nine's ordeal was among the first of its kind encountered during the process of school desegregation, but it was by no means the last. In November 1960, six-year-old Ruby Bridges became the first black student to desegregate a white elementary school in New Orleans. Ruby was one of a number of black students who took a test to determine whether they would be eligible to attend one of the city's white public schools. The test was designed more with the intent to demonstrate that black students were incapable of competing with white students than it was to encourage desegregation. Ruby was one of only six black children in

New Orleans to pass the test and she was assigned to William Frantz School close to her home. Despite numerous efforts by the Louisiana State Legislature to delay school desegregation, Ruby finally enrolled on 14 November, accompanied by federal marshals at the request of the federal District Court.

As in Little Rock, a white mob gathered to try to prevent Ruby's entry into the school, a scene made famous in Norman Rockwell's 1963 painting "The Problem We All Live With," which appeared on the front cover of Look *magazine on 14 January 1964. All the teachers except one, Barbara Henry, a newcomer from Boston, refused to teach Ruby. White parents either withdrew their children from the school immediately or threatened to withdraw them if they were forced to attend Ruby's class. For the entire school year, just Barbara Henry and Ruby studied in a classroom together. Ruby faced ongoing intimidation from school administrators, teachers, and students. Her family was also targeted for retribution, which included her father being fired from his job at a filling station.*

Yet by the end of the school year there were signs that white parents were beginning to relent and accept the seemingly inevitable. White students began to return to the school. The following year, although Barbara Henry's teaching contract was not renewed, Ruby was able to walk to school by herself without the need for federal marshals, and white students attended her second grade class. Ruby finished elementary school before graduating from the desegregated Francis T. Nicholls High School in New Orleans. Ruby's ordeal suggests that the actual experience of desegregated schools was, for white parents and students, far less alarming than their presumed fears about what might happen.

My mother took special care getting me ready for school. When somebody knocked on my door that morning, my mother expected to see people from the NAACP. Instead, she saw four serious-looking white men, dressed in suits and wearing armbands. They were US federal marshals. They had come to drive us to school and stay with us all day. I learned later they were carrying guns.

I remember climbing into the back seat of the marshals' car with my mother, but I don't remember feeling frightened. William Frantz Public School was only five blocks away, so one of the marshals in the front seat told my mother right away what we should do when we got there.

"Let us get out of the car first," the marshal said. "Then you'll get out, and the four of us will surround you and your daughter. We'll walk up to the door together. Just walk straight ahead and don't look back."

When we were near the school, my mother said, "Ruby, I want you to behave yourself today and do what the marshals say."

We drove down North Galvez Street to the point where it crosses Alvar. I remember looking out of the car as we pulled up to the Frantz school. There were barricades and people shouting and policemen everywhere. I thought maybe it was Mardi Gras, the carnival that takes place in New Orleans every year. Mardi Gras was always noisy.

As we walked through the crowd, I didn't see any faces. I guess that's because I wasn't very tall and I was surrounded by marshals. People yelled and threw things. I could see the school building, and it looked bigger and nicer than my old school. When we climbed the high steps to the front door, there were policemen in uniforms at the top. The policemen at the door and crowd behind us made me think this was an important place.

It must be college, I thought to myself.

Once we were inside the building, the marshals walked us up a flight of stairs. The school office was at the top. My mother and I went in and were told to sit in the principal's office. The marshals sat outside. There were windows in the room where we waited. That meant everybody passing by could see us. I remember noticing everyone was white.

All day long, white parents rushed into the office. They were upset. They were arguing and pointing at us. When they took their children to school that morning, the parents hadn't been sure whether William Frantz would be integrated that day or not. After my mother and I arrived, they ran into classrooms and dragged their children out of the school. From behind the windows in the office, all I saw was confusion. I told myself that this must be the way it is in a big school.

The whole first day, my mother and I just waited. We didn't talk to anybody. I remember watching a big, round clock on the wall. When it was 3:00 and time to go home, I was glad. I had thought my new school would be hard, but the first day was easy.

When we left school that first day, the crowd outside was even bigger and louder than it had been in the morning. There were reporters and film cameras and people everywhere. I guess the police couldn't keep them behind the barricades. It seemed to take us a long time to get to the marshals' car.

Later on I learned there had been protestors in front of the two integrated schools the whole day. They wanted to be sure white parents would boycott the school and not let their children attend. Groups of high school boys, joining the protestors, paraded up and down the street and sang new verses to old hymns. Their favorite was "Battle Hymn of the Republic," in which they changed the chorus to "Glory, glory, segregation, the South will rise again." Many of the boys carried signs and said awful things, but most of all I remember seeing a black doll in a coffin, which frightened me more than anything else.

After the first day, I was glad to get home. I wanted to change my clothes and go outside to my friends. My mother wasn't too worried about me because the police had set up barricades at each end of the block. Only local residents were allowed on our street. That afternoon, I taught a friend the chant I had learned: "Two, four, six, eight, we don't want to integrate." My friend and I didn't know what the words meant, but we would jump rope to it every day after school.

My father heard about the trouble at school. That night when he came home from work, he said I was his "brave little Ruby."

Source: Ruby Bridges, *Through My Eyes* (New York: Scholastic Press, 1999), pp. 15–20.

4.8 James Meredith Recalls Entering the University of Mississippi in 1962

As public school desegregation continued at a painfully slow pace amid a good deal of trauma for black students, the struggle to desegregate higher education continued. In 1962, the racial barrier fell at the University of Mississippi. Born, raised, and educated in Mississippi, James Meredith spent nine years in the US Air Force before enrolling at the black Jackson State College in his home state in 1960. The following year, Meredith made one of numerous applications to the white University of Mississippi in Oxford, or "Ole Miss" as it is popularly known. Meredith was initially granted admission until the university discovered that he was black, when it reversed its original decision. In a familiar pattern, Meredith took his case to the lower courts, which all ruled against him, and eventually appealed his case to the US Supreme Court, which ruled in his favor.

When Meredith arrived at the university on 20 September 1962, his entrance was blocked. A riot ensued, leading Attorney General Robert Kennedy to send in 500 federal marshals, and his brother President John F. Kennedy to send in military police, federalized Mississippi National Guard troops, and officials from the US Border Patrol to impose law and order. In the course of the battle, 160 federal marshals were wounded and two people were killed. James Meredith and the federal government persisted, and Meredith was finally enrolled on 1 October 1962. He graduated the following year.

At 5:30 p.m. I landed at the Oxford University airport in my government plane as dusk fell and press cameras popped.

We drove onto the quiet campus through a side entrance and proceeded to my assigned dormitory, Baxter Hall, where I remained with a force of twenty-four United States marshals as bodyguards. I was assigned to a Spartan corner suite in the dormitory.

Now, a series of logistical problems and tactical misjudgments began happening that would combine to unleash a riot and battle in less than three hours. Communications between [Mississippi Governor Ross] Barnett, his state highway patrol, and various state officials in Jackson and Oxford broke down completely. No one was clearly in charge and no one was sure if the state lawmen were supposed to fight the federals or help them.

My federal escorts couldn't find anyone at the school to register me. For lack of any other plan, several hundred marshals simply surrounded the university Lyceum building, the administration building and registration office, for a registration attempt that now looked like it would occur the next day, Monday morning. This served as a decoy to make people think I was in that building so as to divert any attention and violence from me where I was located, one-quarter of a mile away in my dormitory. The ensuing battle would soon be centralized in the attempt to seize the Lyceum back from the federal forces.

As dusk fell, students returning from a football game in Jackson began gradually crowding around the front of the Lyceum building, attracted by the sudden presence of the United States marshals, foot soldiers of the hated federal government now in their midst. They looked like mismatched gladiators ready for battle, as they wore crash helmets and tear gas weapons over suits, blue jeans, and Hawaiian shirts. Their bizarre appearance inflamed the blossoming crowd, and in the rush to deploy ahead of schedule, much of the marshals' equipment was misplaced in the shuffle, including radios, tear gas ammo, and loudspeakers.

As I nonchalantly made my bed and read my newspaper before going to sleep, the original crowd of two hundred white civilians, mostly students, swelled steadily to over one thousand, then toward two thousand whites, including many who were not Ole Miss students. Unaware of Governor Barnett's secret agreement with the Kennedys to stop the Mississippi highway patrol from blocking my entrance onto campus, the crowd was incited by the sight of helmeted marshals with their tear-gas guns cocked skyward, who were first an object of curiosity, which changed rapidly to anger, and hate.

The students were joined by assorted civilians and adults and students from other Mississippi schools, and the group transformed into a mob. They were now taunting and jeering the troops with profanities, racial slurs, and threats. The start of the fifteen hours of violent warfare was at hand. At 7:00 p.m., the spark that started the battle was the arrival of the first groups of news reporters from around the United States and overseas, which agitated the short tempers of the crowd. Newsmen were beaten up, cameras and other equipment smashed. Their cars were overturned and battered.

Simultaneously, the mob pressed toward the shoulder-to-shoulder barricade of marshals around the Lyceum. Rocks, bottles, and anything available were thrown at the marshals and their vehicles. With the marshals under strict orders from RFK [US Attorney General Robert F. Kennedy] not to retaliate by firing back or even drawing their guns, the victory of the mob of white supremacists seemed guaranteed.

Source: James Meredith, with William Doyle, *A Mission from God: A Memoir and Challenge for America* (New York: Atria Books, 2012), pp. 126–8.

Discussion Questions

1. Why did black students bear the burden for desegregating schools in the 1950s and 1960s?
2. What was at stake in the showdown between state and federal power at Little Rock's Central High School in September 1957?
3. Discuss the methods used by white segregationists to oppose desegregation in education. How effective (or not) were those methods, and why?

Further Reading

Anderson, Karen. *Little Rock: Race and Resistance at Central High School* (Princeton University Press, 2010).

Bates, Daisy. *The Long Shadow of Little Rock: A Memoir* (David McKay Company, Inc., 1962).

Bridges, Ruby. *Through My Eyes* (Scholastic Press, 1999).

Dudziak, Mary L. *Cold War Civil Rights: Race and the Image of American Democracy* (Princeton University Press, 2000).

Eagles, Charles W. *The Price of Defiance: James Meredith and the Integration of Ole Miss* (University of North Carolina Press, 2009).

Freyer, Tony A. *Little Rock on Trial:* Cooper v Aaron *and School Desegregation* (University Press of Kansas, 2007).

Jacoway, Elizabeth. *Turn Away Thy Son: Little Rock, the Crisis that Shocked a Nation* (Free Press, 2007).

Kirk, John A. *Redefining the Color Line: Black Activism in Little Rock, Arkansas, 1940–1970* (University Press of Florida, 2002).

Nichols, David. *A Matter of Justice: Eisenhower and the Beginning of the Civil Rights Revolution* (Simon and Schuster, 2007).

Walls LaNier, Carlotta, and Lisa Frazier Page. *A Mighty Long Way: My Journey to Justice at Little Rock Central High School* (One World/Ballantine, 2009).

Chapter 5   The Sit-Ins and the Student Nonviolent Coordinating Committee, 1960

5.1 *Greensboro News and Record*, The Greensboro Four, 1960

On 1 February 1960, four students at North Carolina Agricultural and Technical College in Greensboro – Ezell Blair, Jr, Franklin McCain, Joe McNeil, and David Richmond – went into a downtown Woolworth's department store. The students bought a number of items in the store and then, keeping hold of their receipts, headed to the segregated lunch counter and ordered coffee. The waitress refused to serve them. They demanded to know why, if they could buy goods in other parts of the store, they were then refused service at the lunch counter. The students insisted that they would not leave until they received a satisfactory answer. They stayed until the store closed.

The next day, the four students returned with others from campus to resume the sit-in. Over the following days, more students joined in the protest and initiated more sit-ins at other local stores. By the weekend, the stores decided to close all of their lunch counters. The sit-ins forced the local white business community to address the question of whether segregation was worth the racial unrest and economic damage that came with closed lunch counters and the resultant disruption to businesses in the busy downtown lunch hour. In the end, the city's white businessmen relented and desegregated downtown facilities.

As we saw in Chapter 1, the Congress of Racial Equality (CORE) used sit-ins in Chicago in 1942 to place economic pressure on businesses to desegregate. In the years leading up to the Greensboro sit-ins, at least 16 other cities had experienced sit-in demonstrations. But it was the Greensboro sit-ins that transformed what had previously been a fragmented, tentative, and experimental series of demonstrations into a mass regionwide movement of nonviolent direct action.

The Civil Rights Movement: A Documentary Reader, First Edition. Edited by John A. Kirk.
© 2020 John Wiley & Sons, Inc. Published 2020 by John Wiley & Sons, Inc.

Source: *Greensboro News and Record*, The Greensboro Four – David Richmond, Franklin McCain, Ezell Blair Jr, and Joseph McNeil – on 1 Feb. 1960, http://www.greensboro. com/news/trending/before-video-of-a-starbucks-arrest-images-of-lunch-counter/article_ dfb9c893-a422-538c-8a6a-9f9cd1aed636.html

5.2 Kenneth T. Andrews and Michael Biggs, Map Showing Sit-Ins in the American South, February through April 1960

In direct contrast to the bus boycotts, the sit-ins proved exportable to a large number of other communities. Sit-ins did not require the mobilization of an entire community and they were therefore easier to organize and far simpler to instigate. The week after the Greensboro sit-ins, similar demonstrations occurred in other parts of North Carolina. Then they began to occur in neighboring states, before finally spreading right across the South. From February to April 1960, over 70 communities experienced sit-ins. By the end of the year, over 70,000 students had participated in sit-ins or in other forms of nonviolent direct action and there had been 3,600 arrests.

Sociologists Kenneth T. Andrews and Michael Biggs suggest a number of factors at work that determined the successes of the sit-in movement. Firstly, sit-ins expanded through an interrelated network of southern black colleges that could mobilize student-led action. Secondly, sit-ins proved most successful in places that already had existing movement organizations to lend assistance. Thirdly, sit-ins were most successful in cities and states that operated in a more moderate political climate. Finally, the news media played a vital role in transmitting information about sit-ins from one community to the next.

Yet the sit-in movement was not uniformly successful. In the upper and border South, the sit-ins were more numerous and more effective. In the lower South, where racial lines were drawn more strictly and resistance was more intense, there were fewer sit-ins and those that did take place often did not bring about the same types of changes that occurred elsewhere. Some communities held out against the economic pressure of the sit-ins, while others simply closed their lunch counters altogether rather than desegregate them. Despite these mixed results, the 1960 sit-in movement breathed new dynamism and youthful energy into the civil rights movement and proved an effective opening salvo in an all-out assault on segregation in the years to come.

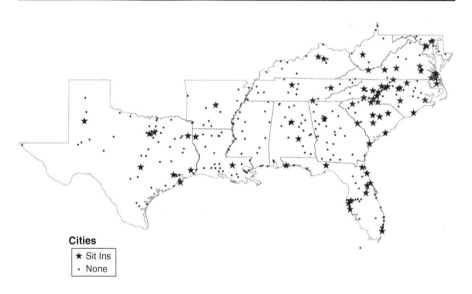

Cities

★ Sit Ins
· None

Source: Kenneth T. Andrews and Michael Biggs, "The Dynamics of Protest Diffusion: Movement Organizations, Social Networks, and News Media in the 1960 Sit-Ins," pp. 752–77 from *American Sociological Review* 71 (October 2006).

5.3 *St. Paul Dispatch-Pioneer Press*, National Association for the Advancement of Colored People Members Picketing outside Woolworth's for Integrated Lunch Counters, 1960

The sit-in movement focused on the South where the large majority of segregated lunch counters were located, but it drew upon national support. In cities outside of the South, marches were held in solidarity with southern black students. There were also economic boycotts of national chain stores that had southern branches.

The National Association for the Advancement of Colored People (NAACP) was at the forefront of mobilizing these demonstrations. Many NAACP leaders were wary of the use of nonviolent direct action and preferred the court-based legal route that the NAACP traditionally followed. Yet the NAACP understood the need to lend assistance to black students, not least since many of those students were the sons and daughters of NAACP members. The NAACP's Legal Defense and Educational Fund (NAACP LDF) provided practical help in raising bond money to bail arrested students out of jail, and in representing students in their subsequent court trials. The sit-ins may have sparked a new movement, but at the same time that new movement depended upon existing organizations and institutions to help nourish and sustain it.

In October 1960, students in Atlanta persuaded Martin Luther King, Jr to participate in a sit-in. King was arrested, and aspiring Democratic presidential candidate John F. Kennedy placed a call to King's wife Coretta offering sympathy and assistance. Soon after, King was released from jail and Kennedy made political capital out of the episode among black voters. Kennedy narrowly won election as president the following month. Though Kennedy ultimately took much more persuading to throw his full support behind the civil rights movement, a connection had been made.

The sit-ins proved successful not only at putting economic pressure on local businesses, but also in bringing national attention to segregation in the South, engaging existing civil rights organizations in the cause, and even in provoking a response from the new president.

Source: *St. Paul Dispatch-Pioneer Press*, NAACP members picketing outside Woolworth's for integrated lunch counters, St Paul, 1960, Minnesota Historical Society, http://collections.mnhs.org/cms/display.php?irn=10747279

5.4 Student Nonviolent Coordinating Committee, Statement of Purpose, 1960

One of the most significant outcomes of the 1960 sit-in movement was the founding of a new civil rights organization, the Student Nonviolent Coordinating Committee (SNCC – pronounced "snick"). Ella Baker, the acting executive director of the Southern Christian Leadership Conference (SCLC), was instrumental in helping to create the new organization. With $800 of SCLC money, Baker held a conference at her alma mater, Shaw University, in Raleigh, North Carolina, on 15–17 April. The keynote speaker was James Lawson, a young minister closely linked to an influential group of students from Nashville who had successfully organized sit-ins in that city and who were in attendance at the conference. Lawson, who drafted SNCC's statement of purpose below, stressed the importance of nonviolent direct action as a tactic and located it firmly within the Judeo-Christian tradition. This seemed very similar to the SCLC, but Lawson, with Ella Baker's support, wanted students to retain their independence through their own organization rather than merely becoming the SCLC's youth council. Martin Luther King, Jr, who also attended the conference, did nothing to block this.

The conference voted to form a "Temporary Student Nonviolent Coordinating Committee." In May 1960, students dropped the "Temporary" label to make SNCC a permanent organization. Nashville student Marion Barry was elected as first SNCC chair. Barry was later elected mayor of Washington, DC serving from 1979 to 1991, and then again from 1995 to 1999. Despite its assertion of independence from the SCLC, SNCC remained closely tied to King's organization. For the early part of its life SNCC's headquarters was based in the SCLC's office in Atlanta. Although the relationship between SNCC and the SCLC was generally a close and friendly one, it could also at times be strained. SNCC looked to push King and the SCLC to take a more forthright stand for civil rights, while King and the SCLC sought to exercise a moderating influence on SNCC. Each side had its own successes and failures in that give and take.

We affirm the philosophical or religious ideal of nonviolence as the foundation of our purpose, the presupposition of our belief, and the manner of our action.

Nonviolence, as it grows from the Judeo-Christian tradition, seeks a social order of justice permeated by love. Integration of human endeavor represents the crucial first step towards such a society.

Through nonviolence, courage displaces fear. Love transcends hate. Acceptance dissipates prejudice; hope ends despair. Faith reconciles doubt.

Peace dominates war. Mutual regards cancel enmity. Justice for all overthrows injustice. The redemptive community supersedes immoral social systems.

By appealing to conscience and standing on the moral nature of human existence, nonviolence nurtures the atmosphere in which reconciliation and justice become actual possibilities.

Although each local group in this movement must diligently work out the clear meaning of this statement of purpose, each act or phase of our corporate effort must reflect a genuine spirit of love and good-will.

Adopted by the Southwide Youth Leadership Conference
Shaw University, Raleigh, NC
April 15–17, 1960

Source: Student Nonviolent Coordinating Committee, Statement of Purpose, 1960, http://www.crmvet.org/docs/sncc5.htm

5.5 Ella J. Baker, "Bigger than a Hamburger," 1960

Ella Baker's enthusiastic role in founding SNCC reflected her growing disillusionment in her association with King and the SCLC. Although she had been instrumental in founding the SCLC, Baker felt that the male-dominated hierarchy of ministers in the organization sidelined her voice and contributions because she was a woman. King fired his initial choice of SCLC executive director in 1959 and handed Baker the job of acting executive director. Baker ran the SCLC office as essentially a one-woman operation, coordinating campaigns, making field trips, preparing the SCLC's newsletter, arranging conventions and board meetings, making reports to King and the SCLC's administrative committee, and compiling complaints about voting discrimination. Exasperated at being left to do all of the work and at the seeming lack of a strategy and direction within the organization, Baker finally challenged King and the board of directors to reexamine the way that the SCLC operated. This produced a number of changes, but none of them significant enough to prevent Baker from leaving in August 1960.

In encouraging the founding of SNCC, Baker hoped that a student-led organization would address what she perceived to be the shortcomings of King and the SCLC. In place of the SCLC's rigid hierarchy, Baker advocated for a "group-centered leadership" to take precedence over a "leader-centered group." Her reference in the below to a "prophetic leader" with "heavy feet of clay" was a barely concealed dig at King. Baker's ideas about grassroots community organizing though building a movement from the bottom-up rather than the top-down, and empowering local leadership in local communities to effect lasting and meaningful change on a day-to-day basis, were of profound influence in the way that SNCC operated. Baker insisted that the civil rights movement should not just be about incremental policy changes, but that it should also lead to a more expansive discussion about rights and responsibilities as they related to citizenship and freedom in modern society.

Raleigh, NC – The Student Leadership Conference made it crystal clear that current sit-ins and other demonstrations are concerned with something much bigger than a hamburger or even a giant-sized Coke.

Whatever may be the difference in approach to their goal, the Negro and white students, North and South, are seeking to rid America of the scourge of racial segregation and discrimination – not only at lunch counters, but in every aspect of life.

In reports, casual conversations, discussion groups, and speeches, the sense and the spirit of the following statement that appeared in the initial newsletter of the students at Barber-Scotia College, Concord, NC, were re-echoed time and again:

"We want the world to know that we no longer accept the inferior position of second-class citizenship. We are willing to go to jail, be ridiculed, spat upon and even suffer physical violence to obtain First Class Citizenship."

By and large, this feeling that they have a destined date with freedom, was not limited to a drive for personal freedom, or even freedom for the Negro in the South. Repeatedly it was emphasized that the movement was concerned with the moral implications of racial discrimination for the "whole world" and the "Human Race."

This universality of approach was linked with a perceptive recognition that "it is important to keep the movement democratic and to avoid struggles for personal leadership."

It was further evident that desire for supportive cooperation from adult leaders and the adult community was also tempered by apprehension that adults might try to "capture" the student movement. The students showed willingness to be met on the basis of equality, but were intolerant of anything that smacked of manipulation or domination.

This inclination toward group-centered leadership, rather than toward a leader-centered group pattern of organization, was refreshing indeed to those of the older group who bear the scars of the battle, the frustrations and the disillusionment that come when the prophetic leader turns out to have heavy feet of clay.

However hopeful might be the signs in the direction of group-centeredness, the fact that many schools and communities, especially in the South, have not provided adequate experience for young Negroes to assume initiative and think and act independently accentuated the need for guarding the student movement against well-meaning, but nevertheless unhealthy, over-protectiveness.

Here is an opportunity for adult and youth to work together and provide genuine leadership – the development of the individual to his highest potential for the benefit of the group.

Many adults and youth characterized the Raleigh meeting as the greatest or most significant conference of our period.

Whether it lives up to this high evaluation or not will, in a large measure, be determined by the extent to which there is more effective training in and understanding of non-violent principles and practices, in group dynamics, and in the re-direction into creative channels of the normal frustrations and hostilities that result from second-class citizenship.

Source: Ella J. Baker, "Bigger than a Hamburger," p. 4 from *The Southern Patriot* 18 (June 1960).

5.6 Robert P. Moses, "Letter from a Mississippi Jail Cell," 1961

If anyone came to personify the grassroots organizing tradition and the spirit of participatory democracy in SNCC, it was the enigmatic Robert P. Moses. Moses was born in New York's black neighborhood of Harlem into a working-class family. Through scholarships, he attended predominantly white elite schools and began a PhD in philosophy at Harvard University before dropping out to help his family after the death of his mother. Moses traveled south to visit with relatives and to join protests after the emergence of the 1960 sit-in movement. For a short time, he worked with the SCLC, where he met Ella Baker. Moses was deeply influenced by Baker's grassroots organizing philosophy and he joined SNCC before heading to Mississippi to work on voter registration campaigns. At the time, many viewed voter registration as a soft touch and slightly old-fashioned compared with the seemingly more edgy and confrontational approach of nonviolent direct action. Moses soon discovered that voter registration in Mississippi was every bit as dangerous as other forms of civil rights activism. When local Mississippian Herbert Lee was killed because of his involvement with voter registration efforts, Moses felt the full weight of the task he had taken on. White Mississippians cast Moses, like his fellow SNCC workers, as an "outside agitator."

In the letter below, Moses recounts the conditions in a Mississippi jail cell after being arrested. Mississippi was, as Moses writes, the "middle of the iceberg," one of the toughest places to crack in terms of voting rights and racial discrimination. To Moses, that was the very reason to be in the state: if SNCC could overcome white supremacy in rural Mississippi, he believed, it could overcome white supremacy anywhere. Moses and other SNCC workers laid the groundwork for later voter registration efforts in Mississippi that received far greater national attention in 1964.

We are smuggling this note from the drunk tank of the county jail in Magnolia, Mississippi. Twelve of us are here, sprawled out along the concrete bunker; Curtis Hayes, Hollis Watkins, Ike Lewis and Robert Talbert, four veterans of the bunker, are sitting up talking – mostly about girls; Charles McDew ("Tell the story") is curled into the concrete and the wall; Harold Robinson, Stephen

Ashley, James Wells, Lee Chester, Vick, Leotus Eubanks, and Ivory Diggs lay cramped on the cold bunker; I'm sitting with smuggled pen and paper, thinking a little, writing a little; Myrtis Bennett and Janie Campbell are across the way wedded to a different icy cubicle.

Later on Hollis will lead out with a clear tenor into a freedom song; Talbert and Lewis will supply jokes; and McDew will discourse on the history of the black man and the Jew. McDew – a black by birth, a Jew by choice and a revolutionary by necessity – has taken on the deep hates and deep loves which America, and the world, reserve for those who dare to stand in a strong sun and cast a sharp shadow.

In the words of Judge Brumfield, who sentenced us, we are "cold calculators" who design to disrupt the racial harmony (harmonious since 1619) of McComb into racial strife and rioting; we, he said, are the leaders who are causing young children to be led like sheep to the pen to be slaughtered (in a legal manner). "Robert," he was addressing me, "haven't some of the people from your school been able to go down and register without violence here in Pike county?" I thought to myself that Southerners are most exposed when they boast.

It's mealtime now: we have rice and gravy in a flat pan, dry bread and a "big town cake"; we lack eating and drinking utensils. Water comes from a faucet and goes into a hole.

This is Mississippi, the middle of the iceberg. Hollis is leading off with his tenor, "Michael, row the boat ashore, Alleluia; Christian brothers don't be slow, Alleluia; Mississippi's next to go, Alleluia." This is a tremor in the middle of the iceberg – from a stone that the builders rejected.

Source: Robert P. Moses, "Letter from a Mississippi Jail Cell," 1961, cited in Peter B. Levy ed., *Let Freedom Ring: A Documentary History of the Modern Civil Rights Movement* (New York and Westport, CT: Praeger, 1992), pp. 94–5.

Discussion Questions

1. How and why were the sit-ins successful at achieving their aim of desegregating lunch counters?
2. What was the purpose of founding yet another new civil rights organization, the Student Nonviolent Coordinating Committee, in 1960?
3. Assess the relationship between younger civil rights activists and organizations and more established leaders and organizations during the sit-in movement.

Further Reading

Carson, Clayborne. *In Struggle: SNCC and the Black Awakening of the 1960s* (Harvard University Press, 1981).

Chafe, William H. *Civilities and Civil Rights: Greensboro, North Carolina and the Black Struggle For Freedom* (Oxford University Press, 1980).

Greenberg, Cheryl, ed. *A Circle of Trust: Remembering SNCC* (Rutgers University Press, 1998).

Halberstam, David. *The Children* (Random House, 1998).

Hogan, Wesley C. *Many Minds, One Heart: SNCC's Dream of a New America* (University of North Carolina Press, 2007).

Morgan, Iwan, and Philip Davies, eds. *From Sit-Ins to SNCC: The Student Civil Rights Movement in the 1960s* (University Press of Florida, 2012).

Morris, Aldon D. *The Origins of the Civil Rights Movement: Black Communities Organizing for Change* (Free Press, 1984).

Murphee, Vanessa. *The Selling of Civil Rights: SNCC and the Use of Public Relations* (Routledge, 2006).

Ransby, Barbara. *Ella Baker and the Black Freedom Movement: A Radical Democratic Vision* (University of North Carolina Press, 2002).

Schmidt, Christopher W. *The Sit-Ins: Protest and Legal Change in the Civil Rights Era* (University of Chicago Press, 2018).

Visser-Maessen, Laura. *Robert Parris Moses: A Life in Civil Rights and Leadership at the Grassroots* (University of North Carolina Press, 2016).

Chapter 6 The Freedom Rides and the Congress of Racial Equality, 1961

6.1 US Supreme Court, *Boynton v. Virginia*, 1960

The 1960 sit-ins were followed in 1961 by another wave of nonviolent direct action protests in the shape of the Freedom Rides. In 1947, in response to the Morgan *(1946) ruling that outlawed segregation on interstate buses, the Journey of Reconciliation tested whether the law was being implemented. In 1961, in response to the* Boynton *(1960) ruling, which further extended the* Morgan *ruling to interstate bus terminal facilities, the Congress of Racial Equality (CORE) held Freedom Rides to test whether that law was being implemented. The origins of the Boynton case lay in a 1958 trip taken by Bruce Boynton, a law student at Howard University in Washington, DC to visit his parents, civil rights activists Sam and Amelia Boynton, in Selma, Alabama. On a stopover in Richmond, Virginia, Boynton sought service at a "whites only" lunch counter at the bus terminal. Boynton was told to move to the black section; he refused and was arrested for trespassing. After spending a night in jail, Boynton was fined $10 by the Richmond Municipal Court. With the assistance of attorneys from the National Association for the Advancement of Colored People Legal Defense and Educational Fund (NAACP LDF), Boynton appealed his case to the US Supreme Court. The Court agreed that since interstate bus journeys operated on a desegregated basis, so too should facilities in bus stations that serviced those interstate bus journeys.*

The basic question presented in this case is whether an interstate bus passenger is denied a federal statutory or constitutional right when a restaurant in a bus terminal used by the carrier along its route discriminates in serving food to the passenger solely because of his color.

The Civil Rights Movement: A Documentary Reader, First Edition. Edited by John A. Kirk.
© 2020 John Wiley & Sons, Inc. Published 2020 by John Wiley & Sons, Inc.

Petitioner, a Negro law student, bought a Trailways bus ticket from Washington, DC, to Montgomery, Alabama. He boarded a bus at 8 p.m. which arrived at Richmond, Virginia, about 10:40 p.m. When the bus pulled up at the Richmond "Trailways Bus Terminal" the bus driver announced a forty-minute stopover there. Petitioner got off the bus and went into the bus terminal to get something to eat. In the station he found a restaurant in which one part was used to serve white people and one to serve Negroes. Disregarding this division, petitioner sat down on a stool in the white section. A waitress asked him to move over to the other section where there were "facilities" to serve colored people. Petitioner told her he was an interstate bus passenger, refused to move and ordered a sandwich and tea. The waitress then brought the Assistant Manager, who "instructed" petitioner to "leave the white portion of the restaurant and advised him he could be served in the colored portion." Upon petitioner's refusal to leave an officer was called and petitioner was arrested and later tried, convicted and fined ten dollars in the Police Justice's Court of Richmond on a charge that he "*Unlawfully* did remain on the premises of the Bus Terminal Restaurant of Richmond, Inc. after having been forbidden to do so" by the Assistant Manager. (Emphasis supplied.) The charge was based on ß 18-225 of the Code of Virginia of 1950, as amended (1958), which provides in part:

"If any person shall *without authority of law* go upon or remain upon the lands or premises of another, after having been forbidden to do so by the owner, lessee, custodian or other person lawfully in charge of such land, [...] he shall be deemed guilty of a misdemeanor, and upon conviction thereof shall be punished by a fine of not more than one hundred dollars or by confinement in jail not exceeding thirty days, or by both such fine and imprisonment." (Emphasis supplied.)

Petitioner appealed his conviction to the Hustings Court of Richmond, where, as in the Police Court, he admitted that he had remained in the white portion of the Terminal Restaurant although ordered not to do so. His defense in both courts was that he had a federal right as an interstate passenger of Trailways to be served without discrimination by this restaurant used by the bus carrier for the accommodation of its interstate passengers. On this basis petitioner claimed he was on the restaurant premises lawfully, not "unlawfully" as charged, and that he remained there with, not "without authority of law." His federal claim to this effect was spelled out in a motion to dismiss the warrant in Hustings Court, which was overruled both before and after the evidence was heard. Pointing out that the restaurant was an integral part of the bus service for interstate passengers such as petitioner, and asserting that refusal to serve him was a discrimination based on color, the motion to dismiss charged that application of the Virginia law to petitioner violated the Interstate Commerce Act and the Equal Protection, Due Process and Commerce Clauses of the Federal Constitution. On appeal the Virginia Supreme Court held that the conviction was "plainly right" and affirmed without opinion, thereby rejecting petitioner's assignments of error based on the same grounds of discrimination set out in his motion to dismiss in Hustings Court but not specifically charging that the discrimination violated the Interstate Commerce Act. We think, however, that the claims of discrimination previously made under the Act are sufficiently closely related to the assignments that were made to be considered within the scope of the issues presented to the State Supreme Court. We granted certiorari because of the serious federal questions raised concerning discrimination based on color.

The petition for certiorari we granted presented only two questions: first, whether the conviction of petitioner is invalid as a burden on commerce in violation of Art. I, ß 8, cl. 3 of the Constitution; and second, whether the conviction violates the Due Process and Equal Protection Clauses of the Fourteenth Amendment. Ordinarily we limit our review to the questions presented in an application for certiorari. We think there are persuasive reasons, however, why this case should be decided, if it can, on the Interstate Commerce Act contention raised in the Virginia courts. Discrimination because of color is the core of the two broad constitutional questions presented to us by petitioner, just as it is the core of the Interstate Commerce Act question presented to the Virginia courts. Under these circumstances we think it appropriate not to reach the constitutional questions but to proceed at once to the statutory issue.

The Interstate Commerce Act, as we have said, uses language of the broadest type to bar discriminations of all kinds. We have held that the Act forbids railroad dining cars to discriminate in service to passengers on account of their color [...]

The manager of the restaurant testified that it was not affiliated in any way with the Trailways Bus Company and that the bus company had no control over the operation of the restaurant, but that while the restaurant had "quite a bit of business" from local people, it was primarily or partly for the service of the passengers on the Trailways bus. This last statement was perhaps much of an understatement, as shown by the lease agreement executed in writing and signed both by the "Trailways Bus Terminal, Inc.," as lessor, and the "Bus Terminal Restaurant of Richmond, Inc.," as lessee. The first part of the document showed that Trailways Terminal was then constructing a "bus station" with built-in facilities "for the operation of a restaurant, soda fountain, and news stand." Terminal covenanted to lease this space to Restaurant for its use; to grant Restaurant the exclusive right to sell foods and other things usually sold in restaurants, newsstands, soda fountains and lunch counters; to keep the terminal building in good repair and to furnish certain utilities. Restaurant on its part agreed to use its space for the sale of commodities agreed on at prices that are "just and reasonable"; to sell no commodities not usually sold or installed in a bus terminal concession without Terminal's permission; to discontinue the sale of any commodity objectionable to Terminal; to buy, maintain, and replace equipment subject to Terminal's approval in writing as to its quality; to make alterations and additions only after Terminal's written consent and approval; to make no "sales on buses operating in and out said bus station" but only "through the windows of said buses"; to keep its employees neat and clean; to perform no terminal service other than that pertaining to the operation of its restaurant as agreed on; and that neither Restaurant nor its employees were to "sell transportation of any kind or give information pertaining to schedules, rates or transportation matters, but shall refer all such inquiries to the proper agents of" Terminal. In short, as Terminal and Restaurant agreed, "the operation of the restaurant and the said stands shall be in keeping with the character of service maintained in an up-to-date, modern bus terminal."

All of these things show that this terminal building, with its grounds, constituted one project for a single purpose, and that was to serve passengers of one or more bus companies – certainly Trailways' passengers. The restaurant area was specifically designed and built into the structure from the beginning to fill the needs of bus passengers in this "up-to-date, modern bus terminal." Whoever may have had technical title or immediate control of the details of the various activities in the terminal, such as waiting-room seating, furnishing of schedule information, ticket sales, and restaurant service, they were all geared to the service of bus companies and their passengers, even though local people who might happen to come into the terminal or its restaurant might also be accommodated. Thus we have a well-coordinated and smoothly functioning plan for continuous cooperative transportation services between the terminal, the restaurant and buses like Trailways that made stopovers there. All of this evidence plus Trailways' use on this occasion shows that Trailways was not utilizing the terminal and restaurant services merely on a sporadic or occasional basis. This bus terminal plainly was just as essential and necessary, and as available for that matter, to passengers and carriers like Trailways that used it, as though such carriers had legal title and complete control over all of its activities. Interstate passengers have to eat, and the very terms of the lease of the built-in restaurant space in this terminal constitute a recognition of the essential need of interstate passengers to be able to get food conveniently on their journey and an undertaking by the restaurant to fulfill that need. Such passengers in transit on a paid interstate Trailways journey had a right to expect that this essential transportation food service voluntarily provided for them under such circumstances would be rendered without discrimination prohibited by the Interstate Commerce Act. Under the circumstances of this case, therefore, petitioner had a federal right to remain in the white portion of the restaurant. He was there under "authority of law" – the Interstate Commerce Act – and it was error for the Supreme Court of Virginia to affirm his conviction.

Because of some of the arguments made here it is necessary to say a word about what we are not deciding. We are not holding that every time a bus stops at a wholly independent roadside restaurant the Interstate Commerce Act requires that restaurant service be supplied in harmony with the provisions of that Act. We decide only this case, on its facts, where circumstances show that the terminal and restaurant operate as an integral part of the bus carrier's transportation service for interstate passengers. Under such circumstances, an interstate passenger need not inquire into documents of title or contractual arrangements in order to determine whether he has a right to be served without discrimination.

The judgment of the Supreme Court of Virginia is reversed and the cause is remanded to that Court for proceedings not inconsistent with this opinion.

Reversed and remanded.

Source: US Supreme Court, *Boynton v. Virginia* 364 US 454 (1960), https://supreme. justia.com/cases/federal/us/364/454/case.html

6.2 Associated Press, Freedom Riders by Burned-Out Bus, 1961

On 4 May 1961, 13 freedom riders—three white women, three white men, and seven black men – divided into two groups and boarded Greyhound and Trailways buses in Washington, DC. The first leg of their journey through Virginia, North Carolina, South Carolina, and Georgia passed largely without incident. After rendezvousing with Martin Luther King, Jr in Atlanta, the two groups set off for Alabama the following morning.

When the Greyhound bus pulled into Anniston, Alabama, an armed white mob was waiting at the terminal to meet the freedom riders. The riders decided not to test facilities there but to move on. When they tried to leave, the mob slashed the bus's tires. The bus limped out of Anniston and ground to a halt on the outskirts of town with the white mob close behind. When the mob arrived, one of its members threw a firebomb on board. The bus burst into flames and the riders were forced to evacuate. An undercover plainclothes state investigator on board kept the white mob back with his revolver drawn, but as the riders poured outside the mob began to attack them. Alabama state troopers belatedly arrived on the scene to escort the injured riders to Anniston Hospital.

An hour later, the Trailways bus pulled into Anniston where three whites boarded, beat up several freedom riders, and physically forced the black riders to the back seats. The whites remained on board for the rest of the journey to Birmingham to make sure that the bus remained segregated.

Source: Associated Press, Freedom Riders sit next to a burned-out Greyhound bus
that was attacked by a mob of white people on the highway after leaving Anniston,
Alabama,https://www.gettyimages.com/detail/news-photo/freedom-riders-sit-
beside-a-burned-out-greyhound-bus-they-news-photo/514901378#/freedom-riders-
sit-beside-a-burnedout-greyhound-bus-they-had-ridden-picture-id514901378

6.3 James Peck Recalls Freedom Riders Being Beaten in Birmingham, Alabama in 1961

*Upon the arrival of the Trailways bus in Birmingham, the freedom riders
encountered an even more savage attack at the hands of members of the local
Ku Klux Klan who, in collusion with the local police force, were allowed a 15-
minute beating of the riders before law enforcement authorities intervened.
Below, James Peck, a white volunteer who had been selected to test the
Birmingham bus terminal lunch counter with black student Charles Person,
recounts his experience of being attacked by the mob. Birmingham's public
safety commissioner T. Eugene "Bull" Connor, who was in charge of the police
department, later explained away the delayed arrival of his men by claiming that
because it was Mother's Day there were fewer police on duty. Despite all of the
difficulties that they had encountered, the freedom riders were determined to
continue their journey the next morning. But bus drivers in Birmingham refused
to transport them. The freedom riders reluctantly decided to abandon their
overland journey and proceeded to New Orleans by plane. Even at the airport
they were delayed by bomb threats.*

When we arrived in Birmingham, we saw along the sidewalk about twenty men with pipes. We saw no cop in sight. And now I'll tell you what, how I remember the date. The next day, Bull Connor, the notorious police chief was asked why there were no police on hand. He said, he replied, it was Mother's Day and they were all visiting their mothers. Well, we got out of the bus and Charles Person, the black student from Atlanta, and I, had been designated to try to enter the lunch counter. We, of course, we didn't get there. This mob seized us and, well, part of it seized me and the other seized Person, and I was unconscious, I'd say, within a minute. I woke up. I came to in an alley way. Nobody was there. A big pool of blood. I looked at that pool of blood, I said, I wonder whether I'm going to live or die. But I was too tired to care. I lay down again. Finally I came too [sic] again, and I looked and a white GI who had come up and said, you look in a bad way. Do you need help? And I looked the other way and Bergman was coming. So I said, no, my friend is coming, he'll help me out. So, Bergman took me in a cab to [Birmingham minister Rev. Fred] Shuttlesworth's home. When Shuttlesworth saw me, he said, man, you need to go to a hospital. And so he called the ambulance and they took me to the hospital and put fifty-three stitches into my head.

Source: Interview with James Peck, conducted by Blackside, Inc. on 26 October 1979, from *Eyes on the Prize: America's Civil Rights Years (1954–1965)*, Washington University Libraries, Film and Media Archive, Henry Hampton Collection, http://digital.wustl.edu/cgi/t/text/text-idx?c=eop;cc=eop;rgn=main;view=text;idno=pec0015.0499.082

6.4 Diane Nash Recalls the Nashville Students' Involvement in the Freedom Rides in 1961

Determined that the Freedom Rides should not be brought to a standstill and end in defeat, a group of Student Nonviolent Coordinating Committee (SNCC) students from Nashville declared that they would continue the protest. The students asked their local Southern Christian Leadership Conference (SCLC) affiliate, the Nashville Christian Leadership Council (NCLC), to pay their bus fares. With great reluctance, since they feared for the students' safety, the NCLC agreed. On 17 May, ten Nashville students arrived in Birmingham. When they tried to board a bus bound for Montgomery they were taken into "protective custody" by local police. Held overnight and for much of the following day, eventually public safety commissioner Connor personally led a convoy that drove the students back to the state line, where they were unceremoniously dumped by the side of the road in the dead of night. The students told Connor that they would see him back in Birmingham by noon the next day. Connor laughed. True to their promise, the students were back in Birmingham the following day to keep their appointment. Yet bus drivers still refused to carry them on the next leg of their journey to Montgomery.

INTERVIEWER: WHAT I WANT TO DO IS, I WANT TO JUMP TO THE FREEDOM RIDES, AND I WANT YOU TO TELL ME ABOUT HEARING ABOUT MONTGOMERY AND THE FIRST RIDES AND STOPPING WITH WHAT THAT DID TO YOU.

Nash: Well, we heard about the Freedom Rides in Nashville, when they were starting, and we all agreed with their purposes and agreed that it was really an important thing for CORE to do. We also were very aware of the fact that taking the route that they were taking, which was down the eastern seacoast, into the deep south, through Georgia, Florida, Alabama and Mississippi, we knew that that was awfully dangerous, and that they would probably meet with violence a number of times. So in Nashville we decided that we would watch them, as they, as the Freedom Ride progressed, and if there were ways that we could help, we'd stand by, and be available. And true enough, that's – well, they were beaten and attacked, many, many times. When the buses were burned in Anniston, on Mother's Day, the Nashville group met and – When those buses were burned in Alabama, since there was such a close kinship, between us and the Freedom Riders, we understood exactly what they were doing, and it was our fight, every bit as much as theirs. It was as though we had been attacked. And a contingency of students left Nashville to go and pick up the Freedom Ride where it had stopped, been stopped. Now, that was really one of the times where I saw people face death. Because nobody went and joined the Freedom Ride without – it would have been really unwise to have gone without realizing that they might not come back. Some of the students that left gave me sealed letters to be mailed, in case they were killed. That's how prepared they were, for death.

INTERVIEWER: WHY DID YOU, WHY DID YOU THINK YOU HAD TO CONTINUE RIDES, THEN?

Nash: You know, if the Freedom Ride had been stopped as a result of violence, I strongly felt that the future of the movement was going to be, just cut short. Because the impression would have been given that whenever a movement starts, all that has to be done is that you attack it, massive violence and the, the blacks would stop. And I thought that was a very dangerous thing to happen. So, under those circumstances, it was really important that the Ride continue. And again, part of the non-violent strategy understands that when that type of negative image is directed at you, one of the important things to do is find ways to convert it to, to positive energy, which we were able to do as a result of continuing.

INTERVIEWER: WHAT DO YOU THINK THAT THE FEDERAL GOVERNMENT WAS GOING TO DO? WAS THERE A PLAN TO THEN FORCE THEM INTO SOME SORT OF ACTION, WAS THAT A PART OF THE PLAN THEN, TO GET THEM TO RESPOND TO –

Nash: As I recall, there was some, different individuals had different feelings about that. Of course, our whole, right – our whole way of operating was that we took ultimate responsibility for what we were going to do, so we made our decisions, and then we told the federal government what that would be. It was felt that they should be advised, in Washington, of what our plans were and what we were going to do, and we certainly made sure that they did know what we were going to do. Some people hoped for protection from the federal government. I – I think Jim Lawson was, he cautioned against relying on hoping for federal protection.

INTERVIEWER: BUT YOU SAID YOU WERE CONSTANTLY IN TOUCH WITH THEM, YOU WOULD CALL THE JUSTICE DEPARTMENT CONSTANTLY.

Nash: Well, as my – the students from Nashville who were going to pick up the Freedom Ride elected me coordinator. And as coordinator, part of my responsibility was to stay in touch with the Justice Department. I was to keep the press informed, the Justice Department, keep the communities that were participating informed, such as Birmingham, Montgomery, Jackson, Nashville, etc. To coordinate the training and recruitment of more people to take up the Freedom Ride, etc. etc., so I advised the Justice Department regularly as to what our plans were, and what kinds of things were happening.

INTERVIEWER: NOW, WHEN THE RIDERS ARE AMBUSHED IN MONTGOMERY, THE SECOND WAVE, WITH JOHN LEWIS, JIM – AND THESE PEOPLE. WHAT DID YOU FEEL ABOUT – DID YOU, DID YOU EXPECT THEM TO BE PROTECTED AT THAT POINT?

Nash: Well, I hoped they would be, of course, everything was so uncertain. We never knew what the situation would be like ten minutes from the time that it was. During the Freedom Ride, in my job as coordinator, I found myself really, that was an intensely emotional time for me, because the people, some of the people I loved most, who were my closest friends, I was very well aware of them – of the fact that when I went to sleep at night, some of them might not be alive the next night. And during that particular time I think I, I cried just every night, profusely. And I needed to, as an energy release. It was so much tension. It was like being at war. And we were very upset when they were attacked and injured, and I remember visiting them in the hospital, and there was so much concern over which of these injuries would be permanent. People really stood to be permanently injured for the rest of their lives.

Source: Interview with Diane Nash, conducted by Blackside, Inc. on 12 November 1985, from *Eyes on the Prize: America's Civil Rights Years (1954–1965)*, Washington University Libraries, Film and Media Archive, Henry Hampton Collection, http://digital.wustl.edu/cgi/t/text/text-idx?c=eop;cc=eop;rgn=main;view=text; idno=nas0015.0267.075

6.5 John Seigenthaler Recalls Events in Birmingham and Montgomery, Alabama in 1961

It required direct federal intervention by Attorney General Robert Kennedy to end the standoff in Birmingham. Kennedy asked the bus company to take the students to Montgomery, telling local bus officials to contact "Mr Greyhound" if necessary to get things moving. Kennedy also managed to secure a grudging assurance from Alabama governor John Patterson that the riders would be afforded state protection. On 20 May, a Greyhound bus left Birmingham bound for Montgomery carrying the Nashville SNCC freedom riders with an escort of 16 Alabama highway patrol cars. When the buses approached Montgomery, the police escort disappeared. A similar scene to the one previously witnessed in Birmingham played out. Local whites were given 15 minutes to beat the freedom riders until the police arrived. Even John Seigenthaler, Robert Kennedy's administrative assistant, who was there simply as an observer, was beaten by the mob as he attempted to intervene. Infuriated that Gov. Patterson had reneged on his promise to safeguard the riders, Robert Kennedy sent US federal marshals to Montgomery to protect them.

Suddenly, [Alabama Gov. John] Patterson flew back into Montgomery and gave me an interview. I drove down to Montgomery and went in to see him. And finally he said, "We can protect them and will." I then left and met with [assistant attorney general John] Doar and while I was with Patterson, we got the president of Southeast Greyhound and the Attorney General [Robert Kennedy] on the line and I had a conversation back and forth. The result of it was that we agreed that the state of Alabama would protect them from Birmingham to Montgomery and from Montgomery to the Mississippi line [...] So, then Doar and I drove back to Birmingham. Bull [Connor] agreed then that if Greyhound would carry them, he would let them out of jail. The understanding though, with [Rev. Fred] Shuttlesworth and the Freedom Riders was that the bus would make a regular run. They would stop at every small town. They wouldn't run an express bus. Well, Greyhound couldn't get a driver to take it on that basis. At any rate, when they got on the bus, Doar and I drove to Montgomery and had breakfast and when we got to the [...] Federal Building, is really the Post Office Building. It adjoins the Greyhound lot. I let John out and he went into the Federal Building. As I drove around the bus station all hell broke loose. The police hadn't provided any protection. John Lewis was on that ride. They were just beating the hell out of them. Two young women were catching it and I bounced up on the curb and got out of the car and tried to get them into my car. They got me and they damn near killed me. I'll tell you, I was in the hospital with a fractured skull. Well, when I woke up there was a lieutenant of police standing beside the car. Doar had stood in the window and watched it all. The FBI took pictures of it. Later they recovered the pipe that I got hit with, which Kennedy gave me framed when I left the Justice Department. But all ambulances were out of service for thirty minutes. It was really a bad time I woke up and I've got blood all over me and you know, and I said, "What happened?" And he said, "Well, you got messed up with these niggers and you got hurt." I said, "You better call Mr Kennedy." So, he very officiously takes out my notebook with all these numbers that I've got in it ... [Gov.] John Patterson, Martin Luther King, Fred Shuttlesworth, the president of Greyhound, Dianne Nash, you know. And he takes out my notebook and says, "Now, what Mr Kennedy is that?" I said, "Well, either the President or the Attorney General." So, he looked at me. I didn't have any identification on me except that notebook. He put it back in his pocket and said, "We'd better get you to the hospital." He took me out of the car, and I don't remember anything after that until maybe hours later and they had me on an X-ray table and I woke up talking to Wizzer White and he said that the President had called. Bob had been out somewhere, I don't [know] where, and he called later and there was a good conversation. At the end of it, he said something like, "How is my popularity down there?" I said, "If you are going to run for public office, don't do it in Alabama." Martin Luther King came in three or four days later and I went out as he came in and they surrounded the building with police to keep people away. It was a bad time. It was the first time that the Kennedy administration used marshals. And I was sort of the excuse for that. "The President's representative was beaten into unconsciousness and left lying in the street for thirty minutes, so therefore, the marshals are coming in to enforce the law."

Source: Oral History Interview with John Seigenthaler, 24 and 26 December 1974. Interview A-0330. Southern Oral History Program Collection (#4007) in the Southern Oral History Program Collection, Southern Historical Collection, Wilson Library, University of North Carolina at Chapel Hill, http://docsouth.unc.edu/sohp/A-0330/excerpts/excerpt_9274.html

6.6 John Lewis Recalls the Bus Journey from Montgomery to Jackson, Mississippi in 1961

Attorney General Robert Kennedy brokered another deal with Gov. Patterson that Alabama National Guardsmen would protect the freedom riders on the last leg of their journey from Montgomery to Jackson, Mississippi. Kennedy also arranged with Mississippi governor James O. Eastland that in exchange for the riders' safe passage through that state they would face arrest when they attempted to use segregated facilities in Jackson. The Kennedy administration wanted the immediate crisis out of the headlines, but as soon as that happened, it lost interest in the plight of the riders. Many of the freedom riders ended up in Hinds County Jail at the mercy of local lawmen outside the glare of media publicity. More civil rights activists from different parts of the country began to flood into Montgomery, taking the ride to Jackson and joining the Nashville students in jail. By the end of the summer, 328 freedom riders were in Mississippi jails. As the jails filled to overflowing, some students were taken either to the county penal farm or to the notorious state penitentiary at Parchman, where squalid conditions and beatings tested their endurance to the limit. The students were placed two to three each in a nine-by-six feet cell and handed badly fitting prison wear. When they sang freedom songs to relieve the boredom, the guards removed their mattresses, meaning that they had to sleep on wire bed frames or on a concrete floor. Below, one of the Nashville students, John Lewis, recalls how events unfolded.

JOHN LEWIS: We arrived in Jackson at the Trailway Bus Station there and we were arrested for refusing to move on, and disorderly conduct, and disturbing the peace. When the city jail got too full, they transferred us to the Hinds County jail and from Hinds County jail we were transferred to Parchman. I will never forget the experience going from Hinds County jail in Jackson to Parchman, the state penitentiary. The jailers came to the cell and they did all of this late at night [...] They had a large van truck and they took all of the male prisoners, black and white, into this van truck. We had been segregated in the city jail, the Hinds County jail. Putting us together in this large van truck was the first integration, I guess. After we got off the bus, they thought of putting black and white people together to transport them to the State Pen. We arrived there and one of the guards said, "Sing your Freedom songs now, we have nig-gers here who will eat you up; sing your Freedom songs." The moment we all started stepping off the van truck, walking to the gate through the gate that leads to maximum security, that's where we were being placed. We had to walk right in and you had to take off all of your clothes. So all of us – seventy-five guys, black and white, because during that period you had students, professors, ministers coming in from all parts of the country to continue the Freedom Ride. And we stood there for at least two hours without any clothes and I just felt that it was an attempt to belittle and dehumanize you. Then they would take us in twos, two blacks and two whites – the segregation started all over again after we got inside the jail – to take a shower. While we were taking a shower, there was a guard standing there with a gun pointed on you while you showered. If you had a beard or a mustache, any hair, you had to shave your beard off, you had to shave your mustache off. After taking the showers in twos, you were placed in a cell and given a Mississippi undershirt and a pair of shorts. During our stay in Mississippi Penitentiary we didn't have any visitors. We were able to write one person a letter. The second day Governor [unknown] came by with some state officials. We all got out within a forty-day period in order to appeal the charges.

INTERVIEWERS: You were there for how long?

JOHN LEWIS: I was there for thirty-seven days.

INTERVIEWERS: And what was the charge?

JOHN LEWIS: Disorderly conduct. We were fined and sentenced. You had the choice, you could pay your fine, and I think the fine was something like two hundred dollars and the number of days must have been something like sixty-six days, but if you got out within forty days you had a right to appeal the case. And most of the people got out within the forty days. I left Mississippi after I got out and came back to Jackson and took a train to Jackson back to Nashville.

Source: Oral History Interview with John Lewis, 20 November 1973. Interview A-0073. Southern Oral History Program Collection (#4007) in the Southern Oral History Program Collection, Southern Historical Collection, Wilson Library, University of North Carolina at Chapel Hill, http://docsouth.unc.edu/sohp/A-0073/menu.html

6.7 The Code of Federal Regulations of the United States of America, Title 49, 1963

Attorney General Robert Kennedy called Martin Luther King, Jr to demand a "cooling-off" period from demonstrations and offered federal help to get the Nashville students out of jail in return for a temporary cessation of the Freedom Rides. King replied that the students intended to take a stand by refusing bail and by staying in jail instead. CORE, along with the SCLC and SNCC, formed a Freedom Rides Coordinating Committee (FRCC) to orchestrate and to fund further Freedom Rides in the summer of 1961. More Freedom Rides tested more facilities across the South and continued to place pressure on the Kennedy administration to

*act. The lesson of the earlier Freedom Rides had been well learned: only through
sustained pressure would the federal government respond. Once demonstrations
were out of the spotlight, any urgency to take action fast disappeared. Although
President John F. Kennedy warned King that continuing the Freedom Rides would
have no impact on his administration's actions, on 29 May Robert Kennedy took
up King's suggestion to petition the Interstate Commerce Commission (ICC), an
independent body that had direct responsibility for interstate travel facilities, to ban
segregation. After holding hearings on the matter, the ICC issued a comprehensive
ban on all forms of segregation in interstate transit and in interstate terminal
facilities, effective 1 November 1961. Although this took time to codify and
enforce, by 1963 substantial progress had been made in desegregating interstate
transport and interstate transportation facilities. The below document contains
some of the new regulations that helped to achieved this.*

Part 180a – Regulations Governing Discrimination in Operations of Interstate Motor Common Carriers of Passengers [Added]

180a.1 Discrimination prohibited.

No motor common carrier of passengers subject to section 216 of the
Interstate Commerce Act shall operate a motor vehicle in interstate or foreign
commerce on which the seating of passengers is based upon race, color, creed,
or national origin.

180a. 2 Sign to be posted in vehicles.

Every motor common carrier of passengers subject to section 216 of the
Interstate Commerce Act shall conspicuously display and maintain, in all vehicles operated by it in interstate or foreign commerce, a plainly legible sign or
placard containing the statement "Seating aboard this vehicle is without regard
to race, color, creed or national origin, by order of the Interstate Commerce
Commission." This () 180a shall cease to be effective on January 1, 1963, unless
such time be further extended by the Interstate Commerce Commission.

180a. 3 Notice to be printed on tickets.

Every motor common carrier of passengers subject to section 216 of the Interstate
Commerce Act shall cause to be printed on every ticket sold by it for transportation
on any vehicle operated in interstate or foreign commerce, a plainly legible notice as
follows: "Seating aboard this vehicle is without regard to race, color, creed or
national origin, by order of the Interstate Commerce Commission." This () 180a
shall cease to be applicable to all tickets sold on or after January 1, 1963.

[...]

180a. 4 Discrimination in terminal facilities.

No motor common carrier of passengers subject to section 216 of the
Interstate Commerce Act shall in the operation of vehicles operated in interstate

or foreign commerce provide, maintain arrangements for, utilize, make available, adhere to any understanding for the availability of, any terminal facilities which are so operated, arranged or maintained as to involve any separation of any portion thereof, or in the use thereof on the basis of race, color, creed or national origin.

180a. 5 Notice to be posted at terminal facilities.

No motor common carrier of passengers subject to section 216 of the Interstate Commerce Act shall in the operation of vehicles in interstate or foreign commerce utilize any terminal facility in which there is not conspicuously displayed and maintained so as to be readily visible to the public a plainly legible sign or placard containing the full text of the regulations in this part. Such sign or placard should be captioned: "Public Notice: Regulations Applicable to Vehicles and Terminal Facilities of Interstate Motor Common Carriers of Passengers, by order of the Interstate Commerce Commission."

180a. 6 Carriers not relieved of existing obligations.

Nothing in this part shall be construed to relieve any interstate motor common carrier of passengers subject to 216 of the Interstate Commerce Act of any of its obligations under the Interstate Commerce Act or its certificate(s) of public convenience and necessity.

180a. 7 Reports of interference with regulations.

Every motor common carrier of passengers subject to section 216 of the Interstate Commerce Act operating vehicles in interstate or foreign commerce shall report to the Secretary of the Interstate Commerce Commission within fifteen (15) days of its occurrence, any interference by any person, municipality, county, parish, state or body politic with its observance of the requirements of the regulations in this part. Such reports shall include a statement of action that such carrier may have taken to eliminate such interference.

180a. 10 Definitions.

For the purpose of regulations in this part the following terms and phrases are defined:

a. *Terminal facilities*: As used in the regulations in this part of the term "terminal facilities" means all facilities, including waiting room, rest room, eating, drinking, and ticket sales facilities which a motor common carrier makes available to passengers of a motor vehicle operated in interstate or foreign commerce as a regular part of their transportation.

b. *Separation*: As used in ()180a. 4, the term separation includes, among other things, the display of any sign indicating that any portion of the terminal facilities are separated, allocated, restricted, provided, available, used, or otherwise distinguished on the basis of race, color, creed or national origin.

Source: The Code of Federal Regulation in the United States of America, Title 49, 1963, https://books.google.com/books?id=Xy6kozIuDiQC&pg=PA65&lpg=PA65&dq= Part+180a%E2%80%94Regulations+Governing+Discrimination+in+Operations+of+ Interstate+Motor+Common+Carriers+of+Passengers+%5BAdded%5D&source=bl& ots=9vpMylBLHk&sig=gTUEMLyJ7Bbi8jAmUyMmpOYYRro&hl=en&sa=X& ved=0ahUKEwiGscSlvuLaAhUjooMKHUdsBMUQ6AEIQzAD#v=onepage&q= Part%20180a%E2%80%94Regulations%20Governing%20Discrimination%20in %20Operations%20of%20Interstate%20Motor%20Common%20Carriers%20of %20Passengers%20%5BAdded%5D&f=false

Discussion Questions

1. Evaluate the importance of the legal distinction between intrastate (within state) and interstate (between states) transportation.
2. Why did the Nashville students believe it was vital for the Freedom Rides to continue after they came to a temporary halt in Birmingham?
3. Explain why the federal government abandoned the freedom riders after they reached Jackson, Mississippi. What did the civil rights movement learn from that experience?

Further Reading

Arsenault, Raymond. *Freedom Riders: 1961 and the Struggle for Racial Justice* (Oxford University Press, 2006).

Barnes, Catherine. *Journey from Jim Crow: The Desegregation of Southern Transit* (Columbia University Press, 1983).

Carson, Clayborne. *In Struggle: SNCC and the Black Awakening of the 1960s* (Harvard University Press, 1981).

Catsam, Derek Charles. *Freedom's Main Line: The Journey of Reconciliation and the Freedom Rides* (University Press of Kentucky, 2009).

Farmer, James. *Lay Bare the Heart: An Autobiography of the Civil Rights Movement* (Arbor House, 1985).

Forman, James. *The Making of Black Revolutionaries* (Open Hand Publishing, 1985).

Halberstam, David. *The Children* (Random House, 1998).

Lewis, John, with Michael D'Orso. *Walking with the Wind: A Memoir of the Movement* (Simon and Schuster, 1998).

Meier, August, and Elliott Rudwick. *CORE: A Study in the Civil Rights Movement, 1942–1968* (Oxford University Press, 1973).

Niven, David. *The Politics of Injustice: The Kennedys, The Freedom Rides, and the Electoral Consequences of a Moral Compromise* (University of Tennessee Press, 2003).

Chapter 7   Albany, Birmingham, and the March on Washington, 1961–3

7.1 Laurie Pritchett Recalls Civil Rights Demonstrations in Albany, Georgia in 1961 and 1962

Albany, in southwest Georgia, became the site of the next major flashpoint in the civil rights movement in late 1961 and early 1962. In August 1961, Charles Sherrod, a worker from the Student Nonviolent Coordinating Committee (SNCC) established a voter registration campaign there. He then helped form a coalition of various local civil rights groups in the city under the umbrella of the Albany Movement, before launching nonviolent direct action demonstrations to desegregate train terminal facilities. As the movement escalated, local leaders invited Martin Luther King, Jr and the Southern Christian Leadership Conference (SCLC) to participate.

King's presence only added to the already existing factionalism in the Albany Movement among its numerous organizations and representatives that did not always see eye-to-eye on the best way forward. These internal movement divisions came up against a white power structure in Albany that coalesced behind chief of police Laurie Pritchett. Pritchett had observed the unfolding civil rights movement and noted that its success depended to a large degree on publicity and framing the narrative of events. He looked to steal the initiative from the movement by portraying himself as a calm-headed and reasonable figure that did not seek direct conflict with demonstrators. When the Albany Movement tried to fill the city's jail with protesters, Pritchett arranged jail space for them in surrounding areas. Denied a dramatic point of confrontation, the movement failed to engage the interest of the federal government in its cause.

The Civil Rights Movement: A Documentary Reader, First Edition. Edited by John A. Kirk.
© 2020 John Wiley & Sons, Inc. Published 2020 by John Wiley & Sons, Inc.

The media declared events in Albany a failure for King, who was forced into a retreat without achieving any tangible gains. This added to criticisms of King by SNCC that he simply turned up in communities seeking headlines and afterwards left local people on their own to fend for themselves. The local movement in Albany continued on without King, but the national spotlight quickly moved elsewhere.

LAURIE PRITCHETT: Now, the Albany movement started prior to that, which was made up of Dr. W.G. Anderson and local blacks. And they had started trying to deal with the city council; they wouldn't talk with them at that time, you know. So Dr. Anderson (well, he's a real close personal friend of mine), the Tates and Manly Tates, Tennessee B. King, Slater King, his brother, all of them started what they called (it was a loose-knit organization at that time) the Albany Movement. Then Charles Sherrard [sic] and some others (I forget), they was with SNCC; they came in. Bonnie Bevonovich – her father was a well-known attorney in New York; I think he handled the Cuban affair – and some other students from Colorado, they came in and joined Sherrard and Jones. And then December 16 – they were pushing for fuller restoration, that's what they were – 1961 [...] And we had prior knowledge to this, and we knew that they were going to make Albany a focal point for some reason. And we'd been training for it and getting ready for whatever. On December 16 they came in on the train; and there wasn't two, there was a group of them. And the population had found out about it; they were all down at the train station.

JAMES RESTON: Yes. Now he's got that listed, yes, as December 10, 1961: "eight SNCC workers, black and white, took Central Georgia Railroad from Atlanta to Albany."

LAURIE PRITCHETT: It was somewhere around there. It might have been the trial that was on December 16; but somewhere along there ...

JAMES RESTON: "Sat together in a white car. Then several hundred Albany blacks gathered at the Union Railway Terminal to meet them. They got off the train, went to the white waiting station and sat down. Chief Pritchett told them to get out. They did, and went to the waiting room." Then he says this about you. He says, "As they were going into the waiting room Chief Pritchett said, 'I told you to get off the streets. You are all under arrest.'"

LAURIE PRITCHETT: No.

JAMES RESTON: And later he quotes your version to the press. "I told the demonstrators to move away from the terminal three times. Then we called the paddy wagon, and I gave the order to arrest them. We will not stand for these trouble-makers coming into our city for the sole purpose of disturbing the peace and quiet in the city of Albany."

LAURIE PRITCHETT: Now that is right. I made that statement. But the arrest resulted from the fact that when they came in, as I say, there was a large group of whites and a large group of blacks in there. And the people who were coming in to pick up passengers and things of this nature couldn't get to the terminal, because they just went into the streets, you know. And we had asked them to disperse out of the streets and onto the sidewalks and the parking lot so that the people could get into taxis and all this business, to pick up passengers. And they refused to do it. And the local blacks moved back; but these people refused to move, and they were arrested. And that's basically what happened.

JAMES RESTON: Now, when you say that you had trained for it, you knew that they were going to make Albany a focal point, what kind of training do you remember you had at that time?

LAURIE PRITCHETT: Well, as you remember, we had information that Dr. King was coming into the Albany Movement with the Southern Christian Leadership. And you know his philosophy was non-violence. So we were going on the same philosophy as that. My men would train on non-violence: not that we had police dogs; they were deactivated. The men were instructed that if they were spit upon, cussed, abused in any way of that nature, that they were not to take their billyclubs out. And they would act in a non-violent approach in that. And this is what they did; you know, there was no bloodshed. It went on from '61 to '64, I think June or July of '64. There was never any violence on the part of over-reaction of the police. We arrested Dr. King twice, I think. We arrested some twenty-four hundred people. There was never any violence on our part. In talking to Dr. King (who was a close personal friend of mine) [...] Well, there was Dwight T. Walker, who was with Dr. King at that time (he's a big preacher in New York now), Andrew Young, who was a legislator from Georgia; Dr. Abernathy; all those were there. And we were real close friends; you know, we sat and talked a lot about it. Even after he left there, I went to Montgomery and seen him. We corresponded with each other for a long time; still get Christmas cards from his wife. But anyway, he said many times that this is what turned them around in Albany. His quote is that, as he stated to the *New York Times* and the *Herald Tribune* and *Newsweek* and *Time* magazine (all of them that was there), it was non-violent, that there wasn't any violence. The federal troops or marshals couldn't come in; they couldn't have accomplished the goal.

JAMES RESTON: Yes. OK, let me carry this on a minute here. "December 12: the trial of the eleven." Now who would that have been, the eleven people involved in the original arrests, the December 10 arrests? "Over four hundred black students march downtown to protest. Police guards with loud speakers order them to disperse." It talks about a fifteen foot alley that ran alongside of City Hall, where they were …

LAURIE PRITCHETT: Let's get this into focus, now, because actually what happened: the mayor at that time was Asa Kelly. He was a judge in Georgia now, and he was a practicing attorney, Asa Kelly. And unknown to anybody, unknown to me or I don't guess any other city council, he had given permission for these blacks to parade in an orderly fashion in downtown. And they did. No one bothered them. The police were there. There were always up in the thousands of whites on one side of the street, and the police were in the middle. And they marched. After they come up, you know, the mayor said he had given permission, so they did. And he told them they had permission to circle the block twice, and then after that they were to go back. And they continued to circle. And then they begin to move off the sidewalk; they were blocking pedestrians. There were so many of them that people couldn't get in or out of the stores on the street. And that's when we asked them to disperse. And I don't think any was arrested that day. That alley they're talking about, they called it Freedom Alley. It was just an alley between the police headquarters and some other buildings, and they called it Freedom Alley, because that's where most of them ended up. And we would book them, fingerprint them, mug them, put them on buses and ship them out. We never did what they intended to do. And King's philosophy, you know, was on Gandhi's, the march to the sea where they just filled the jails to capacity, and no place to put them, and then you've got to turn in to it. Our plans had been made where we had the capability of 10,000 prisoners, and never put a one in our city jail. They were to be shipped out to surrounding cities that were in a circle. And we had fifteen miles, twenty-five miles, forty-five miles on up to about seventy miles that we could ship prisoners to.

JAMES RESTON: Now who worked out that plan?

LAURIE PRITCHETT: I did.

JAMES RESTON: Of course it was your idea to do it that way.

LAURIE PRITCHETT: Yes, because, like I say, I'd studied the thing. I'd read a lot about King and used his … on Gandhi on overpower them by mass arrests. He knew our jail facilities were limited, and he felt if he brought four hundred people, with four hundred arrests we'd have no place to put them. But they'd already bought part of the buses; they were out of business, so the city buses brought the buses in. We'd fill them up, send them to Camilla or surrounding cities around Albany, and they would put them in their jails and we'd leave personnel there to watch them. So we never had any in ours.

JAMES RESTON: Well now, that had to be worked out with who, with the governor?

LAURIE PRITCHETT: No, it was worked out with the local people, and the sheriffs in the surrounding cities, police chiefs in the surrounding cities, the commissioners and local government. And they said, "Look, you're fighting our battle. We know if Albany falls all of us fall, so we're with you." And they didn't charge us for upkeep or anything. We'd have been about sixty miles from Atlanta, the last place we could have kept them. And like I say, we'd have twenty-four hundred.

JAMES RESTON: At this time?

LAURIE PRITCHETT: Oh, over a period of time. You know, we had mass marches in '61, from '61 continuously. We'd arrest seven or eight hundred people in marches every march they made. I guess at one time we had about fifteen hundred in jail at that time.

Source: James Reston interview with Laurie Pritchett, 23 April 1976. Interview B-0027. Southern Oral History Program Collection (#4007), Southern Historical Collection, Wilson Library, University of North Carolina at Chapel Hill, http://docsouth.unc.edu/sohp/B-0027/B-0027.html

7.2 Freedom Singers, "Ain't Gonna Let Nobody Turn Me Around," 1962

A distinctive hallmark of demonstrations in Albany was the use of songs to forge a sense of solidarity among civil rights activists. In one of Charles Sherrod's local SNCC workshops, a group of students formed an ensemble called the Freedom Singers. Many of the freedom songs that the Freedom Singers sang were old slave spirituals with lyrics adapted to reflect contemporary movement concerns. The songs surfaced not only at church meetings, but also on marches, demonstrations, and even in the jails. King called the songs "the soul of the movement." From what became known as "the singing movement" in Albany, the imparting of such songs by the Freedom Singers to other localities soon made them a recurrent and familiar aspect of civil rights struggles across the South. The below Albany Movement song name-checks Albany chief of police Laurie Pritchett and Albany mayor Asa Kelly, as well as "Uncle Toms," a pejorative term used to describe blacks that were perceived as being more interested in appeasing whites than fighting for freedom.

Ain't gonna let nobody, lordy, turn me 'round,
Turn me 'round, turn me 'round,
Ain't gonna let nobody, lordy, turn me 'round.
I'm gonna' keep on a-walkin', gonna' keep on a-talkin',
Marchin' up to freedom land.
Ain't gonna let segregation lordy, turn me 'round,
Turn me 'round, turn me 'round.
Ain't gonna let segregation lordy, turn me 'round,
I'm gonna keep on a-walkin', keep on a-talkin',
Marchin' up to freedom land.
Ain't gonna let no jailhouse lordy, turn me 'round,
Turn me 'round, turn me 'round,
Ain't gonna let no jailhouse, turn me 'round.
Keep on a-walkin', keep on a-talkin',
Marchin' up to freedom land.
Ain't gonna let no nervous Nellie lordy, turn me 'round,
Turn me 'round, turn me 'round.
Ain't gonna let no nervous Nellie lordy, turn me 'round,
Keep on a-walkin', keep on a-talkin',
Marchin' up to freedom land.
Ain't gonna let Chief Pritchett lordy, turn me 'round,
Turn me 'round, turn me 'round,
Ain't gonna let Chief Pritchett lordy,
Turn me 'round,
Keep on a-walkin', keep on a-talkin',
Marchin' up to freedom land.
Ain't gonna let Mayor Kelly lordy, turn me 'round,
Turn me 'round, turn me 'round,
Ain't gonna let Mayor Kelly lordy,
Turn me 'round,
Keep on a-walkin', keep on a-talkin',
Marchin' up to freedom land.
Ain't gonna let no Uncle Tom lordy, turn me 'round,
Turn me 'round, turn me 'round,
Ain't gonna let no Uncle Tom lordy,

Turn me 'round,
Keep on a-walkin', keep on a-talkin',
Marchin' up to freedom land.
Ain't gonna let nobody, lordy, turn me 'round,
Turn me 'round, turn me 'round,
Ain't gonna let nobody, lordy, turn me 'round.
I'm gonna' keep on a-walkin', yeah, keep on a-talkin', yeah,
Marchin' up to freedom land.

Source: *Sing for Freedom: The story of the Civil Rights Movement through its songs* (Smithsonian/Folkways, 1990).

7.3 Alabama Christian Movement for Human Rights, "Birmingham: People in Motion" on Civil Rights Demonstrations in 1962 and 1963

After regrouping from defeat in Albany, King and the SCLC launched their next community-based campaign in Birmingham in 1963. One of the advantages in targeting Birmingham was that it already had a strong SCLC affiliate in the Alabama Christian Movement for Human Rights (ACMHR), led by the fearless and energetic Rev. Fred Shuttlesworth, who had earlier played a role in the Freedom Rides. The city was also undergoing a political transformation. Birmingham had a reputation for hostile and violent race relations, exemplified by public safety commissioner Connor's brutal policing methods. In an attempt to undermine Connor, city businessmen changed the form of city government and held elections for a new mayor. Connor stood for mayor against business representative Albert (not Alfred, as mistakenly identified in the source below) Boutwell. Boutwell won, but in a bid to hold on to power, Connor contested the election.

Amid political confusion, and having fully expected the more moderate Boutwell to be in place by the start of demonstrations, the SCLC launched the Birmingham campaign by orchestrating sit-ins to challenge segregation at lunch counters. A number of problems immediately arose. The demonstrations drew less support than the SCLC anticipated. SCLC executive director Wyatt T. Walker addressed this by holding demonstrations at the busy lunch hour, which attracted considerable residual support from bystanders and made the numbers involved appear far larger than they actually were. White ministers in Birmingham criticized King and the SCLC for not allowing the new city administration time to initiate voluntary reforms. At first, Connor showed restraint in policing demonstrations, seeking to emulate Laurie Pritchett in Albany. Yet Connor's restraint did not last long. On Good Friday, 12 April 1963, King was arrested on a march and placed in jail, bringing the first wave of demonstrations to a head.

It was in early 1962 that the pressure which finally cracked the solid white wall of opposition of the city's power structure began to build up. Community leaders were still refusing even to talk to [Rev. Fred] Shuttlesworth in spite of progress in the courts and mounting support from around the country – but now, a year before the giant Birmingham demonstrations, the people began to move.

In the spring, Birmingham Negro college students and the ACMHR put on an effective selective buying campaign against the downtown stores. Their demands were desegregation of public accommodations and hiring of Negro clerks. Newspapers ignored the boycott but business leaders admitted privately it hurt them badly. Negro leaders claimed it was eighty per cent effective. Connor retaliated by cutting off the city relief payments, most of which go to Negroes. In announcing the decision, Mayor Hanes reportedly remarked: "Birmingham in cutting off the contribution to the surplus food program is demonstrating to the Negro community who their real friends and benefactors are. If the Negroes are going to heed the irresponsible and militant advice of the NAACP and CORE leaders, then I say: let these leaders feed them."

Further pressure developed in April when SNCC, SCEF [the Southern Conference Education Fund] and the ACMHR held the first large integrated public meeting in Birmingham in twenty-five years.

The break came when the Rev. Martin Luther King, Jr announced plans to hold SCLC's 1962 convention in Birmingham. Albany, Ga. was still in the headlines, and in order to avert demonstrations in their own city Birmingham business leaders sent delegates to confer with SCLC. SCLC replied that whether there would be demonstrations in Birmingham was a matter for local civil rights leaders to decide. So Birmingham business leaders were forced to talk to Shuttlesworth for the first time. During these talks it became evident that the white group was split, and that the first beginnings of the moderate white force necessary to Southern social change had emerged.

Business leaders had decided that some changes would have to be made if the city's economy was to avoid drastic damage. They found themselves pitted against the city's political leaders, who were unbending in their extreme segregationist position.

The struggle between the two groups focused on a vote in November 1962 to decide whether to change Birmingham's form of government from commission to city council. The people voted to change to a mayor-council system. It was a clear victory for moderation and a vote against the racist policies of police commissioner Bull Connor and the other two commissioners. In the spring of 1963 Connor was defeated in the mayoralty race and moderate Alfred E. Boutwell elected. Birmingham's Negroes provided the essential majority for Boutwell. The movement had withheld demonstrations until after the election to avoid upsetting the result.

Wherever you live, if you believe in human dignity and brotherhood, Birmingham Negroes are fighting our battle. Birmingham is the strongest bastion of segregation in America. When Equality and Right win there, the key line of segregationist defense will be breached. From then on, victory for human rights will be easier everywhere. As Birmingham goes, so will go your future and the future of your children and grandchildren.

These words appeared in the brochure about Birmingham published by SCEF in 1960. In the spring of 1963, Shuttlesworth and Dr. Martin Luther King, Jr of SCLC decided that the time had come to apply them literally – to wage a campaign to desegregate "the symbol of segregation." They felt that a direct confrontation with the power structure was necessary to realize the goals which had still only been made on paper. "Winning laws is no good if you have no officials to enforce them," Shuttlesworth said. "We decided that people in motion was the best way to correct social ills." More than a year of boycotting downtown stores had split the power structure but failed to win any meaningful concessions. Promises made by the white merchants to avert demonstrations when SCLC held its conference in Birmingham the year before had not been fulfilled. And so the people of Birmingham took to the streets.

The demonstrations began April 2 1963. During the next month Negroes staged massive marches through the downtown sections. More than 2000 children left school to join the marches and go to jail. The marchers were lashed by high pressure fire hoses, bitten by dogs, and imprisoned by the thousands – some as many as six times. The violence reached a peak on May 4 during a clash between police and demonstrators at Kelly Ingram Park.

Source: *Birmingham: People in Motion* (Birmingham: Alabama Christian Movement for Human Rights in cooperation with the Southern Conference Educational Fund, 1966).

7.4 Martin Luther King, Jr, "Letter from Birmingham City Jail," 1963

From his jail cell, King penned the "Letter from Birmingham City Jail," one of his most celebrated writings about the role of nonviolent direct action in the civil rights movement. Stung by the criticisms of local white ministers who questioned the timing of the SCLC's campaign in Birmingham, King defended his tactics. King refuted the "outside agitator" label, pointing out that the SCLC had a regionwide network of support and that its affiliate in Birmingham had invited King and the SCLC to the city. Moreover, King asserted, "We are caught in an inescapable network of mutuality, tied in a single garment of destiny. Whatever affects one directly affects all indirectly." King believed that it was his duty as a Christian minister to take a stand against injustice wherever it reared its head.

King's reference to the Apostle Paul in his letter not only identified King with civil rights evangelism, but also had a bearing on the medium of King's message: Paul, too, had written letters while imprisoned to spread the gospel. King went on to decry the notion that the movement was proceeding too quickly, noting that the long and ongoing struggle for black freedom and equality stretched well beyond the immediate events in Birmingham. King also insisted that nonviolent direct action was used only as a last resort. Collecting the facts, seeking negotiation, and earnestly examining the situation all came first. It was only when injustice proved immovable by any other means that nonviolent direct action became an option, providing the necessary creative tension to bring into plain sight the latent violence that underpinned racial discrimination.

While confined here in the Birmingham city jail, I came across your recent statement calling our present activities "unwise and untimely." Seldom, if ever, do I pause to answer criticism of my work and ideas. If I sought to answer all of the criticisms that cross my desk, my secretaries would be engaged in little else in the course of the day, and I would have no time for constructive work. But since I feel that you are men of genuine good will and your criticisms are sincerely set forth, I would like to answer your statement in what I hope will be patient and reasonable terms.

I think I should give the reason for my being in Birmingham, since you have been influenced by the argument of "outsiders coming in." I have the honor of serving as president of the Southern Christian Leadership Conference, an organization operating in every Southern state, with headquarters in Atlanta, Georgia. We have some eighty-five affiliate organizations all across the South, one being the Alabama Christian Movement for Human Rights. Whenever necessary and possible, we share staff, educational and financial resources with our affiliates. Several months ago our local affiliate here in Birmingham invited us to be on call to engage in a nonviolent direct-action program if such were deemed necessary. We readily consented, and when the hour came we lived up to our promises. So I am here, along with several members of my staff, because we were invited here. I am here because I have basic organizational ties here.

Beyond this, I am in Birmingham because injustice is here. Just as the eighth-century prophets left their little villages and carried their "thus saith the Lord" far beyond the boundaries of their hometowns; and just as the Apostle Paul left his little village of Tarsus and carried the gospel of Jesus Christ to practically every hamlet and city of the Greco-Roman world, I too am compelled to carry the gospel of freedom beyond my particular hometown. Like Paul, I must constantly respond to the Macedonian call for aid.

Moreover, I am cognizant of the interrelatedness of all communities and states. I cannot sit idly by in Atlanta and not be concerned about what happens in Birmingham. Injustice anywhere is a threat to justice everywhere. We are caught in an inescapable network of mutuality, tied in a single garment of destiny. Whatever affects one directly affects all indirectly. Never again can we afford to live with the narrow, provincial "outside agitator" idea. Anyone who lives inside the United States can never be considered an outsider.

You deplore the demonstrations that are presently taking place in Birmingham. But I am sorry that your statement did not express a similar concern for the conditions that brought the demonstrations into being. I am sure that each of you would want to go beyond the superficial social analyst who looks merely at effects and does not grapple with underlying causes. I would not hesitate to say that it is unfortunate that so-called demonstrations are taking place in Birmingham at this time, but I would say in more emphatic terms that it is even more unfortunate that the white power structure of this city left the Negro community with no other alternative.

In any nonviolent campaign there are four basic steps: collection of the facts to determine whether injustices are alive, negotiation, self-purification, and direct action. We have gone through all of these steps in Birmingham. There can be no gainsaying of the fact that racial injustice engulfs this community. Birmingham is probably the most thoroughly segregated city in the United States. Its ugly record of police brutality is known in every section of this country. Its unjust treatment of Negroes in the courts is a notorious reality. There have been more unsolved bombings of Negro homes and churches in Birmingham than in any other city in this nation. These are the hard, brutal, and unbelievable facts. On the basis of them, Negro leaders sought to negotiate with the city fathers. But the political leaders consistently refused to engage in good-faith negotiation.

Source: Martin Luther King, Jr, "Letter from Birmingham City Jail," 16 April 1963, Martin Luther King, Jr Papers Project website, http://mlk-kpp01.stanford.edu/kingweb/liberation_curriculum/pdfs/letterfrombirmingham_wwcw.pdf

7.5 Afro Newspaper/Gado, African-American Protesters Being Attacked by Police Dog in a Street during Segregation Demonstrations, Birmingham, Alabama, 1963

King's imprisonment attracted national publicity, but the difficulties of mobilizing demonstrations on the ground still remained. James Bevel, an SCLC field secretary recruited from the Nashville group of students, identified black high school students in Birmingham as being the most receptive to participating in demonstrations. King was hesitant about using children in the Birmingham campaign. A number of people, ranging from Attorney General Robert Kennedy to Nation of Islam minister Malcolm X, roundly condemned the idea. Placing children in harm's way was fraught with all kinds of moral quandaries and practical difficulties. Without King's consent, Bevel forged ahead anyway.

Bevel mobilized hundreds of school children to participate in marches. Connor deployed police dogs and spray from high-pressure fire hoses that could strip the bark off trees to disperse them. Kelly Ingram Park, close to the movement's meeting point for marches at the Sixteenth Street Baptist Church, provided the stage upon which the street theater of protests unfolded. The highly controversial "Children's Crusade" had its intended impact. The attacks on the children galvanized the black adult community in support. The images of the attacks conveyed by the mass media elicited widespread condemnation of Connor and support for the movement. President John F. Kennedy dispatched representatives to the city to broker an agreement to end the violence in the streets. White businessmen and movement activists sat down together to hammer out a truce that acceded to a number of the movement's demands.

Source: Afro Newspaper/Gado, African-American protesters being attacked by police dog in a street during segregation demonstrations, Birmingham, Alabama, 4 May 1963, https://www.gettyimages.com/license/513540823

7.6 Michael Ochs, Black Children are Attacked by Firefighters with High-Powered Water Hoses during a Protest Against Segregation in Birmingham, Alabama, 1963

Source: Michael Ochs, Black children are attacked by firefighters with high-powered water hoses during a protest against segregation in May 1963 in Birmingham, Alabama, http:// www.gettyimages.com/detail/news-photo/african-american-children-are-attacked-by-dogs-and-water-news-photo/81159913

7.7 President John F. Kennedy, "Report to the American People on Civil Rights," 1963

The truce agreement did not end the violence in Birmingham. As soon as King left the city, the Ku Klux Klan began dynamiting the homes of movement supporters. State troopers clashed in the streets with local blacks. On 11 June, President John F. Kennedy federalized the Alabama National Guard to prevent its use by Alabama governor George Wallace and moved federal troops close to the city. Kennedy used the national guardsmen to desegregate the University of Alabama, with Vivian Malone and James A. Hood becoming the first black students to attend since Autherine Lucy's controversial expulsion in 1956. The same night, Mississippi NAACP field secretary Medgar Evers was shot dead in the drive of his home by white segregationist Byron De La Beckwith.

The president went on television to address the nation about events in Birmingham. Kennedy gave his most unequivocal support for the civil rights movement yet. The president stressed the need for equality under the law in all areas of American life; he acknowledged the debilitating effects of racial discrimination on black Americans and the nation; he insisted that such issues transcended regional and party lines; he pointed to the damaging effects of racial violence on America's world standing in the eyes of other countries; and he referred to civil rights as a "moral issue," saying that he would introduce legislation to abolish segregation and uphold voting rights.

Moving from his previous position of standing on the sidelines and acting only to get demonstrations out of the headlines, Kennedy now placed his support squarely behind the goals of the civil rights movement. He did not live to see the legislation he proposed pass through Congress. In November 1963, Kennedy was assassinated in Dallas, Texas. Kennedy's civil rights legacy now rested on the shoulders of vice president Lyndon B. Johnson, who was sworn in as president to fulfill the rest of Kennedy's term of office.

Good evening, my fellow citizens:

This afternoon, following a series of threats and defiant statements, the presence of Alabama National Guardsmen was required on the University of Alabama to carry out the final and unequivocal order of the United States District Court of the Northern District of Alabama. That order called for the admission of two clearly qualified young Alabama residents who happened to have been born Negro.

That they were admitted peacefully on the campus is due in good measure to the conduct of the students of the University of Alabama, who met their responsibilities in a constructive way.

I hope that every American, regardless of where he lives, will stop and examine his conscience about this and other related incidents. This Nation was founded by men of many nations and backgrounds. It was founded on the principle that all men are created equal, and that the rights of every man are diminished when the rights of one man are threatened.

Today we are committed to a worldwide struggle to promote and protect the rights of all who wish to be free. And when Americans are sent to Viet-Nam or West Berlin, we do not ask for whites only. It ought to be possible, therefore, for American students of any color to attend any public institution they select without having to be backed up by troops.

It ought to be possible for American consumers of any color to receive equal service in places of public accommodation, such as hotels and restaurants and theaters and retail stores, without being forced to resort to demonstrations in the street, and it ought to be possible for American citizens of any color to register and to vote in a free election without interference or fear of reprisal.

It ought to be possible, in short, for every American to enjoy the privileges of being American without regard to his race or his color. In short, every American ought to have the right to be treated as he would wish to be treated, as one would wish his children to be treated. But this is not the case.

The Negro baby born in America today, regardless of the section of the Nation in which he is born, has about one-half as much chance of completing a high school as a white baby born in the same place on the same day, one-third as much chance of completing college, one-third as much chance of becoming a professional man, twice as much chance of becoming unemployed, about one-seventh as much chance of earning $10,000 a year, a life expectancy which is 7 years shorter, and the prospects of earning only half as much.

This is not a sectional issue. Difficulties over segregation and discrimination exist in every city, in every State of the Union, producing in many cities a rising tide of discontent that threatens the public safety. Nor is this a partisan issue. In a time of domestic crisis men of good will and generosity should be able to unite regardless of party or politics. This is not even a legal or legislative issue alone. It is better to settle these matters in the courts than on the streets, and new laws are needed at every level, but law alone cannot make men see right.

We are confronted primarily with a moral issue. It is as old as the scriptures and is as clear as the American Constitution.

The heart of the question is whether all Americans are to be afforded equal rights and equal opportunities, whether we are going to treat our fellow Americans as we want to be treated. If an American, because his skin is dark, cannot eat lunch in a restaurant open to the public, if he cannot send his children to the best public school available, if he cannot vote for the public officials who represent him, if, in short, he cannot enjoy the full and free life which all of us want, then who among us would be content to have the color of his skin changed and stand in his place? Who among us would then be content with the counsels of patience and delay?

One hundred years of delay have passed since President Lincoln freed the slaves, yet their heirs, their grandsons, are not fully free. They are not yet freed from the bonds of injustice. They are not yet freed from social and economic oppression. And this Nation, for all its hopes and all its boasts, will not be fully free until all its citizens are free.

We preach freedom around the world, and we mean it, and we cherish our freedom here at home, but are we to say to the world, and much more importantly, to each other that this is a land of the free except for the Negroes; that we have no second-class citizens except Negroes; that we have no class or caste system, no ghettoes, no master race except with respect to Negroes?

Now the time has come for this Nation to fulfill its promise. The events in Birmingham and elsewhere have so increased the cries for equality that no city or State or legislative body can prudently choose to ignore them.

The fires of frustration and discord are burning in every city, North and South, where legal remedies are not at hand. Redress is sought in the streets, in demonstrations, parades, and protests which create tensions and threaten violence and threaten lives.

We face, therefore, a moral crisis as a country and as a people. It cannot be met by repressive police action. It cannot be left to increased demonstrations in the streets. It cannot be quieted by token moves or talk. It is a time to act in the Congress, in your State and local legislative body and, above all, in all of our daily lives.

It is not enough to pin the blame on others, to say this is a problem of one section of the country or another, or deplore the fact that we face. A great change is at hand, and our task, our obligation, is to make that revolution, that change, peaceful and constructive for all.

Those who do nothing are inviting shame as well as violence. Those who act boldly are recognizing right as well as reality.

Next week I shall ask the Congress of the United States to act, to make a commitment it has not fully made in this century to the proposition that race has no place in American life or law. The Federal judiciary has upheld that proposition in a series of forthright cases. The executive branch has adopted that proposition in the conduct of its affairs, including the employment of Federal personnel, the use of Federal facilities, and the sale of federally financed housing.

But there are other necessary measures which only the Congress can provide, and they must be provided at this session. The old code of equity law under which we live commands for every wrong a remedy, but in too many communities, in too many parts of the country, wrongs are inflicted on Negro citizens and there are no remedies at law. Unless the Congress acts, their only remedy is in the street.

I am, therefore, asking the Congress to enact legislation giving all Americans the right to be served in facilities which are open to the public – hotels, restaurants, theaters, retail stores, and similar establishments.

This seems to me to be an elementary right. Its denial is an arbitrary indignity that no American in 1963 should have to endure, but many do.

I have recently met with scores of business leaders urging them to take voluntary action to end this discrimination and I have been encouraged by their response, and in the last 2 weeks over 75 cities have seen progress made in desegregating these kinds of facilities. But many are unwilling to act alone, and for this reason, nationwide legislation is needed if we are to move this problem from the streets to the courts.

I am also asking Congress to authorize the Federal Government to participate more fully in lawsuits designed to end segregation in public education. We have succeeded in persuading many districts to desegregate voluntarily. Dozens have admitted Negroes without violence. Today a Negro is attending a State-supported institution in every one of our 50 States, but the pace is very slow.

Too many Negro children entering segregated grade schools at the time of the Supreme Court's decision 9 years ago will enter segregated high schools this fall, having suffered a loss which can never be restored. The lack of an adequate education denies the Negro a chance to get a decent job.

The orderly implementation of the Supreme Court decision, therefore, cannot be left solely to those who may not have the economic resources to carry the legal action or who may be subject to harassment.

Other features will be also requested, including greater protection for the right to vote. But legislation, I repeat, cannot solve this problem alone. It must be solved in the homes of every American in every community across our country.

In this respect, I want to pay tribute to those citizens North and South who have been working in their communities to make life better for all. They are acting not out of a sense of legal duty but out of a sense of human decency.

Like our soldiers and sailors in all parts of the world they are meeting freedom's challenge on the firing line, and I salute them for their honor and their courage.

My fellow Americans, this is a problem which faces us all – in every city of the North as well as the South. Today there are Negroes unemployed, two or three times as many compared to whites, inadequate in education, moving into the large cities, unable to find work, young people particularly out of work without hope, denied equal rights, denied the opportunity to eat at a restaurant or lunch counter or go to a movie theater, denied the right to a decent education, denied almost today the right to attend a State university even though qualified. It seems to me that these are matters which concern us all, not merely Presidents or Congressmen or Governors, but every citizen of the United States.

This is one country. It has become one country because all of us and all the people who came here had an equal chance to develop their talents.

We cannot say to 10 percent of the population that you can't have that right; that your children can't have the chance to develop whatever talents they have; that the only way that they are going to get their rights is to go into the streets and demonstrate. I think we owe them and we owe ourselves a better country than that.

Therefore, I am asking for your help in making it easier for us to move ahead and to provide the kind of equality of treatment which we would want ourselves; to give a chance for every child to be educated to the limit of his talents.

As I have said before, not every child has an equal talent or an equal ability or an equal motivation, but they should have the equal right to develop their talent and their ability and their motivation, to make something of themselves.

We have a right to expect that the Negro community will be responsible, will uphold the law, but they have a right to expect that the law will be fair, that the Constitution will be color blind, as Justice Harlan said at the turn of the century.

This is what we are talking about and this is a matter which concerns this country and what it stands for, and in meeting it I ask the support of all our citizens.

Thank you very much.

Source: John F. Kennedy, "Report to the American People on Civil Rights, 11 June 1963," John F. Kennedy Presidential Library and Museum website, http://www.jfklibrary.org/Asset-Viewer/LH8F_oMzvoe6Ro1yEm74Ng.aspx

7.8 John Lewis's Original Text of His March on Washington Speech, 1963

The 1963 March on Washington for Jobs and Freedom was the idea of A. Philip Randolph and Bayard Rustin. The march reprised Randolph's threatened 1941 March on Washington Movement that had moved President Franklin D. Roosevelt to issue Executive Order 8802 banning discrimination in wartime industry and to set up the Fair Employment Practices Committee (FEPC).

Held at the Lincoln Memorial on 28 August, the 1963 event was intended to commemorate the 100th anniversary of President Abraham Lincoln's Emancipation Proclamation and to focus on economic issues facing the black community. As plans evolved, the march lost its "Jobs and Freedom" tag and became solely the "March on Washington." The focus shifted away from economic issues toward placing pressure on Congress to pass civil rights legislation to end racial discrimination in public facilities and accommodations. The march attracted around a quarter of a million people, including many black and white celebrities, movie stars, and singers.

The March on Washington has proved one of the movement's most enduring and celebrated spectacles, and in popular memory the day has become synonymous with Martin Luther King, Jr's "I Have a Dream" speech. However, the feel-good factor that surrounds memories of the march today ignores the simmering tensions that bubbled under the surface at the time. New SNCC chair John Lewis was another of the Nashville group of students placed in a leadership position. His prepared remarks were much more incendiary than King's homily. Lewis criticized the Kennedy administration for doing "too little and too late"; for not stepping up to protect voting rights and civil rights workers facing violence; and for failing to address economic issues. Lewis went on to criticize gradualism and called for radical change and even revolution. In the interests of unity, Lewis was persuaded by other civil rights leaders and the Kennedy administration to tone down the text of his proposed original speech that is provided below. Kennedy administration officials stood in the wings as Lewis spoke, quite literally ready to pull the plug on him if he deviated from the agreement.

We march today for jobs and freedom, but we have nothing to be proud of, for hundreds and thousands of our brothers are not here. They have no money for their transportation, for they are receiving starvation wages, or no wages at all.

In good conscience, we cannot support wholeheartedly the administration's civil rights bill, for it is too little and too late. There's not one thing in the bill that will protect our people from police brutality.

This bill will not protect young children and old women from police dogs and fire hoses, for engaging in peaceful demonstrations. This bill will not protect the citizens in Danville, Virginia, who must live in constant fear in a police state. This bill will not protect the hundreds of people who have been arrested on trumped up charges. What about the three young men in Americus, Georgia, who face the death penalty for engaging in peaceful protest?

The voting section of this bill will not help thousands of black citizens who want to vote. It will not help the citizens of Mississippi, of Alabama and Georgia, who are qualified to vote but lack a sixth-grade education. "ONE MAN, ONE VOTE" is the African cry. It is ours, too. It must be ours.

People have been forced to leave their homes because they dared to exercise their right to register to vote. What is there in this bill to ensure the equality of a maid who earns $5 a week in the home of a family whose income is $100,000 a year?

For the first time in one hundred years this nation is being awakened to the fact that segregation is evil and that it must be destroyed in all forms. Your presence today proves that you have been aroused to the point of action.

We are now involved in a serious revolution. This nation is still a place of cheap political leaders who build their careers on immoral compromises and ally themselves with open forms of political, economic and social exploitation. What political leader here can stand up and say, "My party is the party of principles?" The party of Kennedy is also the party of Eastland. The party of Javits is also the party of Goldwater. Where is *our* party?

In some parts of the South we work in the fields from sunup to sundown for $12 a week. In Albany, Georgia, nine of our leaders have been indicted not by Dixiecrats but by the federal government for peaceful protest. But what did the federal government do when Albany's deputy sheriff beat attorney C.B. King and left him half dead? What did the federal government do when local police officials kicked and assaulted the pregnant wife of Slater King, and she lost her baby?

It seems to me that the Albany indictment is part of a conspiracy on the part of the federal government and local politicians in the interest of expediency.

I want to know, which side is the federal government on?

The revolution is at hand, and we must free ourselves of the chains of political and economic slavery. The nonviolent revolution is saying, "We will not wait for the courts to act, for we have been waiting for hundreds of years. We will not wait for the President, the Justice Department, nor Congress, but we will take matters into our own hands and create a source of power, outside of any national structure, that could and would assure us a victory."

To those who have said, "Be patient and wait," we must say that "patience" is a dirty and nasty word. We cannot be patient, we do not want to be free gradually. We want our freedom, and we want it *now*. We cannot depend on any political party, for both the Democrats and the Republicans have betrayed the basic principles of the Declaration of Independence.

We all recognize the fact that if any radical social, political and economic changes are to take place in our society, the people, the masses, must bring them about. In the struggle, we must seek more than civil rights; we must work for the community of love, peace and true brotherhood. Our minds, souls and hearts cannot rest until freedom and justice exist for *all people*.

The revolution is a serious one. Mr Kennedy is trying to take the revolution out of the streets and put it into the courts. Listen, Mr Kennedy. Listen, Mr Congressman. Listen, fellow citizens. The black masses are on the march for jobs and freedom, and we must say to the politicians that there won't be a "cooling-off" period.

All of us must get in the revolution. Get in and stay in the streets of every city, every village and every hamlet of this nation until true freedom comes, until the revolution is complete. In the Delta of Mississippi, in southwest Georgia, in Alabama, Harlem, Chicago, Detroit, Philadelphia and all over this nation, the black masses are on the march!

We won't stop now. All the forces of Eastland, Barnett, Wallace and Thurmond won't stop this revolution. The time will come when we will not confine our marching to Washington. We will march through the South, through the heart of Dixie, the way Sherman did. We shall pursue our own "scorched earth" policy and burn Jim Crow to the ground – nonviolently. We shall fragment the South into a thousand pieces and put them back together in an image of democracy. We will make the action of the past few weeks look petty. And I say to you, WAKE UP AMERICA!

Source: John Lewis, with Michael D'Orso, *Walking with the Wind: A Memoir of the Movement* (New York: Simon and Schuster, 1998), pp. 216–18.

7.9 Lillian Foscue, "Dead and Injured Taken to Hospital," 1963

The triumphant March on Washington was swiftly eclipsed by tragedy. On 15 September, Sixteenth Street Baptist Church in Birmingham was hit by a dynamite blast. Four young black girls, Addie Mae Collins, Denise McNair, Carole Robertson, and Cynthia Wesley, who had all been attending a Sunday school service, were killed. The city once again exploded with violence as blacks confronted the police. Two blacks were shot dead in the ensuing conflict and many others, black and white, sustained injuries. King arrived in Birmingham the same evening in an attempt to bring calm. The following morning, King demanded federal intervention to protect the black community from further white terrorism. Although President Kennedy roundly condemned the violence, he shied away from direct federal intervention. King later delivered a moving eulogy at the funeral of the four girls in which he referred to them as "the martyred heroines of a holy crusade for freedom and dignity." The day-to-day struggles for civil rights, and their very heavy costs, stood in vivid contrast to the spectacle of the March on Washington. Despite the evident national support for the civil rights movement, white resistance to change in the South remained deeply entrenched. The task of translating popular support into legislation, and then legislation into changes at a grassroots level, still lay ahead.

Dead And Injured Taken To Hospital

BY LILLIAN FOSCUE

A blood-stained sheet covered the slight body on the stretcher.

The group of Negro men and women waiting outside the emergency room at University Hospital silently broke ranks and the body of 14-year-old Adii [sic] Mae Collins was carried away to the undertaker.

"Where's her mother?" someone asked.

Another answered, "Here she comes. She was with another daughter who was hurt. She didn't even know her daughter was dead."

Three other little Negro girls lay at the hospital, covered with plaster dust from crumbled brick that crushed out their lives.

Getting Ready For Choir

Cynthia Wesley, 14, Denise McNair, 11, and Carol [sic] Robertson, 14, had gone to the rear of the church to get ready for a special program at the 11 a.m. service.

Denise and Addi [sic] were putting on their choir robes to sing in the youth choir. Cynthia and Carol were to be among the young people serving as ushers.

The youth service was never held. Dynamite rocked the church, killing the four little girls outright and injuring others. Three persons were admitted to University Hospital. Two Negroes, Sarah Collins, 10, of 233 Sixth-ct, w, sister of the Collins child who was killed, had glass in her eyes, and Sam Ziegler of 2111 11th-av, n, injuries unknown.

Mrs Helen Salter, 150 Brooklane-dr, other person to be admitted, received a concussion and laceration of the ear when a rock was thrown through her car window. Mrs Salter and her son were en route to the airport to meet Mr Salter and were driving along Eighth-av after the explosion.

Had Premonition

Joseph Parish, chairman of the board of trustees of the Sixteenth Street Baptist Church, stood outside the emergency room. Treated for a laceration of the forehead himself, he stayed at the hospital to comfort others.

The pastor, the Rev. John H. Cross, whose 4-year-old daughter was injured, said he couldn't sleep last night. "I had a premonition something was going to happen."

Orzell Billingsly Jr, attorney and member of the church, said he expected trouble Saturday night but not during a church service. "Why would anyone want to kill children?"

A white police officer at the church walked over the intersection at Sixth-av, n and 16th-st glittering with broken glass. All humor was gone from his face as he said, "If I get my hands on the person who did this, I am not sure he'd get to stand trial. I've got kids of my own. This hits home," he declared.

Lesson On Love

Mrs Clevon Phillips, Sunday school teacher of two of the dead children, said bitterly, "We had just finished studying a Bible lesson about Joseph and his forgiving his enemies."

The Sunday school theme at the Sixteenth Street Baptist Church was "the love that forgives."

"We don't condemn the majority of the white people," said the Rev. W.A. Simmons, pastor of New Bethel Baptist Church. He heard the blast and went to find relatives.

"We believe outsiders do these things, not Birmingham people," he said, "but people must make a stand now."

Leads Group Outside

B.H. Wilson Sr, trustee and assistant superintendent of Sunday school, said he led a group of the congregation outside. "It was terrible. People couldn't find their relatives: mothers couldn't find their children.

"The lights went out. Plaster was falling and glass breaking."

Wilson said inside the church the sound of the explosion was muffled.

Persons blocks away heard the explosion, however. M.W. Pippen, grandfather of Denise McNair, heard the blast. He arrived at the church to find his daughter, Mrs Maxine McNair, frantically trying to find Denise. She was dead when they found her.

Pippen, owner of Social Cleaners across the street from the church, stood with his arms folded looking out of the shattered frame of the cleaners' window.

'Never Hurt Anybody'

"It's up to the white people now," he said, dry-eyed. "You know how I feel. My granddaughter, who never hurt any body, gone, and my business wrecked.

"Insurance? I got fire insurance, but I don't know about bomb insurance. I reckon I'm covered."

Denise's mother and father, Mr and Mrs Chris McNair of Rt. 4 are both school teachers. Mr McNair is also a photographer.

Cynthia Wesley, another of the dead children, was the daughter of School Principal Claude Wesley, beginning his first year in charge at Lewis School.

Carol Robertson was the daughter of Mr and Mrs Alvin C. Robertson of 1021 Fifth-st, n, both teachers, and granddaughter of Mrs Sallie M. Anderson, president of the Birmingham Council of Colored PTAs and a member of the Citizens Advisory Committee.

Source: Lillian Foscue, "Dead and Injured Taken to Hospital," *Birmingham Post-Herald*, 16 September 1963, pp. 1, 4, http://bplonline.cdmhost.com/digital/collection/p4017coll2/id/542/rec/24

Discussion Questions

1. Compare and contrast the policing methods of Laurie Pritchett in Albany and T. Eugene "Bull" Connor in Birmingham. Which was more successful, and why? What were the future implications for law enforcement and for the civil rights movement?
2. Assess the role played by freedom songs in the civil rights movement.
3. How important were the media images of the Birmingham campaign? What messages did they convey?
4. Why do you think John Lewis was told to – and agreed to – change the original text of his 1963 March on Washington speech?

Further Reading

Bass, Jonathan S. *Blessed are the Peacemakers: Martin Luther King, Jr, Eight White Religious Leaders, and the 'Letter from Birmingham City Jail'* (Louisiana State University Press, 2001).

D'Emillio, John. *Lost Prophet: The Life and Times of Bayard Rustin* (Free Press, 2003).

Eskew, Glenn T. *But for Birmingham: The Local and National Movements in the Civil Rights Struggle* (University of North Carolina Press, 1997).

Hansen, Drew D. *The Dream: Martin Luther King, Jr and the Speech that Inspired a Nation* (HarperCollins, 2003).

Jones, William P. *The March on Washington: Jobs, Freedom, and the Forgotten History of Civil Rights* (W.W. Norton, 2013).

King, Martin Luther, Jr. *Why We can't Wait* (Harper and Row, 1964).

Manis, Andrew M. *A Fire You can't Put Out: The Civil Rights Life of Birmingham's Fred Shuttlesworth* (University of Alabama Press, 1999).

McWhorter, Dianne. *Carry Me Home: Birmingham, Alabama: The Climatic Battle of the Civil Rights Revolution* (Simon and Schuster, 2001).

Thornton, J. Mills. *Dividing Lines: Municipal Politics and the Struggle for Civil Rights in Montgomery, Birmingham, and Selma* (University of Alabama Press, 2002).

Widdell, Robert W., Jr. *Birmingham and the Long Black Freedom Struggle* (Palgrave Macmillan, 2013).

Chapter 8

The Civil Rights Act of 1964, Freedom Summer, and the Mississippi Freedom Democratic Party, 1964

8.1 US Congress, Civil Rights Act of 1964

President Lyndon B. Johnson was well equipped to take forward the civil rights legislation that Kennedy had proposed. As a Texan, Johnson was considered a southerner, but he was also someone who was sympathetic to civil rights. An admirer of President Franklin D. Roosevelt's New Deal liberalism, Johnson gained first-hand experience of racial and ethnic discrimination while teaching in segregated Mexican-American schools. Unlike the younger and fresh-faced Kennedy, Johnson was a seasoned politician, having served as a US congressman, senator, senate majority whip, and senate Democratic leader. This gave Johnson the necessary political experience and connections to drive civil rights legislation through a normally recalcitrant Congress that was full of powerful southern politicians. The signing into law of the Civil Rights Act of 1964 on 2 July also reflected in no small measure Johnson's political skill in casting the legislation as a tribute to a slain President Kennedy for a nation still in mourning. Of course, the legislation equally rested on the moral force of movement activists' demands at local, state, and national levels, and the movement's successful building of a national public consensus outside of the South in support of civil rights.

The Civil Rights Act of 1964 was a very wide-ranging piece of legislation. Title I tackled voting rights, although not nearly comprehensively enough, which led to separate and more extensive legislation the following year. Title II prohibited discrimination in public accommodations on the basis of "race, color, religion or national origin." Title III prohibited state and local government from denying access to public facilities. Title IV paved the way for a more rigorous enforcement of school desegregation. Title V expanded the role of the Civil Rights Commission, which had been formed by the Civil Rights Act of 1957. Title VI prevented

The Civil Rights Movement: A Documentary Reader, First Edition. Edited by John A. Kirk.
© 2020 John Wiley & Sons, Inc. Published 2020 by John Wiley & Sons, Inc.

discrimination by government agencies in receipt of federal funds. Title VII tackled employment discrimination, including discrimination against women in the workplace. Title VIII required the compilation of voter registration and other voting data in certain geographical areas. Title IX made it easier to move civil rights cases from state to federal courts. Title X established a Community Relations Service to assist in community disputes involving racial discrimination. Title XI dealt with how charges against those in violation of the act were handled.

Title II had the most immediate visible impact, leading to the desegregation of public facilities and accommodations. The Act also significantly led to a change in the focus of the law in civil rights cases away from the Fourteenth Amendment's Equal Protection Clause, which had predominated in the past, to the Constitution's Commerce Clause, which gives the federal government the right to regulate interstate commerce. Through a broad interpretation of the Commerce Clause, the courts successfully extended desegregation from publicly owned facilities to many notionally private establishments as well.

TITLE II – INJUNCTIVE RELIEF AGAINST DISCRIMINATION IN PLACES OF PUBLIC ACCOMMODATION

SEC. 201. (a) All persons shall be entitled to the full and equal enjoyment of the goods, services, facilities, and privileges, advantages, and accommodations of any place of public accommodation, as defined in this section, without discrimination or segregation on the ground of race, color, religion, or national origin.

(b) Each of the following establishments which serves the public is a place of public accommodation within the meaning of this title if its operations affect commerce, or if discrimination or segregation by it is supported by State action:

1. any inn, hotel, motel, or other establishment which provides lodging to transient guests, other than an establishment located within a building which contains not more than five rooms for rent or hire and which is actually occupied by the proprietor of such establishment as his residence;

2. any restaurant, cafeteria, lunchroom, lunch counter, soda fountain, or other facility principally engaged in selling food for consumption on the premises, including, but not limited to, any such facility located on the premises of any retail establishment; or any gasoline station;

3. any motion picture house, theater, concert hall, sports arena, stadium or other place of exhibition or entertainment; and

4. any establishment (A)(i) which is physically located within the premises of any establishment otherwise covered by this subsection, or (ii) within the premises of which is physically located any such covered establishment, and (B) which holds itself out as serving patrons of such covered establishment.

(c) The operations of an establishment affect commerce within the meaning of this title if (1) it is one of the establishments described in paragraph (1) of subsection (b); (2) in the case of an establishment described in paragraph (2) of subsection (b), it serves or offers to serve interstate travelers or a substantial portion of the food which it serves, or gasoline or other products which it sells, has moved in commerce; (3) in the case of an establishment described in paragraph (3) of subsection (b), it customarily presents films, performances, athletic teams, exhibitions, or other sources of entertainment which move in commerce; and (4) in the case of an establishment described in paragraph (4) of subsection (b), it is physically located within the premises of, or there is physically located within its premises, an establishment the operations of which affect commerce within the meaning of this subsection. For purposes of this section, "commerce" means travel, trade, traffic, commerce, transportation, or communication among the several States, or between the District of Columbia and any State, or between any foreign country or any territory or possession and any State or the District of Columbia, or between points in the same State but through any other State or the District of Columbia or a foreign country.

(d) Discrimination or segregation by an establishment is supported by State action within the meaning of this title if such discrimination or segregation (1) is carried on under color of any law, statute, ordinance, or regulation; or (2) is carried on under color of any custom or usage required or enforced by officials of the State or political subdivision thereof; or (3) is required by action of the State or political subdivision thereof.

(e) The provisions of this title shall not apply to a private club or other establishment not in fact open to the public, except to the extent that the facilities of such establishment are made available to the customers or patrons of an establishment within the scope of subsection (b).

SEC. 202. All persons shall be entitled to be free, at any establishment or place, from discrimination or segregation of any kind on the ground of race, color, religion, or national origin, if such discrimination or segregation is or purports to be required by any law, statute, ordinance, regulation, rule, or order of a State or any agency or political subdivision thereof.

SEC. 203. No person shall (a) withhold, deny, or attempt to withhold or deny, or deprive or attempt to deprive, any person of any right or privilege secured by section 201 or 202, or (b) intimidate, threaten, or coerce, or attempt to intimidate, threaten, or coerce any person with the purpose of interfering with any right or privilege secured by section 201 or 202, or (c) punish or attempt to punish any person for exercising or attempting to exercise any right or privilege secured by section 201 or 202.

SEC. 204. (a) Whenever any person has engaged or there are reasonable grounds to believe that any person is about to engage in any act or practice prohibited by section 203, a civil action for preventive relief, including an application for a permanent or temporary injunction, restraining order, or other order, may be instituted by the person aggrieved and, upon timely application, the court may, in its discretion, permit the Attorney General to intervene in such civil action if he certifies that the case is of general public importance. Upon application by the complainant and in such circumstances as the court may deem just, the court may appoint an attorney for such complainant and may authorize the commencement of the civil action without the payment of fees, costs, or security.

(b) In any action commenced pursuant to this title, the court, in its discretion, may allow the prevailing party, other than the United States, a reasonable attorney's fee as part of the costs, and the United States shall be liable for costs the same as a private person.

(c) In the case of an alleged act or practice prohibited by this title which occurs in a State, or political subdivision of a State, which has a State or local law prohibiting such act or practice and establishing or authorizing a State or local authority to grant or seek relief from such practice or to institute criminal proceedings with respect thereto upon receiving notice thereof, no civil action may be brought under subsection (a) before the expiration of thirty days after written notice of such alleged act or practice has been given to the appropriate State or local authority by registered mail or in person, provided that the court may stay proceedings in such civil action pending the termination of State or local enforcement proceedings.

(d) In the case of an alleged act or practice prohibited by this title which occurs in a State, or political subdivision of a State, which has no State or local law prohibiting such act or practice, a civil action may be brought under subsection (a): Provided, That the court may refer the matter to the Community Relations Service established by title X of this Act for as long as the court believes there is a reasonable possibility of obtaining voluntary compliance, but for not more than sixty days: Provided further, That upon expiration of such sixty-day period, the court may extend such period for an additional period, not to exceed a cumulative total of one hundred and twenty days, if it believes there then exists a reasonable possibility of securing voluntary compliance.

SEC. 205. The Service is authorized to make a full investigation of any complaint referred to it by the court under section 204(d) and may hold such hearings with respect thereto as may be necessary. The Service shall conduct any hearings with respect to any such complaint in executive session, and shall not release any testimony given therein except by agreement of all parties involved in the complaint with the permission of the court, and the Service shall endeavor to bring about a voluntary settlement between the parties.

SEC. 206. (a) Whenever the Attorney General has reasonable cause to believe that any person or group of persons is engaged in a pattern or practice of resistance to the full enjoyment of any of the rights secured by this title, and that the pattern or practice is of such a nature and is intended to deny the full exercise of the rights herein described, the Attorney General may bring a civil action in the appropriate district court of the United States by filing with it a complaint (1) signed by him (or in his absence the Acting Attorney General), (2) setting forth facts pertaining to such pattern or practice, and (3) requesting such preventive relief, including an application for a permanent or temporary injunction, restraining order or other order against the person or persons responsible for such pattern or practice, as he deems necessary to insure the full enjoyment of the rights herein described.

(b) In any such proceeding the Attorney General may file with the clerk of such court a request that a court of three judges be convened to hear and determine the case. Such request by the Attorney General shall be accompanied by a certificate that, in his opinion, the case is of general public importance. A copy of the certificate and request for a three-judge court shall be immediately furnished by such clerk to the chief judge of the circuit (or in his absence, the presiding circuit judge of the circuit) in which the case is pending. Upon receipt of the copy of such request it shall be the duty of the chief judge of the circuit or the presiding circuit judge, as the case may be, to designate immediately three judges in such circuit, of whom at least one shall be a circuit judge and another of whom shall be a district judge of the court in which the proceeding was instituted, to hear and determine such case, and it shall be the duty of the judges so designated to assign the case for hearing at the earliest practicable date, to participate in the hearing and determination thereof, and to cause the case to be in every way expedited. An appeal from the final judgment of such court will lie to the Supreme Court.

In the event the Attorney General fails to file such a request in any such proceeding, it shall be the duty of the chief judge of the district (or in his absence, the acting chief judge) in which the case is pending immediately to designate a judge in such district to hear and determine the case. In the event that no judge in the district is available to hear and determine the case, the chief judge of the district, or the acting chief judge, as the case may be, shall certify this fact to the chief judge of the circuit (or in his absence, the acting chief judge) who shall then designate a district or circuit judge of the circuit to hear and determine the case.

It shall be the duty of the judge designated pursuant to this section to assign the case for hearing at the earliest practicable date and to cause the case to be in every way expedited.

SEC. 207. (a) The district courts of the United States shall have jurisdiction of proceedings instituted pursuant to this title and shall exercise the same without regard to whether the aggrieved party shall have exhausted any administrative or other remedies that may be provided by law.

(b) The remedies provided in this title shall be the exclusive means of enforcing the rights based on this title, but nothing in this title shall preclude any individual or any State or local agency from asserting any right based on any other Federal or State law not inconsistent with this title, including any statute or ordinance requiring nondiscrimination in public establishments or accommodations, or from pursuing any remedy, civil or criminal, which may be available for the vindication or enforcement of such right.

Source: US Congress, Civil Rights Act of 1964, http://www.ourdocuments.gov/doc.php ?flash=true&doc=97&page=transcript

8.2 Nina Simone, "Mississippi Goddam," 1964

Mississippi was the epitome of white supremacy and racial injustice: the place where most lynchings occurred, where the first White Citizens' Councils to resist school desegregation were formed, and where state leaders were openly and rabidly resistant to integration. As singer Nina Simone (born in Tryon, North Carolina) put it at the time, "everybody knows about Mississippi Goddam." Mississippi was a place where everything was done slow – the southern drawl of the accent, the rural pace of life in the searing heat, and, above all, the response to anything that indicated possible social change. It was, sociologist James W. Silver wrote in 1964, a "closed society," where dissent from the prevailing social and racial mores was simply not tolerated. This was exactly the sort of place, the Student Nonviolent Coordinating Committee (SNCC) believed, that had to be tackled if civil rights and voting rights were to become a reality everywhere in the United States. Just as Birmingham in 1963 had been a symbol of southern urban injustice and inequality, Mississippi in 1964 became a symbol of southern rural injustice and inequality. SNCC and other civil rights organizations had expected that a regionwide testing of public facilities and accommodations in the wake of the Civil Rights Act of 1964 would be necessary. Yet as desegregation proceeded with less hindrance than expected, the focus quickly shifted to the next major civil rights battleground, the struggle for voting rights.

The name of this tune is Mississippi Goddam
And I mean every word of it
Alabama's gotten me so upset
Tennessee made me lose my rest
And everybody knows about Mississippi Goddam
Alabama's gotten me so upset
Tennessee made me lose my rest
And everybody knows about Mississippi Goddam

Can't you see it
Can't you feel it
It's all in the air
I can't stand the pressure much longer
Somebody say a prayer

Alabama's gotten me so upset
Tennessee made me lose my rest
And everybody knows about Mississippi Goddam

This is a show tune
But the show hasn't been written for it, yet

Hound dogs on my trail
School children sitting in jail
Black cat cross my path
I think every day's gonna be my last

Lord have mercy on this land of mine
We all gonna get it in due time
I don't belong here
I don't belong there
I've even stopped believing in prayer

Don't tell me
I tell you
Me and my people just about due
I've been there so I know
They keep on saying "Go slow!"

But that's just the trouble
"do it slow"
Washing the windows
"do it slow"
Picking the cotton
"do it slow"
You're just plain rotten
"do it slow"
You're too damn lazy
"do it slow"
The thinking's crazy
"do it slow"
Where am I going
What am I doing
I don't know
I don't know

Just try to do your very best
Stand up be counted with all the rest

For everybody knows about Mississippi Goddam
I made you thought I was kiddin' didn't we
Picket lines
School boycotts
They try to say it's a communist plot
All I want is equality
for my sister my brother my people and me
Yes you lied to me all these years
You told me to wash and clean my ears
And talk real fine just like a lady
And you'd stop calling me Sister Sadie
Oh but this whole country is full of lies
You're all gonna die and die like flies
I don't trust you any more
You keep on saying "Go slow!"
"Go slow!"
But that's just the trouble
"do it slow"
Desegregation
"do it slow"
Mass participation
"do it slow"
Reunification
"do it slow"
Do things gradually
"do it slow"
But bring more tragedy
"do it slow"
Why don't you see it
Why don't you feel it
I don't know
I don't know
You don't have to live next to me
Just give me my equality
Everybody knows about Mississippi
Everybody knows about Alabama
Everybody knows about Mississippi Goddam
That's it for now! see ya' later

Source: Nina Simone, *Nina Simone in Concert* (Philips Records, 1964).

8.3 Charles McLaurin, Student Nonviolent Coordinating Committee Field Report, 1964

SNCC began its organizing efforts in Mississippi in 1961. Organizing in rural areas was a very different prospect from the largely city-based campaigns that Martin Luther King, Jr and the Southern Christian Leadership Conference (SCLC) typically ran. Urban areas had larger concentrations of black people to draw upon for collective action. With those numbers came a greater sense of collective security, and in the case of King's campaigns this was reinforced by the ever-present national media attention. In rural areas the black population was more dispersed and therefore more isolated and even more vulnerable to white attacks. The Kennedy brothers and Lyndon B. Johnson believed that guiding the civil rights movement toward voter registration efforts would be less controversial and less confrontational than nonviolent direct action demonstrations. They were wrong. Opposition to voting rights in Mississippi was every bit as violent as opposition to nonviolent demonstrations elsewhere.

In 1962, Robert P. Moses became director of a coalition of civil rights groups, in which SNCC was the dominant influence, called the Council of Federated Organizations (COFO). In 1963, aided by white student volunteers from the North, COFO held a mock "Freedom Vote" to demonstrate that black voters were ready and willing to participate in the electoral process and to have a say in the state's governance – and that the only thing preventing them from doing so was white violence, intimidation, and blatant obstacles to a free and fair vote.

In the source below, SNCC worker Charles McLaurin's February 1964 field report details the sorts of difficulties that Mississippi blacks faced in claiming their voting rights. These included high levels of illiteracy in the black population, a consequence of a segregated school system that consistently underfunded black education; local white control of polling places and procedures for voting, which led to the arbitrary disqualification of black voters; and economic coercion from whites who employed blacks, along with threats of violence and actual physical intimidation.

Civil rights workers believed that in the first instance getting black voters to turn up at the polls and demonstrate a willingness to vote gave lie to claims by whites that blacks showed no interest in casting a ballot. The experience of voting was empowering and emboldening, and a vital first step in engagement with the political process. McLaurin's report testifies to the pivotal role that black women and their networks played in the mobilization of the vote. Even as McLaurin was writing, plans were being made to significantly expand voter registration efforts in Mississippi that summer.

I will start this report with some of the things people are saying and doing; I was on my way to Indianola on Feb. 11, 1964 to carry five old ladies to register. The ladies ranged from 46 years old to 74 years of age. One lady, Mrs Susie Jones, an old lady who lives outside of Ruleville near the Leflore County line, started to talk about things on the plantation and how she as a girl had lived and worked very hard to help her mother and younger sister and brothers.

Mrs Jones cannot read or write, but she wanted to vote. I told her when we get to the courthouse I wanted her to go in and tell Mr C.C. Campbell (the registrar) that she wanted to register to vote and could not read and write. We walked up the steps to the Courthouse behind the others and went into the office together. Mrs Jones told C.C. she wanted to register. When he offered her the application blank, she told him she could not write; at this time I walked up to the desk and asked if I could fill out the form for her. He said "no." I then asked if two persons witnessed her make an X could I sign her name. The registrar said, "If you want to, but I will not pass her." So I signed her name and gave the blank to Campbell.

Later that day, 7 other Negroes were taken to the Courthouse to register, only one could read and write.

That day about 47 people came down to register and of that number only 12 could read and write. The 12 took the test and the others went back to Ruleville.

February 12, 1964: 5 people were taken from Ruleville to Indianola to register; 3 of them lived in plantations outside of Ruleville, and could not read or write. However, they were taken to the Courthouse and told to ask the registrar (C.C. Campbell) to let me fill out the forms for them. He said alway [sic]: "No."

We will not stop carrying down Negroes who cannot read and write because I feel as do the leaders in Ruleville that when these people go down and face the man (C.C. Campbell) that this makes them better than me or anyone else can tell them, that the white people don't love them. Also shows that people (Negroes) would register and vote if they could.

Well after we got back to Ruleville from Indianola, the truck with 24 thousand pounds of food and clothing had arrived; and community people were unloading the boxes and believe it or not of the 12 people moving these boxes 8 were women. Well this sounds bad for us, but the men up here are nothing. The saying around Ruleville is that if you want a job done right, get a woman. Most of the school bus drivers are women.

February 13, 1964, Thursday: About 75 or more people came to the food center at 820 Quiver Street to sign up for food and clothes. 25 of this number went to the Courthouse to register. The people were told to come to a mass meeting at Williams Chapel Church on Friday night at 7:30 p.m. and that people who went down to try and register would be served first and that those who did not go down to register would be last.

<u>Friday morning (Feb. 14)</u>: There were about 300 people at the center to get food. We started carrying them down to Indianola at 8 a.m. and at 4:30 p.m. more than 156 people had gone to Indianola. These people came from every town in Sunflower County and some had walked five and ten miles to Ruleville.

We had the people coming into the Courthouse, but C.C. Campbell would only take in two at a time.

<u>Feb. 15, Saturday</u>: We took six people to the Courthouse and the registrar told us that the office would be closed because the county Lawyers were holding a meeting in the testing room. So we stayed around in the Hall for about 45 minutes and then went back to Ruleville.

There has been someone off every plantation in Sunflower County except Senator James Eastland's plantation. People say that Negroes on Eastland's plantation are in bad shape, but they are afraid to come and get food and clothing.

The people on Ben Flemmine's place where he told them (the Negroes) that "if any nigger goes down to vote I will shoot him like a rabbit." However nine people came off that plantation to try to register to vote. Last year two people had to move off the place when they went down to register and were forced to find themselves places in Ruleville. Soon as Ben finds out about them going down we may have nine more to try and find places for.

Source: Charles McLaurin, SNCC Field Report, Sunflower County, Mississippi, 19 February 1964, Civil Rights Movement Veterans website, http://www.crmvet.org/lets/6402_sncc_sunflower.pdf

8.4 Liz Fusco, "The Mississippi Freedom Schools: Deeper than Politics," 1964

In late 1963, SNCC worker Charles Cobb proposed a network of Freedom Schools as part of community mobilization efforts. In March 1964, he organized a curriculum planning conference in New York with sponsorship from the National Council of Churches. Spelman College history professor Staughton Lynd was appointed director of the Freedom School program. Over the summer of 1964, more than 40 Freedom Schools were established with over 3,000 students enrolled. At one level, the schools fulfilled a very basic need in providing education to black children who attended poorly funded and largely neglected black rural schools. At another level, the Freedom Schools provided important citizenship education in practical matters such as voting rights, civil rights, and economic rights. They also taught students to critically assess and to evaluate the conditions they faced, and how to go about addressing those conditions.

The Freedom Schools welcomed all ages; a number of adults used the classes to make up for the education that they had been denied in the past. Questions, discussion, and self-reflection were encouraged in classrooms rather than the rote memorization of facts and dates. There was also a recreational curriculum that required students to be physically active. Freedom Schools were set up wherever they could find an appropriate space, from outdoor venues like parks to people's homes. Many used churches for classes. In rural areas where students worked in the daytime, night classes were held. The fundamental values underpinning the Freedom School concept were to be open and welcoming to all, and to demonstrate a willingness to shape education to the needs and conditions of local people.

The original plan for Freedom Schools developed from Charles Cobb's dream that what could be done in Mississippi could be deeper, more fundamental, more far-reaching, more revolutionary than voter registration alone: more personal, and in a sense more transforming, than a political program. The validity of the dream is evidenced by the fact that people trying desperately to keep alive while working on voter registration could take seriously the idea that Mississippi needs more than for Negroes to have the right to vote.

The decision to have Freedom Schools in Mississippi seems to have been a decision, then, to enter into every phase of the lives of the people of Mississippi. It seems to have been a decision to set the people free for politics in the only way that people really can become free – and that is totally. It was an important decision for the staff to be making, and so it is not surprising that the curriculum for the proposed schools became everyone's concern. They worked and argued about what should be taught, about what the realities of Mississippi are, and how these realities affect the kids, and how to get the kids to discover themselves as human beings. And then Staughton Lynd, the director, came in to impose a kind of beautiful order on the torment that the curriculum was becoming – torment because it was not just curriculum: it was each person on the staff painfully analyzing what the realities of his world were, and asking himself, with what pain I can only sense, what right he had to let the kids of Mississippi know the truth, and what right he had to keep it from them until now. And because of these sessions, the whole concept of what could be done in Mississippi must have changed. It was because the people trying to change Mississippi were asking themselves what is wrong with Mississippi that the summer project in effect touched every aspect of the lives of the Negroes in Mississippi, and started to touch the lives of whites as well.

As I see it, it was this asking of questions that made the Mississippi summer project different from other voter registration projects and other civil-rights activities everywhere else in the South. And so it is reasonable that the transformations that occurred took place because for the first time in their lives kids were asking questions. The curriculum itself was based on the asking of certain questions, in connection with the kids' interest in their Freedom School teachers (mostly Northern, mostly white, mostly still in college), in connection with Negro History, African culture, and even the academic subjects, as well as in connection with the study of the realities of Mississippi in the light of Nazi Germany in 1935. The so-called "Citizenship Curriculum" set up two sets of questions. The "primary" set was: 1) Why are we (teachers and students) in Freedom Schools? 2) What is the Freedom Movement? 3) What alternatives does the Freedom Movement offer us? The "secondary" set of questions (which seemed to me more important because more personal) was: 1) What does the majority culture have that we want? 2) What does the majority culture have that we don't want? 3) What do we have that we want to keep?

The continual raising of these questions in many contexts may be said to be what the Freedom Schools were about. This was so because in order to answer them it was necessary for the student to confront other questions of who he is, what his world is like, and how he fits into or is alienated from it.

Source: Liz Fusco, "The Mississippi Freedom Schools: Deeper than Politics," from *Liberation*, November 1964, http://www.crmvet.org/info/641100_fusco_fskools.pdf

8.5 Medical Committee for Human Rights, Press Release, 1964

In June 1964, a number of prominent medical professionals, many of whom were parents of students in the Freedom Summer project, formed the Medical Committee for Human Rights (MCHR) in consultation with one of Mississippi's leading black physicians, Dr. Robert Smith. The MCHR formulated a plan to assist in Freedom Summer. Firstly, it administered first aid to civil rights workers. Most white doctors refused to treat civil rights workers in the state, and only some of the already very few black doctors in Mississippi were willing to take that risk for fear of reprisals. Secondly, it helped local people gain access to doctors and hospitals. Like everything else in Mississippi, medical care was comprehensively segregated, with blacks lacking access to basic medical resources. Finally, it supported existing black and white healthcare personnel that were prepared to work with the civil rights movement.

Around 100 medical volunteers participated in the Freedom Summer project, setting up ad hoc medical clinics in community centers and Freedom Schools before founding a permanent base in Mileston, Holmes County. The clinic was governed by the same egalitarian principles of participatory democracy that ran throughout the Freedom Summer projects. A Holmes County Health Association was formed to involve local people in the decision-making process about the healthcare provided at the clinic and to lobby for better equipment and conditions. The MCHR paved the way for other groups that followed, such as the Physicians for Human Rights and the Physicians for a National Health Program. The MCHR was also an early advocate of single-payer universal healthcare insurance. Although active in Mississippi for only two years, the legacy of the MCHR in the state was long lasting: between 1965 and 1971, for example, the black infant mortality rate in Mississippi decreased by 65%.

New York Sunday, July 12, 1964.

Nationally Prominent Doctors Form Mississippi Project

Over the last several days the Medical Committee For Human Rights (Mississippi Project) has been formed by a group of leading physicians across the United States. They were responding to the request of COFO (Council of Federated Organizations) the federation of civil rights groups that are conducting the Mississippi Summer Project.

Its primary purpose is "to insure adequate medical care for the project's volunteer students, clergymen and lawyers, working to this end in cooperation with the local physicians and hospitals." It will be working closely with COFO, the national Council of Churches, and the NAACP.

Besides its concern with medical care for the volunteers, the committee has also indicated that it "hopes to establish a bridge of communication between the civil rights workers and moderate white local residents through its contacts with the local physicians, and through common concern with them for the health of ill or injured volunteers." Another general purpose, as stated by the Committee is "to provide an opportunity for physicians and nurses to serve in witness of their social and moral beliefs in relation to one of the most crucial issues of our time."

The Committee is under the leadership of Elliot Hurwitt, MD, Medical Director; Jerome Tobis, MD, New York Chairman, Executive Committee; and Leslie A. Falk, Pittsburgh Medical Administrator, all of whom have college age children in the COFO project. Prominent sponsors include, Kenneth Clement MD, Cleveland, Montague Cobb MD, Washington DC, Paul Cornely MD, Washington DC, Leo Davidoff MD, New York, James P. Dixon MD, Yellow Springs, Ohio, Alan Guttmacher MD, New York, Emile Holman MD, San Francisco, Louis Lasagna MD, Baltimore, Bernard Lown MD, Boston, John Madden MD, New York, Benjamin Spock MD, Cleveland, Joseph Stokes MD, Philadelphia, Albert Szent-Gyorgyi MD, Woods Hoel, Mass., Paul Dudley White MD, Boston.

The operational plans revolve around an effort to explore the readiness of practicing physicians and hospitals over the state to provide medical care for the volunteers. The committee is confident that most white physicians and most hospitals in the state will be willing to do so and hopes to have its personnel avoid providing medical treatment themselves.

Source: Medical Committee for Human Rights clippings, press releases, 1964–1965, 1967, Quentin Young papers, 1964–1975, Mss 880, Box 4, Folder 8, Wisconsin Historical Society Archives, Madison, Wisconsin.

8.6 FBI Flyer on Disappearance of Civil Rights Workers Andrew Goodman, James Earl Chaney, and Michael Henry Schwerner, 1964

The idea for a Freedom Summer in Mississippi in 1964 grew out of the experiences of the Freedom Vote in 1963. In 1964, voter registration efforts were on an even greater scale. SNCC recruited approximately 1,000 northern college students to assist with voter registration, many of them from white middle and upper class families. After training sessions designed to teach them what to expect in Mississippi – to the extent that was possible – the first group of students headed South. Just a week after their arrival, the disappearance of three young civil rights workers, two white New Yorkers, Andrew Goodman and Michael Schwerner, and black Mississippian James Chaney, underscored the very real and inherent dangers of civil rights activism in the state. Chaney, Goodman, and Schwerner were all affiliated with COFO through the Congress of Racial Equality (CORE). On the evening of 21 June, the three men traveled from Meridian to Longdale to speak with congregation members whose church had been burned down, one of the many intimidation tactics used by whites to discourage voter registration efforts. On the way back, they were pulled over on a traffic stop in Philadelphia. The three men were taken to the local jail and held a number of hours. Upon release, law enforcement officers and local citizens followed them out of the town. They were pulled over once again, but this time they were abducted and driven to another location where they were shot at close range and killed. Their bodies were buried in an earthen dam. Three days later their burnt-out vehicle was found near a swamp.

President Johnson ordered the FBI to investigate in what was initially deemed a missing persons case. It was not until six weeks later that the bodies were discovered. The murders of Chaney, Goodman, and Schwerner received national headlines and planted Freedom Summer firmly in the national consciousness. As some in the movement noted, it had taken the murder of two white northerners to wake up the rest of the country to what had been happening to black Mississippians for decades. The state refused to prosecute the alleged perpetrators of the crime, which included local members of the Ku Klux Klan and county and local law enforcement officers. In 1967, the federal government charged 18 people with civil rights violations, which led to seven convictions, but to only relatively minor sentences. Not until 2005, 41 years after the crime, was Edgar Ray Killen, a local Ku Klux Klan organizer, convicted on three counts of manslaughter and sentenced to 60 years in prison. In 2016, federal and state officials closed the case. Seemingly, Killen will remain the only person to be convicted for the deaths of the three civil rights workers to the full extent of the law.

Source: Poster of Missing Civil Rights Workers, 29 June 1964, https://www.gettyimages.
com/detail/news-photo/missing-persons-poster-displays-the-photographs-of-civil-news-
photo/515177726#/missing-persons-poster-displays-the-photographs-of-civil-rights-
picture-id515177726

8.7 Fannie Lou Hamer Testimony before Credentials Committee of the Democratic National Convention, 1964

Voter registration efforts in Mississippi focused on the goal of seating Mississippi Freedom Democratic Party (MFDP) delegates at the August 1964 Democratic Party National Convention held in Atlantic City, New Jersey. The MFDP insisted that the regular Mississippi Democratic Party delegation was illegitimate because of the electoral corruption that existed in the state. In the summer of 1964, COFO elected 64 MFDP delegates, 60 black and four white, who arrived in Atlantic City with hopes of being seated at the convention. The MFDP made its case to the convention's Credentials Committee on 22 August. One of the most powerful testimonies came from Fannie Lou Hamer, a sharecropper from Sunflower County and a founding member of the MFDP. Hamer spoke about conditions in Mississippi and the intimidation and violence that civil rights workers encountered there. The damning testimony was broadcast on live television to the nation. The Johnson administration hastily arranged its own televised presidential press conference to remove Hamer from the airwaves.

The Democratic Party, seeking to appease the MFDP, proposed a series of compromises. President Johnson was wary of seating the MFDP delegates over the Mississippi Democratic Party regulars since he did not want to widen the rifts in his party over civil rights. The MFDP was offered two seats at the convention, with its other delegates being given "at large" votes, meaning that they could vote but that they would not be recognized as members of the official Mississippi delegation. The MFDP rejected the offer: "We didn't come all this way for two seats," Hamer said. The MFDP delegation left Atlantic City disappointed, while Johnson was nominated as the Democratic Party's candidate in the 1964 presidential election.

Yet the regular Mississippi Democratic Party delegates did not take their seats either. They refused to swear a required loyalty oath to the Democratic Party since they intended to support the Republican Party's candidate Barry Goldwater in the presidential election, throwing their support behind his anti-civil rights platform. Moreover, as a result of the episode, the Democratic Party initiated reforms that meant at the 1968 Democratic National Convention the all-white regular Mississippi Democratic Party delegation was barred and MFDP delegates were seated. Still, the immediate response of the MFDP and other civil rights workers who had supported their cause in 1964 was one of disillusionment with the Democratic Party in particular and with the democratic process in general. Many began to question whether it was possible to achieve their goals through mainstream party politics at all.

Mr Chairman, and the Credentials Committee, my name is Mrs Fanny Lou Hamer, and I live at 626 East Lafayette Street, Ruleville, Mississippi, Sunflower County, the home of Senator James O. Eastland, and Senator Stennis.

It was the 31st of August in 1962 that 18 of us traveled 26 miles to the country courthouse in Indianola to try to register to try to become first-class citizens. We was met in Indianola by policemen, Highway Patrolmens and they only allowed two of us in to take the literacy test at the time.

After we had taken this test and started back to Ruleville, we was held up by the City Police and the State Highway Patrolmen and carried back to Indianola where the bus driver was charged that day with driving a bus the wrong color.

After we paid the fine among us, we continued on to Ruleville, and Reverend Jeff Sunny carried me four miles in the rural area to where I had worked as a timekeeper and sharecropper for 18 years. I was met there by my children, who told me that the plantation owner was angry because I had gone down to try to register. After they told me, my husband came, and said that the plantation owner was raising Cain because I had tried to register, and before he quit talking the plantation owner came, and said, "Fanny Lou, do you know – did Pap tell you what I said?"

And I said, "Yes, sir."

He said, "I mean that." He said, "If you don't go down and withdraw your registration, you will have to leave." [He] said, "Then if you go down and with-draw," he said, "you still might have to go because we are not ready for that in Mississippi."

And I addressed him and told him and said, "I didn't try to register for you. I tried to register for myself." I had to leave that same night.

On the 10th of September 1962, 16 bullets was fired into the home of Mr and Mrs Robert Tucker for me. That same night two girls were shot in Ruleville, Mississippi. Also Mr Joe McDonald's house was shot in.

And June the 9th, 1963, I had attended a voter registration workshop; was returning back to Mississippi. Ten of us was traveling by the Continental Trailway bus. When we got to Winona, Mississippi, which is Montgomery County, four of the people got off to use the washroom, and two of the people – to use the restaurant – two of the people wanted to use the washroom.

The four people that had gone in to use the restaurant was ordered out. During this time I was on the bus. But when I looked through the window and saw they had rushed out I got off of the bus to see what had happened. And one of the ladies said, "It was a State Highway Patrolman and a Chief of Police ordered us out."

I got back on the bus and one of the persons who had used the washroom got back on the bus, too. As soon as I was seated on the bus, I saw when they began to get the five people in a Highway Patrolman's car. I stepped off of the bus to see what was happening and somebody screamed from the car that the five workers was in, and said, "Get that one there." When I went to get in the car, when the man told me I was under arrest, he kicked me.

I was carried to the county jail and put in the booking room. They left some of the people in the booking room and began to place us in cells. I was placed in a cell with a young woman called Miss Ivesta Simpson. After I was placed in the cell I began to hear sounds of licks and screams, I could hear the sounds of licks and horrible screams. And I could hear somebody say, "Can you say, 'yes, sir,' nigger? Can you say 'yes, sir?'" And they would say other horrible names.

She would say, "Yes, I can say 'yes, sir.'"

"So, well, say it."

She said, "I don't know you well enough."

They beat her, I don't know how long. And after a while she began to pray, and asked God to have mercy on those people.

And it wasn't too long before three white men came to my cell. One of these men was a State Highway Patrolman and he asked me where I was from. I told him Ruleville and he said, "We are going to check this."

They left my cell and it wasn't too long before they came back. He said, "You are from Ruleville all right," and he used a curse word. And he said, "We are going to make you wish you was dead."

I was carried out of that cell into another cell where they had two Negro prisoners. The State Highway Patrolmen ordered the first Negro to take the blackjack. The first Negro prisoner ordered me, by orders from the State Highway Patrolman, for me to lay down on a bunk bed on my face. I laid on my face and the first Negro began to beat. I was beat by the first Negro until he was exhausted. I was holding my hands behind me at that time on my left side, because I suffered from polio when I was six years old.

After the first Negro had beat until he was exhausted, the State Highway Patrolman ordered the second Negro to take the blackjack. The second Negro began to beat and I began to work my feet, and the State Highway Patrolman ordered the first Negro who had beat me to sit on my feet – to keep me from working my feet. I began to scream and one white man got up and began to beat me in my head and tell me to hush.

One white man – my dress had worked up high – he walked over and pulled my dress – I pulled my dress down and he pulled my dress back up.

I was in jail when Medgar Evers was murdered.

All of this is on account of we want to register, to become first-class citizens. And if the Freedom Democratic Party is not seated now, I question America. Is this America, the land of the free and the home of the brave, where we have to sleep with our telephones off the hooks because our lives be threatened daily, because we want to live as decent human beings, in America?

Thank you.

Source: Fannie Lou Hamer testimony before Credentials Committee of the Democratic National Convention, 22 August 1964, Atlantic City, New Jersey, http://americanradioworks. publicradio.org/features/sayitplain/flhamer.html

Discussion Questions

1. Compile and analyze a list of obstacles that blacks faced in casting their votes in Mississippi. In what ways could these obstacles be overcome?
2. Assess the significance of the Freedom Schools and the Medical Committee for Human Rights in the 1964 Freedom Summer.
3. Should the MFDP have accepted the compromise offer of two seats at the 1964 Democratic National Convention? Outline the arguments for and against doing so.

Further Reading

Andrews, Kenneth T. *Freedom is a Constant Struggle: The Mississippi Civil Rights Movement and Its Legacy* (University of Chicago Press, 2004).

Cagin, Seth, and Philip Dray. *We are not Afraid: The Story of Goodman, Schwerner and Chaney and the Civil Rights Campaign for Mississippi* (Macmillan, 1988).

Crosby, Emilye. *A Little Taste of Freedom: The Black Freedom Struggle in Claiborne County, Mississippi* (University of North Carolina Press, 2005).

Dittmer, John. *Local People: The Struggle for Civil Rights in Mississippi* (University of Illinois Press, 1994).

Dittmer, John. *The Good Doctors: The Medical Committee for Human Rights and the Struggle for Social Justice in Health Care* (Bloomsbury Press, 2009).

Hale, Jon N. *The Freedom Schools: Student Activists in the Mississippi Civil Rights Movement* (Columbia University Press, 2016).

Harwell, Debbie Z. *Wednesdays in Mississippi: Proper Ladies Working for Radical Change, Freedom Summer 1964* (University Press of Mississippi, 2014).

King, Mary. *Freedom Song: A Personal Story of the 1960s Civil Rights Movement* (William Morrow, 1987).

Lee, Chana Kai. *For Freedom's Sake: The Life of Fannie Lou Hamer* (University of Illinois Press, 1999).

Loevy, Robert D. *To End All Segregation: The Politics of the Passage of the Civil Rights Act of 1964* (University Press of America, 1990).

[Lorenzi] Sojourner, Sue, with Cheryl Reitan. *Thunder of Freedom: Black Leadership and the Transformation of 1960s Mississippi* (University Press of Kentucky, 2013).

Moye, J. Todd. *Let the People Decide: Black Freedom and White Resistance Movements in Sunflower County, Mississippi, 1945–1986* (University of North Carolina Press, 2004).

Payne, Charles. *I've Got the Light of Freedom: The Organizing Tradition and the Mississippi Freedom Struggle* (University of California Press, 1995).

Sanders, Crystal R. *A Chance for Change: Head Start and Mississippi's Black Freedom Struggle* (University of North Carolina Press, 2016).

Todd, Lisa Anderson. *For a Voice and the Vote: My Journey with the Mississippi Freedom Democratic Party* (University of Kentucky, 2015).

Chapter 9   The Selma Campaign and the Voting Rights Act of 1965

9.1 William C. Sullivan (Anonymous), Letter to Martin Luther King, Jr, 1964

Just as Martin Luther King, Jr and the Southern Christian Leadership Conference (SCLC) had used the 1963 Birmingham campaign to highlight the brutality of segregation and to place pressure on the federal government to pass desegregation legislation, in 1965 they used the Selma campaign to highlight the brutality of disenfranchisement and to place pressure on the federal government to pass legislation to enforce and strengthen black voting rights. In Selma, approximately half the population was black, but 99% of registered voters were white. In contrast to the long-term grassroots community organizing model of the Student Nonviolent Coordinating Committee (SNCC), King and the SCLC's trademark was the short-term community mobilization model that sought to bring about dramatic conflict and a federal response. In no small part, this approach was driven by the resources that King and the SCLC had at their disposal. Without SNCC's cadre of student volunteers, with limited funds, and with King's national standing as its greatest asset, the SCLC saw its short-term, intense burst of activism campaigns as its most effective instrument for change.

The increasing efforts by the federal government to prevent such campaigns from taking place were testimony to their effectiveness. The FBI in particular took an interest in King's activities. FBI director J. Edgar Hoover early on decided that King was "no good" and made a number of public criticisms about him. With the approval of Attorney General Robert Kennedy, the FBI began wiretapping King's phones. Then, moving beyond their legal mandate, they began planting illegal bugging devices in King's hotel rooms. In November 1964, the white FBI assistant director William C. Sullivan sent a taped

The Civil Rights Movement: A Documentary Reader, First Edition. Edited by John A. Kirk.
© 2020 John Wiley & Sons, Inc. Published 2020 by John Wiley & Sons, Inc.

collection of such illicitly obtained recordings that allegedly contained dirty jokes, bawdy remarks, and the sound of people engaging in sexual intercourse, to SCLC headquarters. The letter that accompanied it, below, appeared to ask King to commit suicide or to withdraw from public life to prevent him from being exposed as a "fraud." The move seems to have been an attempt to prevent the Selma campaign from taking place. The package finally made it to King's home address in early January 1965, where King's wife, Coretta Scott King, listened to the tape. She dismissed its contents as "just a lot of mumbo jumbo." A 1977 lawsuit by one of King's associates led to a court decision to seal the contents of the recordings until 2027.

KING,

In view of your low grade ... I will not dignify your name with either a Mr or a Reverend or a Dr. and, your last name calls to mind only the type of King such as King Henry the VIII ...

King, look into your heart. You know you are a complete fraud and a great liability to all of us Negroes. White people in this country have enough frauds of their own but I am sure they don't have one at this time anywhere near your equal. You are no clergyman and you know it. I repeat you are a colossal fraud and an evil, vicious one at that. You could not believe in God ... Clearly you don't believe in any personal moral principles.

King, like all frauds your end is approaching. You could have been our greatest leader. You, even at an early age have turned out to be not a leader but a dissolute, abnormal moral imbecile. We will now have to depend on our older leaders like Wilkins, a man of character and thank God we have others like him. But you are done. Your "honorary" degrees, your Nobel Prize (what a grim farce) and other awards will not save you. King, I repeat you are done.

No person can overcome facts, not even a fraud like yourself ... I repeat – no person can argue successfully against facts ... Satan could not do more. What incredible evilness ... King you are done.

The American public, the church organizations that have been helping – Protestant, Catholic and Jews will know you for what you are – an evil, abnormal beast. So will others who have backed you. You are done.

King, there is only one thing left for you to do. You know what it is. You have just 34 days in which to do it (this exact number has been selected for a specific reason, it has definite practical significant [sic]). You are done. There is but one way out for you. You better take it before your filthy, abnormal fraudulent self is bared to the nation.

Source: David J. Garrow, *The FBI and Martin Luther King, Jr: From Solo to Memphis* (New York: W.W. Norton and Co., 1981), pp. 125–6.

9.2 Martin Luther King, Jr, "Letter from a Selma, Alabama, Jail," 1965

In concert with local organizations including the Dallas County Voters League (the county in which Selma was located) and the Dallas County Improvement Association, as well as SNCC, which was already working in the city, King and the SCLC made attempts to register black voters at the county courthouse. Sheriff James G. Clark, who became Selma's equivalent to Birmingham's public safety commissioner Connor in his actions, rough handled and arrested demonstrators. Demonstrations continued, and federal district judge Daniel H. Thomas issued a temporary restraining order against Selma and Dallas County law officials from impeding black voter registration. This did not deter Sheriff Clark and his men from using further heavy-handed policing methods. SCLC staff members felt the time had come to have King submit to arrest to bring the campaign to wider public attention.

On 1 February, King was arrested along with 260 other demonstrators. From his jail cell, King reprised his earlier "Letter from Birmingham City Jail," this time from Selma. King's letter from Selma underscored just how far he and the movement had come over a short period of time. Now, King could write with the authority of a Nobel Peace Prize winner (he accepted the award as the prize's youngest ever recipient in Oslo, Norway in December 1964), get his letter published in the New York Times, *and bring not just national, but international attention to the civil rights movement.*

The demonstrations in Selma began to spread to adjoining counties. The courts issued further orders to help black voter registration and to stop police harassment. President Johnson issued a strong public statement of support. This left the movement in a quandary: should it ease off with demonstrations and give a chance to the new measures put in place by the courts to work, or should it further intensify its efforts to gain more concessions? King insisted, learning from past campaigns, that the momentum should not be lost and that demonstrations should continue. However, as the clashes between police and demonstrators grew more violent in Selma, movement leaders agreed that the locus of protests should begin to shift to the surrounding counties.

On 26 February, in Marion, Perry County, a state trooper shot and killed young black demonstrator Jimmie Lee Jackson. In an effort to quell the escalating violence while still providing an outlet for blacks to vent their frustration, King suggested organizing a mass motorcade to drive from Selma to Montgomery in protest. Later, at the suggestion of local Marion woman Lucy Foster, King and the SCLC decided that movement participants should walk the route from Selma to Montgomery on Sunday, 7 March.

February 1, 1965.

Dear Friends:

When the King of Norway participated in awarding the Nobel Peace Prize to me he surely did not think that in less than sixty days I would be in jail. He, and almost all world opinion will be shocked because they are little aware of the unfinished business in the South.

By jailing hundreds of Negroes, the city of Selma, Alabama, has revealed the persisting ugliness of segregation to the nation and the world. When the Civil Rights Act of 1964 was passed many decent Americans were lulled into complacency because they thought the day of difficult struggle was over.

Why are we in jail? Have you ever been required to answer 100 questions on government, some abstruse even to a political scientist specialist, merely to vote? Have you ever stood in line with over a hundred others and after waiting an entire day seen less than ten given the qualifying test?

THIS IS SELMA, ALABAMA. THERE ARE MORE NEGROES IN JAIL WITH ME THAN THERE ARE ON THE VOTING ROLLS.

But apart from voting rights, merely to be a person in Selma is not easy. When reporters asked Sheriff Clark if a woman defendant was married, he replied, "She's a nigger woman and she hasn't got a Miss or a Mrs in front of her name."

This is the USA in 1965. We are in jail simply because we cannot tolerate these conditions for ourselves or our nation.

We need the help of all decent Americans. Our organization, SCLC, is not only working in Selma, Ala., but in dozens of other Southern communities. Our self-help projects operate in South Carolina, Georgia, Louisiana, Mississippi and other states. Our people are eager to work, to sacrifice, to be jailed – but their income, normally meager, is cut off in these crises. Your help can make the difference. Your help can be a message of unity which the thickest jail walls cannot muffle. With warmest good wishes from all of us.

Sincerely,
MARTIN LUTHER KING, JR

Source: *New York Times*, 5 February 1965, p. 5.

9.3 John Lewis Recalls the Events of "Bloody Sunday" in 1965

The call for a Selma-to-Montgomery march was an inspired moment of movement symbolism but a logistical nightmare. Taking a group of mainly black demonstrators on a 54-mile hike through rural racist counties was both a hazardous and arduous undertaking. Understanding that the symbolism of the march was the most important thing, movement organizers realistically expected little more than to march out of Selma over the Edmund Pettus Bridge for a short distance before being turned back. They would then return to continue the march the following day. There were doubts about whether the march would even make it that far. Knowing how hastily the march had been put together, Alabama governor George Wallace and his aides initially considered calling the movement's bluff and allowing the march to proceed in hopes that it would prove a failure. On second thoughts, they agreed that this was too risky. The very real prospect of serious violence, they believed, would only bring more unwelcome attention to the state. Wallace ordered state troopers to turn back marchers before they could leave Selma.

With the ball back in the movement's court, there were decisions to make. SNCC opposed the march, arguing that it would put local people in harm's way for nothing more than a publicity stunt. The SCLC meanwhile pondered the wisdom of King's participation in the march. Direct threats against King's life were being made and his arrest potentially removed him from events at a critical moment when he could be an effective national lobbyist with the president. The SCLC agreed the march should go ahead, but without King's presence. On the day of the march, 600 movement supporters gathered at Selma's Brown Chapel. State troopers had already been deployed at Edmund Pettus Bridge to prevent the march from leaving Selma. SCLC staff drew lots to see who would lead the march in King's absence. Hosea Williams won the dubious honor. Williams led the march alongside SNCC chair John Lewis who, despite SNCC's reservations about the march, felt a personal responsibility to participate. The marchers wound through Selma's streets before heading to Edmund Pettus Bridge. Below, Lewis recalls what happened next.

When I reached the crest of the bridge, I stopped dead still.

So did Hosea.

There, facing us at the bottom of the other side, stood a sea of blue-helmeted, blue-uniformed Alabama state troopers, line after line of them, dozens of battle-ready lawmen stretched from one side of US Highway 80 to the other.

Behind them were several dozen more armed men – Sheriff Clark's posse – some on horseback, all wearing khaki clothing, many carrying clubs the size of baseball bats.

On one side of the road I could see a crowd of about a hundred whites, laughing and hollering, waving Confederate flags. Beyond them, at a safe distance, stood a small, silent group of black people.

I could see a crowd of newsmen and reporters gathered in the parking lot of a Pontiac dealership. And I could see a line of parked police and state trooper vehicles. I didn't know it at the time, but Clark and Lingo were in one of those cars.

It was a drop of one hundred feet from the top of that bridge to the river below. Hosea glanced down at the muddy water and said, "Can you swim?"

"No," I answered.

"Well," he said, with a tiny half smile, "neither can I."

"But," he added, lifting his head and looking straight ahead, "we might have to."

Then we moved forward. The only sounds were our footsteps on the bridge and the snorting of a horse ahead of us.

I noticed several troopers slipping gas masks over their faces as we approached.

At the bottom of the bridge, while we were still about fifty feet from the troopers, the officer in charge, a Major John Cloud, stepped forward, holding a small bullhorn up to his mouth.

Hosea and I stopped, which brought the others to a standstill.

"*This is an unlawful assembly,*" Cloud pronounced. "*Your march is not conducive to public safety. You are ordered to go back to your church or to your homes.*"

"May we have a word with the major?" asked Hosea.

"*There is no word to be had,*" answered Cloud.

Hosea asked the same question again, and got the same response.

Then Cloud issued a warning: "*You have two minutes to turn around and go back to your church.*"

I wasn't about to turn around. We were there. We were not going to run. We couldn't turn and go back if we wanted to. There were too many people.

We could have gone forward, marching right into the teeth of those troopers. But that would have been too aggressive, I thought, too provocative. God knew what might have happened if we had done that. These people were ready to be arrested, but I didn't want anyone to get hurt.

We couldn't go forward. We couldn't go back. There was only one option left that I could see.

"We should kneel and pray," I said to Hosea.

He nodded.

We turned and passed the word back to begin bowing down in a prayerful manner.

But that word didn't get far. It didn't have time. One minute after he had issued his warning – I know this because I was careful to check my watch – Major Cloud issued an order to his troopers.

"*Troopers,*" he barked. "*Advance!*"

And then all hell broke loose.

Source: John Lewis, with Michael D'Orso, *Walking with the Wind: A Memoir of the Movement* (New York: Simon and Schuster, 1998), pp. 326–7.

9.4 Sheyann Webb Recalls the Events of "Bloody Sunday" in 1965

Eight-year-old Sheyann Webb, who King described as his "smallest freedom fighter" in Selma, was one of the marchers on Edmund Pettus Bridge when, as John Lewis put it, "all hell broke loose." The state troopers, some on horseback, advanced on the marchers with billy clubs, tear gas, and bull whips. They plowed into the marchers to drive them back across the bridge. In a scene of carnage, Hosea Williams picked up Sheyann and carried her to safety. Major John Cloud's

men forced the marchers right back to Brown Chapel, located in the heart of
Selma's black community. The white invasion of the black neighborhood brought
black residents out into the streets. Most of the black residents were not involved
with the local movement or trained in nonviolence. They were armed and ready to
defend their neighborhood. Fearing a bloodbath, the SCLC's Andrew Young did his
best to persuade black residents to get out of the streets. By the time the conflict
ended there were over 70 hospitalizations for various wounds and injuries
including a suspected fractured skull for John Lewis.

All I knew is I heard all this screaming and the people were turning and I saw
this first part of the line running and stumbling back toward us. At that point, I
was just off the bridge and on the side of the highway. And they came running
and some of them were crying out and somebody yelled, "Oh, God, they're killing us!" I think I just froze then. There were people everywhere, jamming against
me, pushing against me. Then, all of a sudden, it stopped and everyone got
down on their knees, and I did too, and somebody was saying for us to pray. But
there was so much excitement it never got started, because everybody was talking and they were scared and we didn't know what was happening or was going
to happen. I remember looking toward the troopers and they were backing up,
but some of them were standing over some of our people who had been knocked
down or had fallen. It seemed like just a few seconds went by and I heard a
shout. "Gas! Gas!" And everybody started screaming again. And I looked and I
saw the troopers charging us again and some of them were swinging their arms
and throwing canisters of tear gas. And beyond them I saw the horsemen starting their charge toward us. I was terrified. What happened then is something I'll
never forget as long as I live. Never. In fact, I still dream about it sometimes.

I saw those horsemen coming toward me and they had those awful masks on;
they rode right through the cloud of tear gas. Some of them had clubs, others had
ropes or whips, which they swung about them like they were driving cattle.

I'll tell you, I forgot about praying, and I just turned and ran. And just as I
was turning the tear gas got me; it burned my nose first and then got my eyes.
I was blinded by the tears. So I began running and not seeing where I was
going. I remember being scared that I might fall over the railing and into the
water. I don't know if I was screaming or not, but everyone else was. People
were running and falling and ducking and you could hear the horses' hooves
on the pavement and you'd hear people scream and hear the whips swishing
and you'd hear them striking people. They'd cry out; some moaned. Women as
well as men were getting hit. I never got hit, but one of the horses went right by
me and I heard the swish sound as the whip went over my head and cracked
some man across the back. It seemed to take forever to get across the bridge. It
seemed I was running up the hill for an awfully long time. They kept rolling
canisters of tear gas on the ground, so it would rise up quickly. It was making

me sick. I heard more horses and I turned back and saw two of them and the riders were leaning over to one side. It was like a nightmare seeing it through the tears. I just knew then I was going to die, and those horses were going to trample me. So I kind of knelt down and held my hands and arms up over my head, and I must have been screaming – I don't really remember.

All of a sudden somebody was grabbing me under the arms and lifting me and running. The horses went by and I kept waiting to get trampled on or hit, but they went on by and I guess they were hitting at somebody else. And I looked up and I saw it was Hosea Williams who had me and he was running but we didn't seem to be moving, and I kept kicking my legs in the air, trying to speed up, and I shouted at him, "Put me down! You can't run fast enough with me!"

But he held on until we were off the bridge and down on Broad Street and he let me go. I didn't stop running until I got home. All along the way there were people running in small groups; I saw people jumping over cars and being chased by the horsemen who kept hitting them. When I got to the apartments there were horsemen in the yards, galloping up and down, and one of them reared his horse up in the air as I went by, and he had his mask off and was shouting something at me.

When I got into the house my momma and daddy were there and they had this shocked look on their faces and I ran in and tried to tell them what had happened. I was maybe a little hysterical because I kept repeating over and over, "I can't stop shaking, Momma, I can't stop shaking," and finally she grabbed me and sat down with me on her lap. But my daddy was like I'd never seen him before. He had a shotgun and he yelled, "By God, if they want it this way, I'll give it to them!" And he started out the door. Momma jumped up and got in front of him shouting at him. And he said, "I'm ready to die; I mean it! I'm ready to die!" I was crying there on the couch, I was so scared. But finally he put the gun aside and sat down. I remember just lying there on the couch, crying and feeling so disgusted. They had beaten us like we were slaves.

Source: Sheyann Webb and Rachel West Nelson (as told to Frank Sikora), from *Selma, Lord, Selma: Girlhood Memories of the Civil Rights Days* (Tuscaloosa: University of Alabama Press, 1980), pp. 95–8.

9.5 Associated Press, An Officer Accosts an Unconscious Woman as Mounted Police Officers Attack Civil Rights Marchers in Selma, Alabama, 1965

Television coverage of events on "Bloody Sunday" made sensational viewing for the nation that evening. The American Broadcasting Company interrupted its feature film about Nazi war criminals, Judgement at Nuremberg, *to show what was happening in Selma. The juxtaposition was a poignant and striking one. The photographs of events in Selma that appeared on the front pages of newspapers the following morning reinforced the national outrage at events. Once more, just as they had done in Birmingham, King and the SCLC had found a way to dramatize the issues in the campaign, to capture national attention and sympathy, and to spur federal action. Condemnation of events in Selma echoed around the country and in Congress. President Johnson's attorney general Nicholas Katzenbach later informed Selma's director of public safety Wilson Baker that "You people [in Selma] passed t[he 1965 Voting Rights Act] on that bridge that Sunday."*

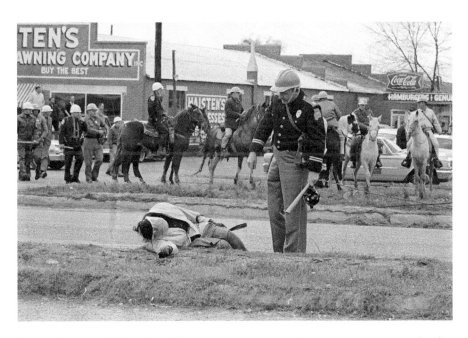

Source: Associated Press, An officer accosts an unconscious woman as mounted police officers attack civil rights marchers in Selma, Alabama in 1965, https://www.gettyimages. com/detail/news-photo/an-officer-accosts-an-unconscious-woman-as-mounted-police-news-photo/514702546#/an-officer-accosts-an-unconscious-woman-as-mounted-police-officers-picture-id514702546

9.6 President Lyndon B. Johnson Addresses Congress on Voting Rights, 1965

Martin Luther King, Jr watched the events of "Bloody Sunday" unfold with pangs of guilt that he was not there to lead the march. King encouraged movement supporters to make their feelings about events known to the president and to Congress and he called upon them to converge on Selma for a second attempt to march to Montgomery the following Tuesday. When King arrived in Selma on Monday in advance of the second march, he discovered that federal judge Frank M. Johnson, Jr wanted the march delayed so that the judge could hold hearings to issue a restraining order against interference with it. Although King did not want to break a federal court order, he decided that the march must proceed as planned. President Johnson sent envoys to Selma to broker an agreement. King agreed to a compromise: the marchers would head to Edmund Pettus Bridge, confront state troopers, but then turn around and head back to Brown Chapel to wait for Judge Johnson's restraining order to be handed down. King hoped this would appease those in the movement calling for the march to take place and those in the federal government calling for its postponement. Adding a further complication, Judge Johnson subsequently issued an order explicitly banning the march.

King nevertheless proceeded to lead 2,000 marchers, black and white, who had traveled to Selma from all over the country, to Edmund Pettus Bridge. As arranged, they marched toward the state troopers. King then kneeled and prayed, before turning the march around and leading it back to Brown Chapel. That night, the Selma campaign suffered its second fatality when white Boston minister Rev. James B. Reeb was attacked and beaten by local white segregationists. Amid the growing tensions, just as President Kennedy had done in the Birmingham campaign, President Johnson appeared on television. This time, it was in a televised address to Congress to proclaim his support for the civil rights movement. Johnson powerfully appropriated the refrain from what had become one of the movement's signature songs, telling Congress "We Shall Overcome." Watching the speech and hearing those words moved King to tears. Selma's Mayor Smitherman reacted very differently. "When he said 'We Shall Overcome' it was just as though somebody had just stuck a knife in your heart," Smitherman said. Like many other white southerners he felt that, "it's over with now [...] our President's sold us out." In his address, Johnson announced that he would introduce a bill to end the widespread disenfranchisement of blacks in the South.

The Constitution says that no person shall be kept from voting because of his race or his color. We have all sworn an oath before God to support and to defend that Constitution. We must now act in obedience to that oath.

Wednesday I will send to Congress a law designed to eliminate illegal barriers to the right to vote.

The broad principles of that bill will be in the hands of the Democratic and Republican leaders tomorrow. After they have reviewed it, it will come here formally as a bill. I am grateful for this opportunity to come here tonight at the invitation of the leadership to reason with my friends, to give them my views, and to visit with my former colleagues.

I have had prepared a more comprehensive analysis of the legislation which I had intended to transmit to the clerk tomorrow but which I will submit to the clerks tonight. But I want to really discuss with you, now, briefly the main proposals of this legislation.

This bill will strike down restrictions to voting in all elections: Federal, State, and local, which have been used to deny Negroes the right to vote.

This bill will establish a simple, uniform standard which cannot be used, however ingeneous the effort, to flout our Constitution.

It will provide for citizens to be registered by officials of the United States Government, if the State officials refuse to register them.

It will eliminate tedious, unnecessary lawsuits which delay the right to vote.

Finally this legislation will ensure that properly registered individuals are not prohibited from voting.

I will welcome the suggestions from all the Members of Congress – I have no doubt that I will get some – on ways and means to strengthen this law and to make it effective. But experience has plainly shown that this is the only path to carry out the command of the Constitution.

To those who seek to avoid action by their National Government in their own communities, who want to and who seek to maintain purely local control over elections, the answer is simple: open your polling places to all your people.

Allow men and women to register and vote whatever the color of their skin.

Extend the rights of citizenship to every citizen of this land.

There is no constitutional issue here. The command of the Constitution is plain.

There is no moral issue. It is wrong, deadly wrong, to deny any of your fellow Americans the right to vote in this country.

There is no issue of States rights or national rights. There is only the struggle for human rights.

I have not the slightest doubt what will be your answer.

But the last time a President sent a civil rights bill to the Congress, it contained a provision to protect voting rights in Federal elections. That civil rights bill was passed after eight long months of debate. And when that bill came to my desk from the Congress for my signature, the heart of the voting provision had been eliminated.

This time, on this issue, there must be no delay, or no hesitation or no compromise with our purpose.

We cannot, we must not, refuse to protect the right of every American to vote in every election that he may desire to participate in. And we ought not and we cannot and we must not wait another eight months before we get a bill. We have already waited a hundred years and more, and the time for waiting is gone.

So I ask you to join me in working long hours – nights and weekends, if necessary – to pass this bill. And I don't make that request lightly. For from the window where I sit with the problems of our country, I recognize that from outside this chamber is the outraged conscience of a nation, the grave concern of many nations, and the harsh judgment of history on our acts.

But even if we pass this bill, the battle will not be over. What happened in Selma is part of a far larger movement which reaches into every section and state of America. It is the effort of American Negroes to secure for themselves the full blessings of American life.

Their cause must be our cause too. Because it's not just Negroes, but really it's all of us, who must overcome the crippling legacy of bigotry and injustice.

And we shall overcome.

Source: Lyndon B. Johnson Presidential Library, http://www.lbjlibrary.org/lyndon-baines-johnson/speeches-films/president-johnsons-special-message-to-the-congress-the-american-promise/

9.7 US Congress, Voting Rights Act of 1965

On Wednesday, 17 March, two days after his address to Congress, President Johnson introduced his promised voting rights bill. Amendment Twenty-Four to the US Constitution had abolished the use of a poll tax in federal elections in 1964. The bill's central proposal was to provide the attorney general with the power to cancel all literacy and voting rights tests and to appoint federal registrars to actively assist black voters. This applied to all areas where less than 50% of the population had been registered voters, or where less than 50% of the population had actually cast ballots in the previous presidential election. The formula covered Alabama, Georgia, Louisiana, Mississippi, North Carolina, South Carolina, and Virginia, although it left out Arkansas, Florida, Tennessee, and Texas. The bill met with swift action in the Senate, but in an indication of the still entrenched power of the southern states in the House of Representatives, and their ability to forestall action from being taken, the bill did not become law until August 1965.

Following the introduction of the bill, the civil rights movement kept pressure on Congress to pass legislation by making plans to finally complete the Selma-to-Montgomery march, beginning Sunday, 21 March. President Johnson issued an executive order federalizing 1,800 members of the Alabama National Guard to protect the marchers; he also sent federal troops, federal marshals, and the FBI. Deputy Attorney General Ramsey Clark was placed in charge of coordinating federal operations on the ground. The march took place peacefully and culminated on Thursday, 25 March, on the steps of Alabama's state capitol building in Montgomery, not far from where King's former church, Dexter Avenue Baptist, was located. King gave a rousing speech that rounded off what many historians have viewed as King's and the SCLC's most successful campaign. A voting rights bill was in Congress, the president had placed his firm support behind the civil rights movement, and thousands of people nationwide, both black and white, had traveled to Selma in support.

Finally, it seemed, the nation had embraced the legitimacy and goals of the movement. Even at that high point, the work that still remained to be done was evident. The day witnessed the third fatality of the campaign when white Detroit housewife Viola Gregg Liuzzo was shot and killed by Ku Klux Klan members in

Lowndes County as she ferried movement workers back to Selma from Montgomery.

The Voting Rights Act of 1965 is a long and complex document. The below extracts indicate some of its key features. Section 2 sought to provide a comprehensive definition of what constituted a denial of voting rights. Section 3 (c) permitted an extension of the coverage of the act to "bail in" jurisdictions subsequently found in violation of its provisions. Section 4 (a) allowed jurisdictions covered by the act to "bail out" of the act's provisions by demonstrating that they had not used any disenfranchisement devices for over five years as determined by a three-judge panel. Section 4 (b) outlines the original "coverage formula" that determined which jurisdictions fell under the act. Section 5 required federal "preclearance" for jurisdictions covered by the Voting Rights Act before they could make any changes to their election laws.

AN ACT To enforce the fifteenth amendment to the Constitution of the United States, and for other purposes.

Be it enacted by the Senate and House of Representatives of the United States of America in Congress assembled, That this Act shall be known as the "Voting Rights Act of 1965."

[...]

SEC. 2. No voting qualification or prerequisite to voting, or standard, practice, or procedure shall be imposed or applied by any State or political subdivision to deny or abridge the right of any citizen of the United States to vote on account of race or color.

[...]

SEC. 3. (c) If in any proceeding instituted by the Attorney General under any statute to enforce the guarantees of the fifteenth amendment in any State or political subdivision the court finds that violations of the fifteenth amendment justifying equitable relief have occurred within the territory of such State or political subdivision, the court, in addition to such relief as it may grant, shall retain jurisdiction for such period as it may deem appropriate and during such period no voting qualification or prerequisite to voting, or standard, practice, or procedure with respect to voting different from that in force or effect at the time the proceeding was commenced shall be enforced unless and until the court finds that such qualification, prerequisite, standard, practice, or procedure does not have the purpose and will not have the effect of denying or abridging the right to vote on account of race or color: Provided, That such qualification, prerequisite, standard, practice, or procedure may be enforced if the qualification, prerequisite, standard, practice, or procedure has been submitted by the chief legal officer or other appropriate official of such State or subdivision to the Attorney General and the Attorney General has not interposed an objection within sixty days after such submission, except that neither the court's finding nor the Attorney General's failure to object shall bar a subsequent action to enjoin enforcement of such qualification, prerequisite, standard, practice, or procedure.

[...]

SEC. 4. (a) To assure that the right of citizens of the United States to vote is not denied or abridged on account of race or color, no citizen shall be denied the right to vote in any Federal, State, or local election because of his failure to comply with any test or device in any State with respect to which the determinations have been made under subsection (b) or in any political subdivision with respect to which such determinations have been made as a separate unit, unless the United States District Court for the District of Columbia in an action for a declaratory judgment brought by such State or subdivision against the United States has determined that no such test or device has been used during the five years preceding the filing of the action for the purpose or with the effect of denying or abridging the right to vote on account of race or color: Provided, That no such declaratory judgment shall issue with respect to any plaintiff for a period of five years after the entry of a final judgment of any court of the United States, other than the denial of a declaratory judgment under this section, whether entered prior to or after the enactment of this Act, determining that denials or abridgments of the right to vote on account of race or color through the use of such tests or devices have occurred anywhere in the territory of such plaintiff. An action pursuant to this subsection shall be heard and determined by a court of three judges in accordance with the provisions of section 2284 of title 28 of the United States Code and any appeal shall lie to the Supreme Court. The court shall retain jurisdiction of any action pursuant to this subsection for five years after judgment and shall reopen the action upon motion of the Attorney General alleging that a test or device has been used for the purpose or with the effect of denying or abridging the right to vote on account of race or color.

SEC. 4. (b) The provisions of subsection (a) shall apply in any State or in any political subdivision of a state which (1) the Attorney General determines maintained on November 1, 1964, any test or device, and with respect to which (2) the Director of the Census determines that less than 50 percentum of the persons of voting age residing therein were registered on November 1, 1964, or that less than 50 percentum of such persons voted in the presidential election of November 1964.

A determination or certification of the Attorney General or of the Director of the Census under this section or under section 6 or section 13 shall not be reviewable in any court and shall be effective upon publication in the Federal Register.

[...]

SEC. 5. Whenever a State or political subdivision with respect to which the prohibitions set forth in section 4(a) are in effect shall enact or seek to administer any voting qualification or prerequisite to voting, or standard, practice, or procedure with respect to voting different from that in force or effect on November 1, 1964, such State or subdivision may institute an action in the United States District Court for the District of Columbia for a declaratory judgment that such qualification, prerequisite, standard, practice, or procedure does not have the purpose and will not have the effect of denying or abridging the right to vote on account of race or color, and unless and until the court enters such judgment no person shall be denied the right to vote for failure to comply with such qualification, prerequisite, standard, practice, or procedure: Provided, That such qualification, prerequisite, standard, practice, or procedure may be enforced without such proceeding if the qualification, prerequisite, standard, practice, or procedure has been submitted by the chief legal officer or other appropriate official of such State or subdivision to the Attorney General and the Attorney General has not interposed an objection within sixty days after such submission, except that neither the Attorney General's failure to object nor a declaratory judgment entered under this section shall bar a subsequent action to enjoin enforcement of such qualification, prerequisite, standard, practice, or procedure. Any action under this section shall be heard and determined by a court of three judges in accordance with the provisions of section 2284 of title 28 of the United States Code and any appeal shall lie to the Supreme Court.

Approved August 6, 1965.

Source: US Congress, Voting Rights Act of 1965, http://www.ourdocuments.gov/doc. php?doc=100&page=transcript

Discussion Questions

1. What does the Selma campaign tell us about the advantages and disadvantages of Martin Luther King, Jr's prominent national profile in the civil rights movement?

2. Why did King choose to defy a federal court order to hold a second march from Selma to Montgomery? Was he right to do so?
3. Assess the significance of President Lyndon B. Johnson's use of the movement's refrain "We Shall Overcome" in his remarks to Congress.

Further Reading

Combs, Barbara Harris. *From Selma to Montgomery: The Long March to Freedom* (Routledge, 2014).

Ellis, Sylvia. *Freedom's Pragmatist: Lyndon Johnson and Civil Rights* (University Press of Florida, 2013).

Garrow, David J. *Protest at Selma: Martin Luther King, Jr, and the Voting Rights Act of 1965* (Yale University Press, 1978).

Garrow, David J. *The FBI and Martin Luther King, Jr: From "Solo" to Memphis* (W.W. Norton, 1981).

Lawson, Steven F. *Black Ballots: Voting Rights in the South, 1944–1969* (Columbia University Press, 1976).

May, Gary. *Bending toward Justice: The Voting Rights Act and the Transformation of American Democracy* (Basic Books, 2013).

O'Reilly, Kenneth. *Racial Matters: The FBI's Secret File on Black America, 1960–1972* (Free Press, 1989).

Stanton, Mary. *From Selma to Sorrow: The Life and Death of Viola Liuzzo* (University of Georgia Press, 1998).

Thornton, J. Mills. *Dividing Lines: Municipal Politics and the Struggle for Civil Rights in Montgomery, Birmingham, and Selma* (University of Alabama Press, 2002).

Webb, Sheyann, and Rachel West Nelson. *Selma, Lord, Selma: Girlhood Memories of the Civil Rights Days* (University of Alabama Press, 1980).

Chapter 10   The Civil Rights Movement outside the South, 1965–75

10.1   Bayard Rustin, "From Protest to Politics," 1965

The passage of the Voting Rights Act of 1965 was a turning point of sorts for the civil rights movement. Along with the Civil Rights Act of 1964, it had helped achieve two of the southern movement's most prominent goals: desegregation and voting rights. Yet essentially, these two pieces of legislation only upheld the almost 100-year-old promises of the Fourteenth and Fifteenth Amendments. Neither piece of legislation eradicated the pervasive racism that existed in American society, nor did they tackle the actual consequences of justice long deferred. Housing discrimination, employment discrimination, still segregated schools, and the policing of the black community, were just some of the issues that the civil rights movement continued to face. How should the movement go about addressing these and other issues? Was it simply a matter of continuing the movement as it had unfolded in the past few years, or did new points of focus require new approaches? And how would whites respond to the changes that had, and continued, to occur? These questions occupied movement activists after 1965 and provoked a range of different answers and responses.

In his perceptive piece below, Bayard Rustin argued that the time had come to move from "protest to politics." Acknowledging the important sacrifices that had already been made to get the country to live up to its basic constitutional promises, Rustin conceded that in many ways the movement's achievements since 1954 had hit racial discrimination in the areas it was least defensible and most vulnerable, and mainly in the southern states. The next set of issues the movement faced was quite different. They applied equally to blacks inside and outside of the South and they involved tackling structural and institutional racism. Rustin argued that a more expansive agenda required a more expansive approach. This meant

The Civil Rights Movement: A Documentary Reader, First Edition. Edited by John A. Kirk.
© 2020 John Wiley & Sons, Inc. Published 2020 by John Wiley & Sons, Inc.

forging broader coalitions, entering into and influencing mainstream politics, and "the building of community institutions or power bases." It also, Rustin said, meant relying less on the nonviolent direct action campaigns of the past, suggesting that he believed such tactics had now reached the limits of their effectiveness.

The decade spanned by the 1954 Supreme Court decision on school desegregation and the Civil Rights Act of 1964 will undoubtedly be recorded as the period in which the legal foundations of racism in America were destroyed. To be sure, pockets of resistance remain; but it would be hard to quarrel with the assertion that the elaborate legal structure of segregation and discrimination, particularly in relation to public accommodations, has virtually collapsed. On the other hand, without making light of the human sacrifices involved in the direct-action tactics (sit-ins, freedom rides, and the rest) that were so instrumental to this achievement, we must recognize that in desegregating public accommodations, we affected institutions which are relatively peripheral both to the American socio-economic order and to the fundamental conditions of life of the Negro people. In a highly industrialized, 20th-century civilization, we hit Jim Crow precisely where it was most anachronistic, dispensable, and vulnerable – in hotels, lunch counters, terminals, libraries, swimming pools, and the like. For in these forms, Jim Crow does impede the flow of commerce in the broadest sense: it is a nuisance in a society on the move (and on the make). Not surprisingly, therefore, it was the most mobility-conscious and relatively liberated groups in the Negro community – lower-middle-class college students – who launched the attack that brought down this imposing but hollow structure.

The term "classical" appears especially apt for this phase of the civil rights movement. But in the few years that have passed since the first flush of sit-ins, several developments have taken place that have complicated matters enormously. One is the shifting focus of the movement in the South, symbolized by Birmingham; another is the spread of the revolution to the North; and the third, common to the other two, is the expansion of the movement's base in the Negro community. To attempt to disentangle these three strands is to do violence to reality. David Danzig's perceptive article, "The Meaning of Negro Strategy," correctly saw in the Birmingham events the victory of the concept of collective struggle over individual achievement as the road to Negro freedom. And Birmingham remains the unmatched symbol of grass-roots protest involving all strata of the black community. It was also in this most industrialized of Southern cities that the single-issue demands of the movement's classical stage gave way to the "package deal." No longer were Negroes satisfied with integrating lunch counters. They now sought advances in employment, housing, school integration, police protection, and so forth.

Thus, the movement in the South began to attack areas of discrimination which were not so remote from the Northern experience as were Jim Crow lunch counters. At the same time, the interrelationship of these apparently distinct areas became increasingly evident. What is the value of winning access to public accommodations for those who lack money to use them? The minute the movement faced this question, it was compelled to expand its vision beyond race relations to economic relations, including the role of education in modern society. And what also became clear is that all these interrelated problems, by their very nature, are not soluble by private, voluntary efforts but require government action – or politics. Already Southern demonstrators had recognized that the most effective way to strike at the police brutality they suffered from was by getting rid of the local sheriff – and that meant political action, which in turn meant, and still means, political action within the Democratic party where the only meaningful primary contests in the South are fought.

And so, in Mississippi, thanks largely to the leadership of Bob Moses, a turn toward political action has been taken. More than voter registration is involved here. A conscious bid for *political power* is being made, and in the course of that effort a tactical shift is being effected: direct-action techniques are being subordinated to a strategy calling for the building of community institutions or power bases. Clearly, the implications of this shift reach far beyond Mississippi. What began as a protest movement is being challenged to translate itself into a political movement. Is this the right course? And if it is, can the transformation be accomplished?

Source: Bayard Rustin, "From Protest to Politics: The Future of the Civil Rights Movement," pp. 25–6 from *Commentary* 39 (February 1965), https://www.com mentarymagazine.com/articles/from-protest-to-politics-the-future-of-the-civil-rights-movement/

10.2 *Chicago Defender*, "Long, Hot Summer Hits Los Angeles," 1965

On 11 August 1965, just five days after President Johnson signed the Voting Rights Act into law, an altercation between local black residents and a white state highway patrolman in the predominantly black district of Watts, Los Angeles, led to an extended outbreak of violence that lasted for six days and resulted in 35 deaths. Racial disturbances in New York, Philadelphia, and Rochester the previous year were forewarnings of the potentially explosive mounting black frustration and anger in America's cities. Many more were to come, in what became known as the "long, hot summers" between 1965 and 1968.

When Martin Luther King, Jr visited Los Angeles, accompanied by, among others, Bayard Rustin, he was appalled at the devastation caused by the riots and the desperation of the local black population living in squalid urban conditions. Few residents appeared receptive to King's message of nonviolence. Instead, they countered with their own "Watts Manifesto" of "Burn, baby, burn." Residents argued that they had been ignored by the southern civil rights movement and ignored by white authorities. The only way for them to attract attention and for their grievances to be taken seriously was a very different sort of direct action, they said: violent, not nonviolent. King later concluded that, "A riot is the language of the unheard." He came away from Watts convinced that the Southern Christian Leadership Conference (SCLC) must now turn its full attention to the plight of urban blacks in America's major cities that had been largely neglected in a hitherto southern-based rural, small town and small city focused movement.

Hundreds of persons streamed into the street in a rock and bottle throwing riot that started when police arrested a drunken driving suspect.

An estimated 70 helmeted policemen aided by motorized units moved shortly before midnight to seal off an eight block area of the predominantly Negro community of Watts on the outskirts of Compton.

Police Capt. Darrell Gates said many of the throng dispersed, but that about 30 or 40 were hurling rocks and other objects at officers in a two-block sector of Avalon Boulevard near 116th Street. Police arrested at least three men, including one who was cheered by bystanders as he was taken to jail.

"We should know in an hour where we stand," Gates said. But the situation remained tense and as he spoke, someone threw a cinder block and bottle that landed a short distance from him at the heavily manned command post.

Inspector Carl Lee said "what we are going to do now is to seal it off and let it sit." He said "too many men have been hit and hurt."

The drunken driving suspect was identified as a Negro, and the arresting California highway patrolmen were white. But police would not describe the disturbance as predominantly racial.

At least a dozen persons were injured, including policemen, three newsmen and one woman.

At the height of the riot, Negroes jeered at helmeted officers with nightsticks and hurled bricks and bottles at police, newsmen and vehicles.

At least 50 to 60 vehicles were damaged, including mobile units from two television stations, police said.

When the disturbance worsened, police charged into the crowd to make it disperse. Then the officers were withdrawn from the area to let the rioters "cool off."

Throughout the night, police brought in suspects for booking. At least 12 persons were booked and another 12 were in custody waiting to be booked. Police said half were charged with felony offenses and the rest with misdemeanor counts.

Police said eight or nine officers suffered minor injuries. One was stabbed and another had his arm fractured by a bottle hurled by a rioter.

Source: "Long, Hot Summer Hits Los Angeles," p. 1 from *Chicago Defender* (National edition), 14 August 1965.

10.3 Whitney M. Young, Jr, "The High Cost of Discrimination," 1965

Among the civil rights organizations operating in the 1960s, the National Urban League (NUL) appeared ideally equipped to tackle the pressing issues found in northern cities. Established in 1910, around the same time as the National Association for the Advancement of Colored People (NAACP), and also headquartered in New York, the NUL was dedicated to pursuing better living conditions and employment opportunities in America's cities, particularly in the North where the great migrations of blacks from the South over the course of the twentieth century had swelled urban populations. In contrast to the NAACP's more high profile political and legal campaigns, the NUL's activities tended to be lower key and less visible to the public. When Whitney Young, Jr became executive director of the NUL in 1961, he made efforts to raise the profile of the organization and to align it more with developments taking place in the rest of the civil rights movement. As a result, the NUL's fund-raising capabilities increased and it joined other civil rights organizations in the 1963 March on Washington.

Building on the NUL's work in urban black communities, Young called for a renewed effort to address black urban poverty and black community underdevelopment. Young argued that helping the black community was beneficial to everyone, not just to black people, since the black population represented a massively underdeveloped resource for the American economy. On the one hand, Young called for uplift in the black community by taking advantage of the civil rights laws that had been passed and the new opportunities that were beginning to open up. On the other hand, Young recognized that blacks could not do this without help. Many years of racial discrimination and its consequences could not easily be swept aside overnight. To aid black community development and to overcome the effects of past racism, Young called for a "National Marshall Plan" that would echo America's investment in devastated post-World War II Europe. This was, Young insisted, not a case of "charity" but a matter of "justice."

A survey by the National Urban League of 68 cities found that the median income of Negroes fell below $4,000 a year in 21 cities and among them were "northern cities" such as Cincinnati, Pittsburgh, and Peoria, Springfield and Champaign-Urbana, in Illinois; Providence, RI; and Western cities like Phoenix, Wichita, and Tulsa. I point this out to illustrate that not only is suffering and squalor widespread in all our cities, but also to highlight the fact that the depressed condition of the Negro minority is holding back the progress and prosperity of all their citizens.

White people, particularly trade union officials, must stop looking at Negroes as competitors and begin seeing us as contributors. We don't just want to compete. We want to *contribute*. We built the South and we are building today, wherever one turns and looks. But unless more of us get the opportunity to get quality schooling and quality training and quality jobs, we are not going to be using our full potential – and America will be the less for it.

So I repeat what I have said before: We must march to the libraries as well as to the picket lines; we must march to the museums and art galleries and places where we learn as well as in the streets. We must accelerate our fight for quality, integrated education because if we fail in this, we fail in all. Civil rights laws are great. They will speed the end of discrimination in industry. But a law is not going to make any man a nuclear physicist. This we have got to do ourselves.

That's why the Urban League's affiliates in 72 cities continuously hammer away at the need for keeping Johnny in school. That's why we set up a National Skills Bank not only to find qualified people for good jobs but to identify the number of men who don't have such skills and need to be retrained.

I said at the beginning that the nation could never repay Negroes for what we have suffered. I am convinced of this. But I also believe that for a brief period of time it can mount to a National Marshall Plan to help us the way Western Europe was helped after World War II. For a time we ought to have families of the poor receiving federal subsidies to boost income levels to the point where they can break out of the poverty cycle. Families that can't afford books aren't going to teach their children to read. Families without enough food on the table aren't going to rear children who are in condition to learn much in school.

The federal, local and state governments, private philanthropies and non-profit agencies of all kinds will have to team up to help us overcome the centuries of deprivation. If the cost of this is $10 billion or $20 billion a year, I say pay it. Even in the short run it will bring to us a savings from what goes down the financial rat hole due to the high cost of discrimination and segregation. A nation which can afford $20 billion to put a man on the moon can do as much to help Negro citizens stand on their own two feet right here on earth. This is not charity, only fundamental justice, a kind of GI Bill of Rights for a people who are each day pulling themselves up by their own bootstraps at an ever increasing speed but who have a long, long way to go.

Source: Whitney M. Young, Jr, "The High Cost of Discrimination," pp. 53–4 from *Ebony*, 1 August 1965, https://books.google.com/books?id=N94DAAAAMBAJ&prin tsec=frontcover&dq=bony+1965&hl=en&sa=X&ved=0ahUKEwj1x9WyroDbAhUPO awKHXdNAVYQ6AEIJzAA#v=onepage&q=ebony%201965&f=false

10.4 Southern Christian Leadership Conference, A Proposal for the Development of a Nonviolent Action Movement for the Greater Chicago Area, 1966

King and the SCLC targeted Chicago for their first northern campaign. Seemingly ignoring Rustin's assertion about the declining efficacy of nonviolent direct action, King appeared to believe that the movement's tactics in the South could easily be transplanted to the North, and that a Chicago campaign could be essentially treated like another Birmingham or Selma campaign.

For many reasons this turned out not to be the case. Northern white allies of the civil rights movement's southern campaigns, among them Chicago's Mayor Richard Daley, white church leaders, and white union leaders, proved less supportive when the movement arrived in their own backyards. Even the federal government was reluctant to get involved. President Johnson knew that his sponsorship of civil rights legislation had lost the Democratic Party support in the South; he was in no mood to alienate allies such as Daley in the North as well. A much-touted white "backlash" to the civil rights movement seemed to be growing in the nation, although in truth there have been very few times in American history when such a backlash to black activism has ever been absent. The black communities King encountered in the North were much different from those in the South. Influential black politicians had existed for a longer time in the North and they too were implicated in the "machine" politics of the cities. On the whole, the black population was more secular than in the South and less inclined to take seriously the authority of a black minister. The sheer scale of the problems and the size of the urban geography in Chicago were greater than King or the SCLC had ever encountered. Chicago was ten times bigger than Birmingham and the task of pinpointing specific issues and places to protest was much tougher.

The SCLC's planning document for the Chicago campaign below provides a list of the multifaceted problems that existed in the city, all combining in a web of pervasive racial discrimination that was exceedingly difficult to untangle. Though King and the SCLC ultimately focused on housing discrimination, the issues involved were far more wide-ranging and complex than any one point of entry. The experience of the Chicago campaign, which King and the SCLC exited without any definitive, lasting concessions, convinced King that new approaches to civil rights needed to be considered.

For the past months the SCLC staff has been working in Chicago trying to apply the SCLC philosophy to the problem of Chicago. Their work has been concerned with strengthening community organizations and recruiting new forces to join in a nonviolent movement, but they have also given a great deal of thought to the crystallization and definition of the problem in Chicago in terms which can be communicated to the man on the street, who is most affected. The Chicago problem is simply a matter of economic exploitation. Every condition exists simply because someone profits by its existence. This economic exploitation is crystallized in the SLUM.

A slum is any area which is exploited by the community at large or an area where free trade and exchange of culture and resources is not allowed to exist. In a slum, people do not receive comparable care and services for the amount of rent paid on a dwelling. They are forced to purchase property at inflated real estate value. They pay taxes, but their children do not receive an equitable share of those taxes in educational, recreational and civic services. They may leave the community and acquire professional training, skills or crafts, but seldom are they able to find employment opportunities commensurate with these skills. And in rare occasions when they do, opportunities for advancement and promotion are restricted. This means that in proportion to the labor, money and intellect which the slum pours into the community at large, only a small portion is received in return benefits. [James] Bevel and our Chicago staff have come to see this as a system of internal colonialism, not unlike the exploitation of the Congo by Belgium.

This situation is true only for Negroes. A neighborhood of Polish citizens might live together in a given geographic area, but that geographic area enters into free exchange with the community at large; and at any time services in that are deteriorate, the citizens are free to move to other areas where standards of health, education and employment are maintained.

As we define and interpret the dynamics of the slum, we see the total pattern of economic exploitation under which Negroes suffer in Chicago and in other northern cities.

1. Education: $266 per year is the average investment per Negro child; per white pupil it is $366 in the city of Chicago. Suburban communities spend anywhere from $450 to $900 per pupil annually. Hence, slum education is designed to perpetuate the inferior status of slum children and prepare them only for menial jobs in much the same way that the South African apartheid education philosophy does for the African.
2. Building Trade Unions: Building trade unions bar Negroes from many employment opportunities which could easily be learned by persons with limited academic training.
3. Real Estate: Real Estate Boards restrict the supply of housing available to Negroes to the result that Negro families pay an average $20 per month more in rent and receive fewer services than persons in other neighborhoods.
4. Banks and Mortgage Companies: Banks and mortgage companies charge higher interest rates and in many instances even refuse to finance real estate in slum communities and transitional communities, making the area easy prey for loan sharks.

5. Slum Landlords: Slum landlords find a most lucrative return on a minimum investment due to inefficient enforcement of city building codes as well as inadequate building codes, over-crowding of living space, and a tax structure on slum property which means the more you let the building run down, the less you pay in taxes.

6. The Welfare System: The welfare system contributes to the breakdown of family life by making it more difficult to obtain money if the father is in the household and subjects families to a dehumanized existence at the hand of impersonal self-perpetuating bureaucracy.

7. Federal Housing Agencies: Federal housing agencies will not insure loans for purchasing real estate in Negro communities and make little money available for financing any low-cost housing or renovation of present housing.

8. The Courts: The courts are organized as a tool of the economic structure and political machine. Judges are political appointees and subject to political influence.

9. The Police: The police are little more than "enforcers" of the present system of exploitation and often demonstrate particular contempt for poor Negroes, so that they are deprived of any sense of human dignity and the status of citizenship in order that they may be controlled and "kept in line."

10. The Political System: The established political system deprives Negroes of political power and, through patronage and pressure, robs the community of its democratic voice in the name of a Democratic Machine.

11. The City Administration: The city administration refuses to render adequate services to the Negro community. Street cleaning, garbage collection and police protection are offered menially, if at all.

12. The Federal Government: The federal government has yet to initiate a creative attempt to deal with the problems of megalopolitan life and the results of the past three centuries of slavery and segregation on Negroes.

Source: "A Proposal by the Southern Christian Leadership Conference for the Development of a Nonviolent Action Movement for the Greater Chicago Area," 1966, Clayborne Carson, David J. Garrow, Gerald Gill, Vincent Harding, and Darlene Clark Hine, eds., *The Eyes on the Prize Civil Rights Reader: Documents, Speeches and Firsthand Accounts From the Black Freedom Struggle* (New York: Viking Penguin, 1991), pp. 291–300.

10.5 Douglas Robinson, "2 Rights Rallies Set Near Chicago," 1966

One notable innovation in the SCLC's Chicago campaign were open housing demonstrations, consisting of marches into white neighborhoods that made visible the problem of racial discrimination in the city's housing practices. This became the most successful attempt at translating southern-style nonviolent direct action into a northern setting. On Martin Luther King, Jr's first open housing march he led a caravan of 600 people in over 100 vehicles into the white Gage Park and Chicago Lawn neighborhoods. Despite a considerable police presence, King encountered a good deal of resistance. Shortly after exiting his vehicle, King was hit in the side of the head by a rock thrown from a white crowd that had gathered to oppose the demonstration. By the end of the march, the police had made 41 arrests and 30 demonstrators had been injured. King told the press that "I have never – even in Mississippi and Alabama, seen mobs as hostile and hate-filled as I've seen in Chicago."

The following day, without consulting King, SCLC workers Jesse Jackson and James Bevel upped the ante by announcing open housing marches in Chicago's Bogan and Cicero neighborhoods, even tougher targets where more violence was expected. The threat of new open housing marches rattled Mayor Daley and he invited civil rights leaders to a "Summit Conference" to try to stop them. When talks broke down, Daley obtained a state court injunction against any further marches. King and Chicago movement representatives eventually brokered a deal with Daley to stop the open housing demonstrations. Daley was worried about the prospect of escalating violence in the city, but so too was King.

A "Summit Agreement" conceded some of the movement's demands, but in vague and general terms. The agreement represented more of a compromise, allowing both sides to claim that they had been involved in give and take and to initiate a retreat, rather than achieving any actual meaningful resolution to the situation. In September 1966, a civil rights bill that included fair housing provisions failed to pass in Congress. The following year, Mayor Daley was reelected with over four-fifths of the black vote.

Civil rights leaders said tonight that they plan two demonstrations this week in white communities that have not experienced such protests before.

The Rev. Jesse Jackson, an aide to the Rev. Dr. Martin Luther King Jr, told a rally that the demonstrations would be held in Bogan, a Chicago neighborhood nine miles southwest of the downtown area, and in Cicero, a suburb west of the city.

Recently, civil rights demonstrations in similar neighborhoods have touched off very angry surges of violence by white residents.

"We expect violence," Mr Jackson said, "but it wouldn't be any more violent than the demonstrations last week."

"The educational system," he told a cheering throng of supporters, "has allowed these white peoples' minds to degenerate."

So far, the Chicago police have prevented screaming white residents from attacking the demonstrators.

In Cicero, however, the demonstrations will have to depend on a police force only a fraction the size of Chicago's unless suburban officials ask the city for assistance.

It was learned authoritatively tonight that state and Federal officials were considering the use of elements of the Illinois National Guard to protect the marchers in Cicero.

In 1951 the suburban community was the scene of a riot touched off when a Negro moved into the area. Since then Cicero has been an all-white community.

Mr Jackson said the dates of the demonstrations protesting segregated housing had not yet been decided. They will take place, he said, "by the weekend."

Earlier in the day, a delegation of white home owners and businessmen met with Mayor Richard J. Daley in an effort to persuade him to appeal to Attorney General Nicholas deB. Katzenbach to "rid the civil rights movement of Communist agitators."

Such action, a spokesman for the group contended, would end demonstrations in white neighborhoods because "the marches will stop by themselves if the Communist agitators are jailed."

The delegation came from the Chicago Lawn-Marquette Park area where a white mob threw bottles and stones at civil rights demonstrators last Friday and where the [sic] Dr. King was struck on the head by a stone.

Source: Douglas Robinson, "2 Rights Rallies Set Near Chicago," p. 25 from *New York Times*, 9 August 1966.

10.6 Associated Press, A Policeman Searches Black Suspects as Buildings are Burned during Unrest Following a Police Operation in Detroit, Michigan, 1967

The urban unrest following the Watts uprising in 1965 continued throughout the "long, hot summers" that followed. In 1967, violence broke out in over 150 cities. Detroit was one of them. On Sunday, 23 July 1967, Detroit police raided an unlicensed after-hours black neighborhood bar, known colloquially as a "blind pig," in the city's Near West Side. Inside, a gathering of 82 blacks was welcoming back two local soldiers who had just returned from the Vietnam War. The police decided to arrest all of the people present. A crowd gathered to protest the arrests and, soon after the police left, looting of nearby stores began. As the Detroit police moved in to stop the looting, the conflict quickly escalated and spread. Fires broke out and the city began to go up in flames. As the situation spiraled out of control, President Johnson authorized the use of federal troops to bring order back to the city, leading to the deployment of the 101st Airborne Division that had been used ten years earlier to escort the Little Rock Nine into Central High School. Gov. George Romney mobilized 8,000 members of the Michigan National Guard. Tanks and machine guns were rolled out into the streets as snipers fired at the police and soldiers. A curfew was put into place as the city began to resemble a war zone. Within 48 hours of troops being deployed, the violence subsided. During the four days of conflict, 43 people were killed, 1,189 were injured, 7,200 were arrested, and 2,000 buildings were destroyed.

Source: Associated Press, A policeman searches black suspects on 25 July 1967 as buildings are burned during unrest following a police operation in Detroit, http://www. gettyimages.com/detail/news-photo/policeman-searches-black-suspects-in-a-detroit-street-on-news-photo/460589916#policeman-searches-black-suspects-in-a-detroit-street-on-july-25-1967-picture-id460589916

10.7 National Advisory Commission on Civil Disorders, *Report of the National Advisory Commission on Civil Disorders,* 1968

In the aftermath of the 1967 urban unrest, President Johnson issued Executive Order 11365 to establish an 11-member commission to look into the causes of the disturbances and to provide recommendations to prevent further outbreaks of violence. In February 1968, the National Advisory Commission on Civil

Disorders – better known as the Kerner Commission after its chair, Gov. Otto Kerner, Jr of Illinois – released its findings after seven months of research. Specifically, Johnson asked the commission to address three basic questions: "What happened? Why did it happen? What can be done to prevent it from happening again and again?"

The answers came in a comprehensive and scathing 426-page assessment examining the effects of racism in American society. The impact of the lack of economic opportunities in the black community and the frustrations that this fueled featured prominently in the report's findings. The report also blamed failed and inadequate federal and state policies in education, welfare, and housing. White racism and white media bias that excluded the viewpoints of black people were likewise identified as issues that needed to be addressed. The report called for nothing short of a fundamental reorientation of American national priorities and values in addressing the needs of the black population. The warning about the consequences of not doing so was spelled out in forthright terms with the report concluding that "Our nation is moving toward two societies, one black, one white – separate and unequal." The Kerner Commission report sold over two million copies. Below is a summary of its findings and conclusions extracted from the report.

No American – white or black – can escape the consequences of the continuing social and economic decay of our major cities.

Only a commitment to national action on an unprecedented scale can shape a future compatible with the historic ideals of American society.

The great productivity of our economy, and a federal revenue system which is highly responsive to economic growth, can provide the resources.

The major need is to generate new will – the will to tax ourselves to the extent necessary, to meet the vital needs of the nation.

We have set forth goals and proposed strategies to reach those goals. We discuss and recommend programs not to commit each of us to specific parts of such programs but to illustrate the type and dimension of action needed.

The major goal is the creation of a true union – a single society and a single American identity. Toward that goal, we propose the following objectives for national action:

* Opening up opportunities to those who are restricted by racial segregation and discrimination, and eliminating all barriers to their choice of jobs, education and housing.
* Removing the frustration of powerlessness among the disadvantaged by providing the means for them to deal with the problems that affect their own lives and by increasing the capacity of our public and private institutions to respond to these problems.

* Increasing communication across racial lines to destroy stereotypes, to halt polarization, end distrust and hostility, and create common ground for efforts toward public order and social justice.

We propose these aims to fulfill our pledge of equality and to meet the fundamental needs of a democratic and civilized society – domestic peace and social justice.

EMPLOYMENT

Pervasive unemployment and underemployment are the most persistent and serious grievances in minority areas. They are inextricably linked to the problem of civil disorder.

Despite growing federal expenditures for manpower development and training programs, and sustained general economic prosperity and increasing demands for skilled workers, about two million – white and nonwhite – are permanently unemployed. About ten million are underemployed, of whom 6.5 million work full time for wages below the poverty line.

The 500,000 "hard-core" unemployed in the central cities who lack a basic education and are unable to hold a steady job are made up in large part of Negro males between the ages of 18 and 25. In the riot cities which we surveyed, Negroes were three times as likely as whites to hold unskilled jobs, which are often part time, seasonal, low-paying and "dead end."

Negro males between the ages of 15 and 25 predominated among the rioters. More than 20 percent of the rioters were unemployed, and many who were employed held intermittent, low status, unskilled jobs which they regarded as below their education and ability.

The Commission recommends that the federal government:

* Undertake joint efforts with cities and states to consolidate existing manpower programs to avoid fragmentation and duplication.
* Take immediate action to create 2,000,000 new jobs over the next three years – one million in the public sector and one million in the private sector – to absorb the hard-core unemployed and materially reduce the level of underemployment for all workers, black and white. We propose 250,000 public sector and 300,000 private sector jobs in the first year.
* Provide on-the-job training by both public and private employers with reimbursement to private employers for the extra costs of training the hard-core unemployed, by contract or by tax credits.

* Provide tax and other incentives to investment in rural as well as urban poverty areas in order to offer to the rural poor an alternative to migration to urban centers.
* Take new and vigorous action to remove artificial barriers to employment and promotion, including not only racial discrimination but, in certain cases, arrest records or lack of a high school diploma. Strengthen those agencies such as the Equal Employment Opportunity Commission, charged with eliminating discriminatory practices, and provide full support for Title VI of the 1964 Civil Rights Act allowing federal grant-in-aid funds to be withheld from activities which discriminate on grounds of color or race.

The Commission commends the recent public commitment of the National Council of the Building and Construction Trades Unions, AFL-CIO, to encourage and recruit Negro membership in apprenticeship programs. This commitment should be intensified and implemented.

EDUCATION

Education in a democratic society must equip children to develop their potential and to participate fully in American life. For the community at large, the schools have discharged this responsibility well. But for many minorities, and particularly for the children of the ghetto, the schools have failed to provide the educational experience which could overcome the effects of discrimination and deprivation.

This failure is one of the persistent sources of grievance and resentment within the Negro community. The hostility of Negro parents and students toward the school system is generating increasing conflict and causing disruption within many city school districts. But the most dramatic evidence of the relationship between educational practices and civil disorders lies in the high incidence of riot participation by ghetto youth who have not completed high school. The bleak record of public education for ghetto children is growing worse. In the critical skills – verbal and reading ability – Negro students are falling further behind whites with each year of school completed. The high unemployment and underemployment rate for Negro youth is evidence, in part, of the growing educational crisis.

We support integration as the priority education strategy; it is essential to the future of American society. In this last summer's disorders we have seen the consequences of racial isolation at all levels, and of attitudes toward race, on both sides, produced by three centuries of myth, ignorance and bias.

It is indispensable that opportunities for interaction between the races be expanded.

We recognize that the growing dominance of pupils from disadvantaged minorities in city school populations will not soon be reversed. No matter how great the effort toward desegregation, many children of the ghetto will not, within their school careers, attend integrated schools.

If existing disadvantages are not to be perpetuated, we must drastically improve the quality of ghetto education. Equality of results with all-white schools must be the goal.

To implement these strategies, the Commission recommends:

* Sharply increased efforts to eliminate de facto segregation in our schools through substantial federal aid to school systems seeking to desegregate either within the system or in cooperation with neighboring school systems.
* Elimination of racial discrimination in Northern as well as Southern schools by vigorous application of Title VI of the Civil Rights Act of 1964.
* Extension of quality early childhood education to every disadvantaged child in the country.
* Efforts to improve dramatically schools serving disadvantaged children through substantial federal funding of year-round compensatory education programs, improved teaching, and expanded experimentation and research.
* Elimination of illiteracy through greater federal support for adult basic education.
* Enlarged opportunities for parent and community participation in the public schools.
* Reoriented vocational education emphasizing work-experience training and the involvement of business and industry.
* Expanded opportunities for higher education through increased federal assistance to disadvantaged students.
* Revision of state aid formulas to assure more per student aid to districts having a high proportion of disadvantaged school-age children.

THE WELFARE SYSTEM

Our present system of public welfare is designed to save money instead of people, and tragically ends up doing neither. This system has two critical deficiencies:

First, it excludes large numbers of persons who are in great need, and who, if provided a decent level of support, might be able to become more productive and self-sufficient. No federal funds are available for millions of men and women who are needy but neither aged, handicapped nor the parents of minor children.

Second, for those included, the system provides assistance well below the minimum necessary for a decent level of existence, and imposes restrictions that encourage continued dependency on welfare and undermine self-respect.

A welter of statutory requirements and administrative practices and regulations operate to remind recipients that they are considered untrustworthy, promiscuous and lazy. Residence requirements prevent assistance to people in need who are newly arrived in the state. Regular searches of recipients' homes violate privacy. Inadequate social services compound the problems.

The Commission recommends that the federal government, acting with state and local governments where necessary, reform the existing welfare system to:

* Establish uniform national standards of assistance at least as high as the annual "poverty level" of income, now set by the Social Security Administration at $3,335 per year for an urban family of four.
* Require that all states receiving federal welfare contributions participate in the Aid to Families with Dependent Children Unemployed Parents program (AFDC-UP) that permits assistance to families with both father and mother in the home, thus aiding the family while it is still intact.
* Bear a substantially greater portion of all welfare costs – at least 90 percent of total payments.
* Increase incentives for seeking employment and job training, but remove restrictions recently enacted by the Congress that would compel mothers of young children to work.
* Provide more adequate social services through neighborhood centers and family-planning programs.
* Remove the freeze placed by the 1967 welfare amendments on the percentage of children in a state that can be covered by federal assistance.
* Eliminate residence requirements.

As a long-range goal, the Commission recommends that the federal government seek to develop a national system of income supplementation based strictly on need with two broad and basic purposes:

* To provide, for those who can work or who do work, any necessary supplements in such a way as to develop incentives for fuller employment;
* To provide, for those who cannot work and for mothers who decide to remain with their children, a minimum standard of decent living, and to aid in the saving of children from the prison of poverty that has held their parents.

A broad system of implementation would involve substantially greater federal expenditures than anything now contemplated. The cost will range widely depending on the standard of need accepted as the "basic allowance" to individuals and families, and on the rate at which additional income above this level is taxed. Yet if the deepening cycle of poverty and dependence on welfare can be broken, if the children of the poor can be given the opportunity to scale the wall that now separates them from the rest of society, the return on this investment will be great indeed.

HOUSING

After more than three decades of fragmented and grossly underfunded federal housing programs, nearly six million substandard housing units remain occupied in the United States.

The housing problem is particularly acute in the minority ghettos. Nearly two-thirds of all non-white families living in the central cities today live in neighborhoods marked with substandard housing and general urban blight. Two major factors are responsible.

First: Many ghetto residents simply cannot pay the rent necessary to support decent housing. In Detroit, for example, over 40 percent of the non-white occupied units in 1960 required rent of over 35 percent of the tenants' income.

Second: Discrimination prevents access to many non-slum areas, particularly the suburbs, where good housing exists. In addition, by creating a "back pressure" in the racial ghettos, it makes it possible for landlords to break up apartments for denser occupancy, and keeps prices and rents of deteriorated ghetto housing higher than they would be in a truly free market.

To date, federal programs have been able to do comparatively little to provide housing for the disadvantaged. In the 31-year history of subsidized federal housing, only about 800,000 units have been constructed, with recent production averaging about 50,000 units a year. By comparison, over a period only three years longer, FHA insurance guarantees have made possible the construction of over ten million middle and upper-income units.

Two points are fundamental to the Commission's recommendations:

First: Federal housing programs must be given a new thrust aimed at overcoming the prevailing patterns of racial segregation. If this is not done, those programs will continue to concentrate the most impoverished and dependent segments of the population into the central-city ghettos where there is already a critical gap between the needs of the population and the public resources to deal with them.

Second: The private sector must be brought into the production and financing of low and moderate rental housing to supply the capabilities and capital necessary to meet the housing needs of the nation.

The Commission recommends that the federal government:

* Enact a comprehensive and enforceable federal open housing law to cover the sale or rental of all housing, including single family homes.
* Reorient federal housing programs to place more low and moderate income housing outside of ghetto areas.
* Bring within the reach of low and moderate income families within the next five years six million new and existing units of decent housing, beginning with 600,000 units in the next year.

To reach this goal we recommend:

* Expansion and modification of the rent supplement program to permit use of supplements for existing housing, thus greatly increasing the reach of the program.
* Expansion and modification of the below-market interest rate program to enlarge the interest subsidy to all sponsors and provide interest-free loans to nonprofit sponsors to cover pre-construction costs, and permit sale of projects to nonprofit corporations, cooperatives, or condominiums.
* Creation of an ownership supplement program similar to present rent supplements, to make home ownership possible for low-income families.
* Federal writedown of interest rates on loans to private builders constructing moderate-rent housing.
* Expansion of the public housing program, with emphasis on small units on scattered sites, and leasing and "turnkey" programs.
* Expansion of the Model Cities program.
* Expansion and reorientation of the urban renewal program to give priority to projects directly assisting low-income households to obtain adequate housing.

CONCLUSION

One of the first witnesses to be invited to appear before this Commission was Dr. Kenneth B. Clark, a distinguished and perceptive scholar. Referring to the reports of earlier riot commissions, he said:

I read that report ... of the 1919 riot in Chicago, and it is as if I were reading the report of the investigating committee on the Harlem riot of '35, the report of the investigating committee on the Harlem riot of '43, the report of the McCone Commission on the Watts riot.

I must again in candor say to you members of this Commission – it is a kind of Alice in Wonderland – with the same moving picture re-shown over and over again, the same analysis, the same recommendations, and the same inaction.

These words come to our minds as we conclude this report.

We have provided an honest beginning. We have learned much. But we have uncovered no startling truths, no unique insights, no simple solutions. The destruction and the bitterness of racial disorder, the harsh polemics of black revolt and white repression have been seen and heard before in this country.

It is time now to end the destruction and the violence, not only in the streets of the ghetto but in the lives of people.

Source: National Advisory Commission on Civil Disorders, *Report of the National Advisory Commission on Civil Disorders*, http://www.eisenhowerfoundation.org/docs/ kerner.pdf

10.8 Ruth Batson Interview on Busing in Boston in the Mid-1970s

School desegregation is often viewed as being mainly a southern issue. Court rulings in the decades after the Brown *decision reinforced that notion by targeting remedies aimed largely at southern school districts. In 1971, the US Supreme Court ruled in the North Carolina case of* Swann v. Charlotte-Mecklenburg Board of Education *that busing – the strategic two-way transportation of black and white students across cities – could be used to achieve racial balance in schools. Busing proved highly controversial. Yet it was in the North, rather than in the South, that one of the first major national flashpoints in resistance to busing occurred.*

Northern schools were frequently just as segregated as southern schools. A common distinction between the segregation that existed in the South and in the North was the claim that in the South segregation occurred because of state laws, which was known as de jure *("in law") segregation, whereas in the North segregation occurred merely because of happenstance, which was known as* de facto *("in fact") segregation. In the North, it was claimed, school segregation reflected established segregated housing patterns, which in turn were the result of individual and private decisions taken by citizens about where to live and therefore beyond the jurisdiction of the courts. More recently, commentators have suggested that the de jure / de facto distinction is an entirely false one, and that de facto segregation was very clearly achieved through discriminatory federal and state actions taken most notably in the area of housing policy.*

The origins of busing in Boston lay in the Massachusetts legislature's enactment of the 1965 Racial Imbalance Act that outlawed segregation in the state's public schools. In 1974, after the National Association for the Advancement of Colored People Legal Defense and Educational Fund (NAACP LDF) filed a lawsuit, federal district judge W. Arthur Garrity, Jr ordered a busing plan to ensure a racial balance of black and white students in Boston public schools. The plan met with ferocious resistance, particularly in Boston's predominantly white working-class Irish-American neighborhoods. Below, local NAACP activist Ruth Batson describes the ordeal of black students who were bused to one such neighborhood in South Boston. Batson was born in Boston's predominantly black Roxbury neighborhood, which was adjacent to South Boston. In the 1950s she was chair of the Public Education Sub-Committee of the NAACP and chair of the NAACP's New England Regional Conference. Throughout the 1960s, Batson led various campaigns to desegregate Boston schools and she remained active in civil rights causes until her death in 2003 at the age of 82.

QUESTION 9

JACKIE SHEARER: Tell me, why were you afraid of reaction in South Boston?

RUTH BATSON: Well, because as a child we had encountered the um, the wrath of um, people in South Boston. And I just felt that they were bigoted. I just felt that they made it very clear that they didn't like Black people. And I was prepared for them not to want um, Black students coming to the school. Plus, which they said it! I mean, they made it very clear. The other thing was that there was absolutely no preparation made for this transition. Um. There were a couple of um, ah, athletes and other people who would go on TV and they would say, you know, "We have a – this thing that we have to, hap – have happen in our city. We're going to be busing kids and so forth and so on. And um, we have to be brave about it." And you say to yourself, "Well, what are they expecting?" Here were little children that were going to a school and they were talking about being brave as if some alien from some planet was coming into the school. I never heard any public official on the state level or on the city level come out and say, "This is a good thing. We should all learn together. We should all live together." There was no encouragement from anybody. I call it complete official neglect. And so therefore there was no preparation being made. Then those of us who knew the police departments and so forth felt that, many of them lived in South Boston. And how were they going to divide their loyalties? And so we felt that this was not going to be a happy occasion, and we were right.

QUESTION 10

JACKIE SHEARER: Can you paint a picture for us of riding a bus to South Boston. Tell us what you saw, what you heard inside the bus, outside the bus.

[...]

RUTH BATSON: Well, um, s – beginning in October I decided I would the ride the buses, along with some of the other team members, to find out for myself, you know, what was happening. We would get reports from team members and from other members of our group ah, like Percy Wilson, who would ride, and a number of people who would ride the buses. Well I hadn't done it so I thought I would do it. And I remember the first morning I got on the bus and the kids were like kids are on a bus – boisterous and happy and having a good time. And then they would sing, "Here We Come Southie, Here We Come." You know, and, just a real raucous occasion. And I remember as you start up that hill going to the um, school seeing signs that people would hold out of windows, or they were on walls and so forth. And um, it really shocked me that this was going on. The other thing that shocked me as we pulled up to the school was the large number of women standing there making noises and making ah, gestures at these children. And you know, it really bothered me because somehow I felt that you know, women would be more understanding, and even if they didn't agree with what was happening, they, they would at least have this motherly feeling or aunterly [sic] feeling, some kind of feeling for these children. So I was amazed at the number of women there. And then, along with the o – these were older women, I'd say, middle aged women that I saw there. Then the other group that I saw, there were a large number of younger men who should have been working in my opinion, you know. They seemed to be in their early twenties. Large number of them. And then the other thing that bothered me was that as we went up the hill and approached the school our students got very, very quiet, where they had been just like any other kid riding the bus, making noise, laughing, talking. Suddenly, as they approached this place they got very, very quiet. And um, then they would have to stay there until the police came over, escorted them out the bus, and in through the metal detectors, into the school. It was ah, I began for the first time to say, "Ruth, maybe you shouldn't have gotten involved. Maybe you shouldn't have urged this desegregation." It, it, it killed me to see our Black students go through that procedure.

Source: Interview with Ruth Batson, conducted by Blackside, Inc. on 8 November 1988, from *Eyes on the Prize II: America at a Racial Crossroads (1965–1985)*, Washington University Libraries, Film and Media Archive, Henry Hampton Collection, http://digital.wustl.edu/e/eii/eiiweb/bat5427.0911.011ruthbatson.html

10.9 Louise Day Hicks, Letter to Congressman John Joseph Moakley, 1975

Resistance to busing in Boston was led by Restore Our Alienated Rights (ROAR), formed by Louise Day Hicks in 1974. ROAR explicitly identified busing as an issue that concerned women's and mother's rights. Indeed, Hicks was a member of the National Organization for Women and a supporter of the Equal Rights Amendment to the US Constitution that looked to secure equal legal protections for women. Born in South Boston and a graduate of Boston University Law School, Hicks was elected to the Boston School Committee in 1961 with the slogan "the only mother on the ballot."

Yet Hicks's feminism did not extend along racial lines. Throughout the 1960s, Hicks refused to listen to black demands for school desegregation. When busing was mandated in Boston by the courts, Hicks and other ROAR members viewed it as an attack on their individual liberties, their right to make choices about their children's futures, and an invasion of their neighborhood schools. The term "forced busing" that Hicks uses in the letter below is indicative of the rhetoric of a perceived oppressive state running roughshod over individual rights.

ROAR used a variety of tactics to win support for its cause: demonstrations, such as a 20,000 strong 1974 march on the Boston State House, and a smaller 1,200 strong 1975 march on Washington; boycotts; sit-ins; letter writing campaigns; publicity stunts, such as burning a wooden bus; and political advocacy. ROAR also engaged in disruption and violence, including pelting buses carrying black students into white neighborhoods with various missiles, taunting black students with racial epithets, and carrying signs with racial slurs on them.

In the end, however, it was the threatened "resegregation" of schools that Hicks warned about in her letter that made the most impact. Busing continued in Boston. In 1987, the courts declared that the city was in compliance with school desegregation laws. By that time, white flight had led to an exodus of white students to the suburbs, leaving a predominantly nonwhite public school system in the city behind. Similar developments have followed nationwide in major urban areas where a recurring pattern of predominantly black public schools and predominantly white private schools in cities, and predominantly white public and private schools in the suburbs and exurbs has emerged, leading to a new era of school resegregation.

Dear Congressman [John Joseph "Joe"] Moakley:

Enclosed for your edification is a recent *Wall Street Journal* article by the incisive young writer, Michael Novak. His arguments against forced busing are not only brilliant and prophetic, but impossible to ignore.

Novak argues that forced busing is immoral because "it goes against the basic social principles of American life: against family, neighborhood, class, ethnic and even educational realities which are so basic they are seldom even voiced."

It appears that Novak has gone one step beyond Professor James Coleman of the University of Chicago. Dr. Coleman has merely reported that the reaction among middle-class white parents to forced busing and the effect that reaction has on black children are sufficient reasons for a second look at the efficacy of this tool of integration.

Novak has given us the cogent and logical explanation for that reaction. It is an explanation devoid of emotionalism; and in all honesty to ourselves and our responsibilities as public servants, business or spiritual leaders, we cannot refuse to consider it in any of our decisions. He foresees an embittered generation that will set the integration movement back twenty years. As a personal note, I have witnessed that bitterness; and I do not want it on my conscience as I am sure you do not.

Parents have come to me in tears because they fear that their children are becoming racists. Somehow we must put an end to this deplorable development before it is too late. We can begin by examining the social realities around us instead of relying on the assumptions of sociologists and their blind followers who would integrate through forced busing to eventually achieve resegregation.

Your comments on Novak's article would be most welcome. Perhaps through the same, we may set Boston, the Nation, and the Civil Rights Movement back on the right track.

Sincerely,
Louise Day Hicks.

Source: Letter from Louise Day Hicks to John Joseph Moakley regarding an anti-busing *Wall Street Journal* article by Michael Novak, 4 August 1975, Congressman John Joseph Moakley Papers, 1926–2001 (MS100), Series 04 District Issues, Box 5, Folder 55, Courtesy of the Moakley Archive, Suffolk University, http://moakleyarchive.omeka.net/items/show/552

Discussion Questions

1. Identify and evaluate the conditions that existed in black communities inside and outside of the South in the mid to late 1960s. What was different about them and what was the same?
2. Why did housing discrimination prove a more difficult issue to address than desegregation and voting rights?

3. What made school busing controversial? Were there any alternatives to ensure school desegregation?

Further Reading

Darden, Joe T., and Richard W. Thomas. *Detroit: Race Riots, Racial Conflicts, and Efforts to Bridge the Racial Divide* (Michigan State University Press, 2013).

Delmont, Matthew F. *Why Busing Failed: Race, Media, and the National Resistance to School Desegregation* (University of California Press, 2016).

Dickerson, Dennis C. *Militant Mediator: Whitney M. Young, Jr* (University Press of Kentucky, 1998).

Finley, Mary Lou, Bernard Lafayette, Jr, James R. Ralph, Jr, and Pam Smith, eds. *The Chicago Freedom Movement: Martin Luther King, Jr and Civil Rights Activism in the North* (University Press of Kentucky, 2015).

Formisano, Ronald P. *Boston against Busing: Race, Class, and Ethnicity in the 1960s and 1970s* (University of North Carolina Press, 1991).

Horne, Gerald. *Fire This Time: The Watts Uprising and the 1960s* (University of Virginia Press, 1995).

McLaughlin, Malcolm. *The Long, Hot Summer of 1967: Urban Rebellion in America* (Palgrave Macmillan, 2014).

Ralph, James R., Jr. *Northern Protest: Martin Luther King, Jr, Chicago, and the Civil Rights Movement* (Harvard University Press, 1993).

Sugrue, Thomas. *Sweet Land of Liberty: The Forgotten Struggle for Civil Rights in the North* (Random House, 2008).

Taylor, Quintard. *In Search of the Racial Frontier: African Americans in the American West, 1528–1990* (W.W. Norton, 1998).

Theoharis, Jeanne, and Komozi Woodard, eds. *Freedom North: Black Freedom Struggles outside the South, 1940–1980* (Palgrave Macmillan, 2003).

Chapter 11   Black Power, 1966

11.1 Robert F. Williams, *Negroes with Guns*, 1962

Although we tend to think of black power as a relatively recent phenomenon, many of its hallmarks – among others, black nationalism, black separatism, and black armed self-defense – have long histories. Black nationalist and separatist ideas have been articulated by, among others, Martin Delaney in The Condition, Elevation, Emigration, and Destiny of the Colored People of the United States, Politically Considered *(1852) in the mid-nineteenth century, Bishop Henry McNeal Turner's "Back to Africa" movement at the turn of the twentieth century, and Marcus Garvey's United Negro Improvement Association (UNIA) in the 1920s. The idea of black armed self-defense was a staple in black rural families where ownership of a shotgun was often the only effective deterrent to white violence.*

In the 1960s, before the black power slogan was popularized, Robert F. Williams was an outspoken proponent of black armed self-defense. Williams became president of the Monroe, North Carolina, National Association for the Advancement of Colored People (NAACP) branch in 1956, and he engaged in desegregation efforts there in the 1950s and 1960s. Encountering growing violence in such endeavors, Williams applied for and received a charter from the National Rifle Association (NRA) to form a local rifle club that he called the Black Armed Guard. The Black Armed Guard was composed of 50–60 men, most of whom, like Williams, were World War II veterans. In 1959, after a Monroe jury acquitted a white man for the attempted rape of a black woman, Williams stood on the courthouse steps and called for black people to "defend themselves even if it is necessary to resort to violence." The NAACP suspended Williams for his comments. When freedom riders came to Monroe in 1961, Williams and his Black Armed Guard rescued them from Klansmen. Amid the chaos, Williams also

The Civil Rights Movement: A Documentary Reader, First Edition. Edited by John A. Kirk.
© 2020 John Wiley & Sons, Inc. Published 2020 by John Wiley & Sons, Inc.

sheltered a white couple from angry blacks, and he was later accused of kidnapping them. Fleeing death threats and charges of kidnapping, Williams moved to Cuba with his wife and two children where he broadcast the news and music radio program "Radio Free Dixie."

The extract below is from Williams's 1962 book Negroes with Guns *which he published in exile and in which he outlined his life story and his thoughts about the civil rights movement and armed self-defense. In 1966, Williams moved to China for three years while it was in the throes of the Cultural Revolution, and he returned to the United States in 1969 where charges against him were dropped and he became an adviser to the US State Department on Chinese relations. Williams died in 1996 at the age of 71 and was buried in his hometown.*

The tactics of non-violence will continue and should continue. We too believed in non-violent tactics in Monroe. We have used these tactics, we've used all tactics. But we also believe that any struggle for liberation should be a flexible struggle. We should not take the attitude that one method alone is the way to liberation. This is to become dogmatic. This is to fall into the same sort of dogmatism practiced by some religious fanatics. We can't afford to develop this type of attitude.

We must use non-violence as a means as long as this is feasible, but the day will come when conditions become so pronounced that non-violence will be suicidal in itself. The day is surely coming when we will see more violence on the American scene. The day is surely coming when some of the same Negroes who have denounced our using weapons for self-defense will be arming themselves. There are those who pretend to be horrified by the idea that a black veteran who shouldered arms for the United States would willingly take up weapons to defend his wife, his children, his home and his life. These same people will one day be loud advocates of self-defense. When violent racism and fascism strike at their families and their homes, not in a token way but in an all-out bloody campaign, then they will be among the first to advocate self-defense. They will justify their position as a question of survival. When it is no longer some distant Negro who is no more than a statistic, no more than an article in a newspaper, when it is no longer their neighbors but them, and when it becomes a matter of personal salvation, then their attitude will change.

As a tactic we use and approve non-violent resistance. But we also believe that a man cannot have human dignity if he allows himself to be abused, to be kicked and beaten to the ground, to allow his wife and children to be attacked, refusing to defend them and himself on the basis that he's so pious, so self-righteous, that it would demean his personality if he fought back.

We know that the average Afro-American is not a pacifist. He is not a pacifist and he has never been a pacifist and he is not made of the type of material that would make a good pacifist. Those who doubt that the great majority of Negroes are not pacifists, just let them slap one. Pick any Negro on any street corner in the USA and they will find out how much he believes in turning the other cheek.

All those who dare to attack are going to learn the hard way that the Afro-American is not a pacifist, that he cannot forever be counted on not to defend himself. Those who attack him brutally and ruthlessly can no longer expect to attack him with impunity.

The Afro-American cannot forget that his enslavement in this country did not pass because of pacifist moral force or noble appeals to the Christian conscience of the slaveholders [...]

It is the nature of the American Negro, the same as all other men, to fight and destroy those things that block his path to a greater happiness in life.

11.2 Malcolm X, "Message to the Grassroots," 1963

The Nation of Islam (NOI), founded by Wallace Fard Muhammad in Detroit in 1930, was one of the inheritors of black nationalist and black separatist traditions. After Fard disappeared under mysterious circumstances in 1934, Elijah Muhammad became the NOI's leader. In the 1950s and 1960s, Malcolm X became the NOI's most prominent public figure. Born in Omaha, Nebraska, in 1925, Malcolm X was originally named Malcolm Little. His father died at an early age and his mother was later committed to a state hospital after suffering a nervous breakdown. Malcolm spent most of his teenage years living with his half-sister in the black Boston neighborhood of Roxbury. In 1943, he moved to Harlem, where he became involved in a life of petty crime. In 1945, Malcolm moved back to Boston where he was arrested and imprisoned with his accomplices for a series of burglaries committed against white families.

It was in prison that Malcolm converted to Islam and joined the NOI, taking on the Malcolm X moniker that signified his unknown family heritage and that disavowed his "slave name" inherited from a former white slave owner. After he was paroled in 1952, Malcolm joined with Elijah Muhammad and became a rising star in the NOI, setting up temples and recruiting members. In 1956, he married Betty Sanders (who then changed her name to Betty X, and later still to Betty Shabazz) and the couple had six children.

By the 1960s, Malcolm's popularity within the NOI caused strains in his relationship with Elijah Muhammad. When he famously described President Kennedy's November 1963 assassination as "chickens coming home to roost" he was publicly censured by the NOI. In March 1964, Malcolm formally broke ties with the NOI and founded the Organization for Afro-American Unity (OAAU). He subsequently made a number of trips overseas, including a pilgrimage to Mecca, the sacred Muslim site in Saudi Arabia, as well as journeys to Africa, France, and the United Kingdom. Following his return to the United States, internecine wrangling with the NOI continued. On 19 February 1965, Malcolm X was assassinated in New York's Audubon Ballroom while preparing to address an audience of OAAU members. NOI members were convicted of the killing. The Autobiography of Malcolm X, the result of a number of interviews conducted with black journalist Alex Haley between 1963 and 1965, was published posthumously and became an instant classic, telling Malcolm's life story and outlining his religious and political philosophy.

An extract from one of Malcolm's speeches below, just before his break with the NOI, reveals his rousing, firebrand, and provocative language, and addresses some of his criticisms of America, white people, and nonviolence.

Look at the American Revolution in 1776. That revolution was for what? For land. Why did they want land? Independence. How was it carried out? Bloodshed. Number one, it was based on land, the basis of independence. And the only way they could get it was bloodshed. The French Revolution – what was it based on? The land-less against the landlord. What was it for? Land. How did they get it? Bloodshed. Was no love lost; was no compromise; was no negotiation. I'm telling you, you don't know what a revolution is. 'Cause when you find out what it is, you'll get back in the alley; you'll get out of the way. The Russian Revolution – what was it based on? Land. The land-less against the landlord. How did they bring it about? Bloodshed. You haven't got a revolution that doesn't involve bloodshed. And you're afraid to bleed. I said, you're afraid to bleed.

As long as the white man sent you to Korea, you bled. He sent you to Germany, you bled. He sent you to the South Pacific to fight the Japanese, you bled. You bleed for white people. But when it comes time to seeing your own churches being bombed and little black girls being murdered, you haven't got no blood. You bleed when the white man says bleed; you bite when the white man says bite; and you bark when the white man says bark. I hate to say this about us, but it's true. How are you going to be nonviolent in Mississippi, as violent as you were in Korea? How can you justify being nonviolent in Mississippi and Alabama, when your churches are being bombed, and your little girls are being murdered, and at the same time you're going to be violent with Hitler, and Tojo, and somebody else that you don't even know?

If violence is wrong in America, violence is wrong abroad. If it's wrong to be violent defending black women and black children and black babies and black men, then it's wrong for America to draft us and make us violent abroad in defense of her. And if it is right for America to draft us, and teach us how to be violent in defense of her, then it is right for you and me to do whatever is necessary to defend our own people right here in this country [...]

Of all our studies, history is best qualified to reward our research. And when you see that you've got problems, all you have to do is examine the historic method used all over the world by others who have problems similar to yours.

And once you see how they got theirs straight, then you know how you can get yours straight. There's been a revolution, a black revolution, going on in Africa. In Kenya, the Mau Mau [the Mau Mau led an anticolonial uprising against the British in Kenya between 1952 and 1964] were revolutionaries; they were the ones who made the word "Uhuru" [the Kenyan word for "freedom"]. They were the ones who brought it to the fore. The Mau Mau, they were revolutionaries. They believed in scorched earth. They knocked everything aside that got in their way, and their revolution also was based on land, a desire for land. In Algeria, the northern part of Africa, a revolution took place. The Algerians were revolutionists; they wanted land. France offered to let them be integrated into France. They told France: to hell with France. They wanted some land, not some France. And they engaged in a bloody battle.

So I cite these various revolutions, brothers and sisters, to show you – you don't have a peaceful revolution. You don't have a turn-the-other-cheek revolution. There's no such thing as a nonviolent revolution. [The] only kind of revolution that's nonviolent is the Negro revolution. The only revolution based on loving your enemy is the Negro revolution. The only revolution in which the goal is a desegregated lunch counter, a desegregated theater, a desegregated park, and a desegregated public toilet; you can sit down next to white folks on the toilet. That's no revolution. Revolution is based on land. Land is the basis of all independence. Land is the basis of freedom, justice, and equality.

The white man knows what a revolution is. He knows that the black revolution is world-wide in scope and in nature. The black revolution is sweeping Asia, sweeping Africa, is rearing its head in Latin America. The Cuban Revolution – that's a revolution. They overturned the system. Revolution is in Asia. Revolution is in Africa. And the white man is screaming because he sees revolution in Latin America. How do you think he'll react to you when you learn what a real revolution is? You don't know what a revolution is. If you did, you wouldn't use that word.

A revolution is bloody. Revolution is hostile. Revolution knows no compromise. Revolution overturns and destroys everything that gets in its way. And you, sitting around here like a knot on the wall, saying, "I'm going to love these folks no matter how much they hate me." No, you need a revolution. Whoever heard of a revolution where they lock arms, as Reverend Cleage was pointing out beautifully, singing "We Shall Overcome"? Just tell me. You don't do that in a revolution. You don't do any singing; you're too busy swinging. It's based on land. A revolutionary wants land so he can set up his own nation, an independent nation. These Negroes aren't asking for no nation. They're trying to crawl back on the plantation.

When you want a nation, that's called nationalism. When the white man became involved in a revolution in this country against England, what was it for? He wanted this land so he could set up another white nation. That's white nationalism. The American Revolution was white nationalism. The French Revolution was white nationalism. The Russian Revolution too – yes, it was – white nationalism. You don't think so? Why [do] you think Khrushchev and Mao can't get their heads together? White nationalism. All the revolutions that's going on in Asia and Africa today are based on what? Black nationalism. A revolutionary is a black nationalist. He wants a nation. I was reading some beautiful words by Reverend Cleage, pointing out why he couldn't get together with someone else here in the city because all of them were afraid of being identified with black nationalism. If you're afraid of black nationalism, you're afraid of revolution. And if you love revolution, you love black nationalism.

Source: Malcolm X, "Message to the Grassroots," from *Malcolm X Speaks: Selected Speeches and Statements*, ed. George Breitman (New York: Pathfinder, 1965), pp. 4–13.

11.3 John Hulett Interview on the Founding of the Lowndes County Freedom Organization (Black Panther Party) in Alabama in 1965

The black panther emblem today has become synonymous with the Black Panther Party for Self-Defense, organized by Huey P. Newton and Bobby Seale in Oakland, California, in 1966. But the black panther emblem, like many other aspects of the black power movement, has its roots in southern soil. Known as "Bloody Lowndes" for the violent nature of race relations there, Lowndes County, Alabama, was 80% black, but it had no black registered voters. Eighty-six white families owned 90% of the land. When the Selma-to-Montgomery march passed through Lowndes County in 1965, Stokely Carmichael, a worker for the Student Nonviolent Coordinating Committee (SNCC), began to encourage local people to mobilize black voters as a first step in translating a black numerical advantage into black political power.

John Hulett, a founder and leader of the Lowndes County Christian Movement for Human Rights (LCCMHR), became the first chair of a newly formed political organization called the Lowndes County Freedom Organization (LCFO). Since Alabama law required political parties to have an emblem, the LCFO chose a black panther and the organization became known as the Black Panther Party. The assertive and determined black panther stood in contrast to the white rooster of the Alabama Democratic Party, which was the political vehicle of white supremacy in the county and state. Seven LFCO candidates ran in the November 1966 elections, although all of them lost.

Nevertheless, the LFCO had a wide-ranging and long-lasting impact. The potential to mobilize local black communities to achieve autonomous black political power inspired Newton and Seale to form the Black Panther Party for Self-Defense. They requested and received permission from the LFCO to appropriate the black panther emblem, although Hulett and other LFCO members later questioned the more explicitly violent rather than assertive connotations that the black panther came to represent on the West Coast. Stokely Carmichael's experiences in Lowndes County influenced his ideas about the black freedom struggle. Carmichael's election as chair of SNCC in 1966 set that civil rights movement organization in a different direction as a black power movement organization.

In 1970, LFCO candidates won office for the first time, including John Hulett, who was elected sheriff of Lowndes County, a position he held for 22 years before serving three terms as a probate judge.

JAMES A. DeVINNEY: I'd like to go back just a little bit in time, even before SNCC came in, even before you started forming the Lowndes County Freedom Organization, just give me a kind of a picture of what Lowndes County was like?

JOHN HULETT: Lowndes County was considered as a total rural county. Real, very poor. Bad roads, you know the school system was very bad, about the worst almost in the nation. There were no jobs available here in this area except farming and sharecropping. Most of the young peoples who finished school, ah, ah, went to school, once they came out of school, they immediately left the South and went, and went North, to try to live, and even to survive, they'd have to take care of the families then at that time. So the, the, Lowndes County was not a good place for young people to live in. Most of the, the adults who lived here, you know, were, were kind of lived under fear most of their lives, because of the some type of treatment, treatment that was given. At a certain age you just didn't go into, if you lived here, and that was just a few people in the county who caused many of our problems. But because of those people were not stopped by other people, it, it caused a, most Black peoples had to live in fear. We had a sheriff during that time, ah, I can never forget, that at night time, and a young man, if he walked the road at night, if you see a car light coming, everybody would just run in the bushes and hide until they come by, it was raining, whatever it was, you stayed out there and waited until that car passed. They thought the sheriff was coming by and maybe would do something to them. There were peoples who had beaten in a numbers of cases, and because of this type of things.

JAMES A. DeVINNEY: When did you make the decision to form an independent political party? How did that come about?

JOHN HULETT: It was sometimes, we decided to form the independent political party because, Stokely Carmichael and Courtland Cox and others who got together and told us, according to the Alabama law, if we didn't like what the Democratic party was doing in this, in our county, or the Republican party, we, we could form our own political organization, and it could become a political party. We looked into the aspects of it. We asked them to do it. And then we came up with a symbol. And during the time, we was trying to come up with a symbol, we had asked Stokely Carmichael, I believe Courtland Cox and some other peoples from our county to, to look at some type of symbol. And when the group came back, they came back with the panther as their symbol. Then we began to, start putting an organization structure together. During that time, I was a, president of the Lowndes County Christian Movement for Human Rights. This was our original organization we had, had for about a year, and then I, I accepted that, you know, they asked me would I take over the political aspects of it. And the, resign from this Lowndes County Christian Movement, and I did. And we were able to pull our people together in both organizations and work together to form our own political organization.

JAMES A. DeVINNEY: What did the Black Panther mean?

JOHN HULETT: The Black Panther party in, in, well, the Black panther itself as a symbol to the organization, was a symbol of the same thing that the rooster was to the Democratic party. It was a symbol that we thought that it was a vicious animal, and who, if we was attacked, it would, it would not back up. That we would fight back if we had to do it. We would move back if we had to move, but we wasn't going to go back into a corner and just stay. And that's why we chose that symbol as a Black panther. We knew that the White people in this county feared the panther also. They didn't want, ah, people to fight back. As long as in a political organization, or as long as people would not fight back, they thought they could just do them like wanted to. But if we decided to fight back, people would take their hands off us. And then, when we chose that symbol as the Black panther, then many of the peoples in our county started saying we were violent during that time, you know, the, now you've got a violent group in Lowndes County who is turned out, who is going to start killing Black pe – White folks. But it wasn't that, it was a political, just a symbol to our organization that we was here to stay and we were going to do whatever needed to be done to survive. And that's what that symbol meant to us.

JAMES A. DeVINNEY: Well, even though SNCC was a non-violent organization, during this time, many of you did start carrying guns and things. How did that work?

JOHN HULETT: We, we carried guns for our own protection, those of who carried guns. One of us who was by ourselves, we would travel by ourselves, and those of us who carried guns, not to bother other peoples, but in case we were attacked by other peoples to protect ourselves. And that's what the purpose of that idea was, to carry a gun. White peoples carry guns in this county, and they were, the law didn't do anything to them about it, so we started tricking out our pickup trucks. Putting our guns in to carry too. And I think they felt that we was ready to, for war, and they decided not to bother us anymore.

JAMES A. DeVINNEY: But you didn't see yourself as violent.

JOHN HULETT: No, we wasn't, we wasn't violent. We wasn't violent people. But we were just some people who was going to protect ourselves in case we were attacked by individuals.

Source: John Hulett interviewed by James A. DeVinney, 18 October 1988, from *Eyes on the Prize II: America at a Racial Crossroads (1965–1985)*, Washington University Digital Gateway Texts http://digital.wustl.edu/e/eii/eiiweb/hul5427.0553.068marc_record_interviewee_process.html

11.4 Stokely Carmichael, "What We Want," 1966

Stokely Carmichael in many ways personified the shift from the civil rights movement to the black power movement among young black activists in the mid-1960s. Born in Port of Spain, Trinidad and Tobago, Carmichael moved to New York (first to Harlem, then to the Bronx) in 1952 at the age of 11. He attended Howard University and while a student there he participated in the 1961 Freedom Rides, serving time in Mississippi's state penitentiary at Parchman. Carmichael later joined the Nonviolent Action Group (NAG) at Howard, which was an affiliate of SNCC. Graduating with a degree in philosophy in 1964, he turned down a graduate scholarship at Harvard to become more active in the civil rights movement, working as a SNCC organizer in Mississippi and Cambridge, Maryland. Carmichael felt a growing sense of disillusionment with mainstream political parties after his experiences with the Mississippi Freedom Democratic Party (MFDP) at the 1964 Democratic National Convention. In 1965, he participated in voting rights demonstrations in Selma, and on the Selma-to-Montgomery march he began working with local black people in Lowndes County to form the LFCO. In May 1966, Carmichael ousted John Lewis as chair of SNCC. The following month, he participated in a March Against Fear from Memphis to Jackson instigated by James Meredith, the man who had desegregated the University of Mississippi in 1962. Along the way, Carmichael began to popularize the chant and slogan of "Black Power."

Under Carmichael's influence, SNCC switched its focus from a reliance on whites and interracialism to a greater emphasis on black people organizing black communities for change. Controversially, at the end of 1966, SNCC voted to expel all white members. Another new direction in SNCC was a rejection of nonviolence as a foundational principle. Carmichael continued to view nonviolence as a useful and strategic tool of protest under certain circumstances, but nothing more than that. Armed self-defense and violence were not excluded from the new-look SNCC in the struggle for black self-determination. Martin Luther King, Jr and others in the civil rights movement looked askance at these developments. King labeled black power a "slogan without a program." To some degree, King's criticism was not unfounded. Black power represented as much a new black sensibility as it was a coherent political and economic program. Carmichael often seemed to delight in playing with the slogan's ambiguity, refusing to nail it down and define its meaning with any precision.

The below article outlines Carmichael's thoughts on black power. His call for "psychological equality" reflects the influence of thinkers like the Martinican anticolonial writer Franz Fanon, who in his 1961 book The Wretched of the Earth *(Grove Press, 1963 translation) wrote about the need of oppressed peoples not only to throw off the shackles of physical oppression, but to also throw off the shackles of psychological oppression that went with it. Fanon argued that in order to be truly liberated, oppressed people needed to actually experience the power of liberation first-hand. In many ways, and through a variety of different expressions, that is what the black power movement sought to do for black people in America: to bestow a feeling of empowerment, agency, and autonomy that had been denied to them in the past.*

To most whites, Black Power seems to mean that the Mau Mau are coming to the suburbs at night. The Mau Mau are coming, and whites must stop them. Articles appear about plots to "get Whitey," creating an atmosphere in which "law and order must be maintained." Once again, responsibility is shifted from the oppressor to the oppressed. Other whites chide, "Don't forget – you're only 10 percent of the population; if you get too smart, we'll wipe you out." If they are liberals, they complain, "What about me – don't you want my help any more?" These are people supposedly concerned about black Americans, but today they think first of themselves, of their feelings of rejection. Or they admonish, "You can't get anywhere without coalitions," when there is in fact no group at present with whom to form a coalition in which blacks will not be absorbed and betrayed. Or they accuse us of "polarizing the races" by our calls for black unity, when the true responsibility for polarization lies with whites who will not accept their responsibility as the majority power for making the democratic process work.

White America will not face the problem of color, the reality of it. The well-intended say: "We're all human, everybody is really decent, we must forget color." But color cannot be "forgotten" until its weight is recognized and dealt with. White America will not acknowledge that the ways in which this country sees itself are contradicted by being black – and always have been. Whereas most of the people who settled this country came here for freedom or for economic opportunity, blacks were brought here to be slaves. When the Lowndes County Freedom Organization chose the black panther as its symbol, it was christened by the press "the Black Panther Party" – but the Alabama Democratic Party, whose symbol is a rooster, has never been called the White Cock Party. No one ever talked about "white power" because power in this country is white. All this adds up to more than merely identifying a group phenomenon by some catchy name or adjective. The furor over that black panther reveals the problems that white America has with color and sex; the furor over Black Power reveals how deep racism runs and the great fear which is attached to it.

Whites will not see that I, for example, as a person oppressed because of my blackness, have common cause with other blacks who are oppressed because of blackness. This is not to say that there are no white people who see things as I do, but that it is black people I must speak to first. It must be the oppressed to whom SNCC addresses itself primarily, not to friends from the oppressing group.

From birth, black people are told a set of lies about themselves. We are told that we are lazy yet I drive through the Delta area of Mississippi and watch black people picking cotton in the hot sun for fourteen hours. We are told, "If you work hard, you'll succeed" but if that were true, black people would own this country. We are oppressed because we are black – not because we are ignorant, not because we are lazy, not because we're stupid (and got good rhythm), but because we're black.

I remember that when I was a boy I used to go to see Tarzan movies on Saturday. White Tarzan used to beat up the black natives. I would sit there yelling, "Kill the beasts, kill the savages, kill 'em!" I was saying: Kill me. It was as if a Jewish boy watched Nazis taking Jews off to concentration camps and cheered them on. Today, I want the chief to beat hell out of Tarzan and send him back to Europe. But it takes time to become free of the lies and their shaming effect on black minds. It takes time to reject the most important lie: that black people inherently can't do the same things white people can do, unless white people help them.

The need for psychological equality is the reason why SNCC today believes that blacks must organize in the black community. Only black people can convey the revolutionary idea that black people are able to do things themselves. Only they can help create in the community an aroused and continuing black consciousness that will provide the basis for political strength. In the past, white allies have furthered white supremacy without the whites involved realizing it – or wanting it, I think. Black people must do things for themselves; they must get poverty money they will control and spend themselves, they must conduct tutorial programs themselves so that black children can identify with black people. This is one reason Africa has such importance: the reality of black men ruling their own nations gives blacks elsewhere a sense of possibility, of power, which they do not now have [...]

Black people do not want to "take over" this country. They don't want to "get Whitey"; they just want to get him off their backs, as the saying goes. The white man is irrelevant to blacks, except as an oppressive force. Blacks want to be in his place, yes, but not in order to terrorize and lynch and starve him. They want to be in his place because that is where a decent life can be had.

But our vision is not merely of a society in which all black men have enough to buy the good things of life. When we urge that black money go into black pockets, we mean the communal pocket. We want to see money go back into the community and used to benefit it. We want to see the cooperative concept applied in business and banking. We want to see black ghetto residents demand that an exploiting landlord or storekeeper sell them, at minimal cost, a building or a shop that they will own and improve cooperatively; they can back their demand with a rent strike, or a boycott, and a community so unified behind them that no one else will move into the building or buy at the store. The society we seek to build among black people, then, is not a capitalist one. It is a society in which the spirit of community and humanistic love prevail. The word "love" is suspect; black expectations of what it might produce have been betrayed too often. But those were expectations of a response from the white community, which failed us. The love we seek to encourage is within the black community, the only American community where men call each other "brother" when they meet. We can build a community of love only where we have the ability and power to do so: among blacks.

As for white America, perhaps it can stop crying out against "black supremacy," "black nationalism," "racism in reverse," and begin facing reality. The reality is that this nation is racist; that racism is not primarily a problem of "human relations" but of an exploitation maintained – either actively or through silence – by the society as a whole. Can whites, particularly liberal whites, condemn themselves? Can they stop blaming us, and blame their own system? Are they capable of the shame which might become a revolutionary emotion?

We have found that they usually cannot condemn themselves, and so we have done it. But the rebuilding of this society, if at all possible, is basically the responsibility of whites – not blacks. We won't fight to save the present society, in Vietnam or anywhere else. We are just going to work, in the way we see fit, and on goals we define, not for civil rights but for all our human rights.

Source: Stokely Carmichael, "What We Want," from *New York Review of Books*, 22 September 1966, http://www.nybooks.com/articles/1966/09/22/what-we-want/

11.5 Black Panther Party, Platform and Program, 1966

When Huey P. Newton and Bobby Seale founded the Black Panther Party for Self-Defense, later shortened to just the Black Panther Party (BPP), its main focus was exercising Second Amendment rights to carry weapons and organizing citizen patrols to monitor the actions of the Oakland Police Department. The gun-toting Panthers with their uniform of black berets and black leather jackets helped to define a black power style and esthetic. In terms of its politics, the party's mixture of revolutionary socialist, anti-imperialist, and black nationalist rhetoric is evident in its ten-point program below. The party later expanded its activities to providing a free breakfast program for children and free community health clinics.

The BPP was not afraid to court controversy and the white press seized on its actions to stoke white fears about a black uprising. In May 1967, thirty people representing the BPP arrived at the California State Capitol holding guns to protest the gun control measures being debated in the California General Assembly. In October 1967, it was alleged that BPP co-founder Huey P. Newton had killed police officer John Frey during an altercation at a traffic stop. Newton was convicted of voluntary manslaughter, although this conviction was later overturned on appeal. While Newton was in prison, the BPP's "Free Huey" campaign received widespread national attention. In April 1968, Eldridge Cleaver, the BPP minister of information, and Bobby Hutton, the 17-year-old BPP national treasurer, were involved in a shootout with Oakland Police. Cleaver was wounded and Hutton was killed.

The forthright rhetoric and actions of the BPP, together with its willingness to directly confront white authority, brought unwelcome attention from the FBI. The FBI's COINTELPRO program (1956–1971) of surveillance, infiltration, and harassment, targeted the BPP and other black power and civil rights groups. The BPP spread across the nation and was especially strong in major urban areas. It also encountered numerous problems, from being vilified in the white press to being wracked with internecine rivalries and conflicts. Run-ins with law enforcement officials led to the deaths of a number of party members. All of these factors precipitated the BPP's decline after reaching a height of membership in 1970, although the party did not formally dissolve until 1982. The BPP was one of the most high profile and enduring manifestations of the black power movement, and its influence – particularly in the realm of popular culture – remains palpable today.

The program is usually divided into one section of ten points entitled "What We Want" and then ten paragraphs explaining these points in a section entitled "What We Believe." For the sake of clarity, we have put each one of the ten points in "What We Want" immediately above its corresponding paragraph in "What We Believe."

WHAT WE WANT

WHAT WE BELIEVE

1. <u>We want freedom. We want power to determine the destiny of our Black Community.</u>

<u>We believe</u> that black people will not be free until we are able to determine our destiny.

2.   <u>We want full employment for our people.</u>

<u>We believe</u> that the federal government is responsible and obligated to give every man employment or a guaranteed income. We believe that if the white American businessmen will not give full employment, then the means of production should be taken from the businessmen and placed in the community so that the people of the community can organize and employ all of its people and give a high standard of living.

3.   <u>We want an end to the robbery by the white man of our Black Community.</u>

<u>We believe</u> that this racist government has robbed us and now we are demanding the overdue debt of forty acres and two mules. Forty acres and two mules was promised 100 years ago as restitution for slave labor and mass murder of black people. We will accept the payment in currency which will be distributed to our many communities. The Germans are now aiding the Jews in Israel for the genocide of the Jewish people. The Germans murdered six million Jews. The American racist has taken part in the slaughter of over fifty million black people; therefore, we feel that this is a modest demand that we make.

4.   <u>We want decent housing, fit for the shelter of human beings.</u>

<u>We believe</u> that if the white landlords will not give decent housing to our black community, then the housing and the land should be made into cooperatives so that our community, with government aid, can build and make decent housing for its people.

5.   <u>We want education for our people that exposes the true nature of this decadent American society. We want education that teaches us our true history and our role in the present-day society.</u>

<u>We believe</u> in an educational system that will give to our people a knowledge of self. If a man does not have knowledge of himself and his position in society and the world, then he has little chance to relate to anything else.

6.   <u>We want all black men to be exempt from military service.</u>

<u>We believe</u> that Black people should not be forced to fight in the military service to defend a racist government that does not protect us. We will not fight and kill other people of color in the world who, like black people, are being victimized by the white racist government of America. We will protect ourselves from the force and violence of the racist police and the racist military, by whatever means necessary.

7.   <u>We want an immediate end to POLICE BRUTALITY and MURDER of black people.</u>

<u>We believe</u> we can end police brutality in our black community by organizing black self-defense groups that are dedicated to defending our black community from racist police oppression and brutality. The Second Amendment to the Constitution of the United States gives a right to bear arms. We therefore believe that all black people should arm themselves for self-defense.

8.   <u>We want freedom for all black men held in federal, state, county and city prisons and jails.</u>

<u>We believe</u> that all black people should be released from the many jails and prisons because they have not received a fair and impartial trial.

9.   <u>We want all black people when brought to trial to be tried in court by a jury of their peer group or people from their black communities, as defined by the Constitution of the United States.</u>

<u>We believe</u> that the courts should follow the United States Constitution so that black people will receive fair trials. The 14th Amendment of the US Constitution gives a man a right to be tried by his peer group. A peer is a person from a similar economic, social, religious, geographical, environmental, historical and racial background. To do this the court will be forced to select a jury from the black community from which the black defendant came. We have been, and are being tried by all-white juries that have no understanding of the "average reasoning man" of the black community.

10.   <u>We want land, bread, housing, education, clothing, justice and peace. And as our major political objective, a United Nations supervised plebiscite to be held throughout the black colony in which only black colonial subjects will be allowed to participate, for the purpose of determining the will of black people as to their national destiny.</u>

When, in the course of human events, it becomes necessary for one people to dissolve the political bonds which have connected them with another, and to assume, among the powers of the earth, the separate and equal station to which the laws of nature and nature's God entitle them, a decent respect to the opinions of mankind requires that they should declare the causes which impel them to the separation.

We hold these truths to be self-evident, that all men are created equal; that they are endowed by their Creator with certain inalienable rights; that among these are life, liberty, and the pursuit of happiness. <u>That, to secure these rights, governments are instituted among men, deriving their just powers from the consent of the governed; that, whenever any form of government becomes destructive of these ends, it is the right of the people to alter or abolish it, and to institute a new government, laying its foundation on such principles, and organizing its powers in such form, as to them shall seem most likely to effect their safety and happiness.</u> Prudence, indeed, will dictate that governments long established should not be changed for light and transient causes; and, accordingly, all experience hath shown, that mankind are more disposed to suffer, while evils are sufferable, than to right themselves by abolishing the forms to which they are accustomed. But, when a long train of abuses and usurpations, pursuing invariably the same object, evinces a design to reduce them under absolute despotism, it is their right, it is their duty, to throw off such government, and to provide new guards for their future security.

Source: *The Black Panther*, Saturday, 19 October 1968, p. 19.

11.6 Larry Neal, "The Black Arts Movement," 1968

The Black Arts Movement (BAM) was, as Larry Neal puts it in the extract below, "the aesthetic and spiritual sister of the Black Power concept." It brought the concerns and sensibilities of the black power movement into poetry, painting, music, theater, and other artistic forms of expression. In doing so, BAM shared the black power movement's core ideals, with an emphasis on the primacy of black people and black peoples' experiences shaping and informing its approach. A leading figure in BAM was poet LeRoi Jones, who after 1967 went by the name Amiri Baraka, the founder of the Black Arts Repertory Theater/School (BARTS) in Harlem, which became one of the hubs of BAM's creative endeavors. Baraka's and other artists' work responded to events such as the assassination of Malcolm X in 1965 and the growing racial violence in the United States, as well as taking their cues from global struggles for freedom and equality, such as the fight against apartheid in South Africa.

BAM also built upon a long and rich heritage of black cultural expression in the United States that had flourished in periods before them, such as the Harlem Renaissance of the 1920s and 1930s, and the more recent On Guard for Freedom political black literary group in Manhattan in the 1960s, in which Baraka and others in BAM had been members. Like the black power movement, BAM spread across the country with its own distinct local expressions: Chicago's Third World Press and Detroit's Broadside Press and Lotus Press published black poets; Cleveland's Karamu House, a neighborhood center and black theater, nurtured BAM in Ohio; and California's Black Dialogue and Soulbook provided literary journals to showcase the work of black poets and authors. BAM included black women's voices, such as playwright and poet Ntozake Shange, and poets Jayne Cortez, Sonia Sanchez, Audre Lorde, and June Jordan. A combination of political disagreements and the commercial success of some artists such as Baraka, Nikki

Giovanni, and Gil Scott-Heron, which led them into more mainstream pursuits, hastened the demise of BAM in the mid-1970s. Yet the movement's influence lived on, with its emphasis on speech and performance evident in later black musical expressions such as rap and hip-hop, and spoken-word and performance poetry.

Larry Neal, the author of the piece below, worked with Baraka to form BARTS, published several influential essays defining and describing the role of BAM, published poetry, and served as arts editor of Liberator *magazine from the mid to late 1960s. Following the award of a prestigious Guggenheim Fellowship in 1970, Neal held an academic post at Yale University and served on the Commission on the Arts and Humanities in Washington, DC, an indication of BAM's influence in the academy. This influence, in turn, helped to pave the way for the emergence of Black Studies as a discipline and the establishment of Black Studies departments on university campuses in the late 1960s and early 1970s.*

The Black Arts Movement is radically opposed to any concept of the artist that alienates him from his community. Black Art is the aesthetic and spiritual sister of the Black Power concept. As such, it envisions an art that speaks directly to the needs and aspirations of Black America. In order to perform this task, the Black Arts Movement proposes a radical reordering of the Western cultural aesthetic. It proposes a separate symbolism, mythology, critique, and iconology. The Black Arts and the Black Power concept both relate broadly to the Afro-American's desire for self-determination and nationhood. Both concepts are nationalistic. One is politics; the other with the art of politics.

Recently, these two movements have begun to merge: the political values inherent in the Black Power concept are now finding concrete expression in the aesthetics of Afro-American dramatists, poets, choreographers, musicians, and novelists. A main tenet of Black Power is the necessity for Black people to define the world in their own terms. The Black artist has made the same point in the context of aesthetics. The two movements postulate that there are in fact and in spirit two Americas – one black, one white.

The Black artist takes this to mean that his primary duty is to speak to the spiritual and cultural needs of Black people. Therefore, the main thrust of this new breed of contemporary writers is to confront the contradictions arising out of the Black man's experience in the racist West. Currently, these writers are re-evaluating Western aesthetic, the traditional role of the writer, and the social function of art. Implicit in this re-evaluation is the need to develop a "black aesthetic."

It is the opinion of many Black writers, I among them, that the Western aesthetic has run its course: it is impossible to construct anything meaningful within its decaying structure. We advocate a cultural revolution in art and ideas. The cultural values inherent in Western history must either be radicalized or destroyed, and we will probably find that even radicalization is impossible. In fact, what is needed is a whole new system of ideas. Poet Don L. Lee expresses it:

We must destroy Faulkner, dick, jane, and other perpetrators of evil. It's time for Du Bois, Nat Turner, and Kwame Nkrumah. As Frantz Fanon points out: destroy the culture and you destroy the people. This must not happen. Black artists are culture stabilizers; bringing back old values, and introducing new ones. Black Art will talk to the people and with the will of the people stop impending "protective custody."

The Black Arts Movement eschews "protest" literature. It speaks directly to Black people. Implicit in the concept of "protest" literature, as brother [black poet Etheridge] Knight has made clear, is an appeal to white morality:

Now any Black man who masters the technique of his particular art form, who adheres to the white aesthetic, and who directs his work toward a white audience is, in one sense, protesting. And implicit in the act of protest is the belief that a change will be forthcoming once the masters are aware of the protestor's "grievance" (the very word connotes begging, supplications to the gods). Only when that belief has faded and protestings end, will Black art begin.

Brother Knight also has some interesting statements about the development of a "Black aesthetic":

Unless the Black artist establishes a "Black aesthetic" he will have no future at all. To accept the white aesthetic is to accept and validate a society that will not allow him to live. The Black artist must create new forms and new values, sing new songs (or purify old ones); and along with other Black authorities, he must create a new history, new symbols, myths, and legends (and purify old ones by fire). And the Black artist, in creating his own aesthetic, must be accountable for it only to the Black people. Further, he must hasten his own dissolution as an individual (in the Western sense) – painful though the process may be, having been breast-fed the poison of "individual experience."

When we speak of a "Black aesthetic" several things are meant. First, we assume that there is already in existence the basis for such an aesthetic. Essentially, it consists of an African-American cultural tradition. But this aesthetic is finally, by implication, broader than that tradition. It encompasses most of the useable elements of the Third World culture. The motive behind the Black aesthetic is the destruction of the white thing, the destruction of white ideas, and white ways of looking at the world.

The new aesthetic is mostly predicated on an Ethics which asks the question: whose vision of the world is finally more meaningful, ours or the white oppressors'? These are basic questions. Black intellectuals of previous decades failed to ask them. Further, national and international affairs demand that we appraise the world in terms of our own interests. It is clear that the question of human survival is at the core of contemporary experience. The Black artist must address himself to this reality in the strongest terms possible. In a context of world upheaval, ethics and aesthetics must interact positively and be consistent with the demands for a more spiritual world.

Consequently, the Black Arts Movement is an ethical movement. Ethical, that is, from the viewpoint of the oppressed. And much of the oppression confronting the Third World and Black America is directly traceable to the Euro-American cultural sensibility. This sensibility, antihuman in nature, has, until recently, dominated the psyches of most Black artists and intellectuals; it must be destroyed before the Black creative artists can have a meaningful role in the transformation of society.

[...]

Implicit in the Black Arts Movement is the idea that Black People, however dispersed, constitute a nation within the belly of white America. This is not a new idea. Garvey said it and the Honorable Elijah Muhammad says it now. And it is on this idea that the concept of Black Power is predicated.

Afro-American life and history is full of creative possibilities, and the movement is just beginning to perceive them. Just beginning to understand that the most meaningful statements about the nature of Western society must come from the Third World of which Black America is a part. The thematic material is broad, ranging from folk heroes like Shine and Stagolee to historical figures like Marcus Garvey and Malcolm X. And then there is the struggle for Black survival, the coming confrontation between white America and Black America. If art is the harbinger of future possibilities, what does the future of Black America portend?

Source: Larry Neal, "The Black Arts Movement," pp. 29–39 from *The Drama Review*, 12:4 (T40-Summer, 1968). © 1968 by the New York University and the Massachusetts Institute of Technology.

11.7   Frances Beale, "Double Jeopardy: To be Black and Female," 1969

Frances M. Beale was born in Binghamton, New York, in 1940. Her mother was a Russian Jewish immigrant and her father was of black and Native American ancestry. Beale's parents' backgrounds and experiences influenced her early antiracist activism. She first worked with the NAACP and then later with SNCC.

Beale shared the concerns of other women in SNCC about the organization's patriarchal assumptions. During the 1964 Freedom Summer, later viewed as a crucible for the emergence of the modern feminist movement, the unequal roles assigned to men and women on the basis of gender sparked intense conversations about sexism in SNCC and the civil rights movement. In 1965, white women activists Casey Hayden and Mary King articulated these concerns in "A Kind of Memo" that was circulated to a number of black and white women activists, and which was published the following year in edited form as "Sex and Caste" in Liberation *magazine. In 1966, the National Organization for Women (NOW) was founded, which still exists today as one of the preeminent feminist organizations in the United States, further extending the conversation about sexism in American society.*

Concerned at the continuing unequal treatment of women in SNCC after its embrace of black power in 1966, Beale founded SNCC's Black Women's Liberation Caucus (BWLC) in 1968. A year later, the caucus formally separated from SNCC and became the Black Women's Alliance (BWA) and then the Third World Women's Alliance (TWWA). Beale's concept of "double jeopardy" in her article below insists that the specific nature of black women's oppression is rooted in the distinct twin shaping forces of racism and sexism. Racism was an experience that black women shared with black men, but, Beale argued, black women's experiences were different from those of black men because they were also mediated by sexism. Black men, Beale claimed, expected black women to be subservient along the lines of traditional gender roles. Deviating from that expectation was viewed as emasculating black men and a distraction from the common struggle for black liberation. Beale asserted that both racism and sexism (and classism) had to be addressed simultaneously, and that one form of oppression should not be considered subordinate to another.

In attempting to analyze the situation of the black woman in America, one crashes abruptly into a solid wall of grave misconceptions, outright distortions of fact and defensive attitudes on the part of many. The system of capitalism (and its after birth ... racism) under which we all live, has attempted by many devious ways and means to destroy the humanity of all people, and particularly the humanity of black people. This has meant an outrageous assault on every black man, woman and child who reside in the United States.

In keeping with its goal of destroying the black race's will to resist its subjugation, capitalism found it necessary to create a situation where the black man found it impossible to find meaningful or productive employment. More often than not, he couldn't find work of any kind. And the black woman likewise was manipulated by the system, economically exploited and physically assaulted. She could often find work in the white man's kitchen, however, and sometimes became the sole breadwinner of the family. This predicament has led to many psychological problems on the part of both man and woman and has contributed to the turmoil that we find in the black family structure [...]

Unfortunately, there seems to be some confusion in the Movement today as to who has been oppressing whom. Since the advent of black power, the black male has exerted a more prominent leadership role in our struggle for justice in this country. He sees the system for what it really is for the most part. But where he rejects its values and mores on many issues, when it comes to women, he seems to take his guidelines from the pages of the Ladies Home Journal.

Certain black men are maintaining that they have been castrated by society but that black women somehow escaped this persecution and even contributed to this emasculation. Let me state here and now that the black woman in America can justly be described as a "slave of a slave." By reducing the black man in America to such abject oppression, the black woman had no protector and was used, and is still being used in some cases, as the scapegoat for the evils that this horrendous system has perpetrated on black men. Her physical image has been maliciously maligned; she has been sexually molested and abused by the white colonizer; she has suffered the worst kind of economic exploitation, having been forced to serve as the white woman's maid and wet nurse for white offspring while her own children were more often than not, starving and neglected. It is the depth of degradation to be socially manipulated, physically raped, used to undermine your own household, and to be powerless to reverse this syndrome.

It is true that our husbands, fathers, brothers and sons have been emasculated, lynched and brutalized. They have suffered from the cruelest assault on mankind that the world has ever known. However, it is a gross distortion of fact to state that black women have oppressed black men. The capitalist system found it expedient to enslave and oppress them and proceeded to do so without signing any agreements with black women.

It must also be pointed out at this time, that black women are not resentful of the rise to power of black men. We welcome it. We see in it the eventual liberation of all black people from this corrupt system under which we suffer. Nevertheless, this does not mean that you have to negate one for the other. This kind of thinking is a product of miseducation; that it's either X or it's Y. It is fallacious reasoning that in order the black man to be strong, the black woman has to be weak.

Those who are exerting their "manhood" by telling black women to step back into a domestic, submissive role are assuming a counter-revolutionary position. Black women likewise have been abused by the system and we must begin talking about the elimination of all kinds of oppression. If we are talking about building a strong nation, capable of throwing off the yoke of capitalist oppression, then we are talking about the total involvement of every man, woman, and child, each with a highly developed political consciousness. We need our whole army out there dealing with the enemy and not half an army.

There are also some black women who feel that there is no more productive role in life than having and raising children. This attitude often reflects the conditioning of the society in which we live and is adopted (totally, completely and without change) from a bourgeois white model. Some young sisters who have never had to maintain a household and accept the confining role which this entails, tend to romanticize (along with the help of a few brothers) this role of housewife and mother. Black women who have had to endure this kind of function as the sole occupation of their life, are less apt to have these utopian visions.

Those who project in an intellectual manner how great and rewarding this role will be and who feel that the most important thing that they can contribute to the black nation is children, are doing themselves a great injustice. This line of reasoning completely negates the contributions that black women have historically made to our struggle for liberation. These black women include Sojourner Truth, Harriet Tubman, Ida B. Wells-Barnett, Mary McLeod Bethune and Fannie Lou Hamer to name but a few.

We live in a highly industrialized society and every member of the black nation must be as academically and technologically developed as possible. To wage a revolution, we need competent teachers, doctors, nurses, electronic experts, chemists, biologists, physicists, political scientists, and so on and so forth. Black women sitting at home reading bedtime stories to their children are just not going to make it.

Source: Frances Beale, "Double Jeopardy: To be Black and Female," 1969, http://www. hartford-hwp.com/archives/45a/196.html

11.8 Angela Davis, *An Autobiography*, 1974

As in the civil rights movement, black women played prominent roles in the black power movement. By the late 1960s, over half of BPP members were women. Angela Davis was one of the BPP's most visible and well-known women activists. Born in Birmingham, Alabama, in 1944, Davis's mother was a teacher and her father was a teacher and businessman. The family lived in a black neighborhood called Dynamite Hill, so named because of the frequent Ku Klux Klan bombings there. In high school, Davis joined SNCC, and later graduated from Brandeis University with a degree in philosophy and French literature. While at Brandies, Davis also spent time studying at the Sorbonne in Paris, where Algerian students introduced her to global perspectives on colonialism and oppression. Abandoning her PhD studies in Germany in 1967, Davis returned to the United States to study and to become active in the black freedom struggle. Davis studied under philosopher, sociologist, and political theorist Herbert Marcuse at the University of San Diego, where she earned a master's degree in philosophy. She also became active in SNCC, the BPP, and the Communist Party. In 1969, the University of California at Los Angeles hired Davis but she was later dismissed at the urging of California governor Ronald Reagan because of her communist affiliation. Davis continued her activism, most notably in her efforts to gain justice for the "Soledad Brothers" – George Jackson, John Clutchette, and Fleeta Drumgo – who stood accused of killing white prison guard John Vincent Mills at California's notorious Soledad Prison in January 1970.

Davis narrates her involvement with the Soledad Brothers case in the extract from her autobiography below. In August 1970, George Jackson's brother, Jonathan Jackson, along with two others, took hostages in a courtroom to try to free a prisoner and to win freedom for the Soledad Brothers. The episode ended in four deaths. Some of the firearms used in the courtroom siege were registered to Davis, who was charged with kidnapping, murder, and conspiracy. Davis became a fugitive from the law on the FBI's Most Wanted list until she was apprehended in October 1971. An international "Free Angela" campaign followed, and she was acquitted of all charges in June 1972. Davis resumed her academic career at San Francisco State University and became a prolific writer, advocate, and activist on issues of race, class, gender, and criminal justice. She ran as a vice presidential candidate on the Communist Party ticket in 1980 and 1984.

Days before his trial for allegedly killing John Vincent Mills, in August 1971 George Jackson was shot and killed by a white guard at San Quentin Prison. The authorities claimed that this was a result of an escape attempt gone wrong, while Jackson supporters maintained that the episode was a setup. In March 1972, the remaining two Soledad Brothers, John Clutchette and Fleeta Drumgo, were acquitted of killing Mills.

Around the middle of February, I picked up the Los Angeles *Times* and noticed on the front page a large photograph of three very striking Black men. Their faces were serene and strong, but their waists were draped in chains. Chains bound their arms to the sides and chains shackled their legs. "They are still trying to impress upon us that we have not yet escaped bondage," I thought. Angry and frustrated, I began to read the story. It was about Soledad Prison.

Soledad Prison was a household word in the Black community. During my last two years in Los Angeles, I must have heard it a million times. There was San Quentin, there was Folsom – and there was Soledad.

Soledad is the Spanish word for solitude. Solitude Prison – this name seemed to expose what the prison was trying to hide. When Josef was living in my apartment, he told me how they had kept him in solitary confinement during most of his imprisonment. He still bore the stamp of Soledad. He still preferred solitude. For hours and often days he would stay on the sunporch which was his bedroom, reading, thinking, alone. And when he talked, it was always in a soft whisper of a voice – as if not to disturb the massive silence that had so long surrounded him.

The L.A. *Times* article reported the indictment of George Jackson, John Clutchette and Fleeta Drumgo for the murder of a guard at Soledad Prison. An entire month had elapsed since the killing took place. Why had it taken so long to return the indictments? I wondered why the author had not commented on this time lag. The article reeked of deception and evasiveness. It seemed that the *Times* was trying to turn public opinion against the accused men even before the trial got started. If one accepted the article on its face, one would have come away with the assumption that the three men were guilty.

During the next days, I kept thinking about the faces of those brothers. Three beautiful virile faces pulled out of the horrible anonymity of prison life.

A few weeks later the Che-Lumumba Club [a communist youth group] was contacted about meeting on the Soledad situation. It was being arranged by the Los Angeles "Committee to Defend the Bill of Rights," which wanted to discuss the mounting of a mass campaign to free the three from Soledad.

I was drowning in work, but I simply couldn't stop thinking about those three haunting faces in the newspaper. I had to attend the meeting; even if I became involved in only a minimal way, at least I would be doing something.

The night of the meeting, Tamu, Patrice Neal – another club member – and I went to the run-down old Victoria Hall. (It had been famous once for its swinging Saturday night dances. Now, in this hall, people were no longer having fun. They were talking about a very serious thing, about liberation.)

About a hundred people answered the call. Though they were predominantly Black, a sizeable number of white people had turned up as well. There were young people, older people and people who were obviously attending their first political meeting. There were those who had to come because they had sons, husbands and brothers in Soledad Prison.

Seated behind the long tables stretched across the front of the hall were Fay Stender, lawyer for George Jackson, George's mother and sisters – Georgia, Penny and Frances Jackson – Inez Williams, Fleeta's mother, and Doris Maxwell, the mother of John Clutchette.

Speaking of Soledad, Fay Stender [George Jackson's attorney] explained from the warden down to the guards, the prison hierarchy had a long history of promoting racial enmity in the prison population. As long as the Black, Chicano and white prisoners were at each other's necks, the prison administration knew they would not have to worry about the serious challenges to their authority.

As in an old southern town, segregation in Soledad Prison was almost total. All activities were arranged so that racial mingling would not occur – or so that when it did occur, the prisoners would be in a posture of battle. With the collaboration of some of the white prisoners, Soledad had developed its own counterpart to the Ku Klux Klan – a group called the "Aryan Brotherhood." Tension in the prison was so thick that even the most innocuous meeting between the races was bound to set off an explosion.

Before January 13, 1970, exercise periods, like everything else, were segregated. On that day, with no explanation, the guards sent Black, Chicano and white prisoners to exercise together in the newly constructed yard. Not a single guard was assigned to accompany them. The explosion was inevitable. A fight erupted between a Black prisoner and a white prisoner, and within a few minutes, there was havoc.

O.G. Miller had the reputation of being a hard-line racist, and was known to be an expert marksman. He was stationed in the gun tower that day. He carefully aimed his carbine and fired several times. Three men fell: W.L. Nolen, Cleveland Edwards, Alvin Miller. They were all black. A few days later the

Montgomery County Grand Jury was convened to hear the case of O.G. Miller. As could have been predicted, he was absolved of all responsibility for the deaths of the three brothers. The Grand Jury ruled that he had done nothing more serious than commit "justifiable homicide."

Source: Angela Davis, *An Autobiography* (New York: Random House, 1974), pp. 250–2.

Discussion Questions

1. Outline and assess the similarities and differences between the civil rights movement and the black power movement.
2. In what ways did gender shape the experiences of individuals in the civil rights and black power movements?
3. Account for the shift in emphasis from nonviolent direct action to other tactics such as armed self-defense in the mid to late 1960s.
4. Discuss the impact of the black power movement on black culture, society, and the arts in the mid to late 1960s.

Further Reading

Carmichael, Stokely, and Charles V. Hamilton. *Black Power: The Politics of Liberation in Black America* (Random House, 1967).

Cobb, Charles E., Jr. *This Nonviolent Stuff'll Get You Killed: How Guns made the Civil Rights Movement Possible* (Basic Books, 2014).

Davis, Angela. *An Autobiography* (Random House, 1974).

Farmer, Ashley D. *Remaking Black Power: How Black Women Transformed an Era* (University of North Carolina Press, 2017).

Jeffries, Hasan Kwame. *Bloody Lowndes: Civil Rights and Black Power in Alabama's Black Belt* (New York University Press, 2009).

Joseph, Peniel E. *Waiting 'Til the Midnight Hour: A Narrative History of the Black Power Movement in America* (Henry Holt, 2006).

Joseph, Peniel E. *Stokely: A Life* (Basic Civitas, 2014).

Marable, Manning. *Malcolm X: A Life of Reinvention* (Viking, 2011).

Seale, Bobby. *Seize the Time: The Story of the Black Panther Party and Huey P. Newton* (Random House, 1970).

Smethurst, James Edward. *The Black Arts Movement: Literary Nationalism in the 1960s and 1970s* (University of North Carolina Press, 2005).

Tyson, Timothy B. *Radio Free Dixie: Robert F. Williams and the Roots of Black Power* (University of North Carolina Press, 1999).

Williams, Robert F. *Negroes with Guns* (Wayne State University Press, reprint 1998).

Chapter 12   Vietnam, Economic Justice, and the Poor People's Campaign, 1967–8

12.1   Robert E. Holcomb Interview on Vietnam War Experiences in the 1960s

The Vietnam War affected black Americans in a number of different ways. By the time of escalating conflict in Vietnam in the mid-1960s, the armed forces included many more blacks than in the past, although their equal acceptance by whites was far from complete. A recurring complaint about the Vietnam War was that black soldiers were drafted and sent into combat roles in disproportionate numbers due to racism in draft boards. This meant black casualties were disproportionately higher, which, in turn, had an impact on the economic wellbeing and self-sufficiency of black families and black communities. There were those who felt that blacks were being used as "cannon fodder" for an unpopular war overseas and that civil rights and black power activists were being targeted by draft boards to get rid of "troublemakers" at home. Some black activists questioned whether black soldiers should be fighting a war for white America against people of color in another country at all, given the persistent and urgent problems of racism at home. At the same time, there were those in President Lyndon B. Johnson's administration who viewed black participation in the military as a means to develop skills and self-esteem that would serve black men well when – or rather, if – they returned to civilian life. The skyrocketing number of unemployed black veterans after the war did not suggest that this was the case. In part, this was a consequence of the disproportionate number of less-than-honorable discharges handed to black soldiers, where racism again, it was charged, played a role. Those who received less-than-honorable discharges struggled to gain access to, or were completely denied access to, the benefits available to other veterans under the GI Bill, in hospital and medical care, and in employment and job training opportunities.

The Civil Rights Movement: A Documentary Reader, First Edition. Edited by John A. Kirk.
© 2020 John Wiley & Sons, Inc. Published 2020 by John Wiley & Sons, Inc.

Tennessee State was a hotbed of social and political unrest in the mid-sixties. Black awareness was on the rise. People like Nikki Giovanni, Kathleen Cleaver, and Rap Brown would be on campus and join our marches. We staged sit-ins at the governor's office and mansion, protesting poor living conditions for black people in the state, some of whom lacked food, decent shelter, and even real toilet facilities. We got into Che Guevara's theories on guerilla warfare, read Mao's little red book, and the revolutionary writings of Camus and Jean-Paul Sartre.

We thought the government was going to begin to be more and more oppressive, especially to black and other minority people. So some of us even took our philosophy to the point that we felt we should arm ourselves and develop skills so that we could survive in the hillsides. We were essentially carrying the student movement into a revolutionary mold.

We wanted the war in Vietnam to cease and desist. We felt that it was an attack on minority people, minority people were being used to fight each other. Some of us would give safe haven to soldiers who went AWOL from Fort Campbell, Kentucky, because they did not want to go to Vietnam. They would hope to stay around the college campus scene until things just blew away. But they wouldn't blow away. You had to do something about it; otherwise, they'd be following you for the rest of your life.

I was arrested for violations of curfew after a riot. And for that and other infractions of school policies aimed at stopping protests, I was expelled. As tensions between the police and the black community continued to rise, I decided to leave Nashville. I just had this feeling that I was under surveillance and one day I'd be walking down the street and someone would roll down his window and I would be shot [...]

I decided to move to New York to continue my art study. Soon afterwards, I got a draft letter. At that point I decided I was going to resist, because I didn't believe in the war [...] I didn't have any problems fighting for capitalism, but I was not interested in fighting for a war in which I would not enjoy the rewards [...]

I was charged with draft evasion. The FBI offered me an option. I could work for them as a plant, an informant, or I could go to the service. For two weeks they kept me locked up in the Federal House of Detention hoping to sweat me into working for them. They wanted to plant me with various black or radical groups, like the Black Panthers, the Student Non-violent Coordinating Committee, and the Symbionese Liberation Army. They said we could start off in New York, but there might be other cities involved. They would provide me with an apartment and a subsistence allowance. For each person that I helped them capture on an outstanding warrant, they would pay me from $1,000 to $3,000. My questions to them were, Would I get concessions against the charge against me, how long would I have to do it, and would I be permitted to carry an arm to protect myself? They offered no promises of leniency or a time when I could get out. And no, I wouldn't be permitted to carry any kind of weapon. I said no deal. I did not want to fulfill that kind of role, especially not unarmed.

Then I went before a federal district court judge and told him I'd prefer to go to war than go to jail or be an informant. He stamped my papers approved to go into the Army.

When they took me to the induction center on Whitehall for the first time, the agent said, "You're not gonna go anywhere are you?"

I said, "No."

He took the manacles off me and left me in the hands of the Army. The Army treated me just as they did any other recruit. They didn't know what my history was. I was free to roam around, so what I did was to roam around and roamed right out of the building.

I got in contact with the lady I was living with, Felice Mosely. I told her I was going into the war, and she got cold feet about waiting for me. We resolved some issues. We broke up. And, after two weeks to rest and recuperate with a friend, I told the FBI to pick me up.

After I finished basic training, they made me a security holdover for two months because they weren't sure whether I'd be subversive to the government in a war situation. I had to go over to the G2 every week to prove to them that I'd be a loyal trooper and fight for the red, white and blue. Finally, they said, "Fine. We're gonna take you through a little more training in AIT school, and from there you'll more than likely go to Vietnam."

But an odd thing happened before I left Fort Gordon, Georgia. I was training some troops on how to fight with a bayonet. One of them came running down the path to stick the dummy with his bayonet. It was a guy I was in college with who had had his ear severely damaged when he was beaten by the Nashville police. I thought to myself they must be taking all of us who were involved in any sort of black political struggle and putting us into the Army as soon as they could so we wouldn't be a problem anymore.

Source: Wallace Terry, *Bloods – Black Veterans of the Vietnam War: An Oral History* (New York: Presidio Press Market Edition, 2006, originally published in New York by Random House, 1984), pp. 201–2, 203–4.

12.2 Student Nonviolent Coordinating Committee, Statement on Vietnam, 1966

There was some initial hesitancy among civil rights organizations and leaders in speaking out against the Vietnam War. The concern revolved around potentially shifting the focus from civil rights activism to antiwar activism and thereby diluting efforts to bring about an end to racial discrimination. Such a stand also risked courting even more controversy and opposition to civil rights. Yet the United States' escalation of troops on the ground in Vietnam from 1965 onward, together with an increasing number of young men drafted to fight the war, led to growing antiwar sentiment in the nation that many civil rights activists felt could not be ignored.

The Student Nonviolent Coordinating Committee (SNCC) agreed at a November 1965 meeting that it would issue a public statement against the war. The catalyst for doing so was the murder of SNCC worker Sammy Younge on 3 January 1966. Younge, a 21-year-old Navy veteran of the Vietnam War, was helping people register to vote at the Macon County Courthouse in Alabama when he and others were threatened with violence. Later that day, Younge was shot and killed in Tuskegee for trying to use a white restroom at a service station. Three days later, SNCC issued its Statement on Vietnam, which explicitly tied civil rights and antiwar activism together. The statement condemned oppressive and interlinked US domestic and foreign policies, including the nation's use of violence against marginalized peoples in flagrant disregard of the law, and the denial of free elections and voting rights. The statement also provided support for draft evasion with encouragement to join the struggle for civil rights in the United States instead.

The antiwar stand came with consequences. Most immediately, four days after the statement was issued, the Georgia House of Representatives voted not to seat SNCC's communications director Julian Bond, who had won election the previous November, because Bond declared his support for SNCC's antiwar statement. Bond successfully appealed the decision to the US Supreme Court, which ruled in Bond v. Floyd *(1966) that he had been denied freedom of speech. The Court ordered the Georgia House of Representatives to seat him. Bond served four terms and helped form the Georgia Black Legislative Caucus. He remained active in civil rights until his death in 2015.*

The Student Nonviolent Coordinating Committee has a right and a responsibility to dissent with United States foreign policy on any issue when it sees fit. The Student Nonviolent Coordinating Committee now states its opposition to the United States' involvement in Vietnam on these grounds:

We believe the United States government has been deceptive in its claims of concern for the freedom of the Vietnamese people, just as the government has been deceptive in claiming concern for the freedom of colored people in other countries such as the Dominican Republic, the Congo, South Africa, Rhodesia, and in the United States itself.

We, the Student Nonviolent Coordinating Committee, have been involved in the black peoples' struggle for liberation and self-determination in this country for the past five years. Our work, particularly in the South, has taught us that the United States government has never guaranteed the freedom of oppressed citizens, and is not yet truly determined to end the rule of terror and oppression within its own borders.

We ourselves have often been victims of violence and confinement executed by United States governmental officials. We recall the numerous persons who have been murdered in the South because of their efforts to secure their civil and human rights, and whose murderers have been allowed to escape penalty for their crimes.

The murder of Samuel Young [sic] in Tuskegee, Alabama, is no different than the murder of peasants in Vietnam, for both Young and the Vietnamese sought, and are seeking, to secure the rights guaranteed them by law. In each case, the United States government bears a great part of the responsibility for these deaths.

Samuel Young was murdered because United States law is not being enforced. Vietnamese are murdered because the United States is pursuing an aggressive policy in violation of international law. The United States is no respecter of persons or law when such persons or laws run counter to its needs or desires.

We recall the indifference, suspicion and outright hostility with which our reports of violence have been met in the past by government officials.

We know that for the most part, elections in this country, in the North as well as the South, are not free. We have seen that the 1965 Voting Rights Act and the 1964 Civil Rights Act have not yet been implemented with full federal power and sincerity.

We question, then, the ability and even the desire of the United States government to guarantee free elections abroad. We maintain that our country's cry of "preserve freedom in the world" is a hypocritical mask, behind which it squashes liberation movements which are not bound, and refuse to be bound, by the expediencies of United States cold war policies.

We are in sympathy with, and support, the men in this country who are unwilling to respond to a military draft which would compel them to contribute their lives to United States aggression in Vietnam in the name of the "freedom" we find so false in this country.

We recoil with horror at the inconsistency of a supposedly "free" society where responsibility to freedom is equated with the responsibility to lend oneself to military aggression. We take note of the fact that 16% of the draftees from this country are Negroes called on to stifle the liberation of Vietnam, to preserve a "democracy" which does not exist for them at home.

We ask, where is the draft for the freedom fight in the United States?

We therefore encourage those Americans who prefer to use their energy in building democratic forms within this country. We believe that work in the civil rights movement and with other human relations organizations is a valid alternative to the draft. We urge all Americans to seek this alternative, knowing full well that it may cost them their lives – as painfully as in Vietnam.

Source: Student Nonviolent Coordinating Committee, Statement on Vietnam, 6 January 1966, https://www.crmvet.org/docs/snccviet.htm

12.3   Martin Luther King, Jr, "Beyond Vietnam: A Time to Break Silence," 1967

The speech that Martin Luther King, Jr delivered to the group "Clergy and Laymen Concerned about Vietnam" at Riverside Church in New York on 4 April 1967 – exactly a year to the day before King's assassination at the Lorraine Motel in Memphis – reveals the shifting nature of King's stance in the last few years of his life. King had remained mostly silent on the issue of the Vietnam War or addressed it only indirectly, focusing on the money that the war took away from poverty programs and its distraction from civil rights issues. This approach consciously avoided criticism of President Johnson's administration that had proved an ally to the movement in the past. King knew that by condemning the war, he would also be alienating Johnson, who was fully committed to the conflict in Vietnam. In his Riverside Church speech, King decided to take that risk. King roundly denounced American conduct in Vietnam and US foreign policy in other parts of the world. Moreover, King connected the moral bankruptcy in US foreign policy with its domestic policies, calling for a "revolution of values" that would see the nation reorient its priorities from profit motives to people. On 25 April, King co-led a peace march of 125,000 people alongside other notable antiwar protesters such as white pediatrician Dr. Benjamin Spock and black entertainer Harry Belafonte. Like SNCC's antiwar stand, King's stand also had consequences: it represented a final break in faltering relations with the Johnson administration – "a naïve black preacher" were the president's dismissive words at hearing King's Riverside speech – and also rankled many of King's former allies in the civil rights movement. One poll showed that only a quarter of the black population backed King's antiwar sentiment. To some, King's speech marked the emergence of a more assertive and less compromising figure than in the past, someone who was determined to follow through on his moral convictions no matter what the cost. To others, it smacked of desperation and ill judgment, indicating a leader who could no longer command a consensus within or between the black and white communities on civil rights issues, as he had previously appeared to do. Certainly, King's speech indicated that his scope was broadening from a narrow focus on civil rights to encompass foreign policy, human rights, and economic justice, which he viewed as an entirely natural extension of his earlier civil rights leadership and consistent with his calling as a Christian minister.

The war in Vietnam is but a symptom of a far deeper malady within the American spirit, and if we ignore this sobering reality ... and if we ignore this sobering reality, we will find ourselves organizing "clergy and laymen concerned" committees for the next generation. They will be concerned about Guatemala – Guatemala and Peru. They will be concerned about Thailand and Cambodia. They will be concerned about Mozambique and South Africa. We will be marching for these and a dozen other names and attending rallies without end, unless there is a significant and profound change in American life and policy.

And so, such thoughts take us beyond Vietnam, but not beyond our calling as sons of the living God.

In 1957, a sensitive American official overseas said that it seemed to him that our nation was on the wrong side of a world revolution. During the past ten years, we have seen emerge a pattern of suppression which has now justified the presence of US military advisors in Venezuela. This need to maintain social stability for our investments accounts for the counterrevolutionary action of American forces in Guatemala. It tells why American helicopters are being used against guerrillas in Cambodia and why American napalm and Green Beret forces have already been active against rebels in Peru.

It is with such activity in mind that the words of the late John F. Kennedy come back to haunt us. Five years ago he said, "Those who make peaceful revolution impossible will make violent revolution inevitable." Increasingly, by choice or by accident, this is the role our nation has taken, the role of those who make peaceful revolution impossible by refusing to give up the privileges and the pleasures that come from the immense profits of overseas investments. I am convinced that if we are to get on the right side of the world revolution, we as a nation must undergo a radical revolution of values. We must rapidly begin ... we must rapidly begin the shift from a thing-oriented society to a person-oriented society. When machines and computers, profit motives and property rights, are considered more important than people, the giant triplets of racism, extreme materialism, and militarism are incapable of being conquered.

A true revolution of values will soon cause us to question the fairness and justice of many of our past and present policies. On the one hand, we are called to play the Good Samaritan on life's roadside, but that will be only an initial act. One day we must come to see that the whole Jericho Road must be transformed so that men and women will not be constantly beaten and robbed as they make their journey on life's highway. True compassion is more than flinging a coin to a beggar. It comes to see that an edifice which produces beggars needs restructuring.

A true revolution of values will soon look uneasily on the glaring contrast of poverty and wealth. With righteous indignation, it will look across the seas and see individual capitalists of the West investing huge sums of money in Asia, Africa, and South America, only to take the profits out with no concern for the social betterment of the countries, and say, "This is not just." It will look at our alliance with the landed gentry of South America and say, "This is not just." The Western arrogance of feeling that it has everything to teach others and nothing to learn from them is not just.

A true revolution of values will lay hand on the world order and say of war, "This way of settling differences is not just." This business of burning human beings with napalm, of filling our nation's homes with orphans and widows, of injecting poisonous drugs of hate into the veins of peoples normally humane, of sending men home from dark and bloody battlefields physically handicapped and psychologically deranged, cannot be reconciled with wisdom, justice, and love. A nation that continues year after year to spend more money on military defense than on programs of social uplift is approaching spiritual death.

America, the richest and most powerful nation in the world, can well lead the way in this revolution of values. There is nothing except a tragic death wish to prevent us from reordering our priorities so that the pursuit of peace will take precedence over the pursuit of war. There is nothing to keep us from molding a recalcitrant status quo with bruised hands until we have fashioned it into a brotherhood.

[...]

We still have a choice today: nonviolent coexistence or violent coannihilation. We must move past indecision to action. We must find new ways to speak for peace in Vietnam and justice throughout the developing world, a world that borders on our doors. If we do not act, we shall surely be dragged down the long, dark, and shameful corridors of time reserved for those who possess power without compassion, might without morality, and strength without sight.

Now let us begin. Now let us rededicate ourselves to the long and bitter, but beautiful, struggle for a new world. This is the calling of the sons of God, and our brothers wait eagerly for our response. Shall we say the odds are too great? Shall we tell them the struggle is too hard? Will our message be that the forces of American life militate against their arrival as full men, and we send our deepest regrets? Or will there be another message – of longing, of hope, of solidarity with their yearnings, of commitment to their cause, whatever the cost? The choice is ours, and though we might prefer it otherwise, we must choose in this crucial moment of human history.

Source: Martin Luther King, Jr, "Beyond Vietnam: A Time to Break Silence," 4 April 1967, Martin Luther King Papers Project, http://mlk-kpp01.stanford.edu/kingweb/publications/speeches/Beyond_Vietnam.pdf

12.4 US Congress, Economic Opportunity Act of 1964

The inextricable link between race and poverty is a long one, but in the 1960s it received fresh attention in the United States. Democratic socialist and political scientist Michael Harrington's 1962 book The Other America: Poverty in the United States *is credited with influencing policymakers in addressing the fact that in the midst of the country's growing economic affluence, up to a quarter of the nation still lived in poverty. The book caught President Kennedy's attention and helped to convince his successor in office, President Johnson, to launch a War on Poverty as part of his broader vision to build a Great Society that was free from poverty and racial injustice. The passage of the Economic Opportunity Act of 1964, among other measures, created an Office of Economic Opportunity (OEO), headed by Kennedy's brother-in-law Sargent Shriver. The OEO launched a number of grassroots Community Action Programs (CAPs) that were charged with ensuring "maximum feasible participation" of the poor in tackling issues of poverty in their communities. This ethos was very much along the lines of SNCC's organizing philosophy, and the CAPs provided funds that sustained and extended civil rights and black power activism at a local level.*

---

508 PUBLIC LAW 88-452-AUG. 20, 1964

Public Law 88-452

AN ACT

To mobilize the human and financial resources of the Nation to combat poverty in the United States.

Be it enacted by the Senate and House of Representatives of the United States of America in Congress assembled, That this Act may be cited as the "Economic Opportunity Act of 1964."

FINDINGS AND DECLARATION OF PURPOSE

SEC.2. Although the economic well-being and prosperity of the United States have progressed to a level surpassing any achieved in world history, and although these benefits are widely shared through-out the Nation, poverty continues to be the lot of a substantial number of our people. The United States can achieve its full economic and social potential as a nation only if every individual has the opportunity to contribute to the full extent of his capabilities and to participate in the workings of our society. It is, therefore, the policy of the United States to eliminate the paradox of poverty in the midst of plenty in this Nation by opening to everyone the opportunity for education and training, the opportunity to work, and the opportunity to live in decency and dignity. It is the purpose of this Act to strengthen, supplement, and coordinate efforts in furtherance of that policy.

[...]

TITLE II – URBAN AND RURAL COMMUNITY ACTION PROGRAMS

PART A – GENERAL COMMUNITY ACTION PROGRAMS

STATEMENT OF PURPOSE

SEC. 201. The purpose of this part is to provide stimulation and incentive for urban and rural communities to mobilize their resources to combat poverty through community action programs.

COMMUNITY ACTION PROGRAMS

SEC. 202. (a) The term "community action program" means a program –

1. which mobilizes and utilizes resources, public or private, of any urban or rural, or combined urban and rural, geographical area (referred to in this part as a "community"), including but not limited to a State, metropolitan area, county, city, town, multicity unit, or multicounty unit in an attack on poverty;
2. which provides services, assistance, and other activities of sufficient scope and size to give promise of progress toward elimination of poverty or a cause or causes of poverty through developing employment opportunities, improving human performance, motivation, and productivity, or bettering the conditions under which people live, learn, and work;
3. which is developed, conducted, and administered with the maximum feasible participation of residents of the areas and members of the groups served; and
4. which is conducted, administered, or coordinated by a public or private nonprofit agency (other than a political party), or a combination thereof.

(b) The Director is authorized to prescribe such additional criteria for programs carried on under this part as he shall deem appropriate.

Source: US Congress, Economic Opportunity Act of 1964, https://www.gpo.gov/fdsys/pkg/STATUTE-78/pdf/STATUTE-78-Pg508.pdf

12.5 George Wiley, "Proposal for the Establishment of an Anti-Poverty Action Center," 1966

A number of non-governmental organizations also responded to poverty in the 1960s. In 1965, the National Urban League's Whitney Young, Jr proposed a massive investment in American cities (see Chapter 10) and in 1966 A. Philip Randolph and Bayard Rustin outlined a "Freedom Budget" to eliminate poverty. One of the largest antipoverty coalitions in the 1960s was the Citizens' Crusade Against Poverty (CCAP) founded in 1963 by United Automobile Workers (UAW) president Walter Reuther. The CCAP was composed of a broad-based coalition of groups that included labor, church, business, and civic organizations. However, tensions mounted in the CCAP over who should lead it and what its demands should be. Just before the CCAP's 1966 convention, George Wiley, a former chemistry professor and a leader in the Congress of Racial Equality (CORE), issued his "Proposal for the Establishment of an Anti-Poverty Action Center," making the case for putting more poor people in leadership positions, pursuing significant income redistribution, and taking a more assertive approach to antipoverty efforts. When his proposal was rebuffed, Wiley resigned from the CCAP and became founder and executive director of the National Welfare Rights Organization (NWRO). The membership of the NWRO, mostly black and mostly female, grew to nearly 25,000 over the next few years and helped to open access to welfare for thousands of eligible families, as well as influencing government welfare policy. In December 1972, Wiley resigned from the NWRO to form a new organization, the Movement for Economic Justice (MEJ), in an effort to build a broader interracial antipoverty coalition. He tragically died in a boating accident less than a year later.

PURPOSES

1. To develop nationwide support for major anti-poverty measures. (e.g. Minimum Wage Bill, pressing for "maximum feasible participation" of the poor in the anti-poverty program; developing a drive for a guaranteed annual income.)
2. To develop nationwide support for significant local anti-poverty movements. (e.g. Delano Grape Strike and its drive for NLRA coverage for agricultural workers.)
3. To provide surveillance of and pressure on federal agencies with programs designed to help the poor. (e.g. monitor activities and policies of OEO, Department of Agriculture, Department of Labor, HUD, HEW, etc.)
4. To be the eyes and ears in Washington for local groups wishing specific information about federal agencies and federal programs. (e.g. respond to local groups' requests for information; check on status of applications before federal agencies at request of local action groups.)
5. Provide advice and assistance to local groups coming to Washington to lobby or to press for support of their programs by federal agencies. (e.g. act as Washington contact for groups planning to come to Washington on poverty issues. Help with housing, location of appropriate government offices, appointments, public relations, etc.)

Source: George Wiley, "Proposal for the Establishment of an Anti-Poverty Action Center," 7 April 1966, George Wiley Papers, box 5, folder 13, State Historical Society of Wisconsin, Madison.

12.6 Richard L. Copley, I **Am** a Man, 1968

Martin Luther King, Jr and the Southern Christian Leadership Conference (SCLC) provided their own response to antipoverty efforts in formulating the Poor People's Campaign (PPC). The PPC was planned as an interracial coalition of the poor that would march on Washington, DC to demand economic justice. In effect, it constituted a reprisal of the 1963 March on Washington, but with a focus that returned to economic issues and with more of a nonviolent direct action component to it.

While preparing the PPC, King was diverted by a labor dispute in Memphis. The black sanitation workers in the city who were members of the local American Federation of State, County and Municipal Employees (AFSCME) union had been on strike since 12 February 1968 because city officials were refusing to negotiate over a "checkoff" system whereby union dues were deducted straight from paypackets. Memphis Mayor Henry

Loeb refused to recognize the predominantly black union at all. Violence erupted at a union march when the police used Mace, tear gas, and billyclubs. A new black community organization, Community on the Move for Equality (COME) was founded, with half of its leaders ministers, to support the strike.

In March 1968, an old friend of King's, James Lawson, the man who had drafted SNCC's Statement of Purpose in 1960 (see Chapter 5), and who was a member of COME, asked King to visit Memphis and to support the movement there. King agreed and addressed an enthusiastic crowd of 15,000 people at Mason Temple on 18 March. He told them that they should engage in a "general work stoppage" to support the strikers and to show black community solidarity. King vowed to return to lead a march in the city on the day of the work stoppage. So convinced was King that the strike highlighted the central idea of the PPC – the profound link between racial and social inequality and poverty – that he declared the march would mark the official beginning of the PPC.

Because of heavy snowfall in Memphis, the march was moved from 22 March to 28 March. When it did finally occur, things quickly descended into chaos. After an unruly and jostling start, looting began to break out on Main Street. Lawson called the march to a halt and hurried King away from the scene. That day, there were 282 arrests, 62 injuries, and the death of 17-year-old Larry Payne who was shot by a Memphis police officer. A curfew was called and 3,800 members of the Tennessee National Guard were brought into service. King was dejected at the outbreak of violence and the potential impact on the PPC. The PPC's opponents were issuing ominous warnings that the campaign would bring similar violence to the nation's capital.

The below photograph depicts striking AFSCME sanitation workers holding their distinctive signs asserting "I Am A Man" which became an enduring image of the dispute in Memphis.

Source: Richard L. Copley, I Am a Man, 1968, AFSCME Communications Department Records, https://reuther.wayne.edu/node/3631

12.7 Dr. Sybil C. Mitchell, "The Invaders: The Real Story" on Memphis Demonstrations in 1968

The march held on 28 March excluded local black power group the Black Organizing Project (BOP), also known as the Invaders (named after the popular science fiction television program at the time), from the planning committee. Some blamed them for the violence. The following day, three members of the Invaders, Charles Cabbage, Calvin Taylor, and Charles Harrington met with King to plead their innocence in the unrest and to offer help in organizing another, this time peaceful march, in exchange for financial help with their community organizing plans. King explained that the SCLC did not have the funds to help, but he promised to make inquiries with other organizations on their behalf. King also enlisted the help of SCLC staff to pave the way for a peaceful march in Memphis, initially scheduled for 5 April and later moved to 8 April.

When King flew into Memphis on 3 April, he learned that federal district judge Bailey Brown had issued a restraining order against march leaders. Six Memphis attorneys agreed to help fight the restraining order. That night an emotional and exhausted King spoke again at Mason Temple. He recounted the history of the movement through the sit-ins, the Freedom Rides, the March on Washington, and SCLC campaigns in Albany, Birmingham, and Selma, along with the other ordeals he and the movement had been through, finishing with a flourish: "But it really doesn't matter to me now, because I've been to the mountaintop ... and I've seen the promised land. I may not get there with you. But I want you to know tonight, that we, as a people will get to the promised land. And so I'm happy tonight. I'm not worried about anything. I'm not fearing any man. Mine eyes have seen the glory of the coming of the Lord."

Early the next evening King was shot and killed on the balcony of the Lorraine Motel by white supremacist James Earl Ray. The city swiftly capitulated to the demands of striking sanitation workers. Congress passed the Civil Rights Act of 1968 containing provisions for fair housing and the protection of civil rights workers. Meanwhile, racial disturbances rocked more than 130 cities in 29 states, resulting in 46 deaths, over 7,000 injuries, and 20,000 arrests, with damage to property estimated at over $100 million.

Charles Cabbage

I was a student at Morehouse College in Atlanta. It was in the middle of the civil rights movement. I was involved in the SCLC and helped to organize the city's only black anti-war group on campus [...] When I returned home to Memphis, John Smith and I formed the Black Organizing Project (BOP). There were high school students, college students, and community organizations coming together. Out of that effort came the Invaders [...] To say that we were militants is to limit our purpose. We tried to plan various strategies to see changes come about. Yes, we were revolutionary – young, black revolutionary men [...] In addition to that last meeting, two others with Dr. King also took place [...] He wanted to solve some problems in his own organization and we were looking at how we could join forces and help one another [...] When he was murdered, it was devastating. How do you prepare for something like that? We had no way of gaining access to the press. We had no power. And the federal government was after us. They knew who we were and had orders to shoot to kill on sight [...] I left Memphis and went to different cities, worked in different places for a while, but I returned home to Memphis eventually. Today, I have grandchildren, and I can tell them how things were and how I tried to make things better for our people.

John Burl Smith

We came out of the Riverside community in South Memphis [...] At that time, there were no black political leaders and no one to train us. We were just trying to bring about change – to see businesses in our communities and make life better for our people. Whites had the power of life and death over us. That had to change [...] I had served in Viet Nam like a good American. I defended my country and had proven myself [...] There was an incident that happened at a gas station [...] You have to remember this was before self-service. This man would pump the gas and then tell you the gas cap was missing, and he'd sell it back to you for a dollar. He had gotten me twice before, and when he did it this particular time, I told him I knew it was my gas cap and to give it back [...] We had words, and I called the police. They looked at him and looked at me, and I am the one who gets arrested. Memphis police were notorious for brutality. No one could do anything about it [...] When we started the Invaders, it was just time. You couldn't see beyond the next minute. Something had to be done. Things had to change [...] But what people don't really know about us was that we were not a bunch of ignorant, street thugs shouting 'black power' and raising our fists. We were college students at LeMoyne-Owen and Memphis State. No one ever really acknowledged that [...]

John Gary Williams

I got involved with the Invaders in January of 1968. It was a natural transition for me. There was an incident over in Viet Nam. An elderly man had a copy of the Stars and Stripes, and it had a picture in there of a Black guy with camouflage on [...] The man showed me the picture, rubbed the skin on my arm and pointed back to the picture. I nodded to him. He was trying to tell me that the man was the same color as I was, and he was dressed for the jungle on the streets of Detroit [...] That gave me the incentive to live from that point on. I didn't have that incentive before because my pop had killed my mom right before I left, and I had no intentions of coming back home alive. Black people over here were fighting for equality. I wanted to get back home and be a part of it [...] The movement with the Invaders was perfect to express my feelings.

We had to stop the madness. Fire hoses and dogs were turned on people for no reason [...] The '60s produced a new breed of black men and women. It was just time. We were in the middle of a revolution. A change had to come about [...] By the time Dr. King had been murdered, we had pretty much calmed down. After jail, I left Memphis, moved to different cities and worked, but I eventually came back home [...] We are no longer the Invaders, but we never stopped pushing for change. We evolved into the men we are today. The fight for justice and equality never ended. It continues even today [...]

Minister Suhkara A. Yahweh

The day Dr. King was crucified was the day I became an Invader. I told John that I was going to work with the Poor People's Campaign in Washington as prime minister of the Invaders. We provided security for that movement [...] I wasn't officially a part of the rebellion when Dr. King came for that first march, but I know that the Invaders were blamed for the violence that broke out. The organization had nothing to do with that, but the blame fell on the Invaders [...] Dr. King had to return to Memphis and lead a peaceful march because he had to prove that the Poor People's March to Washington could be peaceful. After he came here and was killed, I had two purposes as far as the Invaders were concerned: to redeem the name of the organization and to work with the Poor People's Campaign.

Source: Dr. Sybil C. Mitchell, "The Invaders: The Real Story," from *Tri-State Defender* (Memphis), 4 April 2008, http://www.tsdmemphis.com/news/3229

12.8 Ralph David Abernathy Recalls the Poor People's Campaign in 1968

After Martin Luther King, Jr's death, the heavy mantle of leadership for the SCLC and the PPC fell on King's closest friend and confidant Ralph D. Abernathy. Abernathy was a fellow minister and a peer of King's from the Montgomery bus boycott days. Not only did Abernathy provide constant support and friendship for King, but he also in effect became King's own minister to turn to in moments of doubt and hardship. In that capacity, Abernathy was King's number two person. But Abernathy was arguably best suited to that role which he had performed admirably in the past, rather than someone who had been primed to take over and step into King's shoes as a movement leader. When King announced the PPC on 4 December 1967, it consisted of a plan to bring a coalition of blacks, poor whites, Latinos, and American Indians to Washington, DC to set up a shantytown called Resurrection City on the National Mall. This would be followed by a campaign of nonviolent demonstrations and civil disobedience culminating in a mass march. Finally, there would be a national boycott of large corporations to exert pressure on businesses and Congress for economic justice.

Abernathy launched the PPC in Washington, DC on 12 May 1968 and the construction of Resurrection City got underway. Almost 2,600 people from different parts of the country converged on the nation's capital, traveling from their various locales in caravans to maintain their visibility and to advertise the campaign ahead of their arrival. The "Appalachian Trail" brought poor whites and blacks from upper South states; the "Mule Train" brought participants from the rural South; the "San Francisco Caravan" from the West Coast; and the "Indian Trail," which began in Seattle, from western and northern states. Upon arrival, the people in the caravans built Resurrection City out of plywood on 15 acres of West Potomac Park. The city had its own zip code, a city hall, a dispensary, a dining tent, a Soul Center for cultural and recreational activities, and a number of other facilities.

Officially we opened the Poor People's Campaign on May 12, with a rally in Cardozo High School Stadium, located in the heart of Washington's worst black slum. The surrounding area had been devastated by riots following Martin's death, and the stadium rose out of great piles of bricks and rubble that served as a reminder both of Martin's death and of the inevitable consequences of violence, even in the face of such cruel injustices.

Thousands came to hear Coretta King give a stirring speech calling for "black women, white women, brown women and red women – all the women of this nation – [to join] in a campaign of conscience." She called for welfare reform, and a restoration of benefits for women and children, saying: "Our Congress passes laws which subsidize corporation farms, oil companies, airlines and houses for suburbia, but when it turns its attention to the poor, it suddenly becomes concerned about balancing the budget."

She was joined on the platform by my wife, Juanita, and Mrs Robert Kennedy, as well as Mrs Harry Belafonte, Mrs Phillip Hart, and several other prominent women, who supported our efforts by sharing in that moment. It was an impressive kickoff for the campaign; and after the rally a number of us returned to the Mall to begin setting up our model city.

There were Mexican-Americans from the Southwest, American Indians from the Dakotas, Puerto Ricans from New York City, poor blacks and poor whites from all over. They believed deeply and firmly that they had come to find a better life, and they took the idea of their own City on a Hill quite seriously. For the first time in their lives, they were to have their own homes and their own street addresses. You could see the excitement shining in their eyes when we told them what we had in mind.

We had spots staked out along streets named for the heroes of the movement: King Boulevard, Abernathy Street, Fanny Lou Hamer Drive. As they scrambled out of wagons and buses – carrying all their belongings in bundles, cardboard boxes, or cardboard suitcases – we met them, took them to City Hall to register, and then tried to assign them "property" on a first-come, first-served basis.

On May 13, we had a brief dedication ceremony, at which I drove the nails into the first plywood building and then said a few words. I announced that we had come "to plague the Pharaohs of this nation with plague after plague until they agree to give us meaningful jobs and a guaranteed annual income."

I also vowed that our marches and demonstrations in the city would be non-violent, but I warned the government that we were there for the long haul.

"Unlike the previous marches which have been held in Washington," I said, "this march will not last a day, or two days, or even a week. We will be here until the Congress of the United States decide that they are going to do something about the plight of the poor people by doing away with poverty, unemployment, and underemployment in this country."

I pledged that we would stay until Congress adjourned. "And then," I said, "we're going to go where Congress goes, because we have decided that there will be no new business until we first take care of the old business."

Then we sang "We Shall Overcome." Since the Indians had originally owned the land and had suffered greatly at the hands of our government over the years, I symbolically alluded to this injustice by asking an Indian girl for permission to use the land, and she granted it. Then I said, "I declare this to be the site of our new city of hope, Resurrection City, USA."

After this brief ceremony, we began to build the first home on our property for Minnie Lee Hill, who had come from Marks, Mississippi. Mrs Hill was there with eight of her children and she symbolized the need and deprivation that Martin had recognized and responded to in that community.

The "homes" we were building were not, strictly speaking, tents although they were often called that in news stories and although there were some real tents on the site. They were actually, A-frame huts made of plywood. In size, they were about eight by twenty feet, not the Taj Mahal by any means, but with the square footage of a fairly spacious bedroom. Since these had been prefabricated, they were fairly easy to put together, and by nightfall we had constructed about a hundred. We continued, however, by spotlight; and as hammers pounded nails and saws into wood, the city took shape between the marble formality of the Lincoln Memorial and the Washington Monument, its progress evident in the still waters of the reflecting pool. By the next day, Washingtonians were surprised (and probably shocked) to see about six city blocks of raw plywood structures covering the green lawn of the Mall.

We had moved in.

At first the "shacks" had the same unpainted look about them, as if they were made out of huge wooden playing cards leaning against one another. Later, however, the graffiti that decorated them gave each a distinctive character. One was named "Big House of John Hickman." Another contained "Soul Sisters Shirley, Mary, Ruby, Joyce." Still another was called "Cleveland's Rat Patrol." There were also some bearing Spanish names, and a few with pictures drawn on them. We allowed them to write what they wanted to, as long as it wasn't offensive or obscene.

In addition to the individual shacks, we also had a large mess tent where everyone ate, as well as tents that housed doctors, dentists, and a nursery. During the first days, which were sunny, barbers gave free haircuts on a first-come, first-served basis.

We even had our own zip code, 20013.

I was too busy to ponder at length the meaning of all this; but when I stopped to watch these people, I was touched by the eager and grateful way they responded to these services, usually unavailable to them in the towns and cities where they lived. For the first time, many of them felt genuinely part of a real community, something most people take for granted since it is part of our nature as human beings to be social animals rather than loners. We had taken a few of the nation's loners and brought them together with one another – and for a brief while it appeared as if they were going to meld into a genuine family.

Source: Ralph David Abernathy, *And the Walls Came Tumbling Down* (New York: Harper and Row, 1989), pp. 511–14.

12.9 Associated Press, Aerial View of Resurrection City, 1968

For a variety of reasons, Resurrection City and the PPC ran into trouble from the very outset. Young members of street gangs, who were given the job of camp marshals, alienated the Washington press corps that was essential to gaining much-needed favorable publicity. Financial constraints meant that Resurrection City could not be completed to the full extent planned. Ralph Abernathy postponed the mass march originally scheduled for 30 May, a further indication that all was not well, although a series of smaller demonstrations at government offices did take place. The unseasonably rainy weather compounded the difficulties, turning Resurrection City into a mud bath. The problems that plagued poor neighborhoods across the United States also plagued Resurrection City: turf battles between street gangs, protection rackets, and petty theft among them. Within the SCLC, Martin Luther King, Jr's absence prompted bickering and factionalism among remaining staff members whose strong opinions and egos had to some extent been kept in check while King remained the authoritative leader of the organization. The FBI's efforts to disrupt and undermine the civil rights movement in general, and the PPC in particular, continued through its COINTELPRO program.

The planned mass march eventually took place without a hitch on 19 June, but the muted response it received, both from those participating and in the nation at large, only underscored the very different mood of the movement and the nation between the March on Washington in August 1963 and what was called Solidarity Day in June 1968. The conditions, tensions, and problems in Resurrection City only grew worse, and on 24 June, after the permit to construct Resurrection City expired, the authorities shut the camp down. This constituted, in effect, a negotiated settlement with SCLC leaders, who were just as concerned about developments in Resurrection City as the authorities were. The police cleared the grounds in 90 minutes without any conflict arising. Abernathy led one last column of 250 marchers to the US Capitol where he and others were arrested for illegally demonstrating. They were

freed a few days later. With that last act of defiance, the PPC, the SCLC's final
major campaign of the 1960s, came to an end with a whimper rather than a bang.
Although it achieved some modest goals in changing some government policies, the
PPC failed to make the substantive and lasting impact that King had hoped for.

Source: Associated Press, Aerial View of Resurrection City, 1968, https://www.
gettyimages.com/license/514870722

Discussion Questions

1. Were civil rights organizations and leaders right to speak out about the Vietnam War? What were the benefits and costs in doing so?
2. Why did the attention of the civil rights movement shift more broadly toward human rights and economic justice in the late 1960s?
3. Account for the widespread violence that followed nonviolent leader Martin Luther King, Jr's assassination in April 1968.
4. Explain the reasons for the limited success of the Poor People's Campaign.

Further Reading

Abernathy, Ralph David. *And the Walls Came Tumbling Down* (Harper and Row, 1989).

Ashmore, Susan Youngblood. *Carry It On: The War on Poverty and the Civil Rights Movement in Alabama, 1964–1972* (University of Georgia Press, 2008).

Graham, Herman, III. *The Brothers' Vietnam War: Black Power, Manhood, and the Military Experience* (University Press of Florida, 2003).

Hall, Simon. *Peace and Freedom: The Civil Rights and the Antiwar Movements in the 1960s* (University of Pennsylvania Press, 2005).

Honey, Michael K. *Going Down Jericho Road: The Memphis Strike, Martin Luther King's Last Campaign* (W.W. Norton, 2007).

Jackson, Thomas F. *From Civil Rights to Human Rights: Martin Luther King, Jr and the Struggle for Economic Justice* (University of Pennsylvania Press, 2007).

King, Martin Luther, Jr. *Where do We go from Here: Chaos or Community?* (Harper and Row, 1968).

Kornbluh, Felicia. *The Battle for Welfare Rights: Politics and Poverty in Modern America* (University of Pennsylvania Press, 2007).

Lucks, Daniel S. *Selma to Saigon: The Civil Rights Movement and the Vietnam War* (University Press of Kentucky, 2014).

McKnight, Gerald D. *The Last Crusade: Martin Luther King Jr, the FBI, and the Poor People's Campaign* (Westview Press, 1998).

Orleck, Annelise, and Lisa Gayle Hazirjian, eds. *The War on Poverty: A New Grassroots History, 1964–1980* (University of Georgia Press, 2011).

Terry, Wallace. *Bloods – Black Veterans of the Vietnam War: An Oral History* (Random House, 1984).

Chapter 13   Affirmative Action, 1960s–1980s

13.1 President John F. Kennedy, Executive Order 10925, 1961

Starting in the 1960s, the federal government set its sights on tackling discrimination in hiring practices though the ever-evolving concept of affirmative action. In 1960, the election of President John F. Kennedy coincided with the emerging visibility of civil rights demonstrations. Kennedy responded in March 1961 by issuing Executive Order 10925 that established the President's Committee on Equal Employment Opportunity (PCEEO). The new president proclaimed that in so doing he had dedicated his "administration to the cause of equal opportunity in employment by the government or its contractors." Chaired by Vice President Lyndon B. Johnson, the committee was charged with taking "affirmative action to ensure that applicants are employed, and that employees are treated during employment without regard to their race, creed, color, or national origin." It was the young black attorney Hobart Taylor, Jr, who Johnson asked to draft the language for President Kennedy's executive order, alongside future US Supreme Court justices Arthur Goldberg and Abe Fortas, who coined the term "affirmative action." Taylor toyed with using either the term "positive action" or "affirmative action," but he liked the alliterativeness of the latter better.

Precisely what the term meant was unclear. The initial idea of affirmative action was that it would signify a determined stand by the administration to address employment opportunities. Although on the one hand affirmative action asked federal agencies to hire more black people, on the other hand it did not contain any specific guidelines about how to actually go about doing that. Essentially, the idea of affirmative action at this point consisted of a very general directive to pursue a nondiscriminatory hiring policy. As successive presidential administrations and the courts discovered, the idea was anything but simple to translate into practice.

The Civil Rights Movement: A Documentary Reader, First Edition. Edited by John A. Kirk.
© 2020 John Wiley & Sons, Inc. Published 2020 by John Wiley & Sons, Inc.

Under the PCEEO, federal agency contractors were charged with enforcing equal employment opportunities under threat of having contracts canceled if they did not comply. But the PCEEO had no actual enforcement powers and its mandate excluded all employment funded through federal grants and loans that ran into billions of dollars.

ESTABLISHING THE PRESIDENT'S COMMITTEE ON EQUAL EMPLOYMENT OPPORTUNITY

PART III – OBLIGATIONS OF GOVERNMENT CONTRACTORS AND SUBCONTRACTORS

SUBPART A – CONTRACTORS' AGREEMENTS

SECTION 301. Except in contracts exempted in accordance with section 303 of this order, all government contracting agencies shall include in every government contract hereafter entered into the following provisions:

In connection with the performance of work under this contract, the contractor agrees as follows:

1. The contractor will not discriminate against any employee or applicant for employment because of race, creed, color, or national origin. The contractor will take affirmative action to ensure that applicants are employed, and that employees are treated during employment, without regard to their race, creed, color, or national origin. Such action shall include, but not be limited to, the following: employment, upgrading, demotion or transfer; recruitment or recruitment advertising; layoff or termination; rates of pay or other forms of compensation; and selection for training, including apprenticeship. The contractor agrees to post in conspicuous places, available to employees and applicants for employment, notices to be provided by the contracting officer setting forth the provisions of this nondiscrimination clause.

2. The contractor will, in all solicitations or advertisements for employees placed by or on behalf of the contractor, state that all qualified applicants will receive consideration for employment without regard to race, creed, color, or national origin.

3. The contractor will send to each labor union or representative of workers with which he has a collective bargaining agreement or other contract or understanding, a notice, to be provided by the agency contracting officer, advising the said labor union or workers' representative of the contractor's commitments under this section, and shall post copies of the notice in conspicuous places available to employees and applicants for employment.

4. The contractor will comply with all provisions of Executive Order No. 10925 of March 6, 1961, and of the rules, regulations, and relevant orders of the President's Committee on Equal Employment Opportunity created thereby.

5. The contractor will furnish all information and reports required by Executive Order No. 10925 of March 6, 1961, and by the rules, regulations, and orders of the said Committee, or pursuant thereto, and will permit access to his books, records, and accounts by the contracting agency and the Committee for purposes of investigation to ascertain compliance with such rules, regulations, and orders.

6. In the event of the contractor's non-compliance with the nondiscrimination clauses of this contract or with any of the said rules, regulations, or orders, this contract may be cancelled in whole or in part and the contractor may be declared ineligible for further government contracts in accordance with procedures authorized in Executive Order No. 10925 of March 6, 1961, and such other sanctions may be imposed and remedies invoked as provided in the said Executive order or by rule, regulation, or order of the President's Committee on Equal Employment Opportunity, or as otherwise provided by law.

7. The contractor will include the provisions of the foregoing paragraphs (1) through (6) in every subcontract or purchase order unless exempted by rules, regulations, or orders of the President's Committee on Equal Employment Opportunity issued pursuant to section 303 of Executive Order No. 10925 of March 6, 1961, so that such provisions will be binding upon each subcontractor or vendor. The contractor will take such action with respect to any subcontract or purchase order as the contracting agency may direct as a means of enforcing such provisions, including sanctions for noncompliance: Provided, however, that in the event the contractor becomes involved in, or is threatened with, litigation with a subcontractor or vendor as a result of such direction by the contracting agency, the contractor may request the United States to enter into such litigation to protect the interests of the United States.

Source: President John F. Kennedy, Executive Order 10925, https://www.eeoc.gov/eeoc/history/35th/thelaw/eo-10925.html

13.2 US Congress, Title VII of the Civil Rights Act, 1964

In 1963, President Kennedy issued Executive Order 11114 that further developed the idea of affirmative action by extending it to include all federally funded employment, which covered work related to federal grants, loans, and other forms

of financial assistance. Employers, employment agencies, and unions were required to state in all job ads that, "all qualified applicants will receive consideration without regard to race, creed, color, or national origin." The federal government could access records to check compliance with affirmative action mandates and those in breach could have their contracts canceled and be declared ineligible for federal funding in the future.

After Kennedy's November 1963 assassination, President Johnson took his predecessor's embryonic civil rights bill and infused it with bolder and more expansive measures that were enshrined in the Civil Rights Act of 1964. Among its provisions, Title VI wrote Kennedy's Executive Order 11114 into law, while Title VII extended affirmative action to all firms (not just those involved with the federal government and with federal funding and contracts) of 25 or more employees, and established the Equal Employment Opportunities Commission (EEOC) to police those requirements. Notably, for the first time the act also specifically prohibited sex discrimination in employment.

Extending affirmative action to all businesses proved controversial and was the focus of opposition to Title VII inside and outside of Congress. The specter of "reverse discrimination" against whites was raised. Title VII did provide some employment loopholes. Different standards or wages could be applied to employees on the basis of seniority or merit; education and skills tests could be used in hiring and promotion; and Indian tribes, nonprofit and private membership organizations, and smaller firms with less than 25 employees, were all exempt. There were other exceptions under certain circumstances: for example, a French restaurant could advertise for a French cook, a Catholic school could require its teachers to be Catholic, and Girl Scouts could hire only female camp counselors.

In terms of implementation, the new rules applying to companies of less than 25 did not take full effect until 1968, limiting its immediate impact; the seniority principle meant that in recessions the "last hired, first fired" policy could be applied, which had an adverse impact on minority workers who had initially benefited from nondiscriminatory legislation; and the use of education and skills tests disadvantaged blacks who typically had less access to education resources than whites.

TITLE VII – EQUAL EMPLOYMENT OPPORTUNITY

DEFINITIONS

SEC. 701. For the purposes of this title –

(a) The term "person" includes one or more individuals, labor unions, partnerships, associations, corporations, legal representatives, mutual companies, joint-stock companies, trusts, unincorporated organizations, trustees, trustees in bankruptcy, or receivers.

(b) The term "employer" means a person engaged in an industry affecting commerce who has twenty-five or more employees for each working day in each of twenty or more calendar weeks in the current or preceding calendar year, and any agent of such a person, but such term does not include (1) the United States, a corporation wholly owned by the Government of the United States, an Indian tribe, or a State or political subdivision thereof, (2) a bona fide private membership club (other than a labor organization) which is exempt from taxation under section 501(c) of the Internal Revenue Code of 1954: Provided, That during the first year after the effective date prescribed in subsection (a) of section 716, persons having fewer than one hundred employees (and their agents) shall not be considered employers, and, during the second year after such date, persons having fewer than seventy-five employees (and their agents) shall not be considered employers, and, during the third year after such date, persons having fewer than fifty employees (and their agents) shall not be considered employers: Provided further, That it shall be the policy of the United States to insure equal employment opportunities for Federal employees without discrimination because of race, color, religion, sex or national origin and the President shall utilize his existing authority to effectuate this policy.

[...]

EQUAL EMPLOYMENT OPPORTUNITY COMMISSION

SEC. 705. (a) There is hereby created a Commission to be known as the Equal Employment Opportunity Commission, which shall be composed of five members, not more than three of whom shall be members of the same political party, who shall be appointed by the President by and with the advice and consent of the Senate. One of the original members shall be appointed for a term of one year, one for a term of two years, one for a term of three years, one for a term of four years, and one for a term of five years, beginning from the date of enactment of this title, but their successors shall be appointed for terms of five years each, except that any individual chosen to fill a vacancy shall be appointed only for the unexpired term of the member whom he shall succeed. The President shall designate one member to serve as Chairman of the Commission, and one member to serve as Vice Chairman. The Chairman shall be responsible on behalf of the Commission for the administrative operations of the Commission, and shall appoint, in accordance with the civil service laws, such officers, agents, attorneys, and employees as it deems necessary to assist it in the performance of its functions and to fix their compensation in accordance with the Classification Act of 1949, as amended. The Vice Chairman shall act as Chairman in the absence or disability of the Chairman or in the event of a vacancy in that office.

(b) A vacancy in the Commission shall not impair the right of the remaining members to exercise all the powers of the Commission and three members thereof shall constitute a quorum.

(c) The Commission shall have an official seal which shall be judicially noticed.

(d) The Commission shall at the close of each fiscal year report to the Congress and to the President concerning the action it has taken; the names, salaries, and duties of all individuals in its employ and the moneys it has disbursed; and shall make such further reports on the cause of and means of eliminating discrimination and such recommendations for further legislation as may appear desirable.

(e) The Federal Executive Pay Act of 1956, as amended (5 U.S.C. 2201–2209), is further amended –

    1. by adding to section 105 thereof (5 USC 2204) the following clause: "(32) Chairman, Equal Employment Opportunity Commission"; and

    2. by adding to clause (45) of section 106(a) thereof (5 USC 2205(a)) the following: "Equal Employment Opportunity Commission (4)."

(f) The principal office of the Commission shall be in or near the District of Columbia, but it may meet or exercise any or all its powers at any other place. The Commission may establish such regional or State offices as it deems necessary to accomplish the purpose of this title.

(g) The Commission shall have power –

    1. to cooperate with and, with their consent, utilize regional, State, local, and other agencies, both public and private, and individuals;

    2. to pay to witnesses whose depositions are taken or who are summoned before the Commission or any of its agents the same witness and mileage fees as are paid to witnesses in the courts of the United States;

    3. to furnish to persons subject to this title such technical assistance as they may request to further their compliance with this title or an order issued thereunder;

    4. upon the request of (i) any employer, whose employees or some of them, or (ii) any labor organization, whose members or some of them, refuse or threaten to refuse to cooperate in effectuating the provisions of this title, to assist in such effectuation by conciliation or such other remedial action as is provided by this title;

    5. to make such technical studies as are appropriate to effectuate the purposes and policies of this title and to make the results of such studies available to the public;

6. to refer matters to the Attorney General with recommendations for intervention in a civil action brought by an aggrieved party under section 706, or for the institution of a civil action by the Attorney General under section 707, and to advise, consult, and assist the Attorney General on such matters.

(h) Attorneys appointed under this section may, at the direction of the Commission, appear for and represent the Commission in any case in court.

(i) The Commission shall, in any of its educational or promotional activities, cooperate with other departments and agencies in the performance of such educational and promotional activities.

All officers, agents, attorneys, and employees of the Commission shall be subject to the provisions of section 9 of the Act of August 2, 1939, as amended (the Hatch Act), notwithstanding any exemption contained in such section.

Source: US Congress, Title VII, Civil Rights Act of 1964, http://www.ourdocuments. gov/doc.php?doc=97&page=transcript

13.3 President Lyndon B. Johnson, "To Fulfill These Rights," 1965

On 4 June 1965, President Johnson gave the commencement address at Howard University. In the address, Johnson outlined his evolving understanding of civil rights and the nation's responsibilities in the pursuit of black freedom and equality. After noting his administration's considerable legislative achievements, Johnson declared that this was a start, but not enough. Providing opportunity was one thing; actually achieving equality was another. Johnson baldly stated that it had been an "American failure" to address poverty, and black poverty in particular, which, he said, was a specific and distinct consequence of the racially biased injustices of the past. Influenced by assistant labor secretary Daniel Patrick Moynihan's recent report The Negro Family: The Case for Action *(which became more popularly known as "The Moynihan Report"), Johnson pointed toward the breakdown of the black family as in part being responsible for the predicament of black America. The Moynihan Report subsequently received much criticism on a number of grounds for its assumptions and conclusions about black families. There were other less contested problems that Johnson recognized, such as the lack of decent housing, education, healthcare, and employment opportunities for blacks.*

Johnson proposed bringing together a "conference of scholars, and experts, and outstanding Negro leaders" to tackle the issue of how "To Fulfill These Rights"

(an echo of President Truman's earlier commissioned report To Secure These Rights, *referenced in Chapter 1). The necessity of addressing these issues, Johnson suggested, was something that was deeply embedded in the political culture of the United States, and he declared that he would make them "a chief goal of my administration." A White House Conference on Civil Rights was held in early June 1966 and produced a lengthy report. Yet by then the seeming consensus over civil rights in 1965 had begun to unravel in the wake of urban unrest, more forthright and assertive black demands, and an accompanying white "backlash" to further reforms. Moreover, the Vietnam War occupied an increasing amount of Johnson's time, energy, and focus. Nevertheless, Johnson's Howard University commencement address did provide clarification about what he meant by affirmative action. If one sentence encapsulated his approach it was this: "To move beyond opportunity to achievement."*

Dr. Nabrit, my fellow Americans:

I am delighted at the chance to speak at this important and this historic institution. Howard has long been an outstanding center for the education of Negro Americans. Its students are of every race and color and they come from many countries of the world. It is truly a working example of democratic excellence.

Our earth is the home of revolution. In every corner of every continent men charged with hope contend with ancient ways in the pursuit of justice. They reach for the newest of weapons to realize the oldest of dreams, that each may walk in freedom and pride, stretching his talents, enjoying the fruits of the earth.

Our enemies may occasionally seize the day of change, but it is the banner of our revolution they take. And our own future is linked to this process of swift and turbulent change in many lands in the world. But nothing in any country touches us more profoundly, and nothing is more freighted with meaning for our own destiny than the revolution of the Negro American.

In far too many ways American Negroes have been another nation: deprived of freedom, crippled by hatred, the doors of opportunity closed to hope.

In our time change has come to this Nation, too. The American Negro, acting with impressive restraint, has peacefully protested and marched, entered the courtrooms and the seats of government, demanding a justice that has long been denied. The voice of the Negro was the call to action. But it is a tribute to America that, once aroused, the courts and the Congress, the President and most of the people, have been the allies of progress.

LEGAL PROTECTION FOR HUMAN RIGHTS

Thus we have seen the high court of the country declare that discrimination based on race was repugnant to the Constitution, and therefore void. We have seen in 1957, and 1960, and again in 1964, the first civil rights legislation in this Nation in almost an entire century.

As majority leader of the United States Senate, I helped to guide two of these bills through the Senate. And, as your President, I was proud to sign the third. And now very soon we will have the fourth – a new law guaranteeing every American the right to vote.

No act of my entire administration will give me greater satisfaction than the day when my signature makes this bill, too, the law of this land.

The voting rights bill will be the latest, and among the most important, in a long series of victories. But this victory – as Winston Churchill said of another triumph for freedom – "is not the end. It is not even the beginning of the end. But it is, perhaps, the end of the beginning."

That beginning is freedom; and the barriers to that freedom are tumbling down. Freedom is the right to share, share fully and equally, in American society – to vote, to hold a job, to enter a public place, to go to school. It is the right to be treated in every part of our national life as a person equal in dignity and promise to all others.

FREEDOM IS NOT ENOUGH

But freedom is not enough. You do not wipe away the scars of centuries by saying: Now you are free to go where you want, and do as you desire, and choose the leaders you please.

You do not take a person who, for years, has been hobbled by chains and liberate him, bring him up to the starting line of a race and then say, "you are free to compete with all the others," and still justly believe that you have been completely fair.

Thus it is not enough just to open the gates of opportunity. All our citizens must have the ability to walk through those gates.

This is the next and the more profound stage of the battle for civil rights. We seek not just freedom but opportunity. We seek not just legal equity but human ability, not just equality as a right and a theory but equality as a fact and equality as a result.

For the task is to give 20 million Negroes the same chance as every other American to learn and grow, to work and share in society, to develop their abilities – physical, mental and spiritual, and to pursue their individual happiness.

To this end equal opportunity is essential, but not enough, not enough. Men and women of all races are born with the same range of abilities. But ability is not just the product of birth. Ability is stretched or stunted by the family that you live with, and the neighborhood you live in – by the school you go to and the poverty or the richness of your surroundings. It is the product of a hundred unseen forces playing upon the little infant, the child, and finally the man.

PROGRESS FOR SOME

This graduating class at Howard University is witness to the indomitable determination of the Negro American to win his way in American life.

The number of Negroes in schools of higher learning has almost doubled in 15 years. The number of nonwhite professional workers has more than doubled in 10 years. The median income of Negro college women tonight exceeds that of white college women. And there are also the enormous accomplishments of distinguished individual Negroes – many of them graduates of this institution, and one of them the first lady ambassador in the history of the United States.

These are proud and impressive achievements. But they tell only the story of a growing middle class minority, steadily narrowing the gap between them and their white counterparts.

A WIDENING GULF

But for the great majority of Negro Americans – the poor, the unemployed, the uprooted, and the dispossessed – there is a much grimmer story. They still, as we meet here tonight, are another nation. Despite the court orders and the laws, despite the legislative victories and the speeches, for them the walls are rising and the gulf is widening.

Here are some of the facts of this American failure.

Thirty-five years ago the rate of unemployment for Negroes and whites was about the same. Tonight the Negro rate is twice as high.

In 1948 the 8 percent unemployment rate for Negro teenage boys was actually less than that of whites. By last year that rate had grown to 23 percent, as against 13 percent for whites unemployed.

Between 1949 and 1959, the income of Negro men relative to white men declined in every section of this country. From 1952 to 1963 the median income of Negro families compared to white actually dropped from 57 percent to 53 percent.

In the years 1955 through 1957, 22 percent of experienced Negro workers were out of work at some time during the year. In 1961 through 1963 that proportion had soared to 29 percent.

Since 1947 the number of white families living in poverty has decreased 27 percent while the number of poorer nonwhite families decreased only 3 percent.

The infant mortality of nonwhites in 1940 was 70 percent greater than whites. Twenty-two years later it was 90 percent greater.

Moreover, the isolation of Negro from white communities is increasing, rather than decreasing, as Negroes crowd into the central cities and become a city within a city.

Of course Negro Americans as well as white Americans have shared in our rising national abundance. But the harsh fact of the matter is that in the battle for true equality too many – far too many – are losing ground every day.

THE CAUSES OF INEQUALITY

We are not completely sure why this is. We know the causes are complex and subtle. But we do know the two broad basic reasons. And we do know that we have to act.

First, Negroes are trapped – as many whites are trapped – in inherited, gateless poverty. They lack training and skills. They are shut in, in slums, without decent medical care. Private and public poverty combine to cripple their capacities.

We are trying to attack these evils through our poverty program, through our education program, through our medical care and our other health programs, and a dozen more of the Great Society programs that are aimed at the root causes of this poverty.

We will increase, and we will accelerate, and we will broaden this attack in years to come until this most enduring of foes finally yields to our unyielding will.

But there is a second cause – much more difficult to explain, more deeply grounded, more desperate in its force. It is the devastating heritage of long years of slavery; and a century of oppression, hatred, and injustice.

SPECIAL NATURE OF NEGRO POVERTY

For Negro poverty is not white poverty. Many of its causes and many of its cures are the same. But there are differences – deep, corrosive, obstinate differences – radiating painful roots into the community, and into the family, and the nature of the individual.

These differences are not racial differences. They are solely and simply the consequence of ancient brutality, past injustice, and present prejudice. They are anguishing to observe. For the Negro they are a constant reminder of oppression. For the white they are a constant reminder of guilt. But they must be faced and they must be dealt with and they must be overcome, if we are ever to reach the time when the only difference between Negroes and whites is the color of their skin.

Nor can we find a complete answer in the experience of other American minorities. They made a valiant and a largely successful effort to emerge from poverty and prejudice.

The Negro, like these others, will have to rely mostly upon his own efforts. But he just can not do it alone. For they did not have the heritage of centuries to overcome, and they did not have a cultural tradition which had been twisted and battered by endless years of hatred and hopelessness, nor were they excluded – these others – because of race or color – a feeling whose dark intensity is matched by no other prejudice in our society.

Nor can these differences be understood as isolated infirmities. They are a seamless web. They cause each other. They result from each other. They reinforce each other.

Much of the Negro community is buried under a blanket of history and circumstance. It is not a lasting solution to lift just one corner of that blanket. We must stand on all sides and we must raise the entire cover if we are to liberate our fellow citizens.

THE ROOTS OF INJUSTICE

One of the differences is the increased concentration of Negroes in our cities. More than 73 percent of all Negroes live in urban areas compared with less than 70 percent of the whites. Most of these Negroes live in slums. Most of these Negroes live together – a separated people.

Men are shaped by their world. When it is a world of decay, ringed by an invisible wall, when escape is arduous and uncertain, and the saving pressures of a more hopeful society are unknown, it can cripple the youth and it can desolate the men.

There is also the burden that a dark skin can add to the search for a productive place in our society. Unemployment strikes most swiftly and broadly at the Negro, and this burden erodes hope. Blighted hope breeds despair. Despair brings indifferences to the learning which offers a way out. And despair, coupled with indifferences, is often the source of destructive rebellion against the fabric of society.

There is also the lacerating hurt of early collision with white hatred or prejudice, distaste or condescension. Other groups have felt similar intolerance. But success and achievement could wipe it away. They do not change the color of a man's skin. I have seen this uncomprehending pain in the eyes of the little, young Mexican-American schoolchildren that I taught many years ago. But it can be overcome. But, for many, the wounds are always open.

FAMILY BREAKDOWN

Perhaps most important – its influence radiating to every part of life – is the breakdown of the Negro family structure. For this, most of all, white America must accept responsibility. It flows from centuries of oppression and persecution of the Negro man. It flows from the long years of degradation and discrimination, which have attacked his dignity and assaulted his ability to produce for his family.

This, too, is not pleasant to look upon. But it must be faced by those whose serious intent is to improve the life of all Americans.

Only a minority – less than half – of all Negro children reach the age of 18 having lived all their lives with both of their parents. At this moment, tonight, little less than two-thirds are at home with both of their parents. Probably a majority of all Negro children receive federally-aided public assistance sometime during their childhood.

The family is the cornerstone of our society. More than any other force it shapes the attitude, the hopes, the ambitions, and the values of the child. And when the family collapses it is the children that are usually damaged. When it happens on a massive scale the community itself is crippled.

So, unless we work to strengthen the family, to create conditions under which most parents will stay together – all the rest: schools, and playgrounds, and public assistance, and private concern, will never be enough to cut completely the circle of despair and deprivation.

TO FULFILL THESE RIGHTS

There is no single easy answer to all of these problems.

Jobs are part of the answer. They bring the income which permits a man to provide for his family.

Decent homes in decent surroundings and a chance to learn – an equal chance to learn – are part of the answer.

Welfare and social programs better designed to hold families together are part of the answer.

Care for the sick is part of the answer.

An understanding heart by all Americans is another big part of the answer.

And to all of these fronts – and a dozen more – I will dedicate the expanding efforts of the Johnson administration.

But there are other answers that are still to be found. Nor do we fully understand even all of the problems. Therefore, I want to announce tonight that this fall I intend to call a White House conference of scholars, and experts, and outstanding Negro leaders – men of both races – and officials of Government at every level.

This White House conference's theme and title will be "To Fulfill These Rights."

Its object will be to help the American Negro fulfill the rights which, after the long time of injustice, he is finally about to secure.

To move beyond opportunity to achievement.

To shatter forever not only the barriers of law and public practice, but the walls which bound the condition of many by the color of his skin.

To dissolve, as best we can, the antique enmities of the heart which diminish the holder, divide the great democracy, and do wrong – great wrong – to the children of God.

And I pledge you tonight that this will be a chief goal of my administration, and of my program next year, and in the years to come. And I hope, and I pray, and I believe, it will be a part of the program of all America.

WHAT IS JUSTICE

For what is justice?

It is to fulfill the fair expectations of man.

Thus, American justice is a very special thing. For, from the first, this has been a land of towering expectations. It was to be a nation where each man could be ruled by the common consent of all – enshrined in law, given life by institutions, guided by men themselves subject to its rule. And all – all of every station and origin – would be touched equally in obligation and in liberty.

Beyond the law lay the land. It was a rich land, glowing with more abundant promise than man had ever seen. Here, unlike any place yet known, all were to share the harvest.

And beyond this was the dignity of man. Each could become whatever his qualities of mind and spirit would permit – to strive, to seek, and, if he could, to find his happiness.

This is American justice. We have pursued it faithfully to the edge of our imperfections, and we have failed to find it for the American Negro.

So, it is the glorious opportunity of this generation to end the one huge wrong of the American Nation and, in so doing, to find America for ourselves, with the same immense thrill of discovery which gripped those who first began to realize that here, at last, was a home for freedom.

All it will take is for all of us to understand what this country is and what this country must become.

The Scripture promises: "I shall light a candle of understanding in thine heart, which shall not be put out."

Together, and with millions more, we can light that candle of understanding in the heart of all America.

And, once lit, it will never again go out.

Source: *Public Papers of the Presidents of the United States: Lyndon B. Johnson, 1965.* Volume II, entry 301, pp. 635–40. Washington, DC: Government Printing Office, 1966, http://www.lbjlibrary.net/collections/selected-speeches/1965/06-04-1965.html

13.4 Arthur A. Fletcher, "Revised Philadelphia Plan," 1969

In September 1965, President Johnson signed Executive Order 11246 that prohibited "federal contractors and federally assisted construction contractors and subcontractors, who do over $10,000 in Government business in one year from discriminating in employment decisions on the basis of race, color, religion, sex, or national origin." It required such contractors to "take affirmative action to ensure that applicants are employed, and that employees are treated during employment, without regard to their race, color, religion, sex or national origin." A newly created Office of Federal Contract Compliance (OFCC) in the Labor Department oversaw the implementation of the order. In 1967, contract compliance officers Warren Phelan and Bennett Stalvey developed what became known as the Philadelphia Plan. This required prospective contractors in Philadelphia to project the number of nonwhite workers on a jobsite prior to being awarded a contract. Contracting officers could then evaluate these projections along with other factors in determining who to award the contract to. In November 1968, Elmer Staats, Comptroller General of the United States, ruled the Philadelphia Plan illegal under existing procurement law.

The Johnson administration did not get the opportunity to challenge the ruling. The same month, Republican Richard M. Nixon was elected president. Nixon, who appealed to "law and order" policies to curb domestic unrest in the late 1960s and played upon white anxieties that civil rights reforms were going too far and too fast, seemed an unlikely champion of affirmative action. And yet, affirmative action reached its zenith under the Nixon administration. At least in part this was down to political opportunism, with Nixon seeking to divide two staple Democratic constituencies, blacks and white union workers. Blacks supported affirmative action, while white union workers feared it would place white jobs in jeopardy. Black assistant labor secretary Arthur A. Fletcher drew up a Revised Philadelphia Plan that set "specific goals of minority manpower utilization" to raise the percentage of minority workers in various trades. Fletcher described minority workers as blacks, "Orientals, American Indians and people with Spanish surnames."

Both Democrats and Republicans had arrived at roughly the same sort of affirmative action implementation policy. For Democrats, affirmative action was an extension of earlier civil rights policies. For Republicans, it was a way of promoting black capitalism, encouraging black self-sufficiency through economic advancement, and curbing white union influence in the construction industry. The Revised Philadelphia Plan brought criticisms from both the left and right of American politics. Some on the left claimed that it did not go far enough. Some on the right thought it went too far by establishing what they claimed were illegal employment "quotas." The Nixon administration successfully defended the plan against its critics.

1. <u>Purpose</u>
   The purpose of this Order is to implement the provisions of Executive Order 11246, and the rules and regulations issued pursuant thereto, requiring a program of equal employment opportunity by Federal contractors and subcontractors and Federally-assisted construction contractors and subcontractors.

2. <u>Applicability</u>
   The requirements of this Order shall apply to all Federal and Federally-assisted construction contracts for projects the estimated total cost of which exceeds $500,000, in the Philadelphia area, including Bucks, Chester, Delaware, Montgomery and Philadelphia counties in Pennsylvania.

3. <u>Policy</u>
   In order to promote the full realization of equal employment opportunity on Federally-assisted projects, it is the policy of the Office of Federal Contract Compliance that no contracts or subcontracts shall be awarded for Federal and Federally-assisted construction in the Philadelphia area on projects whose cost exceeds $500,000 unless the bidder submits an acceptable affirmative action program which shall include specific goals of

minority manpower utilization, meeting the standards included in the invitation or other solicitation for bids, in trades utilizing the following classifications of employees:

Iron workers
Plumbers, pipefitters
Steamfitters
Sheetmetal workers
Electrical workers
Roofers and water proofers
Elevator construction workers

Source: Arthur A. Fletcher, Revised Philadelphia Plan for Compliance with Equal Employment Opportunity Requirements of Executive Order 11246 for Federally-Involved Construction, 27 June 1969, Records of the AFL-CIO, RG1-038, Box 72, Folder 15, Meany Archives University of Maryland College Park.

13.5 Diane Nilsen Walcott, "Blacks in the 1970's: Did They Scale the Job Ladder?"

The new and more assertive brand of affirmative action promoted by the Johnson and Nixon administrations worked in delivering black upward mobility in the job market, although a number of limitations remained. Complicating the picture was an overall uncertain economic and employment environment in the 1970s as the global economy was hit by a number of recessions.

During the 1970s, more blacks obtained white-collar jobs, particularly in professional and technical, managerial and administrative, and sales and clerical categories, as the ranks of the black middle class grew. This was true for both black men and women. Though this expansion in terms of percentages grew faster than for whites in the 1970s, blacks still represented a disproportionately smaller number of white-collar workers in most sectors, and the jobs they gained tended to be on the lower end of the pay scale. More black men were employed in higher-paid blue-collar jobs such as electricians, painters, plumbers, and metal and printing craftsmen. By 1980, the largest single sector employing black men was skilled craftwork, which had long been the case for white men. The continuing decline in farmworkers and nonfarm laborers, areas where many black workers had been employed in the past, underscored the shifting nature of the job market.

One of the most marked shifts in black women's employment patterns in the 1970s was the drop in private household workers ("domestics") from 16% to 7%. Black women saw the most significant employment gains as accountants, nurses, dieticians and therapists, engineering and science technicians, and vocational and educational counselors. The rates of black women employed as school administrators, insurance agents, and bank officials also increased. In blue-collar occupations, more black women became bus drivers, truck drivers, and delivery persons.

There were also geographic factors that impacted black employment patterns: black men and women experienced better employment prospects in the expanding suburbs, where fewer blacks lived, than in the cities where more blacks were concentrated. In the cities, black women's job prospects were better than those for black men. In short, overall the 1970s witnessed important while still circumscribed and uneven black employment gains.

Source: Diane Nilsen Walcott, "Blacks in the 1970's: Did they scale the job ladder?" pp. 29–38 from *Monthly Labor Review* (June 1982) (tables on p. 30), https://stats.bls.gov/opub/mlr/1982/06/art5full.pdfw

Table 13.1 Employment change by occupation and race, 1972 and 1980, annual averages

[Numbers in thousands]

Occupation	Black employment change, 1972–1980		White employment change, 1972–1980	
	Number	Percent	Number	Percent
Total employment	1,344	17.3	13,306	18.2
White-collar workers	1,185	55.3	10,022	27.4
Professional and technical	354	55.4	3,592	33.8
Managers and administrations	168	69.1	2,639	34.2
Sales	88	51.9	698	13.5
Clerical	580	52.7	3,094	23.8
Blue-collar workers	215	6.8	1,760	7.0
Craft and kindred workers	217	32.3	1,427	14.2
Operatives, except transport	73	5.8	−209	−2.3
Transport equipment operatives	41	9.0	204	7.5
Nonfarm laborers	−116	−14.7	337	10.0
Service workers	21	1.0	1,826	21.2
Private household workers	−238	−41.8	−159	−18.6
Other service workers	259	15.9	1,985	25.6
Farmworkers	−74	−31.9	−302	−10.8
Farm managers	−23	−51.1	−167	−11.4
Farm laborers	−51	−27.3	−116	−9.9

Table 13.2 Percent distribution of employed persons by occupation, race, and sex, 1972 and 1980

Occupation	Black men		White men		Black women		White Women	
	1972	1980	1972	1980	1972	1980	1972	1980
Total employed	4,347	4,704	45,769	5,033	3,406	4,394	27,305	36,043
Percent	100.0	100.0	100.0	100.0	100.0	100.0	100.0	100.0
Professional and technical	6.4	8.2	14.3	16.1	10.6	13.8	14.9	17.0
Managers and administrators	4.0	5.6	14.0	15.3	2.1	3.4	4.8	7.4
Sales	1.7	2.5	6.6	6.4	2.5	2.8	7.8	7.3
Clerical	7.6	8.4	6.8	6.2	22.7	29.3	36.2	36.0
Craft and kindred workers	14.8	17.6	21.2	21.5	.9	1.4	1.3	1.9
Operatives, except transport	17.4	15.5	12.1	10.7	14.8	13.8	12.5	9.4
Transport equipment operatives	10.3	9.9	5.7	5.4	.4	.7	.4	.7
Nonfarm laborers	17.4	13.0	6.8	6.5	.9	1.4	.9	1.2
Farm and farm managers	1.0	.4	3.4	2.6	–	–	.4	.4
Farm laborers and foremen	3.5	2.4	1.7	1.5	1.1	.5	1.5	1.3
Private household workers	.3	.1	–	–	16.4	7.4	3.0	1.9
Other service workers	15.8	16.4	7.3	7.9	27.6	25.4	16.2	16.0

13.6 US Supreme Court, *Regents of the University of California v. Bakke*, 1978

Many early affirmative action programs targeted trades and crafts jobs. But professional white-collar jobs were the more traditional escalator into the middle class. How could minority groups gain those better-paid jobs if they did not possess the professional qualifications to obtain them with?

That question prompted universities and colleges to implement their own affirmative action admission programs to produce qualified candidates for those jobs. Such programs successfully increased the number of minority students in higher education. The University of California at Davis Medical School, for example, accepted 100 students per year and reserved 16 of those places for "disadvantaged" students, a euphemism for minority students. When white student Allan Bakke was turned down for a place in 1972, and then again in 1973, he sued the university on the grounds that his Fourteenth Amendment rights to equal protection under the law had been violated by the university's quota system for minorities. Bakke won his arguments in the lower courts and the University of California Regents appealed the case to the US Supreme Court.

The administration of President James Earl "Jimmy" Carter (a Democrat who was elected in November 1976) filed a brief as amicus curiae *in support of the university's policy. A divided Court produced a divided judgment. The Court upheld Bakke's contention by 5–4 that the use of racial quotas in admissions infringed upon his Fourteenth Amendment rights. But the Court also ruled by 5–4 that the racial and ethnic background of candidates could be taken into account as one element, among others, in the admissions process. In other words, universities could take into account the status of minority students in making admissions decisions, but it could not set aside a designated number of places – a quota – for them. Bakke was admitted to Medical School the following semester. The ruling set a legal principle that would define the extent and limits of affirmative action in higher education admissions policy over the following years.*

In summary, it is evident that the Davis special admissions program involves the use of an explicit racial classification never before countenanced by this Court. It tells applicants who are not Negro, Asian, or Chicano that they are totally excluded from a specific percentage of the seats in an entering class. No matter how strong their qualifications, quantitative and extracurricular, including their own potential for contribution to educational diversity, they are never afforded the chance to compete with applicants from the preferred groups for the special admissions seats. At the same time, the preferred applicants have the opportunity to compete for every seat in the class. The fatal flaw in petitioner's preferential program is its disregard of individual rights as guaranteed by the Fourteenth Amendment. Shelley v. Kraemer, 334 U.S. at 334 U. S. 22. Such rights are not absolute. But when a State's distribution of benefits or imposition of burdens hinges on ancestry or the color of a person's skin, that individual is entitled to a demonstration that the challenged classification is necessary to promote a substantial state interest. Petitioner has failed to carry this burden. For this reason, that portion of the California court's judgment holding petitioner's special admissions program invalid under the Fourteenth Amendment must be affirmed [...]

In enjoining petitioner from ever considering the race of any applicant, however, the courts below failed to recognize that the State has a substantial interest that legitimately may be served by a properly devised admissions program involving the competitive consideration of race and ethnic origin. For this reason, so much of the California court's judgment as enjoins petitioner from any consideration of the race of any applicant must be reversed [...]

With respect to respondent's entitlement to an injunction directing his admission to the Medical School, petitioner has conceded that it could not carry its burden of proving that, but for the existence of its unlawful special admissions program, respondent still would not have been admitted. Hence, respondent is entitled to the injunction, and that portion of the judgment must be affirmed.

Source: US Supreme Court, *Regents of Univ. of California v. Bakke* 438 US 265 (1978), https://supreme.justia.com/cases/federal/us/438/265/case.html#T5/23

13.7 US Supreme Court, *Firefighters Local Union No. 1784 v. Stotts*, 1984

Affirmative action policies increasingly came under attack in the 1980s as American politics took another rightward turn, including the election and reelection of Republican President Ronald Reagan to the White House in 1980 and 1984. The Firefighters v. Stotts *case involved a conflict between affirmative action and seniority policy. Memphis was 40% black, but blacks only held 10% of jobs as firefighters. An affirmative action plan was put into place that increased the number of black firefighters. When a recession hit soon after, the fire department was forced to downsize. Carl Stotts, a black firefighter and union leader, asked the courts to make sure that despite the layoffs the fire department would retain a racially balanced workforce. If the fire department followed its seniority policy, it would lead to a disproportionately larger number of black workers being laid off. The lower courts agreed with Stotts.*

Three white firefighters then sued to reverse the decision. The US Supreme Court agreed to hear their case. The Court ruled 6–3 in favor of the white firefighters, upholding the fire department's seniority policy over the affirmative action plan. The Court said that the seniority policy was not adopted with the intention to discriminate and that it was therefore protected under Title VII of the Civil Rights Act of 1964, which permitted such seniority policies. Much was made at the time of the case being a devastating blow to affirmative action policies in employment. This was not entirely true. The ruling only upheld the seniority policy on very narrow grounds, and that policy was becoming increasingly irrelevant as blacks began to serve in jobs long enough to earn seniority. Still, the ruling was significant in the perception that affirmative action programs could be challenged and a more concerted legal assault on such programs continued in the years after.

The issue at the heart of this case is whether the District Court exceeded its powers in entering an injunction requiring white employees to be laid off, when the otherwise applicable seniority system would have called for the lay-off of black employees with less seniority. We are convinced that the Court of Appeals erred in resolving this issue and in affirming the District Court.

[...]

The Court of Appeals held that, even if the injunction is not viewed as compelling compliance with the terms of the decree, it was still properly entered because the District Court had inherent authority to modify the decree when an economic crisis unexpectedly required layoffs which, if carried out as the City proposed, would undermine the affirmative action outlined in the decree and impose an undue hardship on respondents. This was true, the court held, even though the modification conflicted with a bona fide seniority system adopted by the City. The Court of Appeals erred in reaching this conclusion.

Section 703(h) of Title VII provides that it is not an unlawful employment practice to apply different standards of compensation, or different terms, conditions, or privileges of employment pursuant to a bona fide seniority system, provided that such differences are not the result of an intention to discriminate because of race. It is clear that the City had a seniority system, that its proposed layoff plan conformed to that system, and that, in making the settlement, the City had not agreed to award competitive seniority to any minority employee whom the City proposed to lay off. The District Court held that the City could not follow its seniority system in making its proposed layoffs, because its proposal was discriminatory in effect, and hence not a bona fide plan. Section 703(h), however, permits the routine application of a seniority system absent proof of an intention to discriminate. *Teamsters v. United States*, 431 US 324, 431 US 352 (1977). Here, the District Court itself found that the layoff proposal was not adopted with the purpose or intent to discriminate on the basis of race. Nor had the City, in agreeing to the decree, admitted in any way that it had engaged in intentional discrimination. The Court of Appeals was therefore correct in disagreeing with the District Court's holding that the layoff plan was not a bona fide application of the seniority system, and it would appear that the City could not be faulted for following the seniority plan expressed in its agreement with the Union. The Court of Appeals nevertheless held that the injunction was proper even though it conflicted with the seniority system. This was error.

To support its position, the Court of Appeals first proposed a "settlement" theory, *i.e.,* that the strong policy favoring voluntary settlement of Title VII actions permitted consent decrees that encroached on seniority systems. But, at this stage in its opinion, the Court of Appeals was supporting the proposition that, even if the injunction was not merely enforcing the agreed-upon terms of the decree, the District Court had the authority to modify the decree over the objection of one of the parties. The settlement theory, whatever its merits might otherwise be, has no application when there is no "settlement" with respect to the disputed issue. Here, the agreed-upon decree neither awarded competitive seniority to the minority employees nor purported in any way to depart from the seniority system.

A second ground advanced by the Court of Appeals in support of the conclusion that the injunction could be entered notwithstanding its conflict with the seniority system was the assertion that

"[i]t would be incongruous to hold that the use of the preferred means of resolving an employment discrimination action decreases the power of a court to order relief which vindicates the policies embodied within Title VII and 42 US.C §§ 1981 and 1983."

679 F.2d at 566. The court concluded that, if the allegations in the complaint had been proved, the District Court could have entered an order overriding the seniority provisions. Therefore, the court reasoned,

"[t]he trial court had authority to override the Firefighters' Union seniority provisions to effectuate the purpose of the 1980 Decree."

Ibid.

The difficulty with this approach is that it overstates the authority of the trial court to disregard a seniority system in fashioning a remedy after a plaintiff has successfully proved that an employer has followed a pattern or practice having a discriminatory effect on black applicants or employees. If individual members of a plaintiff class demonstrate that they have been actual victims of the discriminatory practice, they may be awarded competitive seniority and given their rightful place on the seniority roster. This much is clear from *Franks v. Bowman Transportation Co.,* 424 US 747 (1976), and *Teamsters v. United States, supra. Teamsters,* however, also made clear that mere membership in the disadvantaged class is insufficient to warrant a seniority award; each individual must prove that the discriminatory practice had an impact on him. 431 US at 431 US 367–371. Even when an individual shows that the discriminatory practice has had an impact on him, he is not automatically entitled to have a nonminority employee laid off to make room for him. He may have to wait until a vacancy occurs, and if there are nonminority employees on layoff, the court must balance the equities in determining who is entitled to the job. *Teamsters, supra,* at 431 US 371–376. See also *Ford Motor Co. v. EEOC,* 458 US 219, 458 US 236–240 (1982). Here, there was no finding that any of the blacks protected from layoff had been a victim of discrimination, and no award of competitive seniority to any of them. Nor had the parties in formulating the consent decree purported to identify any specific employee entitled to particular relief other than those listed in the exhibits attached to the decree. It therefore seems to us that, in light of *Teamsters,* the Court of Appeals imposed on the parties as an adjunct of settlement something that could not have been ordered had the case gone to trial and the plaintiffs proved that a pattern or practice of discrimination existed.

Our ruling in *Teamsters* that a court can award competitive seniority only when the beneficiary of the award has actually been a victim of illegal discrimination is consistent with the policy behind § 706(g) of Title VII, which affects the remedies available in Title VII litigation. That policy, which is to provide make-whole relief only to those who have been actual victims of illegal discrimination, was repeatedly expressed by the sponsors of the Act during the congressional debates. Opponents of the legislation that became Title VII charged that, if the bill were enacted, employers could be ordered to hire and promote persons in order to achieve a racially balanced workforce even though those persons had not been victims of illegal discrimination. Responding to these charges, Senator Humphrey explained the limits on a court's remedial powers as follows:

"No court order can require hiring, reinstatement, admission to membership, or payment of backpay for anyone who was not fired, refused employment or advancement or admission to a union by an act of discrimination forbidden by this title. This is stated expressly in the last sentence of section 707(e) [enacted without relevant change as § 706(g)] [...] Contrary to the allegations of some opponents of this title, there is nothing in it that will give any power to the Commission or to any court to require [...] firing [...] of employees in order to meet a racial 'quota' or to achieve a certain racial balance. That bugaboo has been brought up a dozen times; but it is nonexistent." 110 Cong.Rec. 6549 (1964).

An interpretative memorandum of the bill entered into the Congressional Record by Senators Clark and Case likewise made clear that a court was not authorized to give preferential treatment to nonvictims.

"No court order can require hiring, reinstatement, admission to membership, or payment of back pay for anyone who was not discriminated against in violation of [Title VII]. This is stated expressly in the last sentence of section [706(g)] ... "

Id. at 7214.

Similar assurances concerning the limits on a court's authority to award make-whole relief were provided by supporters of the bill throughout the legislative process. For example, following passage of the bill in the House, its Republican House sponsors published a memorandum describing the bill. Referring to the remedial powers given the courts by the bill, the memorandum stated:

"Upon conclusion of the trial, the Federal court may enjoin an employer or labor organization from practicing further discrimination and may order the hiring or reinstatement of an employee or the acceptance or reinstatement of a union member. *But title VII does not permit the ordering of racial quotas in businesses or unions ...*"

Id. at 6566 (emphasis added).

In like manner, the principal Senate sponsors, in a bipartisan newsletter delivered during an attempted filibuster to each Senator supporting the bill, explained that,

"[u]nder title VII, not even a court, much less the Commission, could order racial quotas or the hiring, reinstatement, admission to membership or payment of back pay for anyone who is not discriminated against in violation of this title."

Id. at 14465. The Court of Appeals holding that the District Court's order was permissible as a valid Title VII remedial order ignores not only our ruling in *Teamsters,* but the policy behind § 706(g) as well. Accordingly, that holding cannot serve as a basis for sustaining the District Court's order.

Finally, the Court of Appeals was of the view that the District Court ordered no more than that which the City unilaterally could have done by way of adopting an affirmative action program. Whether the City, a public employer, could have taken this course without violating the law is an issue we need not decide. The fact is that, in these cases, the City took no such action, and that the modification of the decree was imposed over its objection.

We thus are unable to agree either that the order entered by the District Court was a justifiable effort to enforce the terms of the decree to which the City had agreed or that it was a legitimate modification of the decree that could be imposed on the City without its consent. Accordingly, the judgment of the Court of Appeals is reversed.

It is so ordered.

Source: US Supreme Court, *Firefighters Local Union No. 1784 v. Stotts* 467 US 561 (1984), https://supreme.justia.com/cases/federal/us/467/561/

Discussion Questions

1. Explain why both Democrat and Republican presidents supported affirmative action in the 1960s and 1970s. Why did this change in the 1980s?
2. Assess the impact of affirmative action policies on black employment patterns in the 1970s.
3. What is the difference between "affirmative action" and "reverse discrimination"?

Further Reading

Anderson, Terry H. *The Pursuit of Fairness: A History of Affirmative Action* (Oxford University Press, 2004).

Ball, Howard. *The* Bakke *Case: Race, Education, and Affirmative Action* (University Press of Kansas, 2000).

Chen, Anthony S. *The Fifth Freedom: Jobs, Politics, and Civil Rights in the United States, 1941–1972* (Princeton University Press, 2009).

Deslippe, Dennis. *Protesting Affirmative Action: The Struggle over Equality after the Civil Rights Revolution* (Johns Hopkins University Press, 2012).

Goldberg, David, and Trevor Griffey, eds. *Black Power at Work: Community Control, Affirmative Action, and the Construction Industry* (ILR Press, 2010).

Golland, David Hamilton. *Constructing Affirmative Action: The Struggle for Equal Employment Opportunity* (University Press of Kentucky, 2011).

Katznelson, Ira. *When Affirmative Action was White: An Untold Story of Racial Inequality in Twentieth-Century America* (W.W. Norton, 2007).

Moreno, Paul D. *From Direct Action to Affirmative Action: Fair Employment Law and Policy in America, 1933–1972* (Louisiana State University Press, 1997).

Rubio, Philip F. *A History of Affirmative Action: 1619–2000* (University Press of Mississippi, 2001).

Yuill, Kevin L. *Richard Nixon and the Rise of Affirmative Action: The Pursuit of Racial Equity in an Era of Limits* (Rowman and Littlefield, 2006).

Chapter 14   Legacies of the Civil Rights Movement

14.1 The Young Lords Organization, 13 Point Program and Platform, 1969

Black activism often provided a template for other minority and marginalized groups to express their voices and concerns. One such group was the Young Lords that began life as a Puerto Rican Chicago street gang and, under the leadership of Jose "Cha-Cha" Jimenez, became politicized and transformed into a Young Lords Organization (YLO). A second chapter of the YLO took root in East Harlem's El Barrio neighborhood in New York and then spread to other cities. The YLO in New York undertook a number of grassroots community programs including community education; a free breakfast program for children; free clothing exchanges; and a day care for working families. As these programs and the 13 Point Program and Platform below suggest, the Young Lords borrowed a good deal in terminology and outlook from the Black Panther Party. In May 1970, the New York YLO formally split from the Chicago group to officially form a Young Lords Party (YLP) that brought together a number of existing Puerto Rican activist groups. The 13 Point Program and Platform was revised, most notably to reflect the desire of the YLP to be more inclusive of women and to be more attentive to gender issues. Following short-lived efforts to organize in Puerto Rico, in 1972 the YLP became the Puerto Rican Revolutionary Worker's Organization (PRRWO) until it disbanded in 1976.

The Civil Rights Movement: A Documentary Reader, First Edition. Edited by John A. Kirk.
© 2020 John Wiley & Sons, Inc. Published 2020 by John Wiley & Sons, Inc.

THE YOUNG LORDS PARTY IS A REVOLUTIONARY POLITICAL PARTY FIGHTING FOR THE LIBERATION OF ALL OPPRESSED PEOPLE.

1 WE WANT SELF-DETERMINATION FOR PUERTO RICANS – LIBERATION OF THE ISLAND AND INSIDE THE UNITED STATES.

For 500 years, first Spain and then united states have colonized our country. Billions of dollars in profits leave our country for the united states every year. In every way we are slaves of the gringo. We want liberation and the Power in the hands of the People, not Puerto Rican exploiters. QUE VIVA PUERTO RICO LIBRE!

2 WE WANT SELF-DETERMINATION FOR ALL LATINOS.

Our Latin Brothers and Sisters, inside and outside the united states, are oppressed by amerikkkan business. The Chicano people built the Southwest, and we support their right to control their lives and their land. The people of Santo Domingo continue to fight against gringo domination and its puppet generals. The armed liberation struggles in Latin America are part of the war of Latinos against imperialism. QUE VIVA LA RAZA!

3 WE WANT LIBERATION OF ALL THIRD WORLD PEOPLE.

Just as Latins first slaved under spain and the yanquis, Black people, Indians, and Asians slaved to build the wealth of this country. For 400 years they have fought for freedom and dignity against racist Babylon (decadent empire). Third World people have led the fight for freedom. All the colored and oppressed peoples of the world are one nation under oppression. NO PUERTO RICAN IS FREE UNTIL ALL PEOPLE ARE FREE!

4 WE ARE REVOLUTIONARY NATIONALISTS AND OPPOSE RACISM.

The Latin, Black, Indian and Asian people inside the u.s. are colonies fighting for liberation. We know that washington, wall street and city hall will try to make our nationalism into racism; but Puerto Ricans are of all colors and we resist racism. Millions of poor white people are rising up to demand freedom and we support them. These are the ones in the u.s. that are stepped on by the rules and the government. We each organize our people, but our fights are against the same oppression and we will defeat it together. POWER TO ALL OPPRESSED PEOPLE!

5 WE WANT COMMUNITY CONTROL OF OUR INSTITUTIONS AND LAND.

We want control of our communities by our people and programs to guarantee that all institutions serve the needs of our people. People's control of police, health services, churches, schools, housing, transportation and welfare are needed. We want an end to attacks on our land by urban removal, highway destruction, universities and corporations. LAND BELONGS TO ALL THE PEOPLE!

6 WE WANT A TRUE EDUCATION OF OUR CREOLE CULTURE AND SPANISH LANGUAGE.

We must learn our history of fighting against cultural, as well as economic genocide by the yanqui. Revolutionary culture, culture of our people, is the only true teaching. LONG LIVE BORICUA! LONG LIVE EL JIBARO!

7 WE OPPOSE CAPITALISTS AND ALLIANCES WITH TRAITORS.

Puerto Rican rulers, or puppets of the oppressor, do not help our people. They are paid by the system to lead our people down blind alleys, just like the thousands of poverty pimps who keep our communities peaceful for business, or the street workers who keep gangs divided and blowing each other away. We want a society where the people socialistically control their labor. VENCEREMOS!

8 WE OPPOSE THE AMERIKKKAN MILITARY.

We demand immediate withdrawal of u.s. military forces and bases from Puerto Rico, Vietnam and all oppressed communities inside and outside the u.s. No Puerto Rican should serve in the u.s. army against his Brothers and Sisters, for the only true army of oppressed people is the people's army to fight all rulers. US OUT OF VIETNAM, FREE PUERTO RICO!

9 WE WANT FREEDOM FOR ALL POLITICAL PRISONERS.

We want all Puerto Ricans freed because they have been tried by the racist courts of the colonizers, and not by their own people and peers. We want all freedom fighters released from jail. FREE ALL POLITICAL PRISONERS!

10   WE WANT EQUALITY FOR WOMEN. MACHISMO MUST BE REVOLUTIONARY... NOT OPPRESSIVE.

Under capitalism, our women have been oppressed by both the society and our own men. The doctrine of machismo has been used by our men to take out their frustrations against their wives, sisters, mothers, and children. Our men must support their women in their fight for economic and social equality, and must recognize that our women are equals in every way within the revolutionary ranks. FORWARD, SISTERS, IN THE STRUGGLE!

11   WE FIGHT ANTI-COMMUNISM WITH INTERNATIONAL UNITY.

Anyone who resists injustice is called a communist by "the man" and condemned. Our people are brainwashed by television, radio, newspapers, schools, and books to oppose people in other countries fighting for their freedom. No longer will our people believe attacks and slanders, because they have learned who the real enemy is and who their real friends are. We will defend our Brothers and Sisters around the world who fight for justice against the rich rulers of this country. VIVA CHE!

12   WE BELIEVE ARMED SELF-DEFENSE AND ARMED STRUGGLE ARE THE ONLY MEANS TO LIBERATION.

We are opposed to violence – the violence of hungry children, illiterate adults, diseased old people, and the violence of poverty and profit. We have asked, petitioned, gone to courts, demonstrated peacefully, and voted for politicians full of empty promises. But we still ain't free. The time has come to defend the lives of our people against repression and for revolutionary war against the businessman, politician, and police. When a government oppresses our people, we have the right to abolish it and create a new one. BORICUA IS AWAKE! ALL PIGS BEWARE!

13   WE WANT A SOCIALIST SOCIETY.

We want liberation, clothing, free food, education, health care, transportation, utilities, and employment for all. We want a society where the needs of our people come first, and where we give solidarity and aid to the peoples of the world, not oppression and racism. HASTA LA VICTORIA SIEMPRE!

Source: 13 Point Program and Platform of the Young Lords Organization (October 1969), pp. 9–11 from *The Young Lords: A Reader*, ed. Darrel Enck-Wanzer (New York and London: New York University Press, 2010), https://www.marxists.org/history/erol/ncm-1/ylp-reader.pdf

14.2 Lacey Fosburgh, "Thousands of Homosexuals hold a Protest Rally in Central Park," 1970

The struggle for gay rights – more expansively known today as Lesbian, Gay, Bisexual, Transgender and Queer/Questioning (LGBTQ+) rights – became increasingly visible and vociferous in the late 1960s and early 1970s. Events that occurred in Greenwich Village's Stonewall Inn in New York in the early morning hours of 28 June 1969 are viewed as a turning point in that struggle. In 1969, the solicitation of gay sex was illegal in New York and in many other cities. Gay bars, such as the Stonewall Inn, provided places of refuge, although they were subject to frequent police harassment. A police raid on 28 June encountered resistance that quickly escalated into an extended conflict lasting five days. The Stonewall uprising served as a galvanizing episode for a more widespread and assertive LGBTQ+ movement not just in the United States but also around the world. Although there were existing organizations that had mobilized in defense of gay rights in the past, such as the Mattachine Society in California, Stonewall inspired the emergence of many new and more emboldened organizations. The protest rally described by New York Times *reporter Lacey Fosburgh below is indicative of the insistence that LGBTQ+ people be "out" – that is open and honest about their sexual orientation and gender identity in public – rather than being forced to lie about their sexual orientation and gender identity and to hide behind closed doors.*

Thousands of young men and women homosexuals from all over the Northeast marched from Greenwich Village to the Sheep Meadow in Central Park yesterday, proclaiming "the new strength and pride of gay people."

From Washington, Boston and Cleveland, from Ivy League colleges, from Harlem, the East Side and the suburbs, they gathered to protest laws that make homosexual acts between consenting adults illegal and social conditions that often make it impossible for them to display affection in public, maintain jobs or rent apartments.

As the group gathered in Sheridan Square before marching up the Avenue of the Americas to hold what the participants described as a "gay-in" in the Sheep Meadow, one of the organizers said a new militancy was developing among homosexuals.

"We're probably the most harassed, persecuted minority group in history, but we'll never have the freedom and civil rights we deserve as human beings unless we stop hiding in closets and in the shelter of anonymity," said 29-year old Michael Brown. He is a founder of the Gay Liberation Front, an activist homosexual organization that has held small demonstrations in Greenwich Village the past year.

"We have to come out into the open and stop being ashamed, or else people will go on treating us as freaks. This march," he went on, "is an affirmation and declaration of our new pride."

Then, chanting, "Say it loud, gay is proud," the marchers held bright red, green, purple and yellow silk banners high in the warm afternoon air and began to move up the avenue.

At the head of the line, which extended for 15 blocks, were about 200 members of the Gay Activists Alliance. They were followed by people representing the Mattachine Society, women's liberation groups, the Queens and 14 other homosexual organizations.

Estimates of the size of the demonstration ranged from that by one police officer, who said casually there were "over a thousand," to organizers who said variously 3,000 and 5,000 and even 20,000.

"We've never had a demonstration like this," said Martin Robinson, 27, a carpenter who is in charge of political affairs for the Gay Activities [sic] Alliance. He walked with others past crowds of people standing in silence on the sidewalks.

"It serves notice on every politician in the state and nation that homosexuals are not going to hide any more. We're becoming militant, and we won't be harassed and degraded any more," Mr Robinson said.

Throughout the demonstrations, first along the Avenue of the Americas and later in the park, where the group sat together, laughing, talking and waving their banners, hundreds of on-lookers gathered.

Some eagerly clicked their cameras, others tittered, many were obviously startled by the scene. There was little open animosity, and some bystanders applauded when a tall pretty girl carrying a sign, "I am a Lesbian," walked by.

Michael Kotis, president of the Mattachine Society, which has about 1,000 members around the country, said that "the gay people have discovered their potential strength and gained a new pride" since a battle on June 29, 1969, between a crowd of homosexuals and policemen who raided the Stonewall Inn, a place frequented by homosexuals at 53 Christopher Street.

"The main thing we have to understand," he added, holding a yellow silk banner high in the air, "is that we're different, but we are not inferior."

Source: Lacey Fosburgh, "Thousands of Homosexuals hold a Protest Rally in Central Park," pp. 1, 29 from *New York Times*, 29 June 1970.

14.3 The Combahee River Collective, The Combahee River Collective Statement, 1977

Struggles for freedom and equality involved navigating multiple and intersecting issues, concerns, and identities. The Combahee River Collective, founded by black feminists and lesbians in Boston, Massachusetts, in 1974, illustrates this. The name of the collective was derived from a daring Combahee River Raid by the former enslaved abolitionist Harriet Tubman in South Carolina in 1863, when she directed a guerrilla action to free 750 enslaved people. Drawing inspiration from Tubman's unique and courageous exploits – the only military campaign orchestrated by a woman in the American Civil War – the Combahee River Collective broke from the National Black Feminist Organization (NFBO) to form a black feminist group that sought to address interrelated issues of race, sexuality, and class. The Combahee River Collective Statement, authored largely by Demita Frazier, Beverly Smith, and Barbara Smith, outlined the collective's concerns and coined what became the influential term of "identity politics." The Combahee River Collective focused on consciousness-raising efforts, gathering information, and providing support networks for women. Though it disbanded in 1980, it is viewed today as an early pioneering model for later intersectional activism.

We are a collective of Black feminists who have been meeting together since 1974. During that time we have been involved in the process of defining and clarifying our politics, while at the same time doing political work within our own group and in coalition with other progressive organizations and movements. The most general statement of our politics at the present time would be that we are actively committed to struggling against racial, sexual, heterosexual, and class oppression, and see as our particular task the development of integrated analysis and practice based upon the fact that the major systems of oppression are interlocking. The synthesis of these oppressions creates the conditions of our lives. As Black women we see Black feminism as the logical political movement to combat the manifold and simultaneous oppressions that all women of color face.

[...]

What We Believe

Above all else, our politics initially sprang from the shared belief that Black women are inherently valuable, that our liberation is a necessity not as an adjunct to somebody else's but because of our need as human persons for autonomy. This may seem so obvious as to sound simplistic, but it is apparent that no other ostensibly progressive movement has ever considered our specific oppression as a priority or worked seriously for the ending of that oppression. Merely naming the pejorative stereotypes attributed to Black women (e.g. mammy, matriarch, Sapphire, whore, bulldagger), let alone cataloguing the cruel, often murderous, treatment we receive, indicates how little value has been placed upon our lives during four centuries of bondage in the Western hemisphere. We realize that the only people who care enough about us to work consistently for our liberation are us. Our politics evolve from a healthy love for ourselves, our sisters and our community which allows us to continue our struggle and work.

This focusing upon our own oppression is embodied in the concept of identity politics. We believe that the most profound and potentially most radical politics come directly out of our own identity, as opposed to working to end somebody else's oppression. In the case of Black women this is a particularly repugnant, dangerous, threatening, and therefore revolutionary concept because it is obvious from looking at all the political movements that have preceded us that anyone is more worthy of liberation than ourselves. We reject pedestals, queenhood, and walking ten paces behind. To be recognized as human, levelly human, is enough.

We believe that sexual politics under patriarchy is as pervasive in Black women's lives as are the politics of class and race. We also often find it difficult to separate race from class from sex oppression because in our lives they are most often experienced simultaneously. We know that there is such a thing as racial-sexual oppression which is neither solely racial nor solely sexual, e.g., the history of rape of Black women by white men as a weapon of political repression.

Although we are feminists and Lesbians, we feel solidarity with progressive Black men and do not advocate the fractionalization that white women who are separatists demand. Our situation as Black people necessitates that we have solidarity around the fact of race, which white women of course do not need to have with white men, unless it is their negative solidarity as racial oppressors. We struggle together with Black men against racism, while we also struggle with Black men about sexism.

We realize that the liberation of all oppressed peoples necessitates the destruction of the political-economic systems of capitalism and imperialism as well as patriarchy. We are socialists because we believe that work must be organized for the collective benefit of those who do the work and create the products, and not for the profit of the bosses. Material resources must be equally distributed among those who create these resources. We are not convinced, however, that a socialist revolution that is not also a feminist and anti-racist revolution will guarantee our liberation. We have arrived at the necessity for developing an understanding of class relationships that takes into account the specific class position of Black women who are generally marginal in the labor force, while at this particular time some of us are temporarily viewed as doubly desirable tokens at white-collar and professional levels. We need to articulate the real class situation of persons who are not merely raceless, sexless workers, but for whom racial and sexual oppression are significant determinants in their working/economic lives. Although we are in essential agreement with Marx's theory as it applied to the very specific economic relationships he analyzed, we know that his analysis must be extended further in order for us to understand our specific economic situation as Black women.

A political contribution which we feel we have already made is the expansion of the feminist principle that the personal is political. In our consciousness-raising sessions, for example, we have in many ways gone beyond white women's revelations because we are dealing with the implications of race and class as well as sex. Even our Black women's style of talking/testifying in Black language about what we have experienced has a resonance that is both cultural and political. We have spent a great deal of energy delving into the cultural and experiential nature of our oppression out of necessity because none of these matters has ever been looked at before. No one before has ever examined the multilayered texture of Black women's lives. An example of this kind of revelation/conceptualization occurred at a meeting as we discussed the ways in which our early intellectual interests had been attacked by our peers, particularly Black males. We discovered that all of us, because we were "smart" had also been considered "ugly," i.e., "smart-ugly." "Smart-ugly" crystallized the way in which most of us had been forced to develop our intellects at great cost to our "social" lives. The sanctions in the Black and white communities against Black women thinkers is comparatively much higher than for white women, particularly ones from the educated middle and upper classes.

As we have already stated, we reject the stance of Lesbian separatism because it is not a viable political analysis or strategy for us. It leaves out far too much and far too many people, particularly Black men, women, and children. We have a great deal of criticism and loathing for what men have been socialized to be in this society: what they support, how they act, and how they oppress. But we do not have the misguided notion that it is their maleness, per se – i.e., their biological maleness – that makes them what they are. As Black women we find any type of biological determinism a particularly dangerous and reactionary basis upon which to build a politic. We must also question whether Lesbian separatism is an adequate and progressive political analysis and strategy, even for those who practice it, since it so completely denies any but the sexual sources of women's oppression, negating the facts of class and race.

Source: Barbara Smith, ed. *Home Girls, A Black Feminist Anthology* (New York: Kitchen Table: Women of Color Press, Inc., 1983), pp. 272, 274–7. Reprinted with permission of Zillah Eisenstein.

14.4 President Ronald Reagan, "Remarks on Signing the Bill Making the Birthday of Martin Luther King, Jr, a National Holiday," 1983

As freedom struggles continued into the 1970s, the 1980s, and beyond, controversies erupted over the memory and meaning of the civil rights movement in the 1950s and 1960s. Efforts were made to create a paid federal holiday in honor of Martin Luther King, Jr to elevate his status (and by extension that of the movement) on a par with the exclusively white figures that were so honored in the United States. Such efforts were met with opposition at a number of levels, and North Carolina's Sen. Jesse Helms led the vanguard in Congress. Among other things, Helms trotted out the long discredited charge that King was a communist and undeserving of the honor. President Ronald Reagan, who eventually signed a holiday bill into law, equivocated on the issue of King's political leanings. Once the King holiday was established in 1983, and first celebrated in 1986, both King and the movement were mostly welcomed into the Parthenon of American historical folklore – although it took 20 years for the last holdout county in the United States to finally officially recognize the holiday.

Opposition to King's and the movement's legacy began to take a different path in seeking to redefine what King and the movement had stood for and meant. For example, King's use of the word "colorblind" as an aspiration for a society that would eventually address and move beyond racial discrimination, was adopted by some as a mandate to simply ignore race altogether. In historicizing the civil rights movement, there were those who were ready to consign it to the past as evidence that the nation had "moved on" from those terrible and racist days, rather than acknowledging the ongoing need to fully realize the movement's goals. By constantly containing King to a soundbite of his "I Have a Dream" speech, many ignored his urging of the nation to tackle the "giant triplets of racism, extreme materialism, and militarism." In honoring the King holiday, in naming streets after King (and other civil rights leaders), and in installing commemorative statues and markers, as well as a host of other forms of historical representation, the legacies of King and the movement are still publicly commemorated and still publicly contested today.

The President. Mrs King, members of the King family, distinguished Members of the Congress, ladies and gentlemen, honored guests, I'm very pleased to welcome you to the White House, the home that belongs to all of us, the American people.

When I was thinking of the contributions to our country of the man that we're honoring today, a passage attributed to the American poet John Greenleaf Whittier comes to mind. "Each crisis brings its word and deed." In America, in the fifties and sixties, one of the important crises we faced was racial discrimination. The man whose words and deeds in that crisis stirred our nation to the very depths of its soul was Dr. Martin Luther King, Jr.

Martin Luther King was born in 1929 in an America where, because of the color of their skin, nearly 1 in 10 lived lives that were separate and unequal. Most black Americans were taught in segregated schools. Across the country, too many could find only poor jobs, toiling for low wages. They were refused entry into hotels and restaurants, made to use separate facilities. In a nation that proclaimed liberty and justice for all, too many black Americans were living with neither.

In one city, a rule required all blacks to sit in the rear of public buses. But in 1955, when a brave woman named Rosa Parks was told to move to the back of the bus, she said, "No." A young minister in a local Baptist church, Martin Luther King, then organized a boycott of the bus company – a boycott that stunned the country. Within 6 months the courts had ruled the segregation of public transportation unconstitutional.

Dr. King had awakened something strong and true, a sense that true justice must be colorblind, and that among white and black Americans, as he put it, "Their destiny is tied up with our destiny, and their freedom is inextricably bound to our freedom; we cannot walk alone."

In the years after the bus boycott, Dr. King made equality of rights his life's work. Across the country, he organized boycotts, rallies, and marches. Often he was beaten, imprisoned, but he never stopped teaching nonviolence. "Work with the faith," he told his followers, "that unearned suffering is redemptive." In 1964 Dr. King became the youngest man in history to win the Nobel Peace Prize.

Dr. King's work brought him to this city often. And in one sweltering August day in 1963, he addressed a quarter of a million people at the Lincoln Memorial. If American history grows from two centuries to twenty, his words that day will never be forgotten. "I have a dream that one day on the red hills of Georgia, the sons of former slaves and the sons of former slave owners will be able to sit down together at the table of brotherhood."

In 1968 Martin Luther King was gunned down by a brutal assassin, his life cut short at the age of 39. But those 39 short years had changed America forever. The Civil Rights Act of 1964 had guaranteed all Americans equal use of public accommodations, equal access to programs financed by Federal funds, and the right to compete for employment on the sole basis of individual merit. The Voting Rights Act of 1965 had made certain that from then on black Americans would get to vote. But most important, there was not just a change of law; there was a change of heart. The conscience of America had been touched. Across the land, people had begun to treat each other not as blacks and whites, but as fellow Americans.

And since Dr. King's death, his father, the Reverend Martin Luther King, Sr, and his wife, Coretta King, have eloquently and forcefully carried on his work. Also his family have joined in that cause.

Now our nation has decided to honor Dr. Martin Luther King, Jr, by setting aside a day each year to remember him and the just cause he stood for. We've made historic strides since Rosa Parks refused to go to the back of the bus. As a democratic people, we can take pride in the knowledge that we Americans recognized a grave injustice and took action to correct it. And we should remember that in far too many countries, people like Dr. King never have the opportunity to speak out at all.

But traces of bigotry still mar America. So, each year on Martin Luther King Day, let us not only recall Dr. King, but rededicate ourselves to the Commandments he believed in and sought to live every day: Thou shall love thy God with all thy heart, and thou shall love thy neighbor as thyself. And I just have to believe that all of us – if all of us, young and old, Republicans and Democrats, do all we can to live up to those Commandments, then we will see the day when Dr. King's dream comes true, and in his words, "All of God's children will be able to sing with new meaning, '… land where my fathers died, land of the pilgrim's pride, from every mountainside, let freedom ring.'"

Thank you, God bless you, and I will sign it.

Source: President Ronald Reagan, "Remarks on Signing the Bill Making the Birthday of Martin Luther King, Jr, a National Holiday," 2 November 1983, The American Presidency Project, http://www.presidency.ucsb.edu/ws/?pid=40708

14.5 Nelson Mandela, "Atlanta Address on Civil Rights," 1990

Black freedom struggles in the United States have always drawn upon influences and inspiration from struggles for freedom and equality around the world. In turn, struggles for freedom and equality around the world have often been influenced and inspired by black freedom struggles in the United States. Alongside Martin Luther King, Jr and Indian independence leader Mohandas K. Gandhi, one of the most famous people of color in the twentieth century who led such a struggle was South African Nelson Mandela.

South Africa's apartheid regime of racial segregation and racial discrimination was similar to that of the American South and was codified into law in 1948 by the white supremacist Afrikaner Nationalist Party. Born in 1918, Mandela joined the African National Congress (ANC) in 1944 and helped form the ANC Youth League (ANCYL) shortly after. Mandela subsequently organized and participated in a number of civil disobedience campaigns against the apartheid regime that led to a series of arrests. When the ANC was banned in 1960, Mandela helped establish Umkhonto weSizwe (Spear of the Nation) that led an armed struggle against apartheid. Mandela was arrested in 1962, and in 1964 he was sentenced to life imprisonment on charges of leaving the country without a permit and inciting workers to strike.

As South Africa began to end its policy of apartheid in the late 1980s and early 1990s, it unbanned the ANC. After 27 years in prison, Mandela was freed in February 1990. That summer, Mandela visited the United States for the first time, making a number of speeches. One of the most poignant was in Martin Luther King, Jr's hometown of Atlanta, where Mandela made explicit the connections between King and the civil rights struggle in the United States and his own and South African struggles for freedom. In 1991, Mandela replaced his ailing friend Oliver Tambo as ANC president. In 1993, he won the Nobel Peace Prize along with white South African president F.W. de Klerk who had helped negotiate an end to apartheid. In 1994, Mandela was elected as president of South Africa, stepping down as promised after one term in office in 1999, while remaining a global icon for freedom and justice. Mandela died in December 2013.

Mrs Coretta Scott King, Dr. John Crecini, Dr. Norman Johnson, Mayor Maynard Jackson, Mr Andrew Young, Dr. Lowery, distinguished guests, sisters and brothers, ladies and gentlemen. I am happy to bring you warm and fraternal greetings from the ANC, the mass democratic movement, and the fighting people of South Africa. In particular, I bring you the very best wishes of our president, Comrade Oliver Tambo. We cannot forget that in 1982 Mayor Maynard Jackson received an ANC delegation led by Comrade Tambo. Since then Mayor Jackson has supported the ANC and our cause. On behalf of our president and myself I thank him for his unwavering support and solidarity

I am doubly happy to be in Atlanta. Atlanta which is the hometown of Dr. Martin Luther King, Jr. And the scene of many civil rights battles. We are also conscious of the fact that in the southern part of this country you have experienced the degradation and inhumanity of slavery and racial discrimination as well as the lynchings and brutal intimidation from those men in white robes. We continue to be inspired by the knowledge that in the face of your own awesome difficulties you are in the forefront of the anti-apartheid movement in this country. Your principled stand demonstrates clearly to us that we are in the midst of fellow freedom fighters, that here we have powerful fighters against racism wherever and whenever it rears its evil head.

The extraordinary reception accorded to us by the people of New York, Boston, Washington, and Atlanta fills us with joy and gives us added strength for the coming battles. I am honored by your presence in the city that gave the world a Dr. Martin Luther King, a giant among giants. Dr. King lit up the firmament of struggle against racism, injustice, poverty, and war. In our prison cells, we felt kinship and affinity with him and were inspired by his indomitable fighting spirit. Even now, twenty-seven years later, I am deeply moved by his outstanding speech at the mammoth march in Washington in 1963. With passion, sincerity, and brilliant eloquence he declared, I quote, "I have a dream that one day on the red hills of Georgia the sons of former slaves and the sons of former slave owners will be able to sit down together at the table of brotherhood. I have a dream that one day even the state of Mississippi, a state sweltering with the heat of injustice, sweltering with the heat of oppression, will be transformed into an oasis of freedom and justice," unquote. As the fervor and applause of the crowd reached a crescendo, Dr. King exclaimed, quote, "Let freedom ring," unquote. Let us all exclaim, Let freedom ring in South Africa. Let freedom ring wherever the people's human rights are trampled upon, let freedom ring.

Dr. King's dreams are now becoming the stuff of reality. At the time he began his anti-racist civil rights crusade there were only 300 elected black officials. Today it fills me with pride to know that there are nearly 6,000 black elected officials in this country. His dreams are suddenly going to see the light of day in our country as well. Dr. King also has the distinction of being the first black American to put the issue of apartheid racism into the middle of the American political agenda. Dr. King rightly deserved the Nobel Peace Prize. We are of course proud that two of our sons, Chief Albert Luthuli and Archbishop Desmond Tutu, were similarly honored. Chief Luthuli was a patient, humble, kind, warm, and compassionate person. He was a brilliant thinker and political strategist. Under his leadership the ANC emerged as a powerful, united, and disciplined mass organization. Both these great freedom fighters were men of honor and noble dignity. Of them we can say the man died but his memory lives on. The man died but his fighting spirit imbues us all. The man died but his ideas and ideals live. Allow me to express our best wishes to Mrs Coretta Scott King.

Brothers and sisters, as you know, apartheid South Africa is skilled in imparity. The unrelenting racist tyranny and the destructive fury of war unleashed on peoples of our region has lead to the death of hundreds of thousands of people and the impoverishment of millions. But our people did not flinch from doing their duty. Prisons, torture, and even death could not and never will cow us into submission. We will never acquiesce in our own apprehension. We will never surrender. We will pursue the struggle until we have transformed South Africa into a united, nonracial, nonsexist democratic country.

Our people who have shed the rivers of blood need democracy; all our people, black and white, need democracy. We are engaged in a life and death struggle to bring into being a future in which all shall, without regard to race, color, creed or sex have the right to vote and to be voted into all elected organs of the state.

Sisters and brothers, we are on the brink of major changes in South Africa. Victory is in sight. But before we reach that promised land we still have to travel a torturous road. Apartheid is still in place. Apartheid continues to imprison, brutalize, maim, and kill our people. Apartheid continues to destroy the future of our children. Apartheid remains a crime against humanity. In this context we say that the sanctions must be maintained. We appeal to you, keep the pressure on apartheid. Keep the pressure on apartheid.

I am happy to report that we had warm, friendly, and fruitful meetings with President Bush and Secretary of State, Mr Baker. It was a meeting of minds on the most important issues determining the future of our country. It gives us great confidence to know that in your country there is developing a national anti-apartheid consensus. From the streets of New York, the institutions of learning in Boston, the churches of Atlanta, and the corridors of power in Washington, the message is clear and very unequivocal. Apartheid must go. It must go now!

This consensus was reached due to the hard and unceasing work of thousands of people, black and white. It is truly an anti-apartheid rainbow coalition. To all of you we say thank you. To all of you we say, we admire you, and above all we love you. Thank you.

Source: "Address by Nelson Mandela," 27 June 1990, Georgia Institute of Technology, in Clayborne Carson, David J. Garrow, Gerald Gill, Vincent Harding, and Darlene Clark Hine, eds., *The Eyes on the Prize Civil Rights Reader: Documents, Speeches and Firsthand Accounts From the Black Freedom Struggle* (New York: Viking Penguin, 1991), pp. 720–2.

14.6 Benjamin Chavis, Jr, "Foreword" *Confronting Environmental Racism: Voices from the Grassroots*, 1999

In 1962, Rachel Carson's influential book Silent Spring *documented the dangers of the widespread use of pesticides in the United States. Concerns about other forms of pollution, dwindling energy resources, and the risks and dangers of nuclear technology, among others, grew as the public became more conscious of such environmental threats. In 1970, the first Earth Day was held that saw millions of Americans demonstrate for environmental reforms. Earth Day became an annual fixture and is now internationally observed. In the 1980s, the environmental justice movement began to draw attention to the specific impact that environmental policies had on communities of color. In 1982, protests led by ministers Walter Fauntroy and Benjamin Chavis against the dumping of toxic wastes in the poor and predominantly black Warren County, North Carolina, led to the coining of the term environmental racism. The term refers, according to a pioneering scholar in the field, Robert Kuehn, to "any environmental policy, practice, or directive that differentially affects or disadvantages (whether intended or unintended) individuals, groups, or communities, based on race or color." In his foreword to a collection of essays edited by another influential scholar in the field, Robert B. Bullard, Chavis elaborates on the concept of environmental racism and its national and international implications.*

Millions of African Americans, Latinos, Asians, Pacific Islanders, and Native Americans are trapped in polluted environments because of their race and color. Inhabitants of these communities are exposed to greater health and environmental risks than is the general population. Clearly, all Americans do not have the same opportunities to breathe clean air, drink clean water, enjoy clean parks and playgrounds, or work in a clean, safe environment.

People of color bear the brunt of the nation's pollution problem. This was the case, for example, in Warren County, North Carolina, in 1982. It is still true today. Warren County is important because activities there set off the national environmental justice movement. The rural, poor, and mostly African-American county was selected for a PCB landfill not because it was an environmentally sound choice, but because it seemed powerless to resist. During the subsequent protests and demonstrations against the landfill, the term "environmental racism" was coined. For the more than 500 protesters who were arrested, the behavior of county authorities was seen as an extension of the institutional racism many of them had encountered in the past – including discrimination in housing, employment, education, municipal services, and law enforcement.

Environmental racism is racial discrimination in environmental policymaking. It is racial discrimination in the enforcement of regulations and laws. It is racial discrimination in the deliberate targeting of communities of color for toxic waste disposal and the siting of polluting industries. It is racial discrimination in the official sanctioning of the life-threatening presence of poisons and pollutants in communities of color. And, it is racial discrimination in the history of excluding people of color from the mainstream environmental groups, decisionmaking boards, commissions, and regulatory bodies.

The United Church of Christ Commission for Racial Justice was among the first national civil rights organizations to raise the question of environmental racism. The Commission's 1987 groundbreaking study *Toxic Wastes and Race* brought national attention to this problem. In preparing the study, the Commission was moving into a new arena – research on environmental injustice. But we already knew then what we know now – injustice might be fought wherever and whenever it is found. The environmental arena is no exception.

Robert D. Bullard's important 1990 book *Dumping in Dixie* examined this type of racism in our nation's own underdeveloped "Third World" region, African-American communities in the South. However, no one segment of the population and no one region has a monopoly on this problem. It is national and international in scope.

Environmental racism does not only involve the siting of toxic waste facilities. This insightful new book, *Confronting Environmental Racism*, extends the analysis and coverage even further to explore the problems of lead, pesticides, and petrochemical plants that have a disproportionately large impact on communities of color. This book also examines sustainable development, job blackmail, discriminatory public policy, and dispute resolution strategies.

As is typical of the environmental justice movement, *Confronting Environmental Racism* has brought together a diverse group of academicians and activists from all across the country to write about these life-and-death environmental justice issues. Many were active participants at the First National People of Color Environmental Leadership Summit. Held in Washington, DC, in October 1991, this Summit brought together more than 650 grassroots and national leaders from all 50 states, the District of Columbia, Puerto Rico, Mexico, and the Marshall Islands. The delegates adopted the "Principles of Environmental Justice," which have since been disseminated throughout the United States and were taken to the 1992 United Nation's Commission on Environment and Development (UNCED) and to parallel Global Forum meetings in Rio de Janeiro. The goal is to have these principles resonate throughout the globe wherever unjust, racist, and nonsustainable environmental and development policies exist.

The struggle for environmental justice has intensified in communities that have become "sacrifice zones." Chicago's southeast neighborhood of Altgeld Gardens has been described as a "toxic doughnut" because it is surrounded by polluting industries. Similar threats exist in East St. Louis, in Louisiana's "Cancer Alley," on Navaho lands where uranium is mined, and in farmworker communities where laborers and their families are routinely poisoned by pesticides.

Environmental justice struggles have now been extended beyond US borders, as threats multiply in the Third World. Many of these threats are beyond the control of the world's poor nations. Toxic wastes, banned pesticides, "recycled" batteries, and scrap metals are routinely shipped to Third World nations by multinational corporations. Further, the atrocious environmental policies of these firms, when operating in the Third World, are well documented. One only needs to look at the environmental record of the nearly 2,000 *maquiladoras* plants that operate on the Mexican side of the US-Mexican border to see the pattern. Environmental justice activists are challenging policies and practices that target wastes and polluting industries for the Third World as well. After all, the international waste and pollution practices of US-based corporations merely reflect the US domestic policy of targeting low-income, disenfranchised communities of color.

The contributors of *Confronting Environmental Racism* make it clear that the environmental justice movement is not an anti-white movement. They document the stories of grassroots leaders who are struggling against unjust, unfair, unethical, and sometimes illegal practices of industry and government. Environmental justice advocates are not saying, "Take the poisons out of our community and put them in a white community." They are saying *no* community should have to live with these poisons. They have thus taken the moral high road and are building a multiracial and inclusive movement that has the potential of transforming the political landscape of this nation.

Source: Benjamin Chavis, Jr, "Foreword," pp. 3–5 from *Confronting Environmental Racism: Voices from the Grassroots*, ed. Robert D. Bullard (Cambridge, MA: South End Press, 1993).

14.7　Congressman John Lewis Supports Renewal of the 1965 Voting Rights Act, 2006

Even as the civil rights movement confronted new issues and fought new battles after the 1960s, older struggles still remained. The Voting Rights Act of 1965 was one of the movement's signal achievements. Many of its provisions were subject to periodic renewal by Congress, which could also adopt amendments to the legislation. These amendments have largely been used to extend and expand the act's coverage to guarantee more voting rights to more people. But starting in the 1980s, there were tussles between the increasingly conservative US Supreme Court and Congress over the Voting Rights Act. In Mobile v. Bolden *(1980), the Court ruled that only explicitly intentional voting discrimination was covered by the act. Congress responded by changing the act to cover voting practices that had any discriminatory effect whatsoever, thereby providing much wider coverage. In 2006, the Voting Rights Act was amended again to counteract the impact of other Court cases that sought to restrict the scope of voting rights protections.*

The 2006 debates in Congress about the Voting Rights Act's provisions were the most contentious since the legislation was passed in 1965. A number of Republicans, whose party held majorities in both the Senate and the House of Representatives, viewed voting rights legislation as primarily favoring the Democrats. Moreover, the debates came within the context of other developments that risked undermining voting rights, such as those outlined by John Lewis, former chair of the Student Nonviolent Coordinating Committee (SNCC), in his speech below, including "redistricting and annexation plans, at-large elections, polling place changes" and particularly the growing number of "voter ID" laws that many viewed as a return to the bad old days of the poll tax that placed unnecessary barriers between voters and the ballot box. Lewis, who had been in Selma in 1965 leading the demonstrations that successfully led to the passage of the Voting Rights Act, now gave first-hand testimony and a living history lesson as an elected Georgia congressman on the floor of the House of Representatives about his and the movement's past struggles and Congress's contemporary responsibilities.

The SPEAKER pro tempore. Under a previous order of the House, the gentleman from Georgia (Mr Lewis) is recognized for 5 minutes.

Mr LEWIS of Georgia. Mr Speaker, the Voting Rights Act was good for America in 1965 and it is good and necessary in 2006. We must strengthen our resolve and complete the job that we began almost a year ago in a bipartisan way and pass the reauthorization of the Voting Rights Act tomorrow without amendment.

The struggle for voting rights was not so long ago. It was not 75 or 100 years ago. It was 41 years ago that this Voting Rights Act was passed. This is not ancient history. Yet so many Members of the House are too young to remember our very dark history of segregation and voting discrimination.

The history of the right to vote in America is a history of conflict, of violence, of struggle for the right to vote. Many people died trying to gain that right. I was beaten and jailed because I stood up for it. The experience of minorities today tell us that the struggle is not over, and that the special provisions of the Voting Rights Act are still necessary.

We do not want to go back to our dark past, and we must not go back. Forty-one years ago it was almost impossible for people of color to register to vote in many parts of the American South, in Georgia, in Alabama, and in Mississippi. Forty-one years ago, the State of Mississippi had a black voting-age population of more than 450,000, and only about 16,000 blacks were registered to vote.

Just 41 years ago, people of color had to pay a poll tax, pass a so-called literacy test in some States in the South. There were black men and women who were professors in colleges and universities, black lawyers and black doctors who were told they could not read or write well enough to register to vote.

They were asked to interpret certain sections of the Constitution in southern States. Some were asked to count the number of bubbles in a bar of soap, others were asked to count the number of jelly beans in a jar.

People stood in unmovable lines for the opportunity to register to vote. In some States voters could register only on 1 or 2 days a month; but those lines never moved, and those would-be voters were never registered. People were beaten, arrested, jailed, people even shot and killed for attempting to register to vote. It was a matter of life and death.

On March 7, 1965, about 600 of us black men and women and a few young children attempted to peacefully march from Selma, Alabama, to Montgomery to the State capitol to dramatize to the Nation and to the world that people of color wanted to register to vote. The world watched as we were met with night-sticks, bullwhips, we were trampled by horses, and tear-gassed.

Eight days after what became known as Bloody Sunday, President Johnson came to this podium and spoke to a joint session of Congress and began by saying, "I speak tonight for the dignity of man and for the destiny of democracy." And during that speech, President Johnson condemned the violence in Selma and called on the Congress to enact a Voting Rights Act. He closed his speech by quoting the rights [sic] of the civil rights movement saying, "And we shall overcome."

I was sitting next to Martin Luther King, Jr, in the home of a local family in Selma, Alabama, as we listened to Lyndon Johnson say, "And we shall overcome." Tears came down his face. And we all cried. Dr. King said, "John, the Voting Rights Act will be passed, and we will make it from Selma to Montgomery."

Congress did pass the Voting Rights Act. On August 6, 1965 it was signed into law.

There was an elderly black man who lived in Selma, Alabama, who after Johnson had signed the Voting Rights Act became registered to vote for the first time. He was 91 years old. He said, "I am registered now. I can die and go home to my Lord."

Today, people no longer meet attack dogs and bullwhips and fire hoses as they demonstrate or attempt to register to vote. Today, the tools of discrimination are not poll taxes and literacy tests. But make no mistake, discrimination still exists. Look at Florida in 2000. Look at Ohio.

The tools of discrimination are much more difficult, but just as dangerous. Today, the discrimination comes in the form of redistricting and annexation plans, at-large elections, polling place changes.

In my own State of Georgia, the legislation went back to a period in our dark history by passing a voter ID law that would make it more difficult for the elderly, the poor and minorities to vote. Both a State and a Federal court jurist have called the law unconstitutional and stopped it from taking effect.

We can do better. We must do better, and pass the Voting Rights Act without amendment tomorrow.

Source: Congressional Record, 109th Congress (2005–2006), https://www.congress.gov/congressional-record/2006/7/12/house-section/article/h5054-2?r=15

14.8 Justice Stephen Breyer Dissenting Opinion in *Parents Involved in Community Schools v. Seattle School District No. 1 et al.*, 2007

Voting rights legislation is not the only one of the movement's notable achievements under threat in the twenty-first century. When the Brown *decision was handed down in 1954 it met with massive resistance. After this was quelled in the years after, most school districts in the South adopted so-called "freedom of choice" desegregation plans that were good enough to satisfy the minimum requirements of the law while continuing to stall on genuine moves to integration.*

In the late 1960s and early 1970s, the courts became more insistent about fulfilling the promise of Brown *as they balked at limited desegregation plans and provided the means, such as busing and the consolidation of school districts, to more proactively pursue school desegregation. The forthright stand of the courts worked. Schools became more integrated in the 1970s and the achievement gap between black and white students began to close as a result. A new wave of resistance to school desegregation followed in the form of "white flight" to predominantly or exclusively white suburbs and exurbs, and the establishment of private schools largely beyond the reach of the law.*

Compounding these difficulties were increasingly conservative courts that rolled back measures previously used to achieve meaningful school desegregation. The Parents Involved *case is a prime example of this. The case involved the use of desegregation plans in Seattle, Washington, and Louisville, Kentucky, that took the student's race into account to achieve greater diversity and/or avoid greater racial isolation of students in school districts. While the Court agreed that seeking diversity and avoiding racial isolation represented a "compelling state interest," a split Court insisted that such plans should be more "narrowly tailored," which in practice meant limiting the parameters and thereby the effectiveness of such plans.*

Justice Stephen G. Breyer's dissent for the minority opinion below (in which he was joined by three other justices, John Paul Stevens, David H. Souter, and Ruth Bader Ginsburg) cites the 2003 Grutter *case in its defense, in which the Court upheld affirmative action admissions policies in higher education on the grounds that it was a compelling state interest to encourage diversity. In an increasingly divided Court on the issue, support for race-conscious school desegregation remedies to right past injustices is more in the balance than ever before.*

Conclusions

To show that the school assignment plans here meet the requirements of the Constitution, I have written at exceptional length. But that length is necessary. I cannot refer to the history of the plans in these cases to justify the use of race-conscious criteria without describing that history in full. I cannot rely upon *Swann*'s statement that the use of race-conscious limits is permissible without showing, rather than simply asserting, that the statement represents a constitutional principle firmly rooted in federal and state law. Nor can I explain my disagreement with the Court's holding and the plurality's opinion, without offering a detailed account of the arguments they propound and the consequences they risk.

Thus, the opinion's reasoning is long. But its conclusion is short: The plans before us satisfy the requirements of the Equal Protection Clause. And it is the plurality's opinion, not this dissent that "fails to ground the result it would reach in law." *Ante,* at 28.

Four basic considerations have led me to this view. *First*, the histories of Louisville and Seattle reveal complex circumstances and a long tradition of conscientious efforts by local school boards to resist racial segregation in public schools. Segregation at the time of *Brown* gave way to expansive remedies that included busing, which in turn gave rise to fears of white flight and resegregation. For decades now, these school boards have considered and adopted and revised assignment plans that sought to rely less upon race, to emphasize greater student choice, and to improve the conditions of all schools for all students, no matter the color of their skin, no matter where they happen to reside. The plans under review – which are less burdensome, more egalitarian, and more effective than prior plans – continue in that tradition. And their history reveals school district goals whose remedial, educational, and democratic elements are inextricably intertwined each with the others. See Part I, *supra*, at 2–21.

Second, since this Court's decision in *Brown*, the law has consistently and unequivocally approved of both voluntary and compulsory race-conscious measures to combat segregated schools. The Equal Protection Clause, ratified following the Civil War, has always distinguished in practice between state action that excludes and thereby subordinates racial minorities and state action that seeks to bring together people of all races. From *Swann* to *Grutter*, this Court's decisions have emphasized this distinction, recognizing that the fate of race relations in this country depends upon unity among our children, "for unless our children begin to learn together, there is little hope that our people will ever learn to live together." *Milliken*, 418 US, at 783 (Marshall, J., dissenting). See also C. Sumner, Equality Before the Law: Unconstitutionality of Separate Colored Schools in Massachusetts, in 2 The Works of Charles Sumner 327, 371 (1849) ("The law contemplates not only that all be taught, but that all shall be taught together"). See Part II, *supra*, at 21–37.

Third, the plans before us, subjected to rigorous judicial review, are supported by compelling state interests and are narrowly tailored to accomplish those goals. Just as diversity in higher education was deemed compelling in *Grutter*, diversity in public primary and secondary schools – where there is even more to gain – must be, *a fortiori*, a compelling state interest. Even apart from *Grutter*, five Members of this Court agree that "avoiding racial isolation" and "achiev[ing] a diverse student population" remain today compelling interests. *Ante*, at 17–18 (opinion of Kennedy, J.). These interests combine remedial, educational, and democratic objectives. For the reasons discussed above, however, I disagree with Justice Kennedy that Seattle and Louisville have not done enough to demonstrate that their present plans are necessary to continue upon the path set by *Brown*. These plans are *more* "narrowly tailored" than the race-conscious law school admissions criteria at issue in *Grutter*. Hence, their lawfulness follows *a fortiori* from this Court's prior decisions. See Parts III–IV, *supra*, at 37–57.

Fourth, the plurality's approach risks serious harm to the law and for the Nation. Its view of the law rests either upon a denial of the distinction between exclusionary and inclusive use of race-conscious criteria in the context of the Equal Protection Clause, or upon such a rigid application of its "test" that the distinction loses practical significance. Consequently, the Court's decision today slows down and sets back the work of local school boards to bring about racially diverse schools. See Part V, *supra*, at 57–63.

Indeed, the consequences of the approach the Court takes today are serious. Yesterday, the plans under review were lawful. Today, they are not. Yesterday, the citizens of this Nation could look for guidance to this Court's unanimous pronouncements concerning desegregation. Today, they cannot. Yesterday, school boards had available to them a full range of means to combat segregated schools. Today, they do not.

The Court's decision undermines other basic institutional principles as well. What has happened to *stare decisis*? The history of the plans before us, their educational importance, their highly limited use of race – all these and more – make clear that the compelling interest here is stronger than in *Grutter*. The plans here are more narrowly tailored than the law school admissions program there at issue. Hence, applying *Grutter*'s strict test, their lawfulness follows *a fortiori*. To hold to the contrary is to transform that test from "strict" to "fatal in fact" – the very opposite of what *Grutter* said. And what has happened to *Swann*? To *McDaniel*? To *Crawford*? To *Harris*? To *School Committee of Boston*? To *Seattle School Dist. No. 1*? After decades of vibrant life, they would all, under the plurality's logic, be written out of the law.

And what of respect for democratic local decisionmaking by States and school boards? For several decades this Court has rested its public school decisions upon *Swann*'s basic view that the Constitution grants local school districts a significant degree of leeway where the inclusive use of race-conscious criteria is at issue. Now localities will have to cope with the difficult problems they face (including resegregation) deprived of one means they may find necessary.

And what of law's concern to diminish and peacefully settle conflict among the Nation's people? Instead of accommodating different good-faith visions of our country and our Constitution, today's holding upsets settled expectations, creates legal uncertainty, and threatens to produce considerable further litigation, aggravating race-related conflict.

And what of the long history and moral vision that the Fourteenth Amendment itself embodies? The plurality cites in support those who argued in *Brown* against segregation, and Justice Thomas likens the approach that I have taken to that of segregation's defenders. See *ante*, at 39–41 (plurality opinion) (comparing Jim Crow segregation to Seattle and Louisville's integration polices); *ante*, at 28–32 (Thomas, J., concurring). But segregation policies did not simply tell schoolchildren "where they could and could not go to school based on the color of their skin," *ante*, at 40 (plurality opinion); they perpetuated a caste system rooted in the institutions of slavery and 80 years of legalized subordination. The lesson of history, see *ante*, at 39 (plurality opinion), is not that efforts to continue racial segregation are constitutionally indistinguishable from efforts to achieve racial integration. Indeed, it is a cruel distortion of history to compare Topeka, Kansas, in the 1950's to Louisville and Seattle in the modern day – to equate the plight of Linda Brown (who was ordered to attend a Jim Crow school) to the circumstances of Joshua McDonald (whose request to transfer to a school closer to home was initially declined). This is not to deny that there is a cost in applying "a state-mandated racial label." *Ante*, at 17 (Kennedy, J., concurring in part and concurring in judgment). But that cost does not approach, in degree or in kind, the terrible harms of slavery, the resulting caste system, and 80 years of legal racial segregation.

*   *   *

Finally, what of the hope and promise of *Brown?* For much of this Nation's history, the races remained divided. It was not long ago that people of different races drank from separate fountains, rode on separate buses, and studied in separate schools. In this Court's finest hour, *Brown* v. *Board of Education* challenged this history and helped to change it. For *Brown* held out a promise. It was a promise embodied in three Amendments designed to make citizens of slaves. It was the promise of true racial equality – not as a matter of fine words on paper, but as a matter of everyday life in the Nation's cities and schools. It was about the nature of a democracy that must work for all Americans. It sought one law, one Nation, one people, not simply as a matter of legal principle but in terms of how we actually live.

Not everyone welcomed this Court's decision in *Brown*. Three years after that decision was handed down, the Governor of Arkansas ordered state militia to block the doors of a white schoolhouse so that black children could not enter. The President of the United States dispatched the 101st Airborne Division to Little Rock, Arkansas, and federal troops were needed to enforce a desegregation decree. See *Cooper* v. *Aaron*, 358 US 1 (1958). Today, almost 50 years later, attitudes toward race in this Nation have changed dramatically. Many parents, white and black alike, want their children to attend schools with children of different races. Indeed, the very school districts that once spurned integration now strive for it. The long history of their efforts reveals the complexities and difficulties they have faced. And in light of those challenges, they have asked us not to take from their hands the instruments they have used to rid their schools of racial segregation, instruments that they believe are needed to overcome the problems of cities divided by race and poverty. The plurality would decline their modest request.

The plurality is wrong to do so. The last half-century has witnessed great strides toward racial equality, but we have not yet realized the promise of *Brown*. To invalidate the plans under review is to threaten the promise of *Brown*. The plurality's position, I fear, would break that promise. This is a decision that the Court and the Nation will come to regret.

I must dissent.

Source: *Parents Involved in Community Schools v. Seattle School District No. 1 et. al.* 551 US 701 (2007), https://supreme.justia.com/cases/federal/us/551/701/dissent2.html

14.9 Joe Raedle, Barack Obama Declares Victory in Presidential Election, 2008

Barack Obama's election as the first black president of the United States in 2008, and his reelection in 2012, was yet another in a line of many black "firsts" in American history. Undoubtedly, President Obama's election was a significant moment. The nation witnessed the first black president to occupy a White House that had been originally built by enslaved people, and some proclaimed, wildly over-optimistically, that it marked the beginning of a "post-racial" nation.

It was an unbearable weight of expectation, which Obama seemed determined to navigate by being scrupulously even-handed in his approach. This disappointed some in the black community who had hoped for much more; they pointed to Obama's interracial upbringing in America's most diverse state of Hawaii as being atypical of the black experience. Yet at times of racial strife, such as the killing of unarmed teenager Trayvon Martin in Miami Gardens, Florida, by George Zimmerman in 2012, and the mass killing of black people at Emanuel American Methodist Episcopal church in Charleston, South Carolina, by Dylann Roof in 2015, Obama was able to reach out to and empathize with black America in ways that no previous president had. Obama at the same time encountered the seemingly ubiquitous white "backlash" to his presidency that ranged from politicians questioning his birthright to be president to a surge in white nationalist groups.

Beyond the racial politics of his presidency, Obama faced huge domestic challenges, such as inheriting one of the worst economic crises in American history, along with foreign policy dilemmas such as fighting terrorism and managing American military commitments in Afghanistan and Iraq. Amid all this, often in a low-key manner, Obama did address some civil rights concerns. The appointment of two black attorneys general in Eric Holder and Loretta Lynch revitalized the Justice Department's civil rights division; Obama commuted vastly more prison sentences than many of his immediate predecessors in office had, indirectly addressing the issue of disproportionate black incarceration rates; and he sought to more strongly enforce anti-discrimination housing policies through the Department of Housing and Urban Development (HUD). Arguably, Obama's crowning achievement was the Affordable Healthcare Act (or "Obamacare" as it became known) that extended healthcare insurance to millions of people and cut the black uninsured rate by a third.

Source: Joe Raedle, Barack Obama Declares Victory in 2008 Presidential Election, https://www.gettyimages.com/event/barack-obama-declares-victory-in-2008-presidential-election-83306963#/president-elect-barack-obama-and-his-wife-michelle-acknowledge-their-picture-id83564833

14.10 Children's Defense Fund, Cradle to Prison Pipeline® Campaign, 2009

Concerns about the use of the criminal justice system as a means to control and discipline people of color still persist. After the abolition of slavery, a convict-leasing system emerged in the South that institutionalized the appropriation of black people as free labor by the criminal justice system. During the black power movement, black activists such as Angela Davis viewed the criminal justice system as playing a pivotal role in the oppression of black people. Many put the continuing disproportionate incarceration of people of color down to the targeted and purposeful criminalization of those communities. An example of this has been described variously as the school-to-prison pipeline, the school-to-prison link, or, as below, by the nonprofit organization the Children's Defense Fund, as the Cradle to Prison Pipeline.

Collectively, all of these terms to some degree express a concern that school discipline increasingly mirrors the criminal justice system though policies such as school disturbance laws, zero tolerance procedures and practices, and the presence of police in schools. The result, it is argued, is a disproportionate number of people of color coming into contact with the criminal justice system at ever earlier ages and sometimes becoming trapped in it for the rest of their lives.

The pipeline is fed by and in turn exacerbates other circumstances that disproportionately impact people of color: poverty, less access to adequate healthcare, less early childcare development, more exposure to substance abuse (and less support to combat it), more mental and emotional difficulties (and less support to tackle them), unequal access to educational opportunities, and an overcrowded juvenile justice system. These interconnected issues are mutually reinforcing, reducing the chances of escaping the pipeline, and further imbedding institutional and structural racism in American society.

The Children's Defense Fund's Cradle to Prison Pipeline Campaign is a national and community crusade to engage families, youth, communities and policy makers in the development of healthy, safe and educated children. Poverty, racial disparities and a culture of punishment rather than prevention and early intervention are key forces driving the Pipeline.

KEY FACTS

A Black boy born in 2001 has a 1 in 3 chance of going to prison in his lifetime; a Latino boy a 1 in 6 chance; and a White boy a 1 in 17 chance. A Black girl born in 2001 has a 1 in 17 chance of going to prison in her lifetime; a Latino girl a 1 in 45 chance; and a White girl a 1 in 111 chance.

Pervasive Poverty – Poverty is the largest driving force behind the Pipeline crisis, exacerbated by race. Black children are more than three times as likely as White children to be born into poverty and to be poor, and are four times as likely to live in extreme poverty. One in 3 Latino babies and 3 in 7 Black babies are born into poverty. More than 1 in 4 Latino children and 1 in 3 Black children are poor. Between 2000 and 2007, the number of poor Latino children increased by 960,000 (to 4.5 million) and the number of poor Black children increased by 323,000 (to 3.9 million).

Inadequate Access to Health Coverage – One out of five Latino children and one out of eight Black children are uninsured, compared to one out of 13 White children. A child is born uninsured every 39 seconds. More than 2,200 children are born uninsured every day. And about 800,000 pregnant women are uninsured, while each year, approximately 28,000 infants die in America before they reach their first birthday.

Gaps in Early Childhood Development – Studies have shown that children who do not get the early intervention, permanence and stability they need are more likely to act out and fail in school because they lack the skills necessary to succeed. Researchers of early childhood emphasize the importance of early childhood nurturing and stimulation to help the brain grow, especially between birth and age seven, and even beyond and thus help children to thrive and to be on a positive path toward successful adulthood. The importance of stimulation in the first years of life is dramatically underlined in the US Department of Education's study of 22,000 kindergartners in the kindergarten class of 1998–99, which found that Black and Hispanic children were substantially behind when they entered kindergarten.

Disparate Educational Opportunities – Children in the most economically depressed communities are at high risk of low achievement and attainment and are often stuck in under-funded, overcrowded schools. Poor urban schools have the highest numbers of teachers who are inexperienced or do not have degrees in the subjects they teach. Eighty-six percent of Black, 83 percent of Latino and 58 percent of White fourth graders cannot read at grade level; and 89 percent of Black, 85 percent of Latino and 59 percent of White 8th graders cannot do math at grade level. Black students are more likely than any other students to be in special education programs for children with mental retardation or emotional disturbance. Black and American Indian children are almost twice as likely as White children to be retained in a grade. The public school suspension rate among Black and American Indian students is almost three times that for Whites. Black, Latino, and American Indian children are more than twice as likely as White children to drop out of school. According to the US Department of Education, only 59 percent of Black and 61 percent of Latino students graduated from high school on time with a regular diploma in 2006. When Black children do graduate from high school, they have a greater chance of being unemployed and a lower chance of going to college full-time than White high school graduates. Only 48,000 Black males earn a bachelor's degree each year, but an estimated 1 in 3 Black men ages 20–29 is under correctional supervision or control. Approximately 815,000 Black males were incarcerated in state or federal prisons or local jails at mid-year 2007.

Intolerable Abuse and Neglect – A child is abused or neglected every 35 seconds. Four in ten of the children who are abused or neglected get no help at all after their initial investigation. More than 800,000 children are in foster care each year, about 513,000 on a single day. Black children represent 32 percent of children in foster care but only 15 percent of all children.

Unmet Mental and Emotional Problems – A Congressional study found 15,000 children in juvenile detention facilities, some as young as 7 years old, solely because community mental health services were unavailable. Studies have reported that as many as three-fourths of incarcerated youth have mental health disorders and about 1 in 5 has a severe disorder. Youths who age out of foster care are less likely to graduate from high school or college and experience more serious mental health problems, including post-traumatic stress disorder, than youths generally. They are less likely to receive adequate health and mental healthcare, and are more likely to experience homelessness, and to be involved in the criminal justice system.

Rampant Substance Abuse – Drugs, tobacco and alcohol lead our children down the wrong path. Disconnected youth, lacking a decent education or high school degree, job training skills, and social support systems or mentors, often resort to self-destructive acts. Unfortunately, alcohol and other substance abuse treatment for youth and for parents and other adults is in too short supply. Only about 10 percent of youth with a substance use disorder receive treatment.

Overburdened, Ineffective Juvenile Justice System – One-size-fits-all zero tolerance school discipline policies are transforming schools into a major point of entry into the juvenile justice system as children are increasingly arrested on school grounds for subjectively and loosely defined behaviors. Black youth are about four times as likely as their White peers to be incarcerated. Black youth are almost five times as likely to be incarcerated as White youth for drug offenses. Of the 1.5 million children with an incarcerated parent in 1999, Black children were nearly nine times as likely and Latino children were three times as likely to have an incarcerated parent as White children. Most juvenile correctional facility programs focus on punishment rather than treatment and rehabilitation, often creating environments that further harden youth. This makes it more difficult for them to productively reintegrate into their families and communities.

Source: Children's Defense Fund, Cradle to Prison Pipeline® Campaign, 19 February 2009, http://www.childrensdefense.org/child-research-data-publications/data/cradle-prison-pipeline-summary-report.pdf

14.11   US Supreme Court, *Shelby County v. Holder*, 2013

The renewal of the 1965 Voting Rights Act by Congress in 2006 did not end the struggle over voting rights in the United States. In Shelby County v. Holder *(2013), the US Supreme Court decided in a split 5–4 decision to invalidate Section 4 (b) of the Voting Rights Act, which contains the coverage formula for jurisdictions subject to preclearance based on their previous history of voter discrimination. In turn, this invalidated Section 5 of the Voting Rights Act that required certain states and local governments to obtain federal preclearance before making any changes to voting laws or practices. Without the coverage formula in Section 4 (b), Section 5 became unenforceable.*

The result of the ruling was a swift and extensive implementation of measures that many people believed were deliberately intended to circumscribe voting rights. Over one thousand polling places were closed, many of them in predominantly black areas, and states variously withdrew online voter registration, early voting, and same-day voter registration, as well as ending other practices that had opened up greater access to voting in the past. Meanwhile, more states have implemented voter identification laws, and they have begun aggressively seeking to remove allegedly ineligible voters from registration rolls.

In his 2006 speech supporting the renewal of the Voting Rights Act cited earlier in this chapter, John Lewis argued that the act was part of recent history and still relevant and urgent. In outlining the Court's decision in Shelby *below, Chief Justice John Roberts asserts exactly the opposite in stating that the act is, essentially, outdated and irrelevant. In a dissenting opinion on the Court written by Justice Ruth Bader Ginsburg, she acknowledged that voter discrimination had decreased in the covered jurisdictions under the act, but also argued that it was precisely because of the act that this had occurred. As Ginsburg put it, "[t]hrowing out preclearance when it has worked and is continuing to work to stop discriminatory changes is like throwing away your umbrella in a rainstorm because you are not getting wet." A divided Congress has so far not been able to agree on a new preclearance formula.*

Chief Justice Roberts delivered the opinion of the Court.

The Voting Rights Act of 1965 employed extraordinary measures to address an extraordinary problem. Section 5 of the Act required States to obtain federal permission before enacting any law related to voting – a drastic departure from basic principles of federalism. And §4 of the Act applied that requirement only to some States – an equally dramatic departure from the principle that all States enjoy equal sovereignty. This was strong medicine, but Congress determined it was needed to address entrenched racial discrimination in voting, "an insidious and pervasive evil which had been perpetuated in certain parts of our country through unremitting and ingenious defiance of the Constitution." South Carolina v. Katzenbach, 383 US 301, 309 (1966). As we explained in upholding the law, "exceptional conditions can justify legislative measures not otherwise appropriate." Id., at 334. Reflecting the unprecedented nature of these measures, they were scheduled to expire after five years. See Voting Rights Act of 1965, §4(a), 79Stat. 438.

Nearly 50 years later, they are still in effect; indeed, they have been made more stringent, and are now scheduled to last until 2031. There is no denying, however, that the conditions that originally justified these measures no longer characterize voting in the covered jurisdictions. By 2009, "the racial gap in voter registration and turnout [was] lower in the States originally covered by §5 than it [was] nationwide." Northwest Austin Municipal Util. Dist. No. One v. Holder, 557 US 193–204 (2009). Since that time, Census Bureau data indicate that African-American voter turnout has come to exceed white voter turnout in five of the six States originally covered by §5, with a gap in the sixth State of less than one half of one percent. See Dept. of Commerce, Census Bureau, Reported Voting and Registration, by Sex, Race and Hispanic Origin, for States (Nov. 2012) (Table 4b).

At the same time, voting discrimination still exists; no one doubts that. The question is whether the Act's extraordinary measures, including its disparate treatment of the States, continue to satisfy constitutional requirements. As we put it a short time ago, "the Act imposes current burdens and must be justified by current needs." Northwest Austin, 557 US, at 203.

[...]

It was in the South that slavery was upheld by law until uprooted by the Civil War, that the reign of Jim Crow denied African-Americans the most basic freedoms, and that state and local governments worked tirelessly to disenfranchise citizens on the basis of race. The Court invoked that history – rightly so – in sustaining the disparate coverage of the Voting Rights Act in 1966. See Katzenbach, supra, at 308 ("The constitutional propriety of the Voting Rights Act of 1965 must be judged with reference to the historical experience which it reflects.").

But history did not end in 1965. By the time the Act was reauthorized in 2006, there had been 40 more years of it. In assessing the "current need[ ]" for a preclearance system that treats States differently from one another today, that history cannot be ignored. During that time, largely because of the Voting Rights Act, voting tests were abolished, disparities in voter registration and turnout due to race were erased, and African-Americans attained political office in record numbers. And yet the coverage formula that Congress reauthorized in 2006 ignores these developments, keeping the focus on decades-old data relevant to decades-old problems, rather than current data reflecting current needs.

The Fifteenth Amendment commands that the right to vote shall not be denied or abridged on account of race or color, and it gives Congress the power to enforce that command. The Amendment is not designed to punish for the past; its purpose is to ensure a better future. See Rice v. Cayetano, 528 US 495, 512 (2000)

("Consistent with the design of the Constitution, the [Fifteenth] Amendment is cast in fundamental terms, terms transcending the particular controversy which was the immediate impetus for its enactment.") To serve that purpose, Congress – if it is to divide the States – must identify those jurisdictions to be singled out on a basis that makes sense in light of current conditions. It cannot rely simply on the past.

Source: US Supreme Court, *Shelby County v. Holder*, 570 US 2 (2013), https://supreme. justia.com/cases/federal/us/570/12-96/#tab-opinion-1970752

14.12 US Supreme Court, *Fisher v. University of Texas*, 2016

Affirmative action in the area of college admissions has survived court scrutiny since the 1980s, but only just. In 2003, the US Supreme Court in Grutter v. Bollinger *upheld the University of Michigan Law School's affirmative action admissions policy on the grounds that promoting diversity was a compelling interest. At the same time, in* Gratz v. Bollinger *(2003), the Court struck down the University of Michigan's point-based undergraduate admissions policy on the grounds that it too closely resembled a quota system. The two cases generally affirmed the earlier* Bakke *decision principle that race could be taken into account in admissions policies, but that universities could not use quotas.*

In 2008, two white students, Abigail Noel Fisher and Rachel Multer Michalewicz, sued the University of Texas at Austin on the grounds that they had failed to gain admission because of racially discriminatory policies. Texas law required the university to accept the top 10% of each Texas high school graduating class and 81% of students were admitted under that requirement. The remaining places were filled in an evaluative process that looked at a number of factors, including a consideration of race.

The lower courts upheld the university's admissions plan on the basis that it met the legal requirements of Grutter v. Bollinger. *On appeal to the US Supreme Court, a 7–1 majority in* Fisher v. University of Texas *(2013) remanded the case back to the Fifth Circuit Court of Appeals on the basis that the lower court had not applied "strict scrutiny" to the admissions policy (that is, it had failed to sufficiently address the issue of compelling interest). The Fifth Circuit heard further oral arguments in the case and again upheld the university's admissions policy. Upon another appeal to the US Supreme Court, the Court split 4–3 in* Fisher v. University of Texas *(2016) upholding the university's admissions policy. Yet as the case syllabus below indicates, such university admissions policies are under more constant observation than ever before. As with public school desegregation plans, "narrow tailoring" is the driving principle in monitoring race-conscious university admissions policies.*

The University of Texas at Austin (University) uses an undergraduate admissions system containing two components. First, as required by the State's Top

Ten Percent Law, it offers admission to any students who graduate from a Texas high school in the top 10% of their class. It then fills the remainder of its incoming freshman class, some 25%, by combining an applicant's "Academic Index" – the student's SAT score and high school academic performance – with the applicant's "Personal Achievement Index," a holistic review containing numerous factors, including race. The University adopted its current admissions process in 2004, after a year-long-study of its admissions process – undertaken in the wake of *Grutter* v. *Bollinger*, 539 US 306, and *Gratz* v. *Bollinger*, 539 US 244 – led it to conclude that its prior race-neutral system did not reach its goal of providing the educational benefits of diversity to its undergraduate students.

Petitioner Abigail Fisher, who was not in the top 10% of her high school class, was denied admission to the University's 2008 freshman class. She filed suit, alleging that the University's consideration of race as part of its holistic-review process disadvantaged her and other Caucasian applicants, in violation of the Equal Protection Clause. The District Court entered summary judgment in the University's favor, and the Fifth Circuit affirmed. This Court vacated the judgment, *Fisher* v. *University of Tex. at Austin*, 570 US ___ (*Fisher I*), and remanded the case to the Court of Appeals, so the University's program could be evaluated under the proper strict scrutiny standard. On remand, the Fifth Circuit again affirmed the entry of summary judgment for the University.

Held: The race-conscious admissions program in use at the time of petitioner's application is lawful under the Equal Protection Clause. Pp. 6–20.

(a) *Fisher I* sets out three controlling principles relevant to assessing the constitutionality of a public university's affirmative action program. First, a university may not consider race "unless the admissions process can withstand strict scrutiny," *i.e.*, it must show that its "purpose or interest is both constitutionally permissible and substantial, and that its use of the classification is necessary" to accomplish that purpose. 570 US, at ___. Second, "the decision to pursue the educational benefits that flow from student body diversity is, in substantial measure, an academic judgment to which some, but not complete, judicial deference is proper." *Id.,* at ___. Third, when determining whether the use of race is narrowly tailored to achieve the university's permissible goals, the school bears the burden of demonstrating that "available" and "workable" "race-neutral alternatives" do not suffice. *Id.,* at ___. Pp. 6–8.

(b) The University's approach to admissions gives rise to an unusual consequence here. The component with the largest impact on petitioner's chances of admission was not the school's consideration of race under its holistic-review process but the Top Ten Percent Plan. Because petitioner did not challenge the percentage part of the plan, the record is devoid of evidence of its impact on diversity. Remand for further factfinding would serve little purpose, however, because at the time of petitioner's application, the current plan had been in effect only three years and, in any event, the University lacked authority to alter the percentage plan, which was mandated by the Texas Legislature. These circumstances refute any criticism that the University did not make good faith efforts to comply with the law. The University, however, does have a continuing obligation to satisfy the strict scrutiny burden: by periodically reassessing the admission program's constitutionality, and efficacy, in light of the school's experience and the data it has gathered since adopting its admissions plan, and by tailoring its approach to ensure that race plays no greater role than is necessary to meet its compelling interests. Pp. 8–11.

(c) Drawing all reasonable inferences in her favor, petitioner has not shown by a preponderance of the evidence that she was denied equal treatment at the time her application was rejected. Pp. 11–19.

(1) Petitioner claims that the University has not articulated its compelling interest with sufficient clarity because it has failed to state more precisely what level of minority enrollment would constitute a "critical mass." However, the compelling interest that justifies consideration of race in college admissions is not an interest in enrolling a certain number of minority students, but an interest in obtaining "the educational benefits that flow from student body diversity." *Fisher I*, 570 US, at ___. Since the University is prohibited from seeking a particular number or quota of minority students, it cannot be faulted for failing to specify the particular level of minority enrollment at which it believes the educational benefits of diversity will be obtained.

On the other hand, asserting an interest in the educational benefits of diversity writ large is insufficient. A university's goals cannot be elusory or amorphous – they must be sufficiently measurable to permit judicial scrutiny of the policies adopted to reach them. The record here reveals that the University articulated concrete and precise goals – *e.g.*, ending stereotypes, promoting "cross-racial understanding," preparing students for "an increasingly diverse workforce and society," and cultivating leaders with "legitimacy in the eyes of the citizenry" – that mirror the compelling interest this Court has approved in prior cases. It also gave a "reasoned, principled explanation" for its decision, *id.*, at ___, in a 39-page proposal written after a year-long study revealed that its race-neutral policies and programs did not meet its goals. Pp. 11–13.

(2) Petitioner also claims that the University need not consider race because it had already "achieved critical mass" by 2003 under the Top Ten Percent Plan and race-neutral holistic review. The record, however, reveals that the University studied and deliberated for months, concluding that race-neutral programs had

not achieved the University's diversity goals, a conclusion supported by significant statistical and anecdotal evidence. Pp. 13–15.

(3) Petitioner argues further that it was unnecessary to consider race because such consideration had only a minor impact on the number of minority students the school admitted. But the record shows that the consideration of race has had a meaningful, if still limited, effect on freshman class diversity. That race consciousness played a role in only a small portion of admissions decisions should be a hallmark of narrow tailoring, not evidence of unconstitutionality. P. 15.

(4) Finally, petitioner argues that there were numerous other race-neutral means to achieve the University's goals. However, as the record reveals, none of those alternatives was a workable means of attaining the University's educational goals, as of the time of her application. Pp. 15–19.

758 F. 3d 633, affirmed.

Source: *Fisher v. University of Texas*, 579 US ____ (2016), https://supreme.justia.com/cases/federal/us/579/14-981/#tab-opinion-3589818

14.13 Janelle Jones, "The Racial Wealth Gap," 2017

A clear-cut, striking, and transparently measurable racial disparity that still exists today is the wealth gap between blacks and whites. This has deep historical roots. Most obviously, there existed for centuries in American history the institution of slavery that specifically denied black people a wage for their labor. State-sanctioned segregation, disenfranchisement, economic exploitation, and racial discrimination perpetuated those economic inequalities.

Housing policy is one significant area of racial discrimination that has helped maintain the wealth gap. The New Deal's Federal Housing Administration (FHA) in the 1930s created affordable loan programs but largely excluded people of color from them. A host of other public policies and private practices resulted in 98% of home loans between 1934 and 1962 going to whites. Homeownership has been one of the most important vehicles for accumulating wealth and privilege among whites in the twentieth century, not only in terms of the rising value of property, but also in the multiple benefits that accrue from living in more affluent neighborhoods.

Although the civil rights movement was successful in eradicating many of the racially discriminatory laws that had existed in the past, the final disappearance of those laws has been a relatively recent development. The abolition of discriminatory laws did little to nothing to address their cumulative impact and effect on black people. Changing the law is one thing; addressing and reversing the very tangible legacy of those discriminatory practices used in the past is quite another.

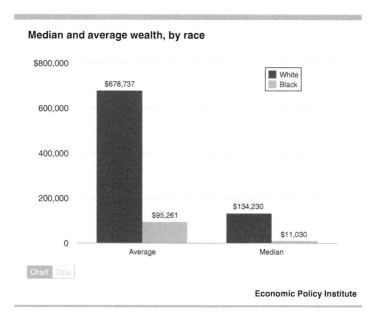

Median and average wealth, by race

Economic Policy Institute

Source: Janelle Jones, "The racial wealth gap: How African-Americans have been shortchanged out of the materials to build wealth," Working Economics Blog, Economic Policy Institute, 13 February 2017, https://www.epi.org/blog/the-racial-wealth-gap-how-african-americans-have-been-shortchanged-out-of-the-materials-to-build-wealth/

14.14 Black Lives Matter, What We Believe, n.d.

How to address racial discrimination and its consequences in the United States? Each generation of black activists has tackled that question, borrowing from past models and experiences, while adapting to the circumstances of their own times. In 2013, three black women, Alicia Garza, Patrisse Cullors, and Opal Tometi founded a movement called #BlackLivesMatter in response to the acquittal of George Zimmerman, a white man who shot and killed the unarmed black teenager Trayvon Martin.

The Black Lives Matter movement has since gone viral, an appropriate term given the movement's Twitter-based hashtag origins and its extensive use of social media. Social media platforms, along with other technological innovations, such as built-in visual and audio recording devices to cell phones that have been used to capture instances of racial discrimination that in the past would have gone undocumented, indicate how a new generation of black activists are appropriating new developments in communications and technology in the struggle for civil rights. This, of course, has always been the case, from the printing press, to radio, to television.

The Black Lives Matter movement has spread in more conventional ways too, growing into a global network with over 40 chapters. As the below list of "What We Believe" indicates, the Black Lives Matter movement draws extensively on many of the civil rights movement's and black power movement's legacies that have been identified in this book, including its continuation of the tradition of movement platforms and programs. The touchstones in the Black Lives Matter manifesto represent a recognizable compendium of those movement legacies, which include: an assertion of black selfhood as an important part of wider justice struggles; an acknowledgment that such struggles in the United States are part of global struggles for freedom and equality; and an attention to issues of intersectionality and an understanding that sexual orientation, gender, economics, disability, religion, age, citizenship status, and geography, among other categories, play vital roles in shaping and defining how people of color (and others) experience discrimination.

The very fact that it is necessary in the twenty-first century for black people to have to assert that Black Lives Matter – and how much vilification and enmity that assertion has encountered in response – is as good an indication as any that the struggle for civil rights, and opposition to it, remains one of the defining issues of our age.

We acknowledge, respect, and celebrate differences and commonalities.

We work vigorously for freedom and justice for Black people and, by extension, all people.

We intentionally build and nurture a beloved community that is bonded together through a beautiful struggle that is restorative, not depleting.

We are unapologetically Black in our positioning. In affirming that Black Lives Matter, we need not qualify our position. To love and desire freedom and justice for ourselves is a prerequisite for wanting the same for others.

We see ourselves as part of the global Black family, and we are aware of the different ways we are impacted or privileged as Black people who exist in different parts of the world.

We are guided by the fact that all Black lives matter, regardless of actual or perceived sexual identity, gender identity, gender expression, economic status, ability, disability, religious beliefs or disbeliefs, immigration status, or location.

We make space for transgender brothers and sisters to participate and lead.

We are self-reflexive and do the work required to dismantle cisgender privilege and uplift Black trans folk, especially Black trans women who continue to be disproportionately impacted by trans-antagonistic violence.

We build a space that affirms Black women and is free from sexism, misogyny, and environments in which men are centered.

We practice empathy. We engage comrades with the intent to learn about and connect with their contexts.

We make our spaces family-friendly and enable parents to fully participate with their children. We dismantle the patriarchal practice that requires mothers to work "double shifts" so that they can mother in private even as they participate in public justice work.

We disrupt the Western-prescribed nuclear family structure requirement by supporting each other as extended families and "villages" that collectively care for one another, especially our children, to the degree that mothers, parents, and children are comfortable.

We foster a queer-affirming network. When we gather, we do so with the intention of freeing ourselves from the tight grip of heteronormative thinking, or rather, the belief that all in the world are heterosexual (unless s/he or they disclose otherwise).

We cultivate an intergenerational and communal network free from ageism. We believe that all people, regardless of age, show up with the capacity to lead and learn.

We embody and practice justice, liberation, and peace in our engagements with one another.

Source: Black Lives Matter, What We Believe, n.d., https://blacklivesmatter.com/about/what-we-believe/

Discussion Questions

1. In what ways are the legacies of the civil rights and black power movements still evident today?
2. In what ways are the legacies of white resistance to black struggles for freedom and equality still evident today?
3. Identify the main achievements of black struggles for freedom and equality in the 1950s and 1960s. What did those struggles fail to achieve, and why?
4. Compare and contrast struggles for black freedom and equality today with those that unfolded in the 1950s and 1960s.

Further Reading

Alexander, Michelle. *The New Jim Crow: Mass Incarceration in the Age of Colorblindness* (New Press, 2010).

Berman, Ari. *Give Us the Ballot: The Modern Struggle for Voting Rights* (Farrar, Straus and Giroux, 2015).

De Jong, Greta. *You can't Eat Freedom: Southerners and Social Justice after the Civil Rights Movement* (University of North Carolina Press, 2016).

Faderman, Lillian. *The Gay Revolution: The Story of Struggle* (Simon and Schuster, 2015).

Joseph, Peniel E. *Dark Days, Bright Nights: From Black Power to Barack Obama* (BasicCivitas Books, 2010).

Khan-Cullors, Patrisse, and asha bandele. *When They Call You a Terrorist: A Black Lives Matter Memoir* (St. Martin's Press, 2018).

Kim, Catherine Y., Daniel J. Losen, and Damon T. Hewitt. *The School-to-Prison Pipeline: Structuring Legal Reform* (New York University Press, 2012).

Kozol, Jonathan. *The Shame of the Nation: The Restoration of Apartheid Schooling in America* (Random House, 2005).

Mandela, Nelson. *Long Walk to Freedom: The Autobiography of Nelson Mandela* (Macdonald Purnell, 1994).

Obama, Barack. *Dreams from My Father: A Story of Race and Inheritance* (Times Books, 1995).

Romano, Renee, and Leigh Raiford, eds. *The Civil Rights Movement in American Memory* (University of Georgia Press, 2006).

Rothstein, Richard. *The Color of Law: A Forgotten History of How Our Government Segregated America* (Liveright, 2018).

Sokol, Jason. *The Heavens Might Crack: The Death and Legacy of Martin Luther King, Jr* (Basic Books, 2018).

Springer, Kimberly. *Living for the Revolution: Black Feminist Organizations, 1968–1980* (Duke University Press, 2005).

Wanzer-Serrano, Darrel. *The New York Young Lords and the Struggle for Liberation* (Temple University Press, 2015).

Zimring, Carl A. *Clean and White: A History of Environmental Racism in the United States* (New York University Press, 2016).

Index

The Civil Rights Movement: A Documentary Reader, First Edition. Edited by John A. Kirk.
© 2020 John Wiley & Sons, Inc. Published 2020 by John Wiley & Sons, Inc.